Kelly's Draftsman

Third (Cumulative) Supplement to Nineteenth Edition

Kelly's Draftsman

Third (Cumulative) Supplement to Nineteenth Edition

by

Roderick Ramage
BSc (Econ)
Solicitor

The supplements

Gillian Cockburn
Solicitor, Cockburns, Guildford

Emma Collins
Solicitor, Mace and Jones, Knutsford

Richard Fearnley
Solicitor, Land Registrar, HM Land Registry

Karl Jackson
Solicitor, Mace & Jones, Manchester

Varun Maharaj
Solicitor, Mace & Jones, Manchester

Michele Phillips
Solicitor, Lupton Fawcett LLP, Leeds

Sally Ramage
Law writer, sallyramage.net

Laurence Target
Solicitor, Trowers & Hamlins LLP, London

The nineteenth edition

Mark Anderson

Gillian Cockburn

Emma Collins

Richard Fearnley

Jackie Heeds

Graham Hill

Karl Jackson

Varun Maharaj

Alison Oakes

Michele Phillips

Andrew Smith

Laurence Target

Victor Warner

 LexisNexis®

Members of the LexisNexis Group worldwide

United Kingdom	LexisNexis, a Division of Reed Elsevier (UK) Ltd, Halsbury House, 35 Chancery Lane, London, WC2A 1EL, and London House, 20–22 East London Street, Edinburgh EH7 4BQ
Australia	LexisNexis Butterworths, Chatswood, New South Wales
Austria	LexisNexis Verlag ARD Orac GmbH & Co KG, Vienna
Benelux	LexisNexis Benelux, Amsterdam
Canada	LexisNexis Canada, Markham, Ontario
China	LexisNexis China, Beijing and Shanghai
France	LexisNexis SA, Paris
Germany	LexisNexis Deutschland GmbH, Munster
Hong Kong	LexisNexis Hong Kong, Hong Kong
India	LexisNexis India, New Delhi
Italy	Giuffrè Editore, Milan
Japan	LexisNexis Japan, Tokyo
Malaysia	Malayan Law Journal Sdn Bhd, Kuala Lumpur
New Zealand	LexisNexis NZ Ltd, Wellington
Poland	Wydawnictwo Prawnicze LexisNexis Sp, Warsaw
Singapore	LexisNexis Singapore, Singapore
South Africa	LexisNexis Butterworths, Durban
USA	LexisNexis, Dayton, Ohio

A CIP Catalogue record for this book is available from the British Library.

ISBN 13: ISBN 9781405744478

Typeset by Letterpart Ltd, Reigate, Surrey

Printed and bound in Great Britain by Hobbs the Printers Ltd, Totton, Hampshire

Visit LexisNexis at www.lexisnexis.co.uk

Publisher's Note

Paragraphs in this supplement update and, where possible, replace in their entirety those published in the nineteenth edition of *Kelly's Draftsman*.

Chapter 9A is a completely new chapter incorporating the changes made by Companies Act 2006. Reference may be made to the existing Chapter 9 as published in the nineteenth edition of the mainwork for the position under the Companies Act 1985.

Preface

This supplement is cumulative with the previous two years'. As it includes the material added by the 2007 and 2008 supplements, the 2008 supplement booklet can be discarded. The main changes made in the 2009 supplement deal with the Companies Act 2006 coming wholly into force (chapters 2, 4, 9A, 12 Boilerplate, Companies and Partnership, inter alia), corporate manslaughter, safeguarding vulnerable persons and the repeal of the statutory grievance and dispute resolution procedures (chapter 10 Employment), company, pension and tax law changes (chapter 13 Sale of shares and businesses), new Land Registry forms and vacant possession when persons other than the sellers are in possession (chapter 25 Sale of land), energy efficiency (chapter 23 Leases and Tenancy Agreements), and the tax treatment of trusts (chapters 14, 19 and 20 Assents, Trusts and trustees, and Wills). The cumulative alteration and additions are as follows.

4 Formal parts

Attestation of documents by companies as altered by the Companies Act 2006.

9 Companies and 9A Companies under the Companies Act 2006

Chapter 9 is based on the law before the coming into force of the 2006 Act. Chapter 9A is the same chapter rewritten to take account of the coming into force on 1 October 2009 of the Companies Act 2006 and the Companies (Model Articles) Regulations 2008, SI 2008/3229 (which replace the Companies (Tables A to F) Regulations 1985, SI 1985/805 and set out the new model articles for companies).

10 Employment

The prospective repeal (three cheers!), at the time of the 2008 supplement, of the statutory disciplinary and grievance procedures, has now become actual, and is reflected in this supplement, which, amongst other matters includes a note to the Health and Safety Policy about the Corporate Manslaughter and Corporate Homicide Act 2007, which came into force on 6 April 2008, and a draft policy document under the Safeguarding Vulnerable Groups Act 2006. It still contains a note of minor revision brought about Tony Blair's electoral promise, which was delivered (increasing statutory annual leave), and guidance notes and a checklist for recruitment checks to avoid falling foul of sections 15 to 25 of the Immigration, Asylum and Nationality Act 2006 which came into force on 29 February 2008. The first supplement dealt mainly with retirement and the Employment Equality (Age) Regulations 2006, SI 2006/1031.

12 Partnership

The 2008 supplement contained provisions about age discrimination and documents about the NHS Pension Scheme 24 hour retirement policy, and the current supplement mainly adds a table of forms for filing at Companies House in connection with limited and limited liability partnerships, and a note discussing whether a partner in an LLP can also be an employee.

13 Sale of shares and businesses

This supplement reflects a number of tax changes, the coming into force of the Companies Act 2006 (including the lifting of restrictions on financial assistance in respect of private companies) and pension law changes affecting multi-employer schemes.

14, 17, 19, 20 Wills, trusts and associated private client chapters

The alterations here stem from tax changes and developing practice to reflect the changes.

16 Family

The one alteration in this chapter is a clause about lasting powers of attorney, which themselves were mentioned in the 2007 supplement.

18 Powers of attorney

The only addition to this chapter is a power of attorney by a company for the execution of documents, prompted by the Companies Act 2006. The legislature's professed aim to make life easier, so far as the formalities of running small companies are concerned, is undermined by its actions. The new provisions, as an example, for the execution of documents by companies are prescriptive (see chapter 4 above) making it attractive to provide for execution by an attorney of a company, and here too the Companies Act 2006 section 47 enacts that a company may give powers of attorney to execute documents in the United Kingdom, which the rest of us thought they could do already. Perhaps the draftsman of this section remembers, as a child, being present at the opening of the Connah's Quay Sports & Recreation Centre, which had already been in use for several months, when, as he cut the ribbon, the Duke of Edinburgh declared it more open than it was before.

23 Leases

The main excitement in the field of landlord and tenant in 2008 is to do with tenants' deposits, for which this supplement includes a notice of prescribed information and a rent deposit agreement. If your nerves are strong you will also find a new clause for insertion in a lease to give rights to mortgagees in respect of forfeiture for want of repair. An addition in the present supplement is a clause and note about the Energy Performance of Buildings (Certificates and Inspections) (England and Wales) Regulations 2007, SI 2007/991.

25 Sale of land

Additional prescribed Land Registry forms and a change to form TR1 are noted. Two additional clauses deal with vacant possession when the property is occupied by persons other than the sellers, one to ensure vacant possession and the other, which in passing, might be attractive to anyone not unattracted to the idea of providing a HIP.

26 Associations

For no better reason than that a classic car club to which I belongs supports a supplier of spare parts, precedents have been provided for use by proprietors' clubs, not for the usual reason of drinking, but to support a commercial business, which might not otherwise not be viable.

Finally, my thanks to the *Kelly* team. The aim of the supplement is not to record every change in the law or practice, but to pick out those which are likely to be of use to practitioners. Therefore the advice of some contributors that nothing need be mentioned at this stage is as valuable as the contributions of new material by others. In this supplement I am grateful for new material from Michele Phillips (Sale of shares and businesses), Gilliam Cockburn (wills, trusts etc), Laurence Target (landlord and tenant and sale of land), Karl Jackson and Varun Maharaj (Sale of land) and my wife Sally Ramage for advice about corporate manslaughter and safeguarding vulnerable persons.

Roderick Ramage

Copehale Coppenhall Stafford S19 9BW www.law-office.co.uk

723rd anniversary of the death of King John

Summary Contents of the 19th edn

Contents

Contents

Contents

Table of Statutes

Table of Statutory Instruments

Table of Cases

2 Standard Clauses

FORMS

Background/recitals

Recital of company and capital

x The (*Party-B*) is a company limited by shares incorporated under the   [2–022]
Companies Act 2006 with a capital of £(…) ((…) pounds) divided into
(*number*) ordinary shares of £(…) each [and (*number*) [rate] per cent cumulative preference shares of £(…) each].

3 Declarations (statutory) and Statements

PRECEDENTS

[3–189] **19   Declaration by company secretary as to charges, receivership and winding up and other matters**

[3–193] 3 Particulars of all charges created by the Company which are registrable under Chapter 1 in Part 25 of the Companies Act 2006 have been sent to the Registrar of Companies for registration and are recorded in the Company's charges register.

4 Formal part of documents

Document date and parties[1]

(Document) by one person [deed poll]

[3] All parties should be properly and fully named, and in the case of a company or a limited liability partnership there should always be included its registration number. Furthermore, the registration number is required by HM Land Registry under the Land Registration Rules 2003, SI 2003/1417, r 181. A misdescription of a company's name in a contract will not enable the company to avoid it: *F Goldsmith (Sicklesmere) Ltd v Baxter* [1970] Ch 85, [1969] 3 All ER 773; but the doctrine of misnomer may not apply if the identity of one of two possible parties cannot be ascertained from the document: *Dumford Trading AG v OAO Atlantrybflot* [2005] EWCA Civ 24, [2005] All ER (D) 231 (Jan). As to the civil and criminal consequences of a failure to comply with the requirements to disclose company names in Companies Act 2006, s 82, see ss 83, 84 of the 2006 Act. As other jurisdictions (overseas as well as Scotland) use the term 'Limited' and its abbreviation 'Ltd', it is prudent also to include the place of registration: see [4–007]. — [4–002]

Testimonium: agreement under hand by company

AS WITNESS the hand of [(*name*) the managing director (*or as the case may be*) (*or*) (*name*) and (*name*) authorised signatories[1]] on behalf of (*name*) Ltd [pursuant to a resolution of its board dated (*date*)[2]] on the date first above written. — [4–019]

[1] From 1 April 2008 documents are executed by companies, if not under common seal, by either a single signature witnessed or two signatures, as to which see [4–035B] and [4–035C] and the notes to them. — [4–020]
[2] Whilst, in favour of a person dealing with a company in good faith, a transaction decided on by the directors is deemed to be within the capacity of the company and the directors (Companies Act 2006, s 40), the prudent person dealing with a company should ascertain that the directors have decided on a transaction. In practice a certified copy of the resolution or certificate that the resolution has been passed is sufficient. An enquiry on this point is more important than the inclusion of these words. See attestation clause [4–046] and the note to it. See also Companies [9–593] and [9–595].

Attestation

AGREEMENTS

A witness is not generally necessary for the execution of an instrument under hand (in contrast to the need for a witness to a deed – see [4–039]), but may be thought desirable as evidence of execution. At common law one witness is sufficient to prove the execution of any deed or document; but a power of attorney to deal with government securities or for use abroad must be attested by two witnesses notwithstanding this rule, as in the first case there is a statutory requirement to that effect and in the second case its production may be required in evidence in a foreign country where two witnesses are necessary. Some statutory provisions as to attestations are: — [4–034]

— Bills of Sale: Bills of Sale Act 1878, s 10, and Bills of Sale Act (1878) Amendment Act 1882, ss 8, 10.

— Corporations and incorporated companies: Law of Property Act 1925, s 74, Companies Act 2006, ss 44–48, Corporate Bodies' Contracts Act 1960, s 1, and Local Government Act 1972, s 135, Industrial and Provident Societies Act 1965, s 29.

— Deeds exercising powers of appointment where special formalities are prescribed by the instrument creating the power: Law of Property Act 1925, s 159.

Attestation: agreement under hand by a company — two signatures[1]

[4-035A]   SIGNED on behalf of (*name*) Ltd by (*name*)   (*signature*)
and (*name*) two of its [directors (*or*)
authorised signatories]

(*signature*)

[4-035B]   [1]   Under CA 2006, s 44 a document is executed by a company by the affixing of its common seal or if it is signed on its behalf by two authorised signatories or by a director in the presence of a witness. Authorised signatories are every director of the company and the company secretary, if the case of a private company, if it has one. This is a very restrictive provision, and it may be more convenient for companies to execute documents by an attorney, whether they are documents in writing or deeds: see [4-048] below. For a suitable power of attorney see [18-091A] in this supplement.

Attestation: agreement under hand by a company — one signature[1]

[4-035C]   SIGNED on behalf of (*name*) Ltd by (*name*) | (*signature*)
a director [*or other authorised signatory*] in
the presence of

(*signature of witness*)
(*address and description*)

[4-035D]   [1]   See note 1 in [4-035B] above.

Attestation: agreement under hand by a limited liability partnership[1]

[4-036]   SIGNED on behalf of (*name*) LLP by (*name*) | (*signature*)
a director [*or other authorised signatory*] in
the presence of

(*signature of witness*)
(*address and description*)

[4-037]   [1]   Under CA 2006, s 43 a contract may be made by a company by writing under its common seal, or on behalf of a company, by any person acting under its authority, express or implied, and any formalities required by law in the case of a contract made by an individual also apply, unless a contrary intention appears, to a contract made by or on behalf of a company. This section applies also to limited liability partnerships: Limited Liability Partnerships Regulations 2001, SI 2001/1090, reg 4, Sch 2, Pt I. See note at [4-020]. The Companies Act 2006 (Commencement No 5, Transitional Provisions and Savings) Order 2007, SI 2007/3495, brings CA 2006, s 44 (execution of documents) into force from 1 April 2008, but by reg 12 (savings), 'Nothing in this Order affects any provision of the 1985 Act ... as applied by the Limited Liability Partnerships Regulations 2001'.

DEEDS

[4-039]   Note: The Law of Property (Miscellaneous Provisions) Act 1989, s 1(1)(b) abolishes any rule of law requiring a seal for the valid execution of an instrument as a deed by an individual. The corresponding provisions for companies were in the Companies Act 1989, s 130 which inserted s 36A into the Companies Act 1985 and are now in the Companies Act 2006, s 44. These provisions had been further amended by the Regulatory Reform (Execution of Deeds and Documents) Order 2005, SI 2005/1906. A deed must describe itself as a deed, and attestation by a witness and delivery are necessary. For the prescribed forms of execution of deeds, see the Land Registration Rules 1925, SI 1925/1093, Sch 3, as added to by the Land Registration Rules 1997, SI 1997/3037, r 2(4), Sch 4.

Attestation: deed executed by company[1] with common seal

(a) if in accordance with the provisions of the Model Articles[2]:   [4–042]

SEALED with the common seal of (*name*) Ltd and signed by (*name of authorised person*) was affixed in the presence of:	(*common seal*)

(*signature*)

(*signature of witness*)

(*address and description*)

(b) If in the accustomed form under regulation 101 of the 1985 version of Table   [4–042A]
A:

THE COMMON SEAL of (*name*) Ltd was affixed in the presence of:	(*common seal*)

(*signature*)

director

(*signature*)

secretary

[1]   Note that, unlike s 44, which was brought into force on 1 April 2008, s 45 (common seal) of   [4–043]
the Companies Act 2006 was not brought into force until 1 October 2009.
    By Companies Act 2006, s 45, a company need not have a seal. By s 44 a company may execute a document by affixing its common seal or signature in accordance with that section, and, by s 46, a company executes a document as deed by executing it and delivering it as a deed.
    See Law of Property Act 1925, s 74, as substituted by reg 2 of SI 2006/1906, by which in favour of a purchaser it is deemed that a deed has been duly executed by a corporation aggregate if its seal is affixed in the presence of and attested by the board of directors, council or other governing body of the corporation or one such member and the clerk, secretary or other permanent officer of the corporation or his deputy.
[2]   The 2006 Act does not state how the seal is to be affixed. The model articles in the schedules to the Companies (Model Articles) Regulations 2008, SI 2008/3229 provide, unless the directors otherwise decide, for a document to which the common seal is affixed to be signed by at least one authorised person in the presence of a witness who attests the signature: SI 2008/3229 Sch 1 reg 49 (private companies limited by shares), Sch 2 reg 35 (private companies limited by guarantee) and Sch 3 reg 81 (pubic companies).

Attestation: deed executed by company[1] without or not using common seal —
alternative version by single signature

SIGNED AS A DEED by (*name*) Ltd by (*name*) a director [*or other authorised signatory*] in the presence of	(*signature*)	[4–045A]

(*signature of witness*)
(*address and description*)

[1]   See [4–043], note 1.   [4–045B]

9 Companies

PRELIMINARY NOTES

[9–002A] The revised timetable, printed at [9A–002], shows that the full implementation of the Companies Act 2006 has been extended to 2009. Until the Act if fully in force, the appropriate version of this chapter (Chapter 9 in respect of the law under the CA 1985 and Chapter 9A as though the CA 2006 were fully in force) must be used according to the extent to which the CA 2006 has been brought into force.

CHANGES TO TABLE A RESULTING FROM THE COMPANIES ACT 2006

[9–002B] Various regulations have made modifications to Tables A etc as a result of the Companies Act 2006. Although Tables A etc will cease to be the default forms on 1 October 2009, when the relevant provision of ss 18 to 20 of the 2006 Act is expected to come into force, articles of association of companies then in existence which incorporate or by default are Table A etc, will continue to incorporate or be whichever Table applies: CA 2006, s 20(2). Indeed companies still exist whose articles are still based on the 1948 and earlier versions of Table A.

A new version of Table A as altered is set out at [9–012A].

The following are minor revisions to the precedent articles of association in [9–039] in respect of companies formed or adopting Table A on or after 1 October 2007 and before 1 October 2009.

EXTRAORDINARY RESOLUTIONS AND EXTRAORDINARY GENERAL MEETINGS

[9–002C] Under the CA 2006, meeting other than an annual general meeting are general meetings and resolutions are either ordinary or special: CA 2006, ss 280, 281 in force 1 October 2007.

In precedent 5 [9–039] (articles of association) article 20 [9–062] substitute 'special' for 'extraordinary' for companies formed with or adopting Table A on and after 1 October 2007. Companies intending to exercise the power given by this article on and after that date but with the articles in its original form ought first to alter it to make this substitution.

CHAIRMAN'S CASTING VOTE AT A GENERAL MEETING

[9–002D] BERR's opinion is that a chairman's casting vote at a general meeting is incompatible with the definition in CA 2006, s 282(1). Therefore it has, by SI 2007/2826, reg 3 removed article 50 from Table A, which provided for the chairman to have a casting vote. Whether this is good law is moot, but is the law. That it is inconsistent with what has been established law, since at least 1 October 1906 when the chairman's casting vote was first included in Table A (reg 58 of SR&O 1906/596 L15), is shown by CA 2006, s 23A inserted by SI 2007/3495, which enacts that any provision in a company's articles, which immediately before 1 October 2007 provided for a casting vote, 'continues to have effect notwithstanding sections 281(3) and 282'. The corresponding provisions in the three model articles, to be introduced on 1 October 2009 are also removed.

This applies only to general meetings and not to meeting of the directors, at which the chairman may still have a casting vote.

In precedent 5 [9–039] (articles of association) article 11 [9–053] is omitted for companies formed with or adopting Table A on and after 1 October 2007.

MEMBERS' RESOLUTIONS IN WRITING

Precedent 5 [9–039] (articles of association) is not altered, but in respect of resolutions in writing first circulated on and after 1 October 2007, use the form in supplement [9A–286] and the note to it in [9A–287] and not that in [9–279].

[9–002E]

RETIREMENT OF DIRECTOR BY ROTATION

By SI 2007/2541 reg 13 the provisions in Table A for retirement by rotation of directors of a private company are omitted with effect on 1 October 2007

[9–002F]

In precedent 5 [9–039] (articles of association) article 18 [9–060] is omitted for companies formed with or adopting Table A on and after 1 October 2007.

TABLE A AS AMENDED CONSEQUENT ON THE COMPANIES ACT 2006

TABLE A AS AMENDED CONSEQUENT ON THE COMPANIES ACT 2006[1]

[9–012A]

The Companies Acts 1985 and 2006

Table A

regulations for management

of a company limited by shares

INTERPRETATION

1 In these regulations:

[9–012AA]

'the Act'	means the Companies Act 1985 including any statutory modification or re-enactment thereof for the time being in force [and any provisions of the Companies Act 2006 for the time being in force[2]].
'the articles'	means the articles of the company.
'clear days'	in relation to the period of a notice means that period excluding the day when the notice is given or deemed to be given and the day for which it is given or on which it is to take effect..
'communication'	means the same as in the Electronic Communications Act 2000.

'electronic communication'	means the same as in the Electronic Communications Act 2000.
'executed'	includes any mode of execution.
'office'	means the registered office of the company.
'the holder'	in relation to shares means the member whose name is entered in the register of members as the holder of the shares.
'the seal'	means the common seal of the company.
'secretary'	means the secretary of the company or any other person appointed to perform the duties of the secretary of the company including a joint, assistant or deputy secretary.
'the United Kingdom'	means Great Britain and Northern Ireland.

Unless the context otherwise requires, words or expressions contained in these regulations bear the same meaning as in the Act but excluding any statutory modification thereof not in force when these regulations become binding on the company.

SHARE CAPITAL

[9–012AB] **2** Subject to the provisions of the Act and without prejudice to any rights attached to any existing shares, any share may be issued with such rights or restrictions as the company may by ordinary resolution determine.

[9–012AC] **3** Subject to the provisions of the Act, shares may be issued which are to be redeemed or are to be liable to be redeemed at the option of the company or the holder on such terms and in such manner as may be provided by the articles.

[9–012AD] **4** The company may exercise the powers of paying commissions conferred by the Act. Subject to the provisions of the Act, any such commission may be satisfied by the payment of cash or by the allotment of fully or partly paid shares or partly in one way and partly in the other.

[9–012B] **5** Except as required by law, no person shall be recognised by the company as holding any share upon any trust and (except as otherwise provided by the articles or by law) the company shall not be bound by or recognise any interest in any share except an absolute right to the entirety thereof in the holder.

SHARE CERTIFICATES

[9–012BA] **6** Every member, upon becoming the holder of any shares, shall be entitled without payment to one certificate for all the shares of each class held by him (and, upon transferring a part of his holding of shares of any class, to a certificate for the balance of such holding) or several certificates each for one or more of his shares of any class, to a certificate for the balance of such holding) or several certificates each for one or more of his shares upon payment for every certificate after the first of such reasonable sum as the directors may determine. Every certificate shall be sealed with the seal and shall specify the number, class and distinguishing numbers (if any) of the shares to which it relates and the amount or respective amounts paid up thereon. The company shall not be bound to issue more than one certificate for shares held jointly by several persons and delivery of a certificate to one joint holder shall be a sufficient delivery to all of them.

7 If a share certificate is defaced, worn-out, lost or destroyed, it may be renewed on such terms (if any) as to evidence and indemnity and payment of the expenses reasonably incurred by the company in investigating evidence as the directors may determine but otherwise free of charge, and (in the case of defacement or wearing-out) on delivery up of the old certificate. **[9–012BB]**

LIEN

8 The company shall have a first and paramount lien on every share (not being a fully paid share) for all moneys (whether presently payable or not) payable at a fixed time or called in respect of that share. The directors may at any time declare any share to be wholly or in part exempt from the provisions of this regulation. The company's lien on a share shall extend to any amount payable in respect of it. **[9–012BC]**

9 The company may sell in such manner as the directors determine any shares on which the company has a lien if a sum in respect of which the lien exists is presently payable and is not paid within fourteen clear days after notice has been given to the holder of the share or to the person entitled to it in consequence of the death or bankruptcy of the holder, demanding payment and stating that if the notice is not complied with the shares may be sold. **[9–012BD]**

10 To give effect to a sale the directors may authorise some person to execute an instrument of transfer of the shares sold to, or in accordance with the directions of, the purchaser. The title of the transferee to the shares shall not be affected by any irregularity in or invalidity of the proceedings in reference to the sale. **[9–012C]**

11 The net proceeds of the sale, after payment of the costs, shall be applied in payment of so much of the sum for which the lien exists as is presently payable, and any residue shall (upon surrender to the company for cancellation of the certificate for the shares sold and subject to a like lien for any moneys not presently payable as existed upon the shares before the sale) be paid to the person entitled to the shares at the date of the sale. **[9–012CA]**

CALLS ON SHARES AND FORFEITURE

12 Subject to the terms of allotment, the directors may make calls upon the members in respect of any moneys unpaid on their shares (whether in respect of nominal value or premium) and each member shall (subject to receiving at least fourteen clear days' notice specifying when and where payment is to be made) pay to the company as required by the notice the amount called on his shares. A call may be required to be paid by instalments. A call may, before receipt by the company of any sum due thereunder, be revoked in whole or part and payment of a call may be postponed in whole or part. A person upon whom a call is made shall remain liable for calls made upon him notwithstanding the subsequent transfer of the shares in respect whereof the call was made. **[9–012CB]**

13 A call shall be deemed to have been made at the time when the resolution of the directors authorising the call was passed. **[9–012CC]**

[9-012CD] **14** The joint holders of a share shall be jointly and severally liable to pay all calls in respect thereof.

[9-012D] **15** If a call remains unpaid after it has become due and payable the person from whom it is due and payable shall pay interest on the amount unpaid from the day it became due and payable until it is paid at the rate fixed by the terms of allotment of the share or in the notice of the call or, if no rate is fixed, at the appropriate rate (as defined by the Act) but the directors may waive payment of the interest wholly or in part.

[9-012DA] **16** An amount payable in respect of a share on allotment or at any fixed date, whether in respect of nominal value or premium or as an instalment of a call, shall be deemed to be a call and if it is not paid the provisions of the articles shall apply as if that amount had become due and payable by virtue of a call.

[9-012DB] **17** Subject to the terms of allotment, the directors may make arrangements on the issue of shares for a difference between the holders in the amounts and times of payment of calls on their shares.

[9-012DC] **18** If a call remains unpaid after it has become due and payable the directors may give to the person from whom it is due not less than fourteen clear days' notice requiring payment of the amount unpaid together with any interest which may have accrued. The notice shall name the place where payment is to be made and shall state that if the notice is not complied with the shares in respect of which the call was made will be liable to be forfeited.

[9-012DD] **19** If the notice is not complied with any share in respect of which it was given may, before the payment required by the notice has been made, be forfeited by a resolution of the directors and the forfeiture shall include all dividends or other moneys payable in respect of the forfeited shares and not paid before the forfeiture.

[9-012E] **20** Subject to the provisions of the Act, a forfeited share may be sold, re-allotted or otherwise disposed of on such terms and in such manner as the directors determine either to the person who was before the forfeiture the holder or to any other person and at any time before sale, re-allotment or other disposition, the forfeiture may be cancelled on such terms as the directors think fit. Where for the purposes of its disposal a forfeited share is to be transferred to any person the directors may authorise some person to execute an instrument of transfer of the share to that person.

[9-012EA] **21** A person any of whose shares have been forfeited shall cease to be a member in respect of them and shall surrender to the company for cancellation the certificate for the shares forfeited but shall remain liable to the company for all moneys which at the date of forfeiture were presently payable by him to the company in respect of those shares with interest at the rate at which interest was payable on those moneys before the forfeiture or, if no interest was so payable, at the appropriate rate (as defined in the Act) from the date of forfeiture until payment but the directors may waive payment wholly or in part or enforce payment without any allowance for the value of the shares at the time of forfeiture or for any consideration received on their disposal.

[9-012EB] **22** A statutory declaration by a director or the secretary that a share has been forfeited on a specified date shall be conclusive evidence of the facts stated in it as against all persons claiming to be entitled to the share and the declaration shall (subject to the execution of an instrument of transfer if necessary) constitute a good title to the share and the person to whom the share is disposed of shall not be bound to see to the application of the consideration, if any, nor shall his title to the share be affected by any irregularity in or invalidity of the proceedings in reference to the forfeiture or disposal of the share.

TRANSFER OF SHARES

23 The instrument of transfer of a share may be in any usual form or in any other form which the directors may approve and shall be executed by or on behalf of the transferor and, unless the share is fully paid, by or on behalf of the transferee. [9–012EC]

24 The directors may refuse to register the transfer of a share which is not fully paid to a person of whom they do not approve and they may refuse to register the transfer of a share on which the company has a lien. They may also refuse to register a transfer unless: [9–012ED]
— it is lodged at the office or at such other place as the directors may appoint and is accompanied by the certificate for the shares to which it relates and such other evidence as the directors may reasonably require to show the right of the transferor to make the transfer;
— it is in respect of only one class of shares; and
— it is in favour of not more than four transferees.

25 If the directors refuse to register a transfer of a share, they shall within two months after the date on which the transfer was lodged with the company send to the transferee notice of the refusal. [9–012F]

26 The registration of transfers of shares or of transfers of any class of shares may be suspended at such times and for such periods (not exceeding thirty days in any year) as the directors may determine. [9–012FA]

27 No fee shall be charged for the registration of any instrument of transfer or other document relating to or affecting the title to any share. [9–012FB]

28 The company shall be entitled to retain any instrument of transfer which is registered, but any instrument of transfer which the directors refuse to register shall be returned to the person lodging it when notice of the refusal is given. [9–012FC]

TRANSMISSION OF SHARES

29 If a member dies the survivor or survivors where he was a joint holder, and his personal representatives where he was a sole holder or the only survivor of joint holders, shall be the only persons recognised by the company as having any title to his interest; but nothing herein contained shall release the estate of a deceased member from any liability in respect of any share which had been jointly held by him. [9–012FD]

30 A person becoming entitled to a share in consequence of the death or bankruptcy of a member may, upon such evidence being produced as the directors may properly require, elect either to become the holder of the share or to have some person nominated by him registered as the transferee. If he elects to become the holder he shall give notice to the company to that effect. If he elects to have another person registered he shall execute an instrument of transfer of the share to that person. All the articles relating to the transfer of [9–012G] shares shall apply to the notice or instrument of transfer as if it were an instrument of transfer executed by the member and the death or bankruptcy of the member had not occurred.

[9–012GA] **31** A person becoming entitled to a share in consequence of the death or bankruptcy of a member shall have the rights to which he would be entitled if he were the holder of the share, except that he shall not, before being registered as the holder of the share, be entitled in respect of it to attend or vote at any meeting of the company or at any separate meeting of the holders of any class of shares in the company.

ALTERATION OF SHARE CAPITAL

[9–012GB] **32** The company may by ordinary resolution—
— increase its share capital by new shares of such amount as the resolution prescribes;
— consolidate and divide all or any of its share capital into shares of larger amount than its existing shares;
— subject to the provisions of the Act, sub-divide its shares, or any of them, into shares of smaller amount and the resolution may determine that, as between the shares resulting from the sub-division, any of them may have any preference or advantage as compared with the others; and
— cancel shares which, at the date of the passing of the resolution, have not been taken or agreed to be taken by any person and diminish the amount of its share capital by the amount of the shares so cancelled.

[9–012GC] **33** Whenever as a result of a consolidation of shares any members would become entitled to fractions of a share, the directors may, on behalf of those members, sell the shares representing the fractions for the best price reasonably obtainable to any person (including, subject to the provisions of the Act, the company) and distribute the net proceeds of sale in due proportion among those members, and the directors may authorise some person to execute an instrument of transfer of the shares to, or in accordance with the directions of, the purchaser. The transferee shall not be bound to see to the application of the purchase money nor shall his title to the shares be affected by any irregularity in or invalidity of the proceedings in reference to the sale.

[9–012GD] **34** Subject to the provisions of the Act, the company may by special resolution reduce its share capital, any capital redemption reserve and any share premium account in any way.

PURCHASE OF OWN SHARES

[9–012H] **35** Subject to the provisions of the Act, the company may purchase its own shares (including any redeemable shares) and, if it is a private company, make a payment in respect of the redemption or purchase of its own shares otherwise than out of distributable profits of the company or the proceeds of a fresh issue of shares.

GENERAL MEETINGS

[9–012HA] **36** [   ][3]

[9–012HB] **37** The directors may call general meetings and, on the requisition of members pursuant to the provisions of the Act, shall forthwith proceed to convene [a] general meeting [in accordance with the provisions of the Act[4]]. If there are not within the United Kingdom sufficient directors to call a general meeting, any director or any member of the company may call a general meeting.

NOTICE OF GENERAL MEETINGS

[*private companies*][5] [9–012HC]

38 General meetings shall be called by at least fourteen clear days' notice but a general meeting may be called by shorter notice if it is so agreed:
—   by a majority in number of the members having a right to attend and vote being a majority together holding not less than ninety per cent, in nominal value of the shares giving that right.

The notice shall specify the time and place of the meeting and the general nature of the business to be transacted and.

Subject to the provisions of the articles and to any restrictions imposed on any shares, the notice shall be given to all the members, to all persons entitled to a share in consequence of the death or bankruptcy of a member and to the directors and auditors.

[*public companies*][6] [9–012HD]

38 An annual general meeting shall be called by at least twenty-one clear days' notice. All other general meetings shall be called by at least fourteen clear days' notice but a general meeting may be called by shorter notice if it is so agreed:
—   in the case of an annual general meeting, by all the members entitled to attend and vote thereat; and
—   in the case of any other meeting by a majority in number of the members having a right to attend and vote being a majority together holding not less than ninety-five per cent, in nominal value of the shares giving that right.

The notice shall specify the time and place of the meeting and the general nature of the business to be transacted and, in the case of an annual general meeting, shall specify the meeting as such.

Subject to the provisions of the articles and to any restrictions imposed on any shares, the notice shall be given to all the members, to all persons entitled to a share in consequence of the death or bankruptcy of a member and to the directors and auditors.

39 The accidental omission to give notice of a meeting to, or the non-receipt of notice of a meeting by, any person entitled to receive notice shall not invalidate the proceedings at that meeting. [9–012I]

PROCEEDINGS AT GENERAL MEETINGS

40 No business shall be transacted at any meeting unless a quorum is present. [Save in the case of a company with a single member[7]] two persons entitled to vote upon the business to be transacted, each being a member or a proxy for a member or a duly authorised representative of a corporation, shall be a quorum. [9–012IA]

41 If such a quorum is not present within half an hour from the time appointed for the meeting, or if during a meeting such a quorum ceases to be [9–012IB] present, the meeting shall stand adjourned to the same day in the next week at the same time and place or to such time and place as the directors may determine.

[9–012IC] **42** The chairman, if any, of the board of directors or in his absence some other director nominated by the directors shall preside as chairman of the meeting, but if neither the chairman nor such other director (if any) be present within fifteen minutes after the time appointed for holding the meeting and willing to act, the directors present shall elect one of their number to be chairman and, if there is only one director present and willing to act, he shall be chairman.

[9–012ID] **43** If no director is willing to act as chairman, or if no director is present within fifteen minutes after the time appointed for holding the meeting, the members present and entitled to vote shall choose one of their number to be chairman.

[9–012J] **44** A director shall, notwithstanding that he is not a member, be entitled to attend and speak at any general meeting and at any separate meeting of the holders of any class of shares in the company.

[9–012JA] **45** The chairman may, with the consent of a meeting at which a quorum is present (and shall if so directed by the meeting), adjourn the meeting from time to time and from place to place, but no business shall be transacted at an adjourned meeting other than business which might properly have been transacted at the meeting had the adjournment not taken place. When a meeting is adjourned for fourteen days or more, at least seven clear days' notice shall be given specifying the time and place of the adjourned meeting and the general nature of the business to be transacted. Otherwise it shall not be necessary to give any such notice.

[9–012JB] **46** A resolution put to the vote of a meeting shall be decided on a show of hands unless before, or on the declaration of the result of, the show of hands a poll is duly demanded. Subject to the provisions of the Act, a poll may be demanded:
—   by the chairman; or
—   by at least two members having the right to vote at the meeting; or
—   by a member or members representing not less than one-tenth of the total voting rights of all the members having the right to vote at the meeting; or
—   by a member or members holding shares conferring a right to vote at the meeting being shares on which an aggregate sum has been paid up equal to not less than one-tenth of the total sum paid up on all the shares conferring that right;
and a demand by a person as proxy for a member shall be the same as a demand by the member.

[9–012JC] **47** Unless a poll is duly demanded a declaration by the chairman that a resolution has been carried or carried unanimously, or by a particular majority, or lost, or not carried by a particular majority and an entry to that effect in the minutes of the meeting shall be conclusive evidence of the fact without proof of the number or proportion of the votes recorded in favour of or against the resolution.

48 The demand for a poll may, before the poll is taken, be withdrawn but only with the consent of the chairman and a demand so withdrawn shall not be taken to have invalidated the result of a show of hands declared before the demand was made. **[9–012JD]**

49 A poll shall be taken as the chairman directs and he may appoint scrutineers (who need not be members) and fix a time and place for declaring the result of the poll. The result of the poll shall be deemed to be the resolution of the meeting at which the poll was demanded. **[9–012K]**

50 [—][8] **[9–012KA]**

51 A poll demanded on the election of a chairman or on a question of adjournment shall be taken forthwith. A poll demanded on any other question shall be taken either forthwith or at such time and place as the chairman directs not being more than thirty days after the poll is demanded. The demand for a poll shall not prevent the continuance of a meeting for the transaction of any business other than the question on which the poll was demanded. If a poll is demanded before the declaration of the result of a show of hands and the demand is duly withdrawn, the meeting shall continue as if the demand had not been made. **[9–012KB]**

52 No notice need be given of a poll not taken forthwith if the time and place at which it is to be taken are announced at the meeting at which it is demanded. In any other case at least seven clear days' notice shall be given specifying the time and place at which the poll is to be taken. **[9–012KC]**

53 [—][9] **[9–012KD]**

VOTES OF MEMBERS

54 Subject to any rights or restrictions attached to any shares, on a show of hands every member who (being an individual) is present in person [or by proxy[10]] or (being a corporation) is present by a duly authorised representative [or by proxy], [unless the proxy (in either case) or the representative is] himself a member entitled to vote, shall have one vote and on a poll every member shall have one vote for every share of which he is the holder. **[9–012L]**

55 In the case of joint holders the vote of the senior who tenders a vote, whether in person or by proxy, shall be accepted to the exclusion of the votes of the other joint holders; and seniority shall be determined by the order in which the names of the holders stand in the register of members. **[9–012LA]**

56 A member in respect of whom an order has been made by any court having jurisdiction (whether in the United Kingdom or elsewhere) in matters concerning mental disorder may vote, whether on a show of hands or on a poll, by his receiver, curator bonis or other person authorised in that behalf appointed by that court, and any such receiver, curator bonis or other person may, on a poll, vote by proxy. Evidence to the satisfaction of the directors of the authority of the person claiming to exercise the right to vote shall be deposited at the office, or at such other place as is specified in accordance with the articles for the deposit of instruments of proxy, not less than 48 hours before the time appointed for holding the meeting or adjourned meeting at which the right to vote is to be exercised and in default the right to vote shall not be exercisable. **[9–012LB]**

[9-012LC] **57** No member shall vote at any general meeting or at any separate meeting of the holders of any class of shares in the company, either in person or by proxy, in respect of any share held by him unless all moneys presently payable by him in respect of that share have been paid.

[9-012LD] **58** No objection shall be raised to the qualification of any voter except at the meeting or adjourned meeting at which the vote objected to is tendered, and every vote not disallowed at the meeting shall be valid. Any objection made in due time shall be referred to the chairman whose decision shall be final and conclusive.

[9-012M] **59** On a poll votes may be given either personally or by proxy. A member may appoint more than one proxy to attend on the same occasion.

[9-012MA] [*private companies*][11]

60 The appointment of a proxy shall be, executed by or on behalf of the appointor and shall be in the following form (or in a form as near thereto as circumstances allow or in any other form which is usual or which the directors may approve):

'   Limited

I/We,   , of   being a member/ members   of   the   above-named   company,   hereby   appoint
                 of   ,   or   failing   him,
                 of   , as my/our proxy to vote in my/our name[s] and on my/our behalf at the general meeting of the company to be held on   20   , and at any adjournment thereof.
Signed on   20   .'

[9-012MB] [*public companies*][12]

60 The appointment of a proxy shall be, executed by or on behalf of the appointor and shall be in the following form (or in a form as near thereto as circumstances allow or in any other form which is usual or which the directors may approve):-

'   PLC

I/We,   , of   , being a member/ members   of   the   above-named   company,   hereby   appoint
                 of   ,   or   failing   him,
                 of   , as my/our proxy to vote in my/our name[s] and on my/our behalf at the annual and any other general meeting of the company to be held on   20   , and at any adjournment thereof.
Signed on   20   .'

[9-012MC] [*private companies*][13]

61 Where it is desired to afford members an opportunity of instructing the proxy how he shall act the appointment of a proxy shall be in the following form (or in a form as near thereto as circumstances allow or in any other form which is usual or which the directors may approve):

'   Limited

I/We   , of   , being a member/ members of the above named company, hereby appoint   of
                 ,   or   failing   him,   of
                 , as my/our proxy to vote in my/our name[s] and on

my/our behalf at the general meeting of the company, to be held on
20   , and at any adjournment thereof.
This form is to be used in respect of the resolutions mentioned below as
follows:
Resolution No. 1 *for *against
Resolution No. 2 *for *against.
*Strike out whichever is not desired.
Unless otherwise instructed, the proxy may vote as he thinks fit or abstain
from voting.
Signed this   day of   20   .'

[*public companies*][14]   [9–012MD]

61 Where it is desired to afford members an opportunity of instructing the
proxy how he shall act the appointment of a proxy shall be in the following
form (or in a form as near thereto as circumstances allow or in any other form
which is usual or which the directors may approve):-
'   PLC
I/We   , of   ,
being a member/members of the above named company, hereby appoint
                              of   , or   failing   him,
                              of   , as my/our proxy to vote in
my/our name[s] and on my/our behalf at the annual and other general
meeting of the company, to be held on   20   , and at any
adjournment thereof.
This form is to be used in respect of the resolutions mentioned below as
follows:
Resolution No 1 *for *against
Resolution No 2 *for *against.
*Strike out whichever is not desired.
Unless otherwise instructed, the proxy may vote as he thinks fit or abstain
from voting.
Signed this   day of   20   .'

62 The appointment of a proxy and any authority under which it is executed   [9–012N]
or a copy of such authority certified notarially or in some other way approved
by the directors may:

— in the case of an instrument in writing be deposited at the office or at
such other place within the United kingdom as is specified in the
notice convening the meeting or in any instrument of proxy sent out by
the company in relation to the meeting not less than 48 hours before
the time for holding the meeting or adjourned meeting at which the
person named in the instrument proposes to vote; or

— in the case of an appointment contained in an electronic communication, where an address has been specified for the purpose of receiving
electronic communications—

(i)   in the notice convening the meeting, or
(ii)   in any instrument of proxy sent out by the company in relation
to the meeting, or
(iii)   in any invitation contained in an electronic communication to
appoint a proxy issued by the company in relation to the
meeting,

be received at such address not less than 48 hours before the time for
holding the meeting or adjourned meeting at which the person named
in the appointment proposes to vote;

— in the case of a poll taken more than 48 hours after it is demanded, be deposited or received as aforesaid after the poll has been demanded and not less than 24 hours before the time appointed for the taking of the poll; or

— where the poll is not taken forthwith but is taken not more than 48 hours after it was demanded, be delivered at the meeting at which the poll was demanded to the chairman or to the secretary or to any director;

and an appointment of proxy which is not deposited, delivered or received in a manner so permitted shall be invalid.

In this regulation and the next, 'address', in relation to electronic communications, includes any number or address used for the purposes of such communications.

[9–012NA] **63** A vote given or poll demanded by proxy or by the duly authorised representative of a corporation shall be valid notwithstanding the previous determination of the authority of the person voting or demanding a poll unless notice of the determination was received by the company at the office or at such other place at which the instrument of proxy was duly deposited or, where the appointment of the proxy was contained in an electronic communication, at the address at which such appointment was duly received before the commencement of the meeting or adjourned meeting at which the vote is given or the poll demanded or (in the case of a poll taken otherwise than on the same day as the meeting or adjourned meeting) the time appointed for taking the poll.

NUMBER OF DIRECTORS

[9–012NB] **64** Unless otherwise determined by ordinary resolution, the number of directors (other than alternate directors) shall not be subject to any maximum but shall be not less than two.

ALTERNATE DIRECTORS

[9–012NC] **65** Any director (other than an alternate director) may appoint any other director, or any other person approved by resolution of the directors and willing to act, to be an alternate director and may remove from office an alternate director so appointed by him.

[9–012ND] **66** An alternate director shall be entitled to receive notice of all meetings of directors and of all meetings of committees of directors of which his appointor is a member, to attend and vote at any such meeting at which the director appointing him is not personally present and generally to perform all the functions of his appointor as a director in his absence but shall not be entitled to receive any remuneration from the company for his services as an alternate director. But it shall not be necessary to give notice of such a meeting to an alternate director who is absent from the United Kingdom.

[9–0120] **67** An alternate director shall cease to be an alternate director if his appointor ceases to be a director; but, if a director retires by rotation or otherwise but is reappointed or deemed to have been reappointed at the meeting at which he retires, any appointment of an alternate director made by him which was in force immediately prior to his retirement shall continue after his reappointment.

68 Any appointment or removal of an alternate director shall be by notice to the company signed by the director making or revoking the appointment or in any other manner approved by the directors.

69 Save as otherwise provided in the articles, an alternate director shall be deemed for all purposes to be a director and shall alone be responsible for his own acts and defaults and he shall not be deemed to be the agent of the director appointing him.

POWERS OF DIRECTORS

70 Subject to the provisions of the Act, the memorandum and the articles and to any directions given by special resolution, the business of the company shall be managed by the directors who may exercise all the powers of the company. No alteration of the memorandum or articles and no such direction shall invalidate any prior act of the directors which would have been valid if that alteration had not been made or that direction had not been given. The powers given by this regulation shall not be limited by any special power given to the directors by the articles and a meeting of directors at which a quorum is present may exercise all powers exercisable by the directors.

71 The directors may, by power of attorney or otherwise, appoint any person to be the agent of the company for such purposes and on such conditions as they determine, including authority for the agent to delegate all or any of his powers.

DELEGATION OF DIRECTORS' POWERS

72 The directors may delegate any of their powers to any committee consisting of one or more directors. They may also delegate to any managing director or any director holding any other executive office such of their powers as they consider desirable to be exercised by him. Any such delegation may be made subject to any conditions the directors may impose, and either collaterally with or to the exclusion of their own powers and may be revoked or altered. Subject to any such conditions, the proceedings of a committee with two or more members shall be governed by the articles regulating the proceedings of directors so far as they are capable of applying.

APPOINTMENT AND RETIREMENT OF DIRECTORS

[*private companies*]

73, **74** and **75** [   ][15]

[*public companies*]

73 At the first annual general meeting all the directors shall retire from office, and at every subsequent annual general meeting one-third of the directors who are subject to retirement by rotation or, if their number is not three or a multiple of three, the number nearest to one-third shall retire from office; but, if there is only one director who is subject to retirement by rotation, he shall retire.

74 Subject to the provisions of the Act, the directors to retire by rotation shall be those who have been longest in office since their last appointment or reappointment, but as between persons who became or were last reappointed directors on the same day those to retire shall (unless they otherwise agree among themselves) be determined by lot.

[9–012PD] **75** If the company, at the meeting at which a director retires by rotation, does not fill the vacancy the retiring director shall, if willing to act, be deemed to have been reappointed unless at the meeting it is resolved not to fill the vacancy or unless a resolution for the reappointment of the director is put to the meeting and lost.

[9–012Q] **76** No person *other than a director retiring by rotation*[16] shall be appointed or reappointed a director at any general meeting unless:
— he is recommended by the directors; or
— not less than fourteen nor more than thirty-five clear days before the date appointed for the meeting, notice executed by a member qualified to vote at the meeting has been given to the company of the intention to propose that person for appointment or reappointment stating the particulars which would, if he were so appointed or reappointed, be required to be included in the company's register of directors together with notice executed by that person of his willingness to be appointed or reappointed.

[9–012QA] **77** Not less than seven nor more than twenty-eight clear days before the date appointed for holding a general meeting notice shall be given to all who are entitled to receive notice of the meeting of any person (*other than a director retiring by rotation at the meeting*)[17] who is recommended by the directors for appointment or reappointment as a director at the meeting or in respect of whom notice has been duly given to the company of the intention to propose him at the meeting for appointment or reappointment as a director. The notice shall give the particulars of that person which would, if he were so appointed or reappointed, be required to be included in the company's register of directors.

[9–012QB] **78** *Subject as aforesaid*[18], the company may by ordinary resolution appoint a person who is willing to act to be a director either to fill a vacancy or as an additional director and may also determine the rotation in which any additional directors are to retire.

[9–012QC] **79** The directors may appoint a person who is willing to act to be a director, either to fill a vacancy or as an additional director, provided that the appointment does not cause the number of directors to exceed any number fixed by or in accordance with the articles as the maximum number of directors. *A director so appointed shall hold office only until the next following annual general meeting and shall not be taken into account in determining the directors who are to retire by rotation at the meeting. If not reappointed at such annual general meeting, he shall vacate office at the conclusion thereof.*[19]

[9–012QD] [*private companies*]

   80 [   ][20]

[9–012R] [*public companies*]

   80 Subject as aforesaid, a director who retires at an annual general meeting may, if willing to act, be reappointed. If he is not reappointed, he shall retain office until the meeting appoints someone in his place, or if it does not do so, until the end of the meeting.

DISQUALIFICATION AND REMOVAL OF DIRECTORS

81 The office of a director shall be vacated if: [9-012RA]

—   he ceases to be a director by virtue of any provision of the Act or he becomes prohibited by law from being a director; or

—   he becomes bankrupt or makes any arrangement or composition with his creditors generally; or

—   he is, or may be, suffering from mental disorder and either:

(i)   he is admitted to hospital in pursuance of an application for admission for treatment under the Mental Health Act 1983 or, in Scotland, an application for admission under the Mental Health (Scotland) Act 1960, or

(ii)   an order is made by a court having jurisdiction (whether in the United Kingdom or elsewhere) in matters concerning mental disorder for his detention or for the appointment of a receiver, curator bonis or other person to exercise powers with respect to his property or affairs; or

—   he resigns his office by notice to the company; or

—   he shall for more than six consecutive months have been absent without permission of the directors from meetings of directors held during that period and the directors resolve that his office be vacated.

REMUNERATION OF DIRECTORS

82 The directors shall be entitled to such remuneration as the company may   [9-012RB]
by ordinary resolution determine and, unless the resolution provides otherwise, the remuneration shall be deemed to accrue from day to day.

DIRECTORS' EXPENSES

83 The directors may be paid all travelling, hotel, and other expenses properly   [9-012RC]
incurred by them in connection with their attendance at meetings of directors or committees of directors or general meetings or separate meetings of the holders of any class of shares or of debentures of the company or otherwise in connection with the discharge of their duties.

DIRECTORS' APPOINTMENTS AND INTERESTS

84 Subject to the provisions of the Act, the directors may appoint one or more   [9-012RD]
of their number to the office of managing director or to any other executive office under the company and may enter into an agreement or arrangement with any director for his employment by the company or for the provision by him of any services outside the scope of the ordinary duties of a director. Any such appointment, agreement or arrangement may be made upon such terms as the directors determine and they may remunerate any such director for his services as they think fit. Any appointment of a director to an executive office shall terminate if he ceases to be a director but without prejudice to any claim to damages for breach of the contract of service between the director and the company. A managing director and a director holding any other executive office shall not be subject to retirement by rotation.

85 Subject to the provisions of the Act, and provided that he has disclosed to   [9-012S]
the directors the nature and extent of any material interest of his, a director notwithstanding his office:

—   may be a party to, or otherwise interested in, any transaction or arrangement with the company or in which the company or in which the company is otherwise interested;

— may be a director or other officer of, or employed by, or a party to any transaction or arrangement with, or otherwise interested in, any body corporate promoted by the company or in which the company is otherwise interested; and

— shall not, by reason of his office, be accountable to the company for any benefit which he derives from any such office or employment or from any such transaction or arrangement or from any interest in any such body corporate and no such transaction or arrangement shall be liable to be avoided on the ground of any such interest or benefit.

[9–012SA] **86** For the purposes of regulation 85:

— a general notice given to the directors that a director is to be regarded as having an interest of the nature and extent specified in the notice in any transaction or arrangement in which a specified person or class of persons is interested shall be deemed to be a disclosure that the director has an interest in any such transaction of the nature and extent so specified; and

— an interest of which a director has no knowledge and of which it is unreasonable to expect him to have knowledge shall not be treated as an interest of his.

DIRECTORS' GRATUITIES AND PENSIONS

[9–012SB] **87** The directors may provide benefits, whether by the payment of gratuities or pensions or by insurance or otherwise, for any director who has held but no longer holds any executive office or employment with the company or with any body corporate which is or has been a subsidiary of the company or a predecessor in business of the company or of any such subsidiary, and for any member of his family (including a spouse and a former spouse) or any person who is or was dependent on him, and may (as well before as after he ceases to hold such office or employment) contribute to any fund and pay premiums for the purchase or provision of any such benefit.

PROCEEDINGS OF DIRECTORS

[9–012SC] **88** Subject to the provisions of the articles, the directors may regulate their proceedings as they think fit. A director may, and the secretary at the request of a director shall, call a meeting of the directors. It shall not be necessary to give notice of a meeting to a director who is absent from the United Kingdom. Questions arising at a meeting shall be decided by a majority of votes. In the case of an equality of votes, the chairman shall have a second or casting vote. A director who is also an alternate director shall be entitled in the absence of his appointor to a separate vote on behalf of his appointor in addition to his own vote.

[9–012SD] **89** The quorum for the transaction of the business of the directors may be fixed by the directors and unless so fixed at any other number shall be two. A person who holds office only as an alternate director shall, if his appointor is not present, be counted in the quorum.

[9–012T] **90** The continuing directors or a sole continuing director may act notwithstanding any vacancies in their number, but, if the number of directors is less than the number fixed as the quorum, the continuing directors or director may act only for the purpose of filling vacancies or of calling a general meeting.

91 The directors may appoint one of their number to be the chairman of the board of directors and may at any time remove him from that office. Unless he is unwilling to do so, the director so appointed shall preside at every meeting of directors at which he is present. But if there is no director holding that office, or if the director holding it is unwilling to preside or is not present within five minutes after the time appointed for the meeting, the directors present may appoint one of their number to be chairman of the meeting.   [9–012TA]

92 All acts done by a meeting of directors, or of a committee of directors, or by a person acting as a director shall, notwithstanding that it be afterwards discovered that there was a defect in the appointment of any director or that any of them were disqualified from holding office, or had vacated office, or were not entitled to vote, be as valid as if every such person had been duly appointed and was qualified and had continued to be a director and had been entitled to vote.   [9–012TB]

93 A resolution in writing signed by all the directors entitled to receive notice of a meeting of directors or of a committee of directors shall be as valid and effectual as it if had been passed at a meeting of directors or (as the case may be) a committee of directors duly convened and held and may consist of several documents in the like form each signed by one or more directors; but a resolution signed by an alternate director need not also be signed by his appointor and, if it is signed by a director who has appointed an alternate director, it need not be signed by the alternate director in that capacity.   [9–012TC]

94 Save as otherwise provided by the articles, a director shall not vote at a meeting of directors or of a committee of directors on any resolution concerning a matter in which he has, directly or indirectly, an interest or duty which is material and which conflicts or may conflict with the interests of the company unless his interest or duty arises only because the case falls within one or more of the following paragraphs: [9–012TD]
—   the resolution relates to the giving to him of a guarantee, security, or indemnity in respect of money lent to, or an obligation incurred by him for the benefit of, the company or any of its subsidiaries;
—   the resolution relates to the giving to a third party of a guarantee, security, or indemnity in respect of an obligation of the company or any of its subsidiaries for which the director has assumed responsibility in whole or part and whether alone or jointly with others under a guarantee or indemnity or by the giving of security;
—   his interest arises by virtue of his subscribing or agreeing to subscribe for any shares, debentures, or other securities of the company or any of its subsidiaries, or by virtue of his being, or intending to become, a participant in the underwriting or sub-underwriting of an offer of any such shares, debentures, or other securities by the company or any of its subsidiaries for subscription, purchase or exchange;
—   the resolution relates in any way to a retirement benefits scheme which has been approved, or is conditional upon approval, by the Board of Inland Revenue for taxation purposes.
For the purposes of this regulation, an interest of a person who is, for any purpose of the Act (excluding any statutory modification thereof not in force when this regulation becomes binding on the company), connected with a

director shall be treated as an interest of the director and, in relation to an alternate director, an interest of his appointor shall be treated as an interest of the alternate director without prejudice to any interest which the alternate director has otherwise.

[9–012U] **95** A director shall not be counted in the quorum present at a meeting in relation to a resolution on which he is not entitled to vote.

[9–012UA] **96** The company may by ordinary resolution suspend or relax to any extent, either generally or in respect of any particular matter, any provision of the articles prohibiting a director from voting at a meeting of directors or of a committee of directors.

[9–012UB] **97** Where proposals are under consideration concerning the appointment of two or more directors to offices or employments with the company or any body corporate in which the company is interested the proposals may be divided and considered in relation to each director separately and (provided he is not for another reason precluded from voting) each of the directors concerned shall be entitled to vote and be counted in the quorum in respect of each resolution except that concerning his own appointment.

[9–012UC] **98** If a question arises at a meeting of directors or of a committee of directors as to the right of a director to vote, the question may, before the conclusion of the meeting, be referred to the chairman of the meeting and his ruling in relation to any director other than himself shall be final and conclusive.

SECRETARY

[9–012UD] **99** Subject to the provisions of the Act, the secretary shall be appointed by the directors for such term, at such remuneration and upon such conditions as they may think fit; and any secretary so appointed may be removed by them.

MINUTES

[9–012V] **100** The directors shall cause minutes to be made in books kept for the purpose:
— of all appointments of officers made by the directors; and
— of all proceedings at meetings of the company, of the holders of any class of shares in the company, and of the directors, and of committees of directors, including the names of the directors present at each such meeting.

THE SEAL

[9–012VA] **101** The seal shall only be used by the authority of the directors or of a committee of directors authorised by the directors. The directors may determine who shall sign any instrument to which the seal is affixed and unless otherwise so determined it shall be signed by a director and by the secretary or by a second director.

DIVIDENDS

[9–012VB] **102** Subject to the provisions of the Act, the company may by ordinary resolution declare dividends in accordance with the respective rights of the members, but no dividend shall exceed the amount recommended by the directors.

103 Subject to the provisions of the Act, the directors may pay interim [9–012VC] dividends if it appears to them that they are justified by the profits of the company available for distribution. If the share capital is divided into different classes, the directors may pay interim dividends on shares which confer deferred or non-preferred rights with regard to dividend as well as on shares which confer preferential rights with regard to dividend, but no interim dividend shall be paid on shares carrying deferred or non-preferred rights if, at the time of payment, any preferential dividend is in arrear. The directors may also pay at intervals settled by them any dividend payable at a fixed rate if it appears to them that the profits available for distribution justify the payment. Provided the directors act in good faith they shall not incur any liability to the holders of shares conferring preferred rights for any loss they may suffer by the lawful payment of an interim dividend on any shares having deferred or non-preferred rights.

104 Except as otherwise provided by the rights attached to shares, all [9–012VD] dividends shall be declared and paid according to the amounts paid up on the shares on which the dividend is paid. All dividends shall be apportioned and paid proportionately to the amounts paid up on the shares during any portion or portions of the period in respect of which the dividend is paid; but, if any share is issued on terms providing that it shall rank for dividend as from a particular date, that share shall rank for dividend accordingly.

105 A general meeting declaring a dividend may, upon the recommendation of [9–012W] the directors, direct that it shall be satisfied wholly or partly by the distribution of assets and, where any difficulty arises in regard to the distribution, the directors may settle the same and in particular may issue fractional certificates and fix the value for distribution of any assets and may determine that cash shall be paid to any member upon the footing of the value so fixed in order to adjust the rights of members and may vest any assets in trustees.

106 Any dividend or other moneys payable in respect of a share may be paid [9–012WA] by cheque sent by post to the registered address of the person entitled or, if two or more persons are the holders of the share or are jointly entitled to it by reason of the death or bankruptcy of the holder, to the registered address of that one of those persons who is first named in the register of members or to such person and to such address as the person or persons entitled may in writing direct. Every cheque shall be made payable to the order of the person or persons entitled or to such other person as the person or persons entitled may in writing direct and payment of the cheque shall be a good discharge to the company. Any joint holder or other person jointly entitled to a share as aforesaid may give receipts for any dividend or other moneys payable in respect of the share.

107 No dividend or other moneys payable in respect of a share shall bear [9–012WB] interest against the company unless otherwise provided by the rights attached to the share.

108 Any dividend which has remained unclaimed for twelve years from the [9–012WC] date when it became due for payment shall, if the directors so resolve, be forfeited and cease to remain owing by the company.

ACCOUNTS

[9-012WD] **109** No member shall (as such) have any right of inspecting any accounting records or other book or document of the company except as conferred by statute or authorised by the directors or by ordinary resolution of the company.

CAPITALISATION OF PROFITS

[9-012X] **110** The directors may with the authority of an ordinary resolution of the company:
—   subject as hereinafter provided, resolve to capitalise any undivided profits of the company not required for paying any preferential dividend (whether or not they are available for distribution) or any sum standing to the credit of the company's share premium account or capital redemption reserve;
—   appropriate the sum resolved to be capitalised to the members who would have been entitled to it if it were distributed by way of dividend and in the same proportions and apply such sum on their behalf either in or towards paying up the amounts, if any, for the time being unpaid on any shares held by them respectively, or in paying up in full unissued shares or debentures of the company of a nominal amount equal to that sum, and allot the shares or debentures credited as fully paid to those members, or as they may direct, in those proportions, or partly in one way and partly in the other: but the share premium account, the capital redemption reserve, and any profits which are not available for distribution may, for the purposes of this regulation, only be applied in paying up unissued shares to be allotted to members credited as fully paid;
—   make such provision by the issue of fractional certificates or by payment in cash or otherwise as they determine in the case of shares or debentures becoming distributable under this regulation in fractions; and
—   authorise any person to enter on behalf of all the members concerned into an agreement with the company providing for the allotment to them respectively, credited as fully paid, of any shares or debentures to which they are entitled upon such capitalisation, any agreement made under such authority being binding on all such members.

NOTICES

[9-012XA] **111** Any notice to be given to or by any person pursuant to the articles (other than a notice calling a meeting of the directors) shall be in writing or shall be given using electronic communications to an address for the time being notified for that purpose to the person giving the notice.
In this regulation, 'address', in relation to electronic communications, includes any number or address used for the purposes of such communications.

[9-012XB] **112** The company may give any notice to a member either personally or by sending it by post in a prepaid envelope addressed to the member at his registered address or by leaving it at that address or by giving it using electronic communications to an address for the time being notified to the company by the member. In the case of joint holders of a share, all notices shall be given to the joint holder whose name stands first in the register of members in respect of the joint holding and notice so given shall be sufficient notice to all the joint holders. A member whose registered address is not within the United Kingdom and who gives to the company an address within the United Kingdom at which notices may be given to him, or an address to which notices may be sent using electronic communications, shall be entitled to have notices given to him at that address, but otherwise no such member shall be entitled to receive any notice from the company.

In this regulation and the next, 'address', in relation to electronic communications, includes any number or address used for the purposes of such communications.

113 A member present, either in person or by proxy, at any meeting of the company or of the holders of any class of shares in the company shall be deemed to have received notice of the meeting and, where requisite, of the purposes for which it was called. **[9–012XC]**

114 Every person who becomes entitled to a share shall be bound by any notice in respect of that share which, before his name is entered in the register of members, has been duly given to a person from whom he derives his title. **[9–012XD]**

115 Proof that an envelope containing a notice was properly addressed, prepaid and posted shall be conclusive evidence that that the notice was given. Proof that a notice contained in an electronic communication was sent in accordance with guidance issued by the Institute of Chartered Secretaries and Administrators shall be conclusive evidence that the notice was given. A notice shall, be deemed to be given at the expiration of 48 hours after the envelope containing it was posted or, in the case of a notice contained in an electronic communication, at the expiration of 48 hours after the time it was sent. **[9–012Y]**

116 A notice may be given by the company to the persons entitled to a share in consequence of the death or bankruptcy of a member by sending or delivering it, in any manner authorised by the articles for the giving of notice to a member, addressed to them by name, or by the title of representatives of the deceased, or trustee of the bankrupt or by any like description at the address, if any, within the United Kingdom supplied for that purpose by the persons claiming to be so entitled. Until such an address has been supplied, a notice may be given in any manner in which it might have been given if the death or bankruptcy had not occurred. **[9–012YA]**

WINDING UP

117 If the company is wound up, the liquidator may, with the sanction of [a special[21]] resolution of the company and any other sanction required by the Act, divide among the members in specie the whole or any part of the assets of the company and may, for that purpose, value any assets and determine how the division shall be carried out as between the members or different classes of members. The liquidator may, with the like sanction, vest the whole or any part of the assets in trustees upon such trusts for the benefit of the members as he with the like sanction determines, but no member shall be compelled to accept any assets upon which there is a liability. **[9–012YB]**

INDEMNITY

118 Subject to the provisions of the Act but without prejudice to any indemnity to which a director may otherwise be entitled, every director or **[9–012YC]**

other officer or auditor of the company shall be indemnified out of the assets of the company against any liability incurred by him in defending any proceedings, whether civil or criminal, in which judgment is given in his favour or in which he is acquitted or in connection with any application in which relief is granted to him by the court from liability for negligence, default, breach of duty or breach of trust in relation to the affairs of the company.

[9–012YD]

1 Table A as prescribed by the Companies (Tables A to F) Regulations 1985, SI 1985/805) and has been amended by:
— the Companies (Tables A to F) (Amendment) Regulations 1985, SI 1985/1052;
— the Companies Act 1985 (Electronic Communications) Order 2000, SI 2000/3373;
(and as a consequence of the Companies Act 2006)
— the Companies (Tables A to F) (Amendment) Regulations 2007, SI 2007/2541 (1 October 2007);
— the Companies (Tables A to F) (Amendment) (No 2) Regulations 2007, SI 2007/2826 (1 October 2007); and
— (for completeness, but it amends Tables C and E and not A) the Companies (Tables A to F) (Amendment) Regulations 2008, SI 2008/739 (6 April 2008).
The version of Table A produced here shows in square brackets or italics the alterations made as a consequence of the Companies Act 2006, all previous alterations having been incorporated in the text, and is the default version for companies formed on and after 1 October 2007.

2 Inserted by SI 2007/2541, reg 3 from 1 October 2007.
3 Ceases to have effect by SI 2007/2541, reg 5 with effect 1 October 2008.
4 Altered by SI 2007/2541, reg 5 with effect 1 October 2008, as a consequence of the expression 'extraordinary general meeting' becoming obsolete.
5 Altered in respect of private companies by SI 2007/2541, reg 9 with effect 1 October 2008.
6 Altered in respect of public companies by SI 2007/2541, reg 20 with effect 1 October 2008.
7 Altered in respect of private companies by SI 2007/2541, reg 10 with effect 1 October 2008.
8 Ceases to have effect by SI 2007/2826, reg 3 with effect 1 October 2008.
9 Ceases to have effect by SI 2007/2541, reg 6 with effect 1 October 2008.
10 All three phrases in square brackets inserted by SI 2007/2826, reg 4 with effect 1 October 2008.
11 Altered in respect of private companies by SI 2007/2541, reg 11 with effect 1 October 2008.
12 Altered in respect of public companies by SI 2007/2541, reg 21 with effect 1 October 2008.
13 Altered in respect of private companies by SI 2007/2541, reg 12 with effect 1 October 2008.
14 Altered in respect of public companies by SI 2007/2541, reg 22 with effect 1 October 2008.
15 Cease to have effect in respect of private companies by SI 2007/2541, reg 13 with effect 1 October 2008.
16 Words in italics omitted in respect of private companies by SI 2007/2541, reg 14 with effect 1 October 2008.
17 Words in italics omitted in respect of private companies by SI 2007/2541, reg 15 with effect 1 October 2008.
18 Words in italics omitted in respect of private companies by SI 2007/2541, reg 16 with effect 1 October 2008.
19 Words in italics omitted in respect of private companies by SI 2007/2541, reg 17 with effect 1 October 2008.
20 Cease to have effect in respect of private companies by SI 2007/2541, reg 18 with effect 1 October 2008.
21 Altered by SI 2007/2541, reg 7 with effect 1 October 2008, as a consequence of the extraordinary resolutions becoming obsolete.

9A Companies

INTRODUCTION TO THE COMPANIES ACT 2006

The Companies Act 2006 ('CA 2006') contains 1300 sections and 16 schedules and received Royal Assent on 8 November 2006. The government had said that all parts of it will be in force by 1 October 2008, but much was not implemented until 1 October 2009: see table below. This chapter has been revised on the assumption that the Act is in force and that the model articles of association will be in the form of the drafts which have been published. The corresponding chapter in the nineteenth edition is therefore not yet superseded, but will be when the CA 2006 is wholly in force. [9A–001]

IMPLEMENTATION TABLE

The following is an outline of the CA 2006. The dates in the third column were taken from the implementation timetable provided by the DTI in July 2007 and published in first supplement to the nineteenth edition. The dates in the fourth column are taken from the BERR (formerly the DTI, now known as BIS) timetable in September 2008 and have been met. Only the following provisions have not been brought into force: s 22(2), s 327(2)(c), s 330(6)(c), Sch 9, Pt 2 and two sets of repeals in Sch 16. [9A–002]

Part (sections)	Provisions	Implementation (original)	Implementation (Sept 2008) if changed
1 (ss 1–6)	General introductory provisions	1 October 2008	1 October 2009
	s 2	6 April 2007	
2 (ss 7–16)	Company formation	1 October 2008	1 October 2009
3 (ss 17–38)	A company's constitution	1 October 2008	1 October 2009
	ss 29, 30	1 October 2007	
4 (ss 39–52)	A company's capacity and related matters	1 October 2008	1 October 2009
	s 44	6 April 2008	
5 (ss 53–85)	A company's name	1 October 2008	1 October 2009
	ss 69 to 74	1 October 2008	

	ss 82 to 85	1 October 2008	
6 (ss 86–88)	A company's registered office	1 October 2008	1 October 2009
7 (ss 89–111)	Re-registration as a means of altering a company's status	1 October 2008	1 October 2009
8 (ss 112–144)	A company's members	1 October 2008	1 October 2009
	ss 116 to 119	1 October 2007	
	ss 121 & 126	6 April 2008	
9 (ss 145–153)	Exercise of members' rights	1 October 2007	
10 (ss 154–259)	A company's directors	1 October 2007	
	ss 155–159, 162–167, 175–177, 182–187, 240–246	1 October 2008	
	ss 154, 160, 161, 168–174, 178–181, 188–239, 247–259	1 October 2007	
	ss 162–167, 240–246	1 October 2008	1 October 2009
	ss 180(1), (2) (in part), and (4)(b), and 181(2) and (3)		1 October 2008
	ss 182–187		1 October 2008
	ss 240–247		1 October 2009
11 (ss 260–269)	Derivative claims and proceedings by members	1 October 2007	
12 (ss 270–280)	Company secretaries	6 April 2008	1 October 2009
	s 270(3)(b)(ii)		1 October 2009
	ss 275–279		1 October 2009
13 (ss 281–361)	Resolutions and meetings, and, related to this, sections 485–488 of Part 16 Audit	1 October 2007	

	ss 308, 209, 333	20 January 2007	
	ss 327(2)(c) and 330(6)(c) are not being commenced for the time being		
14 (ss 362–379)	Control of political donations and expenditure	1 October 2007	
	Provisions relating to independent election candidates	1 October 2007	1 October 2008
	Part 14 comes into force in Northern Ireland on 1 November, except for provisions relating to independent election candidates		
15 (ss 380–474)	Accounts and reports	6 April 2008	
	s 417	1 October 2007	
	s 463 (for reports and statements first sent to members and others after that date	20 January 2007	
16 (ss 475–539)	Audit	6 April 2008	
	ss 485–488	1 October 2007	
17 (ss 540–657)	A company's share capital	1 October 2008	1 October 2009
	s 544		6 April 2008
	ss 641(1)(a) and (2)–(6), 642–644, 652(1) and (3) and 654		6 April 2008
18 (ss 658–737)	Acquisition by limited company of its own shares	1 October 2008	1 October 2009
	Repeal of the restrictions under the Companies Act 1985 on financial assistance for acquisition of shares in private companies, including the 'whitewash' procedure	1 October 2008	

19 (ss 738–754)	Debentures	6 April 2008	
20 (ss 755–767)	Private and public companies	6 April 2008	
21 (ss 768–790)	Certification and transfer of securities	6 April 2008	
22 (ss 791–828)	Information about interests in a company's shares	20 January 2007	
	ss 811(4), 812, 814	1 October 2008	
23 (ss 829–853)	Distributions	6 April 2008	
24 (ss 854–859)	A company's annual return	1 October 2008	1 October 2009
25 (ss 860–894)	Company charges	1 October 2008	1 October 2009
26 (ss 895–901)	Arrangements and reconstructions	6 April 2008	
27 (ss 902–941)	Mergers and divisions of public companies	6 April 2008	
28 (ss 942–992)	Takeovers etc	6 April 2007	
29 (s 993)	Fraudulent trading	1 October 2007	
30 (ss 994–999)	Protection of members against unfair prejudice	1 October 2007	
31 (ss 1000–1034)	Dissolution and restoration to the register	1 October 2008	1 October 2009
32 (ss 1035–1039)	Company investigations: amendments	1 October 2007	
33 (ss 1040–1043)	UK companies not formed under the Companies Acts	1 October 2008	1 October 2009
	s 1043	6 April 2007	
34 (ss 1044–1059)	Overseas companies	1 October 2008	1 October 2009
35 (ss 1060–1120)	The registrar of companies	1 October 2008	1 October 2009
	s 1063 (in respect of England, Wales and Scotland)	6 April 2007	
	ss 1068(5), 1077–1080, 1085–1092, 1102–1107, 1111	1 January 2007	

36 (ss 1121–1133)	Offences under the Companies Acts	With relevant provisions	
	s 1124	1 October 2007	
	s 1126		6 April 2008
37 (ss 1134–1157)	Companies: supplementary provisions	With relevant provisions	
	s 1137(1), (4)(b) and (6)		30 Septem- ber 2007
	ss 1143–1148	20 January 2007	
	s 1157	1 October 2008	
38 (ss 1158–1174)	Companies: interpretation	With relevant provisions	
	ss 1161, 1162, 116, 1165, 1169 and 1172		6 April 2008
	s 1167		30 Septem- ber 2007
	s 1170	6 April 2007	
39 (ss 1175–1181)	Companies: minor amendments	6 April 2007	1 April 2008
	s 1175 (only for Pt 1 of Schedule 9)	1 January 2008	1 April 2008
	ss 1180, 1181	1 October 2008	1 October 2009
40 (ss 1182–1191)	Company directors: foreign disqualification etc	1 October 2008	1 October 2009
41 (ss 1192–1208)	Business names	1 October 2008	1 October 2009
42 (ss 1209–1264)	Statutory auditors	6 April 2008	
	ss 1241–1244		1 October 2009
43 (ss 1265–1273)	Transparency obligations and related matters	Royal Assent	
44 (ss 1274–1283)	Miscellaneous provisions		
	ss 1274, 1276	Royal Assent	
	s 1275		1 October 2009

	ss 1277–1280, 1283	1 October 2008	
	s 1281	6 April 2007	
	s 1282	6 April 2008	
45 (ss 1284–1287)	Northern Ireland	With relevant provisions	
46 (ss 1288–1297)	General supplementary provisions	Royal Assent	
	s 1295	With relevant provisions	
47 (ss 1298–1300)	Final provisions	Royal Assent	

[9A–003] The CA 2006 is said to be the largest piece of legislation ever passed by Parliament. It was granted Royal Assent on 8 November 2006. It restates existing companies legislation, introduces wide-ranging reforms and seeks to enhance corporate governance, shareholder engagement and modernise companies' decision-making processes.

The part and section numbers given in the heading below are not exclusive of all the relevant provisions but are only an indication of the main relevant ones.

MEMORANDUM OF ASSOCIATION — PART 2 S 8 — 1 OCTOBER 2009

[9A–004] Under the CA 2006, the role of the memorandum of association is fundamentally changed, as the articles are effectively the only constitutional document and the memorandum becomes the incorporation document, containing the names of subscribers, the fact that they wish to form a company, that they agree to become members of the company, and, if the company has a share capital, to take at least one share each. The memorandum will no longer be a tool for the operation of the company but is a document which, with specified statements, must be delivered to the registrar with an application for the registration of a company

SHARE CAPITAL — PART 2 S 10, PART 17 S 554 — 1 OCTOBER 2009

[9A–005] From October 2008, new companies will not be required to specify their authorised share capital. A statement of capital and initial shareholdings must be delivered to the registrar on the application to register a company and further allotments registered within two months of each allotment. For existing companies, authorised share capital will continue to operate as a restriction in the articles.

For private companies with one class of shares, directors will be able to allot further shares of that class, subject to any rights or pre-emption in either the articles or the CA 2006, without prior authorisation from members, unless prohibited from doing so by the articles.

MODEL ARTICLES — PART 3 S 18 — 1 OCTOBER 2009

Three sets of model articles will be prescribed in the place of Table A, for [9A–006] private companies limited by shares, private companies limited by guarantee and public companies limited by shares. Companies can choose to exclude some or all of the model articles. Existing companies will still be subject to the articles which were in force at the time the company was registered or subsequently altered, but may, if they wish, adopt the new model articles by passing appropriate special resolution. New companies registering from October 2008 will have the appropriate new model articles as default, unless they choose to register different articles. Articles can be drafted to be entrenched in that certain provisions can only be amended if specific conditions are met or procedures followed, which may be altered only by procedures which are more restrictive than a special resolution.

OBJECTS — PART 3 S 31 — 1 OCTOBER 2009

Objects will not be necessary as the default position under the CA 2006 [9A–007] (s 31(1)) is that a company's objects are unrestricted. If a company adopts an object which states that the purpose of the company is something other than the benefit of its members, the directors' duty under s 172(1) will be to achieve that purpose instead of promoting the success of the company for the benefit of its members.

EXECUTION OF DOCUMENTS — PART 4 S 44 — 6 APRIL 2008

(Effectively re-enacting and modifying the CA 1985 as amended by [9A–008] SI 2005/1906.) A company still may have a seal but is not required to do so. Documents are executed by a company either by affixing its common seal or by signature. The latter requires either signatures of two authorised signatories or one director alone in the presence of a witness. Every director and the secretary are authorised signatories, but this is not exclusive. If the document is a deed it must be executed in the same way but must be delivered as a deed.

NAME — PART 5 S 77 — 1 OCTOBER 2009

A company can now set its own procedure in its articles for changing its name. [9A–009] Anyone may now object to a company's name if it either interferes with a name in which they have goodwill or is so similar to such a name that it will suggest a link between them and the company which is misleading. A company may be directed to change its name if an objection is upheld.

PUBLICATION OF NAME AND DETAILS — PART 5 S 82 — 1 OCTOBER 2006 (BUT EFFECTIVELY SI 2006/3429 — 1 JANUARY 2007)

See also The Companies Act Registrar, Languages, Trading and Disclosures [9A–010] Regulations 2006, SI 2006/3429, in force from 1 January 2007. The name of a company must appear legibly in a sign outside all business premises. The company name must appear on all business communications including emails and electronic documents. A company's website must include the company's place of registration, its registration number and registered office address, its geographic address and email address and the name of the organisation with which the customer is contracting. Any such difference between the organisation's name and its trading name should be explained. It is not sufficient to include a 'contact us' form without also providing an email address and geographic address somewhere easily accessible on the site. If the business is a member of a trade or professional association, membership details, including any registration number, should be provided. If the business has a VAT number, it should be stated.

DIRECTORS — PART 10 — 1 OCTOBER 2007

[9A–011]   The CA 2006, s 172 provides a statutory statement of directors' duty to promote the success of the company for the benefit of its members as a whole. This will apply from 1 October 2007 but the codified duty to avoid conflicts of interests and the duty not to accept benefits from third parties and the duty to declare interests in proposed transactions or arrangements with the company, will not apply until 1 October 2008. Most other aspects of Part 10 will also apply from 1 October 2007, including those relating to directors' appointment and removal; transactions with directors requiring members' approval; directors' service contracts; and directors' liabilities and indemnities.

Sections 188 and 189, on directors' long-term service agreements, come into force on 1 October 2007 and decrease the length of a director's service agreement which require shareholder approval from five years to two years. Loans, quasi-loans and credit transactions to or in favour of directors (ss 197–214) are no longer prohibited but are now subject to member approval if there is inadequate disclosure. Breaches continue to be rectifiable by the members (s 239).

The provisions of ss 232–238 (previously in the Companies (Audit, Investigations and Community Enterprise) Act 2004), allowing companies to indemnify their directors and to advance funds to them to meet defence costs, are restated without significant amendment and extended to allow a corporate trustee of an occupational pension scheme (or a member of its group) to indemnify its directors against liability incurred in connection with the company's activities as trustee of the scheme, other than fines, penalties or the costs of defending criminal proceedings in which the director is convicted. At present, the rules do not allow such indemnities, meaning that directors of corporate trustees may be in a worse position than non-corporate trustees, who can be indemnified out of the scheme's assets. The exception that allows companies to lend money to their directors to fund their defence costs will be extended to cover not just proceedings relating to the company but also relating to any associated companies. There are also new requirements relating to the keeping of copies of relevant indemnities and making them available to members.

Chapter 8 (ss 240–246) contains provision for the disclosure in limited circumstances of the residential addresses of directors, which, where there is a risk of violence or intimidation, are omitted from public inspection. All directors will file a service address and their home addresses will be kept separately both by the company and Companies House: see also Companies (Particulars of Usual Residential Address) (Confidentiality Orders) Regulations 2002, SI 2002/912

DERIVATIVE ACTIONS — PART 11 S 260 — 1 OCTOBER 2007

[9A–012]   The CA 2006 provides, as from 1 October 2007, a framework for shareholders to bring a claim on behalf of a company against directors who are in breach of duty or have been negligent. Executive and non-executive directors, shadow directors and former directors are all 'directors' for these purposes. Shareholders will need the consent of the court to bring a claim, and damages will be owed to the company, rather than to the shareholders themselves.

COMPANY SECRETARY — PART 12 S 270 — 6 APRIL 2008

From 6 April 2008, private companies will no longer be obliged to have a company secretary. If they no longer wish to have a company secretary, they need do nothing, except terminate the appointment of the secretary. Section 274(b) states that a director or person authorised by the directors can do anything required to be done by or to the secretary. A company secretary that remains has the same status as previously. [9A-013]

RESOLUTIONS — PART 13 SS 282, 283 — 1 OCTOBER 2007

Extraordinary resolutions no longer exist, so there are only two types of resolutions: ordinary, which require a simple majority, and special, which require a majority of 75%, or, in either case, a higher percentage if specified in the company's articles. [9A-014]

MEETINGS — PART 13 SS 307 AND 336 — 1 OCTOBER 2007

There is no obligation for private companies to hold annual general meetings. All company meetings are now on 14 day notice (as from 1 October 2007) except annual general meetings, for which 21 days' notice is required, unless the articles state otherwise, but the 28-day special notice procedure for the removal of directors and auditors is retained (s 312). [9A-015]

ACCOUNTS — PART 15 S 442 — 6 APRIL 2008

The time for a company to file its accounts has been reduced from ten to nine months for a private company and from seven to six for a public one. Annual accounts need to be sent out prior to a general meeting. Annual accounts must be sent to members by the time they are due to be filed with the Registrar of Companies. [9A-016]

AUDITORS — PART 16 S 487 — 6 APRIL 2008

Many companies continue to be exempt from audit. The auditor of a private company may be deemed to be re-appointed automatically for the following year, unless the company takes steps to end his appointment or not less than 5% of the members object. Auditor's liability can be limited for a financial year by ordinary resolution. [9A-017]

REDUCTION OF CAPITAL — PART 17 S 642 — 1 OCTOBER 2009

Private companies may in future reduce their capital by a special resolution with a statement by each of the directors, that the company is solvent. This procedure is subject to any provision in the articles restricting or prohibiting reduction of capital. The procedure is the same as for redemption or purchase of its own shares. Before the CA 2006, a reduction of share capital required court approval. [9A-018]

FINANCIAL ASSISTANCE — PART 46 S 1295 (REPEALS) AND (FOR PUBLIC COMPANIES) PART 18 S 677 — 1 OCTOBER 2008

[9A–019] The CA 2006 repeals the prohibition against private companies from giving financial assistance for the purchase of their own shares but substantially replaces and restates the CA 1985 restrictions on public companies and, if solvency requirements are met, to do so out of capital.

ELECTRONIC COMMUNICATIONS — (THROUGHOUT, EG SS 308, 333) PART 37 S 1145 — IN FORCE WITH THE RELEVANT PROVISIONS AND SCHEDULES 4 (TO THE COMPANY) AND 5 (BY THE COMPANY)

[9A–020] A company may provide information to members electronically or on a website, as alternative to hard copy, but the recipients must agree to it being done in this way. A company may therefore propose an appropriate resolution or change to its articles. Each time new information is made available on the website, the company must inform the relevant members of this by hard copy or electronic communication. Shareholders are entitled to request hard copies of documents or information (s 1145).

FLOATING CHARGE — PART 44 S 1282

[9A–021] As from 1 October 2008, the rule in *re Leyland Daf* [2004] UKHL 9, [2004] 1 BCLC 281 is reversed so that liquidators will be able to recover liquidation expenses from floating charge assets, if the assets in the liquidation are insufficient. This already happens in administration and puts the position back to what it used to be, before *re Leyland Daf.*

The CA 2006, s 1282 inserts a new s 176ZA into the Insolvency Act 1986 on the payment of expenses of winding up. The Act is not retrospective and so will not affect distributions that have already been made on the basis of *Leyland Daf* but the legislative changes will, in future liquidations, affect realisations of floating charges under debentures whether or not granted in reliance upon *Leyland Daf.*

CRIMINAL LIABILITIES

[9A–022] Part 36 of the CA 2006 contains specific criminal offences (ss 1121–1131). Also, Part 29 of the Act (s 993) creates an offence of fraudulent trading exactly in the terms as set out in CA 1985, s 458. In *Re Gerald Cooper Chemicals Ltd* [1978] Ch 262, Templeman J said, at 267, that a single transaction could suffice. Dishonesty is an essential element in fraudulent trading.

Directors can also be charged with the offence of false accounting as per Theft Act 1968, s 18, which remains in force as well as the Fraud Act. Section 18 of the Theft Act 1968 states: 'The maximum sanction for approving defective reports and accounts is an unlimited fine of the company. The maximum prison term for directors for fraudulent trading has been increased from seven to ten years.'

The offence of destruction, mutilation or falsification of company documents in the CA 1985 is amended by s 1124 of and Sch 3 to the CA 2006. It is one of the most serious offences and is punishable by up to seven years' imprisonment and an unlimited fine.

In addition to the provisions of the CA 2006, the Corporate Manslaughter and Corporate Homicide Act 2007 gained Royal Assent on 26 July 2007, and the Fraud Act 2006, s 12, sets out certain circumstances in which company officers are liable for an offence committed by a body corporate. Section 12 provides that if persons who have a specified corporate role, 'consent or connive' with the commission of an offence under the Fraud Act 2006 by their body corporate, those persons as well as the company, will be guilty of an offence.

Where the only victims of an offence are the company or its members, the company itself should not be liable for the offence. But where the members of the company are only some of the potential victims, the company itself should be liable. A director or other officer of the company will be personally liable where he authorises, permits, participates in, or fails to take all reasonable steps to prevent the offence.

PRELIMINARY NOTE

The Companies Act 2006 is in this chapter referred to as the 'CA 2006', the Companies Act 1985 as the 'CA 1985', and the Insolvency Act 1986 as 'IA 1986'.

[9A–023]

COMMUNICATIONS TO AND FROM COMPANIES

The CA 2006 contains extensive provisions about the service of documents etc, mainly in Part 37 (ss 1134–1157 and Schedules 4 and 5).

[9A–024]

SERVICE OF DOCUMENTS

A document may be served on a company registered under this Act by leaving it at, or sending it by post to, the company's registered office: CA 2006, s 1139(1). Except for the very limited case of the definition of 'current address' in CA 2006, s 423 (duty to circulate annual accounts and reports), the means of communication from a company to its members is governed by the articles of association, in which the same provision appears in substantially the same form in all three models:

[9A–025]

— means of communication to be used—private (shares) regulation 45, private (guarantee) regulation 33 and public regulation 82; and

— addresses and other contact details—private (shares) regulation 46, private (guarantee) regulation 34 and public regulation 83; with the addition

— in the case of public companies, regulation 84 (failure to notify contact details).

At the risk of a dangerous oversimplification, communications can be in hard copy form (with delivery by hand or post), in electronic form or by means of a website. The model articles provide for anything to be sent to a member at his or her address registered in the register of members, unless the member and the company have agreed that another means of communication is to be used, and the member has supplied the company with the information it needs in order to be able to use that other means of communication.

AUTHENTICATION OF DOCUMENTS

[9A–026] A document or information sent or supplied by a person to a company is, by CA 2006, s 1146, sufficiently authenticated:

— if in hard copy form (by s 1168, the CA 2006's term for paper) it is signed by the person sending or supplying it; and

— if in electronic form is sufficiently authenticated if the identity of the sender is confirmed in a manner specified by the company, or, where no such manner has been specified by the company, if the communication contains or is accompanied by a statement of the identity of the sender and the company has no reason to doubt the truth of that statement.

As ordinary internet communications are notoriously insecure, the default provision for authentication in electronic form is particularly open to abuse, and companies ought not to use it unless they specify a secure means of communication.

MEETINGS, NOTICE AND RESOLUTIONS

1 MEETINGS (OF MEMBERS)

(*a*) *Annual general meeting*

[9A–027] CA 2006, s 336. See [9A–282] and the note to it. Note that the requirement to hold annual general meetings applies only to public companies. A private company may but is not required to hold an AGM: there is no provision for annual general meetings in the draft model for private and guarantee companies.

(*b*) *Other general meetings*

[9A–028] There is no statutory definition of other meetings, although the CA 2006, s 301 states how a resolution of the members may be passed at a general meeting. The expression 'extraordinary general meeting' will become obsolete: in the CA 2006 it appears only in the reference to the CA 1985, s 368 in CA 2006, s 972 (transitional provision).

2 NOTICES[1]

[9A–029] (a) Annual general meetings (public company only)—21 days (CA 2006, s 307(2)(a)), or longer if required by the articles (CA 2006, s 307(3), but may be less if all the members entitled to attend agree to shorter notice (CA 2006, s 337(2));

(b) Other general meetings of limited companies—14 days (CA 2006, s 307(1) if private and s 307(2)(b) if public) or longer if required by the articles (CA 2006, s 307(3)); there is no longer any different provision for unlimited companies;

(c) General meetings to consider a special resolution—the CA 2006 does not require a different notice period than for other resolutions;

(d) General meetings to consider an elective resolution—elective resolution (thankfully) no longer exist;

(e) Special notice to the company (see [9A–317])—28 days: CA 2006, s 312.

(f) Short notice
— for meetings of a public company with consent of a majority of 95% of the nominal value of the shares giving a right to attend and vote: CA 2006, s 307(5)(b), (6); and

— for meetings of a private company with consent of a majority of 90% of the nominal value of the shares giving a right to attend and vote or such higher percentage not exceeding 95 as is specified in the articles: CA 2006, s 307(5)(a), (6).

3 RESOLUTIONS

(a) Ordinary

Section 282 defines an 'ordinary resolution', which was not defined in the CA 1985, as a resolution passed by a simple majority.

[9A–030]

(b) Special

Section 283 defines a special resolution as one passed by a majority of not less than 75%. Special resolutions are now required by a company for the following purposes:

[9A–031]

— section 21: to amend (the move to plain English has lost alter) its articles;
— section 78: to change its name;
— section 88: to amend the register in respect of Welsh companies;
— section 90: to enable a private company to re-register as public;
— section 105: to re-register an unlimited company as limited;
— section 97: to re-register a public company as private;
— section 569: disapplication of pre-emption rights—private company with only one class of shares;
— section 570: disapplication of pre-emption rights—directors acting under general authorisation;
— section 571: disapplication of pre-emption rights by special resolution;
— section 573: disapplication of the statutory pre-emption rights—sale of treasury shares;
— section 626: reduction of capital in connection with redenomination;
— section 573: disapplication of the statutory pre-emption rights—sale of treasury shares;
— section 626: reduction of capital in connection with redenomination;
— section 630: variation of class rights—companies having a share capital;
— section 631: variation of class rights—companies without a share capital;
— section 641: circumstances in which a company may reduce its share capital;
— section 694: authority for off-market purchase;
— section 697: variation of contract for off-market purchase;
— section 700: release of company's rights under contract for off-market purchase;
— section 716: payment by company for own shares out of capital;

Required under the Insolvency Act 1986 for the following purposes:
— section 84(1)(a) and (b): to be wound up voluntarily;
— section 110(3): in a members' voluntary winding up to authorise the liquidator to receive, for distribution amongst members, shares, policies or other like interests in another company acquiring the whole or part of the business of the company being wound up; and
— section 122(1)(a): to be wound up by the court.

(*c*)   *Majority of not less than three-quarters*

[9A–032]   The following, being neither ordinary nor special, are resolutions requiring a majority of not less than three quarters:
—   section 630: variation of class rights: companies with a share capital; and
—   section 631: variation of class rights: companies without a share capital.

(*d*)   *Extraordinary*

[9A–033]   There is no requirement for extraordinary resolutions in the CA 2006, and the only mention of them is in the reference in s 972 to s 378 of the CA 1985.

PRECEDENTS

PRE FORMATION DOCUMENTS

[9A–034]   ## 1   Agreement for formation of a company to acquire a business or property belonging to one of the parties[1]

DATE AND PARTIES

[9A–035]   THIS AGREEMENT is made on (*date*) between (*name*) of (*address*) ('(*Party-A*)') and (*name*) of (*address*) ('(*Party-B*)').

DEFINITIONS

[9A–036]   **1** In this (*document*) the following terms shall have the following meanings.

'Sale Agreement'	means an agreement in agreed terms intended to be made between the (*Party-A*) and the Company for the sale of the Business to the Company.
'Business'	means the business carried on by the (*Party-B*) of the [manufacture and supply of (*description*) products] under the name (*name*).
'Company'	means a company intended to be formed or acquired by the parties to acquire the Business as a going concern.
'Deceased'	means the first of the parties to die.
'Effective Notice'	means written notice served by the Personal Representatives on the Survivor or by the Survivor on the Personal Representatives during the lifetime of the Survivor and on or before whichever is the later of the expiry of: — (*number*) months after the Deceased's death; or — (*number*) months after the grant of representation to the Deceased's estate.
'Personal Representatives'	means the Deceased's personal representatives.
'Sale Shares'	means [all (*or*) (amount)%] of the shares in the Company's capital registered in the Deceased's name at the date of [his] death.

'Survivor'	means the survivor of the parties after the Deceased's death.
'in agreed terms'	in relation to any document means in the form of the draft annexed to this agreement or as agreed in writing between the parties.
'clause' and 'schedule'	mean respectively clauses or schedules in this agreement unless the context shows a contrary meaning.
'comply with'	includes 'observe and perform'.
'parties'	means the parties to this agreement.

FORMATION OF COMPANY

2.1 The parties (*or*) (*Party-A*) shall procure the incorporation of the Company.   [9A–037]

2.2 The Company shall be called '(*name*) Ltd' if that name is available for registration or by such other available name as is agreed between the parties or in default of agreement as the (*Party-A*) selects.

2.3 The Company's articles of association shall be in agreed terms and shall be subscribed by the parties or their respective nominees each of whom shall agree in the memorandum to take one share of £[1] in the Company's capital.[2]

DIRECTORSHIPS ETC

3 Each of the parties shall procure that: [9A–038]
—   they are appointed the sole first directors of the Company [and that the (*Party-B*) is appointed its first secretary];[3]
—   while any of them is a member of the Company [he] shall not be removed from office as director [or secretary] of the Company;
—   the (*Party-A*) shall be the Company's chairman [so long as [he] remains a director of the Company (*or*) until the close of the first annual general meeting whereupon the (*Party-B*) shall be chairman and from then on each of them shall be the Company's chairman in alternate years starting at the close of each annual general meeting]; and
—   so long as [either (*or*) any] of the parties is entitled to remain a director of the Company in accordance with this clause the maximum number of directors of the Company shall not exceed two [*or whatever is the number of parties to the agreement*].

SHARE CAPITAL

4.1 The Company's initial issued share capital shall be £(...) ((...) pounds) divided into (*number*) £[1] shares.   [9A–039]

4.2 Immediately on the incorporation of the Company the (*Party-B*) shall deliver to the Company an application for the allotment to [him] for cash at par of [(*number*) [ordinary] £[1] shares in the Company's capital (*or*) the number of [ordinary] £[1] shares in the Company's capital which is equal to the number of shares to be allotted to the (*Party-A*) pursuant to clause (*number*) of the Sale Agreement] payable [in full (*or*) as to £(...) ((...) pounds) per share on allotment and £(...) ((...) pounds) not more than (*number*) months after allotment].   [9A–040]

[9A–041] **4.3** The Company shall make simultaneous allotments of the shares to be allotted to the parties respectively[4] in accordance with the Sale Agreement[5] and clause [4.2].

LOANS

[9A–042] **5.1** Immediately on the incorporation of the Company the (*Party-B*) shall advance to the Company £(…) ((…) pounds) in cash [and the (*Party-A*) shall advance to the Company £(…) ((…) pounds) in part consideration for the sale of the Business pursuant to the Sale Agreements[6]].

5.2 The Company shall issue to the maker of each advance within (*number*) days of the date of this agreement a debenture[7] in agreed terms.

SALE AGREEMENT[8]

[9A–043] **6.1** The applications for shares and advances shall be conditional on the (*Party-A*) and the Company entering into the Sale Agreement within (*number*) weeks of the incorporation of the Company but shall be otherwise unconditional and the (*Party-B*) shall not withdraw the application and neither of the parties refuse to make the advances.

6.2 As soon as the (*Party-B*) has applied to the Company for shares and paid the subscription money for them in accordance with clause [4.2] the (*Party-A*) and the Company shall enter into the Sale Agreement.

SERVICE AGREEMENTS[9]

[9A–044] **7** As soon as is reasonably practicable after incorporation of the Company the parties shall procure that the Company offers to the (*Party-A*) an executive directorship of the Company under a service agreement in agreed terms and offers to the (*Party-B*) a directorship of the Company under a contract in agreed terms.

SHARE SALE ON DEATH[10]

[9A–045] **8** On the death of the first to die of the parties the Personal Representatives may by an Effective Notice require the Survivor to buy or be required by the Survivor to sell the Sale Shares to the Survivor in either case free from incumbrances. The provisions in the Company's articles of association shall apply mutatis mutandis to any sale of shares under this clause.

PERFORMANCE OF OBLIGATIONS[11]

[9A–046] **9** Each of the parties shall do everything for the time being in [[his] (*or*) his or her] power to procure that anything [reasonably] intended or needed to be done under this (*document*) by a person who is not a party to it is done promptly by that person.

COSTS

[9A–047] **10** The Company shall bear the reasonable costs fees and expenses of respectively (*name*) & Co of (*address*) [solicitors] and (*name*) & Co of (*address*) [accountants] relating to the preparation of this agreement, the formation of the Company and the sale of the business to the Company.

NOTICES

11.1 Any notice given under this deed shall be in writing and may be served: [9A–048]
—   personally;
—   by registered or recorded delivery mail;
—   [by email or [telex or] facsimile transmission (the latter confirmed by telex or post[1])]; or
—   by any other means which any party specifies by notice to the others.

11.2 Each party's address for the service of notice shall be [his] above mentioned address or such other address as [he] specifies by notice to the others [and until otherwise specified by notice those email addresses for the service of notices are as follows:
—   [(*Party-A*)] [*email address*] etc].

11.3 A notice shall be deemed to have been served:
—   if it was served in person, at the time of service;
—   if it was served by post, 48 hours after it was posted[; and
—   if it was served by email or [telex or] facsimile transmission, at [09.00 on the first working day after] the time of transmission].

11.4 [No notices may be served by email, [telex or] facsimile transmission.]

INTERPRETATION

12.1 Except where the context renders it absurd or impossible every reference   [9A–049]
to any party to this (*document*) shall include his or her successors in title and personal representatives, by and against whom this agreement shall be enforceable as if they had been originally named as parties.

12.2 In this (*document*):
—   words expressed in any gender shall where the context so requires or permits include any other gender;
—   words importing persons shall include bodies corporate and partnerships and other incorporated bodies and vice versa;
—   words expressed in the singular shall where the context so requires or permits include the plural; and
—   where any party is more than one person:
      —   that party's obligations in this (*document*) shall take effect as joint and several obligations;
      —   anything in this (*document*) which applies to that party shall apply to all of those persons collectively and each of them separately;
      —   the benefits contained in this (*document*) in favour of that party shall take effect as conferred in favour of all of those persons collectively and each of them separately; and
      —   the receipt of the survivor of joint holders of this (*document*) shall be a good discharge to the (*Party-A*).

12.3 The headings to clauses [and the table of clauses and marginal notes] are inserted for ease of reference only and shall not affect the construction of this (*document*).

12.4 References in this (*document*) to anything which any party is required to do or not to do shall include [his] acts, defaults and omissions, whether:
—   direct or indirect;

— on his own account; or

— for or through any other person; and

— those which he permits or suffers to be done or not done by any other person.

12.5 The effect of all obligations affecting the (*Party-B*) under this (*document*) is cumulative and no obligation shall be limited or modified by any other of those obligations unless there is in this (*document*) an express limitation or modification.

[9A–050]   **12.6** Nothing contained in this agreement shall in any way affect the free exercise by any person of [his] powers as a director of the Company.[12]

[attestation clauses]

[9A–051]

1   For a form of agreement for sale of the assets and goodwill of a business see [9A–177].

2   It was usual for each of the subscribers to agree in the old type of memorandum of association to take up one share, and is likely to be so under the new forms, but instead some or all of the subscribers may agree to take a greater number of shares. Only one subscriber is necessary: CA 2006, s 7.

3   There is no longer any necessity for a private company to have a company secretary: CA 2006, s 270 and see [9A–013].

4   Taxation of Chargeable Gains Act 1992, s 162, provides that, where a business is sold as a going concern together with the whole assets (or the whole assets other than cash) in exchange or partly in exchange for shares, any gain accruing to the transferor on the disposal of the business will not be treated as a chargeable gain to the extent that the consideration for the transfer consists of shares. Accordingly, the exclusion from the sale of any asset, except cash, will disqualify the transferors from relief under the provisions mentioned above, and the payment of the consideration in a form other than shares may give rise to a chargeable gain on the disposal of the business to the extent provided by that paragraph.

5   By CA 2006, s 555(3)(a) the return of allotments must contain the prescribed information. The Act itself contains no equivalent to the requirement in CA 1985, s 88(2)(b) and (3), for the contract for sale, where shares are issued for a consideration other than cash. If the company is public, it must not enter into an agreement with a subscriber to the memorandum within the 'initial period (two years starting with the issue of a trading certificate under s 761' for the transfer of non-cash assets equal to one tenth or more of the company's assets, unless the valuation and approval procedures of CA 2006, ss 599 and 600 have been complied with: CA 2006, s 598.

6   The provision of loans by the prospective members of the company may sometimes be of advantage since it may facilitate the withdrawal by those members at a later date of any capital, which has become surplus to the company's requirements, without paying a dividend, invoking the procedures to enable the company to buy its own shares ([9A–487]), or reducing its capital ([9A–481] to [9A–484]), any of which may involve a tax liability. However, if part of the price for the business is satisfied by a loan, the relief mentioned in note 4 above will be lost.

7   If the debentures are not drafted and agreed at this stage, or none are to be issued, it will be necessary to set out in this agreement the principal terms of the loans. For a debenture, see Mortgages [24–144].

8   For a sale agreement, see [9A–177].

9   See Employment [10–230] or [10–367].

10   The object of this clause is to prevent the beneficiaries under the will or intestacy of a deceased shareholder finding themselves locked in a company, and also to enable the surviving party to compel the personal representatives to sell to him the shares of the deceased party. The clause can be extended to apply on a party reaching a specified age or becoming unfit for a prolonged period to perform his duties as a full-time employee of the company.

     The terms of an agreement on these lines between more than two parties will vary with the particular circumstances. In such cases care must be taken to ensure that fractions of shares will not arise, or if they do, will not give one party a substantial unintended advantage: this difficulty can sometimes best be avoided by providing for the shares in question to be converted into stock.

11   Only if the promissors are to be the sole shareholders can this clause be effective in all circumstances. If, for example, the promissors are only a majority of the members, and the directors are other than they, the promissors might be able to perform their undertaking only

by carrying resolutions in general meeting, which may not be for the benefit of the members as a whole and hence ineffective: *Greenhalgh v Arderne Cinemas Ltd* [1951] Ch 286, [1950] 2 All ER 1120, CA (change in the articles to deprive a minority of pre-emption rights); *Clemens v Clemens Bros Ltd* [1976] 2 All ER 268 (issue of shares to reduce a minority to under 25%).

¹² The object of this clause is to state expressly what is implied by law, namely that any party to the agreement who becomes a director, will remain free to exercise his powers as a director in accordance with the fiduciary nature of his office whilst, subject to any contract to the contrary, in his capacity as a member he may vote as he chooses at a general meeting: see *Northern Counties Securities Ltd v Jackson & Steeple Ltd* [1974] 2 All ER 625, [1974] 1 WLR 1133.

2 Nomination by promoters of new company of intended first directors, secretary and situation of registered office¹

[9A–052]

(*name*) Ltd — a proposed new company

We the subscribers to the memorandum of association of the Company:

1   appoint ourselves to be its first directors;

2   nominate (*name*), one of ourselves, to be its first secretary; and

3   state that its registered office will be at (*address*).

Dated (*date*)

Signed

(*subscribers*)

¹   In straightforward cases the promoters and subscribers will be the same persons. There is frequently no need for a formal formation agreement and, if the parties wish to document their agreement at all, this document suffices at the pre-incorporation stage. The memorandum of association must be in prescribed form and state that the subscribers wish to form a company agree to become members of it and, if it has a share capital, agree to take at least one share each: CA 2006, s 8. The articles of association are no longer required to be signed by the subscriber to the memorandum.

[9A–053]

3 Checklist for application to registrar for the registration of a company¹

[9A–054]

It is assumed that an application form will be promulgated, but in the meantime the following is a summary of what will be required by CA 2006, s 9.

section of CA 2006	*statement, information or document*
9(2)(a)	the company's proposed name
9(2)(b)	whether the company's registered office is to be situated in England and Wales (or in Wales), in Scotland or in Northern Ireland
9(2)(c)	whether the liability of the members of the company is to be limited, and if so whether it is to be limited by shares or by guarantee

section of CA 2006	statement, information or document
9(2)(d)	whether the company is to be a private or a public company
9(3)	if the application is delivered by a person as agent for the subscribers to the memorandum of association, his name and address
9(4)(a)	in the case of a company that is to have share capital, a statement of capital and initial shareholdings (see s 10)
9(4)(b)	in the case of a company that is to be limited by guarantee, a statement of guarantee (see s 11)
9(4)(c)	a statement of the company's proposed officers (see s 12)
9(5)(a)	a statement of the intended address of the company's registered office
9(5)(b)	a copy of any proposed articles of association (to the extent that these are not supplied by the default application of Model Articles: see s 20)

[9A–055]   [1]   By CA 2006, s 9, the memorandum must be delivered to the registrar with an application for registration, the documents required by that section and a statement of compliance. The application must be delivered to the registrar of companies for England and Wales, if the registered office of the company is to be situated in England and Wales (or in Wales), to the registrar of companies for Scotland, if the registered office of the company is to be situated in Scotland, or to the registrar of companies for Northern Ireland, if the registered office of the company is to be situated in Northern Ireland: CA 2006, s 9(6).

ARTICLES OF ASSOCIATION

[9A–056]   **4   Articles of association of a private company limited by shares incorporating the model articles for public companies—full set of regulations with alternatives but without pre-emption rights on transfers[1]**

PRELIMINARY AND INTERPRETATION

[9A–057]   **1.1** In these articles the following terms shall have the following meanings.

'2006 Act'	means the Companies Act 2006.
'Controlling Interest'	means shares conferring over 50% of the total votes capable of being cast on a poll at the Company's general meetings.
'Restricted Shares'[2]	means £[1] shares in the Company's capital ranking pari passu with the ordinary shares, except that:
	— no dividend shall be paid on any Restricted Share in excess of £[1,000]; and

	— on a winding up of the Company no payment in respect of surplus assets shall be paid on any Restricted Share in excess of £[10,000].

'Controlling Shareholder' means a member or members holding between them a Controlling Interest.

'Model Articles' means the model articles in Schedule 3 to the Companies (Model Articles) Regulations 2008.

'Transfer' as a noun includes the renunciation[3] or other disposal of shares allotted or rights in respect of shares granted to a member and any transfer or other act of or relating to a beneficial interest in any share, or any rights attached to any share[4] and the verb 'to transfer' shall be construed accordingly.

1.2 The Model Articles for private companies in Schedules 1 and 2 to the Companies (Model Articles) Regulations 2008 are excluded in their entirety. Except as mentioned in these articles the regulations contained in the Model Articles shall apply to the Company. [9A–058]

1.3 In the first line of regulation 1 of the Model Articles between the words 'in the articles' and ', and unless the context' there shall be inserted the words 'and in any articles adopting them'. [9A–058A]

1.4 Where there is any conflict between these regulations and the provisions of the Model Articles, these regulations shall prevail [and, where there is any conflict between regulation (*number*) of these articles and the other regulations of these articles, regulation (*number*) shall prevail].[5] [9A–059]

1.5 No provision of these articles which is expressed to be an entrenched provision may be altered or revoked, unless whichever of conditions A and B is expressed to apply to it are satisfied. Condition A is that the alteration or revocation is made by a resolution passed by all the members entitled to vote on it. Condition B is that the alteration or revocation is made by a special resolution to which the every member, who at the date of the resolution holds not less than [15]% of the issued ordinary shares in the Company's capital, had consented in writing.[6] [9A–060]

OBJECTS

[**2** The objects of the Company are [*describe*].[7]] [9A–061]

NUMBER OF DIRECTORS[8]

3 The number of directors shall be not less than [two] and not more than [seven]. [9A–062]

POWERS AND DUTIES OF DIRECTORS

4 Regulation 4 of the Model Articles is omitted and replaced by the following regulation 4. [9A–063]

4 The directors shall not without the previous sanction of [an ordinary (*or*) a special] resolution of the Company (and shall procure that the directors of any subsidiary of the Company will not without the previous sanction of a special resolution of the Company carry out any such transaction in relation to the subsidiary):[9]

> — sell or dispose of the Company's business or the shares of any of the Company's subsidiaries or any part of the business or shares or any interest in land or buildings where a substantial part of the Company's business is for the time being carried on;
> — acquire any business;
> — acquire or dispose of any shares in any company;
> — make any investment whose capital value (whenever payable) exceeds £(…) ((…) pounds);
> — exercise its borrowing powers in any way which causes or might cause its total borrowings to exceed £(…) ((…) pounds); or
> — dismiss or engage or alter the terms of employment of any director or any manager whose emoluments are or exceed £(…) ((…) pounds) p a.

[9A–064]   *(or)*

4 In regulation 3 of the Model Articles the word 'special' shall be deleted and the word 'ordinary' substituted for it.

PROCEEDINGS OF DIRECTORS

[9A–065]   **5.1** The directors shall meet not less than [once in every month *(or)* [four times] in every year] and may meet as often as they think necessary. At least [four] clear days' prior notice, which may be oral, shall be given to all directors of the time and place of all meetings of directors unless all directors indicate their willingness to accept shorter notice.

[9A–066]   **5.2** The directors may fix for each year dates, times and places on and at which meetings are to be held, and, if these particulars have been given in writing to all the directors not less than [one month] before the first of those meetings, no further notice need be given of them.

[9A–067]   **5.3** Any corporation which is a director of the Company may by a resolution of its directors or other governing body authorise such person as it thinks fit to act as its representative at any meeting of the Company's directors, and the person so authorised shall be entitled to exercise on behalf of the corporation which he or she represents such powers and duties as the corporation could exercise if it were an individual director of the Company.[10]

[9A–068]   **5.4** Regulation 9 of the Model Articles is altered as follows:
(a)   inserting the word 'orally after communicate in sub-paragraph 9(1)(b);
(b)   deleting sub-paragraph (2);[11] and
(c)   inserting at the end of sub-paragraph (3) the words 'and if there is no agreement the meeting shall be deemed to take place where the largest group of those participating is assembled or if there is no such group where the chairman of the meeting then is'.

[9A–069]   **5.5** In regulation 14(1) of the Model Articles the words 'the chairman or other director chairing the meeting' shall be deleted and there shall be inserted in its place the words 'no person'. [This is an entrenched provision to which condition A applies.][12]

[9A–070]   **5.6** For so long as any member of the Company [holds over 50% of the issued shares in the company's capital *(or)* is the Controlling Shareholder] he or she shall be the chairman of the directors and shall have such number of votes as enables him or her to carry or defeat any proposal for a resolution of the directors.[13]

5.7 The quorum at meetings of the directors shall be two holding together over 50% of the Company's issued share capital, and regulation 9 of the Model Articles shall be construed accordingly.

5.8 If at any meeting of the directors called by not less than [four] days' written notice a quorum is not present within half an hour of the time appointed for the meeting, the director present, if he or she or the person appointing him or her as an alternate or the person appointing him or her under regulation 25 of the Model Articles [and (*number*)[14]] holds not less than 50% of the issued share capital of the Company, shall be a quorum.

5.9 The number of votes exercisable by each director on any resolution of the directors shall equal the number of votes being capable of being cast by him or her on a poll at a general meeting of the Company[15] and if he or she is not a member of the Company he or she shall have [no (*or*) one] vote as a director.[16]

5.10 A director who has been appointed under regulation [9.3] [and (*number*)[17]] shall have the number of votes which would be capable of being cast by the person appointing him or her to be a director if that person were a director in addition to any votes which he or she may exercise in his or her own right.

5.11 No resolution in writing may be passed by the directors except by the agreement of all of them.

UNANIMOUS DECISIONS[18]

6.1 A decision of the directors is taken in accordance with this regulation when all eligible directors indicate to each other by any means that they share a common view on a matter.

6.2 Such a decision may take the form of a resolution in writing, copies of which have been signed by each eligible director or to which each eligible director has otherwise indicated agreement in writing.

6.3 References in this regulation to eligible directors are to directors who would have been entitled to vote on the matter had it been proposed as a resolution at a directors' meeting.

6.4 A decision may not be taken in accordance with this regulation if the eligible directors would not have formed a quorum at such a meeting.

RESOLUTIONS IN WRITING

7 A resolution in writing signed by all[19] the directors entitled to receive notice of a meeting of directors or of a committee of directors shall be as valid and effectual as it if had been passed at a meeting of directors or (as the case may be) a committee of directors duly convened and held and may consist of several documents in the like form each signed by one or more directors; but a resolution signed by an alternate director need not also be signed by his appointor and, if it is signed by a director who has appointed an alternate director, it need not be signed by the alternate director in that capacity. Articles 17 and 18 of the Model Articles do not apply to the Company.[20]'

(*or, if regulations 17 and 18 are retained*)

7 The requirements of regulation 17 of the Model Articles do not apply to a resolution in writing which is passed by the agreement of all the directors who would have been entitled to vote on it at a meeting.[21]

CONFLICTS OF INTEREST

[9A–078] **8** Regulation 15 of the Model Articles shall be altered:[22]
(a)   by the insertion of the words 'the directors has complied in full with his obligations under Section 177 of the 2006 Act and' at the start of sub-paragraph (3)(a);
(b)   the word 'ordinary' in sub-paragraph (3)(a) is deleted and replaced by the word 'special';
(*or*)
(b)   the words 'the company by ordinary resolution disapplies' in regulation 16(3)(a) are deleted and replaced by the words 'the directors disapply';
(c)   the following shall be added as sub-paragraph (7):
'(7) the Company may by [ordinary (*or*) special] resolution ratify any transaction undertaken in breach of this article.'

(*or*)[23]

8 Regulation 16 of the Model Articles does not apply to the Company. Subject to the provisions of the 2006 Act, and if he has disclosed to the directors the nature and extent of any material interest of his, a director notwithstanding his office:
(a)   may be a party to, or otherwise interested in, any transaction or arrangement with the Company or in which the Company is otherwise interested;
(b)   may be a director or other officer of, or employed by, or a party to any transaction or arrangement with, or otherwise interested in, any body corporate promoted by the Company or in which the company is otherwise interested; and
(c)   shall not, by reason of his office, be accountable to the company for any benefit which he derives from any such office or employment or from any such transaction or arrangement or from any interest in any such body corporate and no such transaction or arrangement shall be liable to be avoided on the ground of any such interest or benefit.

APPOINTMENT AND RETIREMENT OF DIRECTORS

[9A–079] **9.1** The directors shall not be subject to retirement by rotation, and accordingly regulation 20 of the Model Articles shall not apply to the Company, and all other references in Model Articles to rotation shall be disregarded.[24]

(*or, if retirement by rotation is to be retained*)

[9A–080] **9.1** Regulation 20 of the Model Articles is altered by the addition to is of the following as sub-paragraph (3).
(3) If the company, at the meeting at which a director retires under sub-paragraphs (1) or (2) of this article does not fill the vacancy the retiring director shall, if willing to act, be deemed to have been reappointed unless at the meeting it is resolved not to fill the vacancy or unless a resolution for the reappointment of the director is put to the meeting and lost.[25]

9.2 The Company may by a resolution passed by a majority of not less than [55]%[26] remove any director before the expiration of his or her period of office, and may by an ordinary resolution appoint another director in his or her place. A person so appointed shall be subject to retirement at the same time as if he or she had become a director on the day on which the director in whose place he or she is appointed was last elected a director.[27]

9.3 A holder of not less than [15]% of the issued ordinary shares in the Company's capital shall have such number of votes as exceeds by one vote the number of votes required to be cast whether on a show of hands or a poll or a resolution in writing:

(a) to pass a resolution for the appointment as a director of himself or any other person as nominee for him or her;

(b) to defeat a proposal for a resolution for the removal from office as a director of him or her or any nominee of his or hers; or

(c) to defeat a proposal for a resolution for the deletion or alteration of this clause or the cancellation or alteration of these articles of association or any other act which would have the same or a similar effect.[28]

[This is an entrenched provision to which condition B in regulation 1.5 of these articles applies.]

(*or*)

9.3 Any [Controlling Shareholder (*or*) member or members holding over [50%] of the Company's issued share capital] may at any time by written notice to the Company do all or any of the following:

— vary the number of directors of the Company;

— appoint one or more additional directors; and

— remove one or more directors from office.

9.4 Regulation 22 of the Model Articles is altered by the addition of the following sub-paragraph (g).

(g) that person receives notice signed by all the other directors stating that that person should cease to be a director.[29]

ALTERNATE DIRECTORS

10 Any person as is mentioned in regulations 24 to 26 in the Model Articles, may act as an alternate director for more than one director. An alternate director shall be entitled at any meeting of the directors or of any committee of the directors to one vote for every director whom he or she represents in addition to his or her own vote (if any) as a director, but he or she shall count as only one for the purpose of determining whether a quorum is present.

ASSOCIATE DIRECTORS[30]

11.1 The directors may from time to time appoint any person employed by the Company to be an associate director of the Company for such period and on such terms as they think fit.

11.2 The directors may revoke the appointment of any associate director without notice and that associate director shall not be entitled to any claim for compensation or otherwise as a result of a revocation or to any reason for it.

11.3 Neither the appointment of an associate director nor the revocation of his or her appointment shall (unless otherwise agreed) affect his or her existing terms and conditions of employment, remuneration or other rights, benefits or duties and he or she shall not (unless otherwise agreed) be entitled to any extra remuneration or other benefits by virtue of his or her appointment as an associate director.

[9A–088] **11.4** The appointment of an associate director shall be automatically revoked if he or she ceases to be employed by the Company.

[9A–089] **11.5** An associate director shall not have access to the Company's accounts and books (including minute books relating to minutes of meetings of the directors) and shall not be entitled to receive notice of or to attend or vote at meetings of the directors. References to directors in the articles shall not include any associate director.

[9A–090] **11.6** The directors may enter into any contracts or arrangements and transact any business without the knowledge or approval of any associate director, but no contract, arrangement or transaction shall be carried out which would impose any personal liability on any associate director except with his or her consent.

COMPANY SECRETARY[31]

[9A–091] **12** The company shall have a secretary appointed by the directors for such term, at such remuneration and upon such conditions as they think fit; and any secretary so appointed may be removed by them. [If no other person is appointed as secretary references in the Model Articles to the company secretary shall be treated as references to the chairman of the directors.]

ANNUAL GENERAL MEETINGS[32]

[9A–091A] **13** The Company shall hold annual general meetings in accordance with the provision of the 2006 Act, except Section 335(3),(4), which would apply to it if it were a public company.

(*or*)

[9A–091B] **13.1** The Company shall hold a general meeting as its annual general meeting in each period of six months beginning with the day following its accounting reference date (in addition to any other meetings held during that period).

13.2 The business of the annual general meeting shall include declaring a dividend, the consideration of the accounts, balance sheets, and the reports of the directors and auditors, the election of directors in the place of those retiring and the appointment of, and the fixing of the remuneration of, the auditors.

PROCEEDINGS AT GENERAL MEETINGS

[9A–091C] **14.1** The majority required to agree short notice of meetings of the Company is 95%.[33]

[9A–091D] **14.2** Regulation 29 of the Model Articles is altered by inserting the word 'orally' after communicate in sub-paragraph (1);[34]

[9A–092] **14.3** The quorum at meetings of the Company shall be two persons holding together [a Controlling Interest (*or*) over 50% of the issued shares in the Company's capital], and regulation 29 of the Model Articles shall be construed accordingly.[35]

14.4 If such a quorum is not present within half an hour from the time appointed for the meeting, or if during a meeting such a quorum ceases to be present, the meeting shall stand adjourned to the same day in the next week at the same time and place or to such time and place as the directors determine. [If at the adjourned meeting a quorum is not present within half an hour from the time appointed for the meeting, the member present, if he or she [is a Controlling Shareholder (*or*) holds over 50% of the Company's issued share capital], shall be a quorum.]³⁶ [9A–093]

14.5 Regulation 34 of the Model Articles is renumbered 34(1) and the following is inserted at regulation 34(2):³⁷ [9A–094]
(2)   If equal numbers of votes are cast for and against a resolution, whether on a show of hands or on a poll, the chairman of the meeting has a casting vote in addition to any other votes he is otherwise entitled to cast on that resolution.
[This is an entrenched provision to which condition A applies.]³⁸‴

RESOLUTIONS IN WRITING³⁹

15.1 No resolution in writing may be passed except by the agreement of all the persons entitled to vote on it.⁴⁰ [9A–095]

15.2 The period in CA 2006 Section 297 for agreeing to a written resolution is [seven] days.⁴¹ [9A–095b]

SHARES

16.1 The amount of capital which may be issued by the Company shall not exceed £[100,000] [and no shares may be issued except ordinary shares of £[1] each.⁴² [This is an entrenched provision to which condition [A (*or*) B] in regulation 1.5 of these articles applies.] [9A–096]

16.2 All references to uncertificated shares and share warrants in the Model Articles shall be disregarded, and regulations 50, 51 and 64 shall not apply to the Company.⁴³ [9A–097]

16.3 In regulation 43 (power to issue shares) of the Model Articles the word 'ordinary' shall be deleted and the word 'special' shall be substituted for it.⁴⁴ [9A–098]

16.4 Regulation 44 of the Model Articles shall not apply to the Company.⁴⁵ [9A–098a]

16.5 The lien conferred by regulations 52 and 53 of the Model Articles shall be extended to apply to all shares (whether part or fully paid) registered in the name of any person indebted or under any liability to the Company, whether he or she is the sole registered holder of them or one of two or more joint holders, and shall be extended to the amount of his or her debt or liability. [9A–099]

16.6 The directors may not exercise any power of the Company to allot shares or to grant rights to subscribe for or to convert any security into shares except in accordance with these articles.⁴⁶ [9A–100]

16.7 The directors are authorised for [five] years from the date on which these articles are adopted to exercise the power of the Company generally and without conditions to allot shares in the Company or to grant rights to subscribe for or to convert any security into shares up to a maximum amount of £(…) ((…) pounds).⁴⁷ [9A–101]

[9A-102] **16.8** Section 561 of the 2006 Act (existing shareholders' right of pre-emption) shall not apply to the Company.[48]

[9A-103] **16.9** Regulation 44 of the Model Articles shall not apply to the Company.[49]

INFORMATION ABOUT INTERESTS IN SHARES

[9A-104] **17.1** The directors may at any time require any person whose name is entered in the register of members of the Company to furnish them with any information, supported (if the directors so require) by a statutory declaration, which they consider necessary for the purpose of determining whether or not the Company is a close company within the meaning of the Income and Corporation Taxes Act 1988.

[9A-105] **17.2** If that person fails to comply with any such request by the directors to the satisfaction of the directors within a period of one month from the date of the request, then and until the request is complied with that person shall not be entitled to attend and vote at any meeting of the Company and no dividends declared on the shares in the Company held by that person shall be paid to him or her until he or she has so complied. All such dividends shall in the meantime be retained by the Company without any liability to pay interest on them.

TRANSFER OF SHARES

[9A-106] **18** The directors may, in their absolute discretion and without assigning any reason, decline to register any transfer of any share, whether or not it is a fully paid share.[50]

TRANSMISSION OF SHARES

[9A-107] **19** The directors may at any time give notice requiring any person becoming entitled to a share in consequence of the death or bankruptcy of a member or who is otherwise a transmittee for the purposes of regulation 66 of the Model Articles to exercise the choice under sub-paragraph (1)(a) of that regulation and, if the notice is not complied with within thirty days, the directors may withhold payment of all dividends and other moneys payable in respect of the share until the requirements of the notice have been complied with, and sub-paragraph (1)(b) of that regulation shall be modified accordingly.

DIVIDENDS

[9A-108] **20** Except in respect of capital which expressly gives to its holders to right to receive dividends, it is not intended that the Company will declare and pay dividends on any of its share capital, and no member shall have any right to and dividend or to require the directors or members to consider whether any dividend should be recommended or paid.[51]

CHANGE OF NAME

[9A-109] **21** [The Company may change its name by an ordinary resolution.

(*or*)

21 The Company may change its name by a resolution passed by all the persons entitled to attend and vote at the meeting at which the resolution was proposed and may not be changed by a special resolution.

(*or*)

21 The Company may change its name by a written notice served on it by its holding company (as defined in Section 1261 of the 2006 Act)].[52]

[1] This precedent is based on the model regulations contained in the Companies (Model Articles) Regulations 2008, SI 2008/3229, Sch 3. A company must have articles of association and, unless it is a company to which model articles apply by s 20, must register articles of association: CA 2006, s 18. In so far as there are no articles or its provisions are not modified or excluded, the relevant model articles in force at the date of its registration shall apply to a company on its formation: CA 2006, s 20. The three models in SI 2008/3229 are for private companies limited by shares, private companies limited by guarantee and public companies limited by shares. Whilst the aim of the legislation is to simplify the formalities applicable to a private companies appears laudable (and will probably be effective for one person companies), the private company articles may be fool's gold in all cases where there are two or more shareholders, whose different interests must be accommodated and protected.

 Whilst in theory it might be intended that private companies with two or more shareholders and more than the simplest capital structure should adopt the 'short and simple' model for private companies and add to them, perhaps by incorporating some articles from the public company articles (e g for alternate directors and part paid shares), this approach would result in adding so much to the model articles, that in practice it is probably preferable to adopt the public company articles and cut them down and modify them as necessary. Therefore this precedent, although intended for use by private companies, is based on the model for public companies. It should be treated as a 'menu' containing a number of regulations for differing circumstances. It contains regulations commonly found useful in the articles of association of private companies, which can be used in various combinations, for various circumstances, including overriding powers for a controlling shareholder, some protection for substantial minority shareholders and simple built-in deadlock provisions, where there are two members with equal shareholdings. The deadlock (achieved simply by the exclusion of casting votes and the retirement of directors by rotation — but with the private company articles achievable by excluding the power to make a casting vote rule (see [9A–069]) is deliberate, on the basis that there is more incentive for equal partners to find a solution to disagreements if neither is able to outvote the other. A simple and generally effective means of avoiding deadlock, if so desired, is to omit the regulations in [9A–069] and [9A–094], and to include the regulation in [9A–513] or [9A–070]. The limitations on the power of a majority holder with over 50% and under 75% of the voting power is discussed in *Clemens v Clemens Bros Ltd* [1976] 2 All ER 268.

 Although the articles operate as a contract between the company and each member (CA 2006, s 33), the principle of freedom of contract does not permit a company to be bound by the provisions of a shareholders' agreement, which would have the effect of altering the articles or fetters its power to alter the articles: *Russell v Northern Bank Development Corpn Ltd* [1992] 3 All ER 161, [1992] BCLC 1016, HL.

[2] See [9A–404], note 1.

[3] A renunciation of bonus shares (and, by analogy, of shares issued by way of rights) is not a transfer: *Re Pool Shipping Co Ltd* [1920] 1 Ch 251.

[4] A transfer in breach of pre-emption provisions in the articles of association is invalid: *Tett v Phoenix Property and Investment Co Ltd* [1984] BCLC 599. These words are required because a transfer of a beneficial interest is not otherwise a transfer which would trigger the pre-emption provisions under the regulation in [9A–111] (*Safeguard Industrial Investments Ltd v National Westminster Bank Ltd* [1982] 1 All ER 449, [1982] 1 WLR 589, CA) and accordingly, a member might by a declaration of trust or a voting agreement be able to enable a non-member to have effective enjoyment of the benefits of membership. See also *Theakston v London Trust plc* [1984] BCLC 390.

[5] Sometimes one shareholder, who is possibly also a lender, requires special provisions, which do not apply to the other members, or there are regulations which cease to apply, for example, when convertible shares or loan stock are converted into shares. It is often convenient to gather all the special provisions in a separate part of the articles, which, when appropriate, can be removed in its entirety.

[6] CA 2006, s 22 enables the articles to provide for specified provisions to be entrenched, so they may be altered or repealed only by conditions or procedures more stringent than those applicable to a special resolution. In this precedent the provisions for weighted voting on a member's directorship [9A–082] and excluding casting votes [9A–069] and [9A–094] are, as examples, expressed to be entrenched.

7   CA 2006 states: 'Unless a company's articles specifically restrict the objects of the company, its objects are unrestricted'. This article is therefore not necessary and may even be undesirable in the case of a commercial company. The codification of directors' duties by CA 2006, s 172 restates the principle that a director's duty is to 'promote the success of the company for the benefits of its members as a whole' and lists matters to which he or she must have regard. Subsection (2) substitutes any other 'purpose other than the benefit of its members' for promoting the success of the company. Therefore an object to manufacture and sell widgets means that the directors' duties are not to promote the success of the company, which might require the abandonment of the widget market, but to manufacture and sell widgets. Therefore, whilst the use of an objects clause may be invaluable for a charitable or other public interest company, it could be very damaging to a commercial company.

8   The model articles do not provide for maximum or minimum numbers of directors. CA 2006, s 154 requires a private company to have at least one director and a public company at least two.

9   Regulation 2 of the model articles provides that the directors are responsible for the management of the company and for that purpose may exercise all the powers of the company. Regulation 3 reserves powers to the shareholders by special resolution to direct that the directors take of refrain from taking specific action. Regulation 6 in this precedent may be required, eg, where the proprietors do not manage the business but wish to reserve certain powers normally within the board's authority. A special resolution should be specified if the balance of voting rights either on the board or by 50% plus one vote at a general meeting would put a large minority shareholder at risk.

10   Use only if a body corporate is or is to be director of the company. Section 323 of the CA 2006 gives corporations a statutory right to appoint representatives to attend meetings of members and creditors, but the right does not extend to meetings of directors.

11   Regulation 7 as drawn would permit a meeting to take place if the sole means of communications were, eg, fax or internet. Whilst this might suit some companies, the alterations in (a) and (b) would make the ability of the participants to speak to and hear each other a condition for a meeting being held.

12   This is the regulation number in the model articles for a public company: the corresponding number for private companies (shares and guarantee) is 13. The object of this regulation and the regulation in [9A–094] is to remove the chairman's casting vote and the consequent built-in advantage accruing to one side when the votes are otherwise split equally. A deadlock could not be broken by a court order for a meeting under CA 1985, s 371 (re-enacted as CA 2006, s 306): *Ross v Telford* [1998] 1 BCLC 82, CA. As to 'entrenched' see note 6 above.

13   For an alternative see example (6) in [9A–264].

14   See [9A–082], [9A–083] and [9A–374].

15   Controlling shareholders often overlook the fact that they may be a minority on the board of directors, over which they may have no control, and that directors have only one vote per person. There can be a considerable delay before a controlling shareholder can regain control of a board: eg a member's request under CA 2006, ss 168, 169 followed after 21 days by 14 days' notice of a general meeting making delay at least 35 clear days, with the s 168 special notice procedure running in parallel. Whether or not the controlling shareholders have power to appoint and remove directors (as under the regulation in [9A–083]) it is a useful safeguard to have weighted voting as in either this regulation or those in [9A–074] and [9A–080].

16   The alternative of one vote is to avoid the risk of a board of directors with no votes if none of them is a member.

17   See [9A–082], [9A–083] and [9A–374].

18   The articles under the heading 'Unanimous decisions' are taken unaltered from the model regulations for private companies. For modifications to these articles see [9A–167] and the notes to it.

19   Under regulations 17 and 18 in the model articles, written resolutions may be passed by the same majorities as are required at a meeting. A reason for unanimity, or a larger majority than normal, is that there may be no opportunity on a written resolution for a debate and exchange of views about the motion, which might affect how votes are cast, and therefore a written resolution is inappropriate on a controversial matter on which votes are likely to be split. This regulation also does away with the additional bureaucratic requirement of regulations 17 and 18 of the model articles, but only if the resolution is passed unanimously. They leave the option of passing a written resolution by a majority if those requirements are complied with.

20   This regulation is a copy of regulation 93 in the 1985 Table A (SI 1985/805) and is intended to give the directors a less prescriptive system than that contained in the model articles.

21   The purpose of this regulation is to remove the prescriptive procedural formalities of the model articles if all the directors sign the resolution.

22 While the simplicity of regulation 15 in the model articles is welcome in contrast with the corresponding provisions of Table A, a director's duties under this must be read in conjunction with CA 2006, ss 175–177. Although the effect of this regulation can be to enable the director to vote on any matter in which he is interested, but it does not relieve him from his duty of good faith towards the company, under which he must act at all times in the interests of the company. A director must account for any private profit which he makes as a result of his fiduciary position (*Regal (Hastings) Ltd v Gulliver* (1942) [1967] 2 AC 134n, [1942] 1 All ER 378, HL) or where that duty conflicts with his private interests, even though the company could not have profited (*Industrial Development Consultants Ltd v Cooley* [1972] 2 All ER 162, [1972] 1 WLR 443).

23 The more relaxed regime in the following alternative is a copy of regulation 85 in the 1985 Table A.

24 Retirement by rotation in a private company is usually at best a nuisance and at worst a trap for the unwary or unlucky, who, in a boardroom dispute, might find him- or herself permanently off the board just because it is his or her turn to retire.

25 The trap in note 24 above is exacerbated by the lack of any provision in the model articles for automatic re-election of retiring directors. This article is a slightly altered copy of regulation 75 in the 1985 Table A. For resolutions see [9A–521] and [9A–538].

26 The figure of 55 as the percentage majority is arbitrary and of no significance, except that the majority is not a simple majority and so the resolution is not ordinary, as defined in CA 2006, s 282, as amended by SI 2009/1632. It is, presumably, a 'particular majority' within the meaning of CA 2006, s 29(c), so that the resolution is part of the company's constitution and a copy of it must be forwarded to the Registrar of Companies under s 30 and accompany every copy of the articles issued by the company.

27 By this regulation the company may remove a director from office without the special notice procedure of the CA 2006, s 168. That section does not provide the only way of removing a director: what it does is to provide a procedure for removing directors which applies notwithstanding anything to the contrary in the articles or any contract with the director. This regulation will also enable a company to remove a director by a written resolution, which would otherwise be prohibited by CA 2006, s 288(2)(a): see the note in [9A–287]. The figure of 55 as the percentage majority is arbitrary and of no significance, except that the majority is not a simple majority and so the resolution is not ordinary, as defined in CA 2006, s 282.

28 This regulation is intended to protect a substantial minority shareholder against removal from the board by a majority. The figure of 15% may be altered according to the circumstances of the company. Such a clause as this is not in contravention of CA 2006, s 168: *Bushell v Faith* [1970] AC 1099, [1970] 1 All ER 53, HL. As to entrenched provisions see article 4 [9A–060] and the note to it. In view of the director's rights under sub-paragraph (c), it is not necessary for this provision to be entrenched, but this illustrates how entrenchment might be used.

29 This sub-paragraph was in the original draft of each of the model articles but omitted from subsequent drafts and the final versions. For a notice by the directors see [3.24.15].

30 It is a common practice for companies to attempt, as by this regulation, to create a class of persons whose members are not directors but are, as senior employees, given the title of director. It is a moot point whether these attempts are effective. If the names of the 'non-director directors' are to appear on the company's letter headings etc they must be distinguished from the 'real' directors: eg '(*name*) divisional director sales'. Directors and shadow directors are defined in CA 2006, ss 250 and 251. Persons accepting such office should be aware of the potential personal risks of directorship, including wrongful etc trading under the IA 1986, s 214 and the Company Directors Disqualification Act 1986. In *SMC Electronics Ltd v Akhter* [2001] 1 BCLC 433, CA it was held that an employee with the title 'director of sales' but who was not a director had ostensible authority to bind the company to a contract.

31 A private company is not required to have a company secretary: CA 2006, s 270. Although the numerous references to a secretary in the model articles for public companies may indicate that a private company adopting those articles has a secretary, the effect of s 270(3)(b) is that this is not necessarily so, and an article such as this, if wanted, put the question beyond doubt.

32 CA 2006, s 336 requires public companies to hold annual general meetings and, in the absence of any statutory requirement or prohibition, private companies may but are not required to hold them. Annual general meetings can be little more that an unnecessary formality and a nuisance to single member and quasi partnership companies, but if a private company chooses to hold annual general meeting and to provide for them in the articles, which is likely to be the case of companies with more than a handful or fewer members, especially if there is any separation of management from membership, the choices are to use the statutory

provisions applicable to public companies, whose provision might be too rigorous or write bespoke provisions. The business of the annual general meeting in the bespoke alternative is based on regulation 52 of the 1948 Table A.

33 As to short notice of meeting of a company, see [3.24.04] and the note to it.

34 See note 13 above.

35 Except in the case of a one member company, at meeting of which one qualifying person is a quorum, the quorum at general meeting is, subject to the articles, two qualifying persons. A qualifying person is an individual who is a member, an authorised representative or a corporation or the proxy of a member. See CA 2006, s 318. By this regulation a quorum will be two members holding over 50% of the issued shares. A meeting held without a quorum is a nullity: *Re London Flats Ltd* [1969] 2 All ER 744, [1969] 1 WLR 711. If a majority or one of two members is deliberately absent in order to frustrate the meeting the aggrieved members may apply to the court to order a meeting to be called and to direct if necessary that one member can constitute the meeting: CA 2006, s 306: see *Re Opera Photographic Ltd* [1989] 1 WLR 634.

CA 2006, s 318 provides that the quorum is two, subject to the articles, but in the case of a company limited by shares or guarantee with only one member, one member present in person or by proxy is a quorum

36 This article, with the addition of the optional sentence in square brackets, is based on regulation 40 of the 1985 version of Table A and is intended to provide a solution to a meeting being or becoming inquorate.

37 The object of this regulation is to introduce or, in the case of a company, which had such a right immediately before 1 October 2010 but subsequently removed it, restore the chairman's casting vote at a general meeting, which BERR (now BIS) removed from the original draft of the model articles: for a discussion about the casting vote of a chairman of general meetings, see preliminary note [9A–000].

38 As to 'entrenched' see note 6 above.

39 There is no provision in the model articles for written resolution of the members. The CA 2006 may have removed the misguided rigmarole introduced by the CA 1989 (as mitigated by the Deregulation (Resolutions of Private Companies) Order 1996, SI 1996/1471), but has instead given us thirteen sections (ss 288–300) of procedures and restrictions in the name of simplification. The CA 2006 expressly provides for private companies to pass resolutions in writing but makes no provision for public companies to do so. There is no need for the articles to contain a power to pass resolutions in writing, but if they do, any provision in the articles is void if it would prevent any resolution required or provided for by any enactment from being passed in writing: CA 2006, s 300. There is, therefore, no restriction on the kind of resolution which may be passed in writing, but by s 288(2) a written resolution may not be passed to remove a director from office before the expiry of his term of office under s 168 (but this restriction would not apply to a removal under the power in regulation 9.2 above) or to remove an auditor from office under s 510.

Every person, who would have been entitled to vote on the resolution, at the time at which the first copy of the resolution is sent or submitted to the member, is an eligible member: CA 2006, s 289. If the directors propose (sic) a written resolution, the company must send a copy to every eligible member at so far as is practicable the same time or by submitting it or copies of it to them in turn, and may do so in hard copy, by email or by website: CA 2006, s 291(1)–(3).

A written resolution is passed when the required majority of eligible members have signified their agreement to it: CA 2006, s 296(4).

All the shareholders acting together can do anything intra vires the company, notwithstanding the lack of any notice, meeting or written and signed document: *Cane v Jones* [1981] 1 All ER 533, [1980] 1 WLR 1451, applying Buckley J in *Re Duomatic Ltd* [1969] 2 Ch. 365 at 373, [1969] 1 All ER 161 at 168. In the light of this decision there should be little doubt that resolutions of the company, if unanimous, can be passed in any way, written (whether hard copy or electronic) or oral, that the parties agree, regardless of the statutory formalities.

40 In the absence of this provision, written resolution may be passed by the same majorities as are required at a meeting. A reason for unanimity, or a larger majority than normal, is that there may be no opportunity on a written resolution for a debate and exchange of views about the motion, which might affect how votes are cast, and therefore a written resolution is inappropriate on a controversial matter on which votes are likely to be split. See [9A–286] and the following forms. Note that the CA 2006 makes no provision for a public company to pass a resolution in writing (but these articles are for a private company using the public company model articles). See also [9A–298], note 1.

41 See [9A–095b] The default period, if none is specified in the articles, is 28 days: CA 2006, s 297(1)(b).

42 There is no requirement in the CA 2006 for a company to have an authorised capital and no provision in the model articles for it to have capital of any particular amount. For the purposes of CA 2006 a company's capital is its issued capital shown in the statement of capital filed on its incorporation under s 10(2) as updated on subsequent changes in capital (allotments of shares, s 555(3); sub-division and consolidation, s 619(2); reconversion of stock into shares, s 621(2); redenomination, s 625(2) and reduction of capital on redenomination, s 627(2) — but not on any other reduction of capital).

It may be useful for some companies to provide in the articles a mechanism akin to an authorised capital in order to establish the number and rights of shares which the members intend to have available for allotment, for which this regulation is a suggestion. The government is expected to make transitional provisions for existing companies. If these provisions abolish the authorised capital for existing companies, those who wish to retain it may need to add a regulation such as this into their articles. For an alternative see [9A–366].

'Ordinary shares' are defined in CA 2006, s 560(1) as shares other than shares that as respects dividends and capital carry a right to participate only up to a specified amount in a distribution.

43 Although the Uncertificated Securities Regulations 2001, SI 2001/3755, made under CA 1989, s 207 do not apply expressly to public companies, their operation through Euroclear UK & Ireland Ltd (formerly known as CRESTCo Ltd) is limited to quoted companies, which are necessarily public. Similarly there is nothing in CA 2006, ss 779 and 780, which prevents a private company from issuing warrants, most owners of private companies wish to control the transfer of shares and are therefore unlikely to give directors power to issue a bearer security transferable by delivery.

44 This regulation is designed to protect a minority shareholder with over 25% of the equity from increases in capital enforced by the majority shareholder, although a minority shareholder in this position may, even without such regulation, be able to rely on *Clemens v Clemens Bros Ltd* [1976] 2 All ER 268.

45 Regulation 44 permits the payment of commissions on the subscription for shares in accordance with CA 2006, s 553. Although directors are of course not obliged to exercise a power such as this, it may be felt in many private companies that it is better not to have the power at all.

46 This regulation reflects CA 2006, s 550, under which directors of a private company with only one class of shares may exercise any power of the company to allot shares or convert securities into shares except to the extent that they are prohibited by the articles. A decision whether to include this regulation and the following two depends substantially on the intended balance of power between the members and the directors.

47 This provision ought not to be used if the company has only one class of shares and the members wish to rely on the statutory power in CA 2006, s 550 (see note 47 above), but should be used if the members wish to have degree of control over the directors' exercise of this power. It may be contained in a resolution or contained in the articles. The authority given by it may not be for longer than five years, but may be renewed: CA 2006, s 551. The power in CA 1985, s 80A for a private company, by an elective resolution, to give an authority for an indefinite period is not repeated in the CA 2006: the authority given by this regulation or by resolution may be reviewed or varied at any time and may be given by an ordinary resolution of the company: see CA 2006, s 551.

48 In the case of a private company with only one class of shares, the pre-emption provision of CA 2006, s 561 may be disapplied or applied with modifications by a special resolution or a provision contained in the articles: CA 2006, s 569. The directors of a public or private company who are generally authorised to allot shares (CA 2006, s 551) may be given similar power by the articles or a special resolution: CA 2006, ss 570, 571.

49 Regulation 44 permits the payment of commissions on the subscription for shares in accordance with CA 2006, s 553. Although directors are of course not obliged to exercise a power such as this, it may be felt in many private companies that it is better not to have the power at all.

50 The model articles for private companies regulation 24(5) gives a power to the directors to refuse to refuse to register the transfers, which could be used as an alternative to this article. Most private companies will require this regulation, whether or not the pre-emption rights in [9A–111] are adopted.

51 A failure to pay a dividend can be a ground for an order to wind up a company on the just and equitable ground: *Re a Company (No 00370 of 1987), ex p Glossop* [1988] 1 WLR 1068; *Re S Weller & Sons Ltd* [1990] Ch 682, [1989] 3 WLR 923. This regulation is intended to avoid such claims.

52 CA 2006, s 77 enables a company to changes its name by special resolution or any other means provided for by the company's articles. See [9A–253].

[9A–111] **5 Pre-emption rights on transfers of shares — transfer notice procedure — basic regulations for inclusion in articles[1]**

PART 1: DEFINITIONS

[9A–112] **1** In this regulation the following terms shall have the following meanings.

'Acceptance'	means (as appropriate) either a written notice by the Company under regulation 2.6 [*see* [9A–119]] or an acceptance by a Relevant Member in response to an Offer Notice.
'Buyer'	means:
	— a Relevant Member who signs an Acceptance; or
	— the Company in respect of any shares which the directors decide it will buy.
['Controlling Interest'[2]	means shares conferring over 50% of the total votes capable of being cast on a poll at the Company's general meetings.]
'Price Date'	means the date on which the Price is agreed or assessed.
'Relevant Event'	means:
	— any transfer or purported transfer of any share in the Company except in accordance with these articles;
	— the death or making of a bankruptcy order against or the passing of any resolution or making of an order to wind up any member;
	— the appointment of any administrator of any member or receiver or administrative receiver of any assets of any member; or
	— the termination of the employment or directorship of any employee or director of the Company who is a member.
'Relevant Members'	means members of the Company other than the Seller [who hold one or more shares of the same class as the Sale Shares].
'Offer Notice'	means a written notice from the Company to the Relevant Members served not less than seven days after the Price has been notified to the Seller stating:
	— the number of Sale Shares available;
	— the price per share;
	— the number provisionally allocated to the member;
	— that the member is entitled to state the maximum number (if any) which he wishes to buy; and
	— that the member is entitled to state the number (if any) of shares which he wishes to buy in addition to the allocated number.

'Transfer Notice'	means a written notice given or a notice deemed to be given by the Seller to the Company stating in the former case the number of Sale Shares he wishes to transfer and (if any) the name of the proposed buyer and the price for the Sale Shares.
'Price'	means:

[— if the sale is pursuant to regulation [x] [ie the circumstances in [9A–145] or [9A–149]] the price stated in the Offer;³]

— the price agreed between the Seller and the directors of the Company; or

— the price assessed under regulation 4.

'Seller'	means the holder or holders of Sale Shares in respect of which a Transfer Notice is given or deemed to have been given.
['Controlling Shareholder'	means a member or members holding between them a Controlling Interest.]
'Sale Shares'	means all the shares in the Company's capital:

— in the Transfer Notice if actually given by the Seller; or

— registered in the Seller's name or in which he or she has a beneficial interest if the Transfer Notice is deemed to have been given.

PART 2: PROCEDURE

2.0 If a member wishes to transfer a share or a Relevant Event occurs the following procedure shall apply so far as is appropriate in the circumstances of each transaction. [9A–113]

2.1 The Seller shall give a Transfer Notice to the Company or (if a Relevant Event occurs) the Company shall give written notice to the Seller stating that he or she is deemed to have given a Transfer Notice. [9A–114]

2.2 The Company and the Seller shall try to agree the Price. [9A–115]

2.3 If the Price is not agreed within one month starting on the date on which the Transfer Notice is or is deemed to be given it shall be assessed under Part 4 of this regulation. [9A–116]

2.4 The directors shall notify the Seller of the Price of the Sale Shares not later than seven days after the Price Date. [9A–117]

2.5 A Transfer Notice actually given by the Seller may not be withdrawn by him except by written notice to the Company within fourteen days of the Price Date stating that he or she does not agree the Price as fixed under Part 4 of this regulation. A Transfer Notice deemed to be given pursuant to a Relevant Event cannot be withdrawn. [9A–118]

2.6 The Sale Shares may be bought by the Company at the Price. The directors shall determine whether and if so how many of them the Company will buy and if they do so determine they shall (not later than twenty-eight days from the Price Date) notify the Seller by an Acceptance of the number of Sale Shares to be bought by the Company. [9A–119]

[9A–120] **2.7** The directors shall without delay provisionally allocate the Sale Shares not to be bought by the Company to the Relevant Members in proportion (as nearly as may be) to the number of shares in the same class as the Sale Shares held by them at close of business on the day of the Transfer Notice. The directors may at their discretion allocate to Relevant Members any shares not being capable of being divided exactly amongst the Relevant Members.

[9A–121] **2.8** On completing the allocation under regulation 2.7 and in any event not later than twenty eight days from the Price Date the directors shall issue the Offer Notices in accordance with the allocation.

[9A–122] **2.9** Relevant Members who wish to buy Sale Shares shall send an Acceptance to the Company not later than fourteen days after service of the Offer Notice.

[9A–123] **2.10** The directors on receipt of Acceptances shall allocate the Sale Shares amongst the Buyers:

— firstly in proportion (as nearly as may be) to the number of shares in the same class as the Sale Shares held by them at the close of business on the day of the Transfer Notice [except that, if the Company has a Controlling Shareholder, the directors shall not allocate any shares to any other person until the number of shares, for which an offer to buy has been made by the Controlling Shareholder, has been satisfied in full[4]];

— secondly in respect of any shares not so allocated amongst those Buyers whose Acceptances were in respect of a maximum number exceeding the shares allocated to them under the allocation mentioned above in proportion between such members on the basis mentioned above until either all the Sale Shares have been so allocated or all Acceptances have been satisfied in full; and

— finally any Sale Shares not taken by any Buyer or not otherwise disposed of under these regulations may be allocated by the directors as they think fit to any member of the Company;

but no Sale Shares may be allocated to any Buyer in excess of the maximum number (if any) stated by any Buyer that he is willing to buy.

PART 3: COMPLETION

[9A–124] **3.1** As soon as is possible the directors shall write to each Buyer and the Seller:

— notifying the Buyer of the number of shares allocated to him and the amount payable by him (to be paid by a cheque in favour of the Company);

— sending to the Seller transfers for the Sale Shares; and

— requiring the cheques, transfers and share certificates (or an indemnity in such form as the directors require for any Sale Share whose certificate is not delivered to them) to be sent to the Company within seven days.

[9A–125] **3.2** The directors [may complete any transfer of Sale Shares when the Price for it has been received (*or*) shall not complete any transfer of Sale Shares unless they have received the Price for all the Sale Shares].[5]

[9A–126] **3.3** On each completion of a sale and purchase of Sale Shares the directors shall:

— enter the Buyer in the register of members;

— send a certificate to each Buyer for the Sale Shares bought by him;
— send a remittance to the Seller for the Sale Shares; and
— send to the Seller a certificate for any Sale Shares not transferred to Buyers.

PART 4: PRICE

4 If the price is not fixed in any other way it shall be assessed: [9A–127]

— by [the Company's auditor (*or*) an accountant to be selected by the Seller and the Company or in default of agreement within 14 days starting on the date of the Transfer Notice to be nominated by the President for the time being of the Institute of Chartered Accountants on the application of the first of them to apply to him];
— as a fair price for the Sale Shares [disregarding[6] (*or*) having regard to] the absence of any dividend or other return to the shareholders and the fact that the shares to be valued represent a majority or a minority interest in the Company's share capital or when registered will result in any person's interest in the Company's share capital becoming a majority.

[*or as an alternative*]
— as a fair price per share on the basis of a valuation of the whole of the Company's issued share capital of the same class as the Sale Shares on an open market sale between a willing buyer and willing seller dealing with each other at arm's length at the date of the Transfer Notice and multiplying valuation by the number of the Sale Shares and dividing it by the number of issued shares in the same class.

PART 5: ADMINISTRATION

5.1 The process culminating with the service of an Acceptance shall constitute a contract between the Seller and the Buyer for the sale at the Price of a number of Sale Shares to be determined by the directors in accordance with these regulations. [9A–128]

5.2 No part of the Price shall be paid to the Seller until he has delivered to the Company all necessary transfers and certificates and indemnities. Until the Price is paid to the Seller it shall be held by the Company in a designated trust account for his benefit and if because of any act or omission by the Seller it remains in that account at the end of five years from the date of the Transfer Notice the directors may at any time resolve that it be forfeited by and belong to the Company free from all claims of the Seller. [9A–129]

5.3 If the Seller fails to execute a transfer of the Sale Shares any director designated by a resolution of the directors shall be attorney of the Seller with full power to execute, complete and deliver in the name and on behalf of the Seller a transfer or transfers of the Sale Shares to the Buyers. A transfer under this clause may be registered notwithstanding that the certificate for any Sale Share has not been delivered to the directors or that the price or part of it has not been paid to the Seller. [9A–130]

5.4 If the Price is fixed by any person under regulation [4] he or she shall certify it to the Company in writing and shall act as an expert and not an arbitrator.[7] [9A–131]

[9A–132]   **5.5** After a Transfer Notice has been served the Seller shall have such number of votes as exceeds by one vote the number of votes required to be cast whether on a show of hands or a poll or a resolution in writing to defeat a proposal for a resolution for the deletion or alteration of any regulation affecting his or her rights as a Seller or the cancellation or alteration of these articles of association or any other act which would have the same or a similar effect.

[9A–133]   **5.6** The Seller shall not be entitled to exercise any right to vote at any meeting of the Company or its directors after service of a Transfer Notice except under regulation 5.5 [and at a meeting under regulation (*number*)[8]].

PART 6: EXCLUDED TRANSFERS

[9A–134]   **6** Regulations [2] to [5] shall not apply to and the directors shall be bound to register:

—   any transfer to an existing member of the Company;

—   any transfer approved by a [resolution in writing signed by each director or by an ordinary (*or*) special resolution of the Company];[9]

—   any request by a person becoming entitled to a share in consequence of the death or bankruptcy of a member to be registered as the holder of such shares;[10]

—   any transfer by a personal representative to any person or persons absolutely entitled to the shares transferred under the will or intestacy of a deceased member;[11]

—   any transfer to the spouse of the transferor or any direct ascendant, descendant or collateral relative of the transferor;[12]

—   any transfer to the trustees of a family settlement made by a transferor (that is to say a settlement under which none other than all or any of the transferor or his or her spouse and issue (including issue not yet born) is entitled to a beneficial interest);[13]

—   any transfer by a trustee to a beneficiary;[14]

—   any transfer by a trustee to a new trustee;[15]

—   any transfer by a corporate shareholder to an associated company (that is to say any holding company or subsidiary company of such corporate shareholder and any other subsidiary company of any such holding company) but any act by which the transferee ceases to be an associated company shall take effect as a Relevant Event;

—   any transfer of an 'A' share from one holder of an 'A' share to another holder of an 'A' share or of a 'B' share from one holder of a 'B' share to another holder of a 'B' share;[16] and

—   one transfer by a Controlling Shareholder of one share to any person as his or her nominee and any subsequent transfer of that share to any other person nominated by the Controlling Shareholder.

[9A–135]   [1]   This set of regulations, which includes its own additional definitions, is intended to be capable of being inserted en block into the articles of association in precedent [9A–056]. The entire set can be accessed through the key number [9A–111]. Whilst it is possible to omit the whole of these regulations and rely entirely on the regulation in [9A–106] in order to restrict transfers, it is generally found to be desirable to include procedure to control transfers of shareholdings. For notices under these regulations, see forms [9A–444] to [9A–465]. This set ([9A–112] to [9A–134]) provides for the intending seller of shares to serve a transfer notice on the directors, typically when two or more persons form a company as quasi-partners, whilst the example in precedent [9A–136] envisages cases where members of a family owned company permit shares to be taken by one or more employees and enables the directors to serve a transfer notice to compel a member in certain circumstances to sell his shares. The additional clauses [9A–145] enable a sale of the member's shares to a third party. The final example ([9A–149]) is a variation of the first and allows for a controlling shareholder to sell the whole of the company's capital to a third party, but only if the third party's offer is not matched by the minority shareholders. This regulation contains a number of alternative provisions and is more extensive than may be required in many cases. Therefore care must be taken to select only those parts which are appropriate to the circumstances.

2   See note 4 below.

3   Include this sub-paragraph only in the 'sale of a conflicting interest' version of the regulation contemplated by [9A–149], which can be added after 'Excluded Transfers'.

4   Include the words in brackets and the definitions of Controlling Interest and Controlling Shareholder only if there is a controlling shareholder and the more stringent controls of [9A–136] are not required.

5   The second alternative is intended to prevent the buyers from acquiring only some of the seller's shares (e g enough to enable the buyer to obtain control) and leave him with an unsaleable reduced holding.

6   If the 'disregarding' formula is used, the value of the shares will be the proportion of the whole value of the company equal to the proportion of the issued share capital being transferred. This appears to be the basis of valuation which is appropriate in some shareholders' petition cases: *Re Company A (No 004475 of 1982)* [1983] Ch 178, [1983] 2 All ER 36 and *Re Bird Precision Bellows Ltd* [1986] Ch 658, [1985] 3 All ER 523, CA. The 'having regard to' formula is likely, in the case of a minority which will not give control to the transferee, to result in the shares being valued at a substantial discount below assets value.

7   Where the parties agree upon a procedure to determine a price or value and express that the person, who makes the determination, acts as an expert and not an arbitrator, they are electing for a measure of certainty but in doing so lose the right to impeach the valuation on the grounds of a mistake, even a negligent mistake: *Baber v Kenwood Manufacturing Co Ltd* (1977) 121 Sol Jo 606, CA. Where the valuation by an expert includes the reasons (a speaking valuation) it may be impugned if it was made on an erroneous basis (*Burgess v Purchase & Sons (Farms) Ltd* [1983] Ch 216, [1983] 2 All ER 4) or if the expert had departed from the instructions given to him (*Jones v Sherwood Computer Services plc* [1992] 2 All ER 170, [1992] 1 WLR 277, CA). The expert must beware that since he is not fulfilling some judicial or quasi-judicial role, he is not immune from an action for negligence: *Palacath Ltd v Flanagan* [1985] 2 All ER 161. See also 'pendulum' arbitration clause, Arbitration [5–094].

8   See the seller's escape route in [9A–154].

9   See [9A–497].

10   This exception should be omitted if it is intended to keep ownership of the shares to those who are its directors or present members. The definition of Relevant Event [9A–112] must be altered appropriately if this exception is used.

11   See note 10 above.

12   See note 10 above.

13   See note 10 above.

14   See note 10 above.

15   See note 10 above.

16   Include only if the regulation in [9A–368] is used.

6   Power for company or controlling shareholder to buy member's shares on death, end of employment etc — additional regulations for inclusion in articles[1]

[9A–136]

x.1 In this clause the following terms shall have the following meanings.

[9A–137]

'Relevant Event'   means:

— any notice by the Vendor to the Company of his or her wish to transfer any share;

— any transfer or purported transfer of any share in the Company except in accordance with this clause;

— the death or bankruptcy of any member;

— the passing of any resolution or making of an order to wind up any member;

	— the appointment of any administrator, receiver or administrative receiver of any assets of any member; or
	— the termination of the employment or directorship of any employee or director of the Company who is a member.
'Buyer'	means the Company or any other person named as such by the directors.
'Transfer Notice'	means a written notice given by the Buyer to the Seller of the exercise of the Buyer's right to buy the Sale Shares.
'Price'	means:
	— the price agreed between the Seller and the directors of the Company; or
	— the price assessed under regulation [x.4].
'Seller'	means any person in respect of whom a Relevant Event occurs or the personal representative, trustee, receiver or liquidator of any such person.
'Sale Shares'	means all the shares in the Company registered in the name of the Seller or in which the Seller has a beneficial interest.
'Transfer'	means the renunciation or other disposal of or dealing with shares allotted or rights in respect of shares granted to a member and the verb 'to transfer' shall be construed accordingly.

[9A–138] **x.2** Nothing in this clause shall apply to any share registered in the name of a Controlling Shareholder.[2]

[9A–139] **x.3** At any time on or after the occurrence of a Relevant Event the Buyer shall have the right to buy the Sale Shares to be exercised by the service of a Transfer Notice on the Seller. If the Buyer is not the Company he shall send a copy of the Transfer Notice to the Company.

[9A–140] **x.4** If the Price is not agreed within one month from the date of the Transfer Notice it shall be assessed by the Company's auditor acting as an expert and not an arbitrator having regard to the absence of any dividend or other return to the shareholders and the fact that the shares to be valued represent a minority interest in the Company's share capital.[3]

[9A–141] **x.5** On the Price being assessed and notified to the Seller, the Seller shall be bound to transfer the Sale Shares to the Buyer on payment of the price to the directors. If he or she fails to do so the chairman of the directors, or failing him or her another director nominated by the directors shall be deemed to be the Seller's duly appointed attorney with full power to execute, complete and deliver in the name and on behalf of the Seller a transfer or transfers of the Sale Shares to the Buyer.

[9A–142] **x.6** No part of the Price shall be paid to the Seller until he or she has delivered to the Company all necessary transfers and certificates and indemnities. Until the Price is paid to the Seller it shall be held by the Company in a designated trust account for his benefit and if because of any act or omission by the

Seller within five years from the date of the Transfer Notice it shall be forfeited by and belong to the Company free from all claims of the Seller.

x.7 The Seller shall not be entitled to exercise any right to vote at any meeting of the Company or its directors after service of a Transfer Notice.

[9A-143]

1   This regulation is intended to be used on its own as an alternative to [9A–111]. See [9A–135], note 1.
2   'Controlling Shareholder' as defined in [9A–112].
3   See [9A–135], note 6.

[9A-144]

7   Articles: Additional pre-emption regulations for sale of transferring member's shares to third party[1]

[9A-145]

ADDITIONAL DEFINITIONS

x.1 In this clause the following terms shall have the following meanings.

[9A-146]

'Independent Buyer'	means any person who is not and who has not been within the 12 months before the date of the Offer:
	— a member of the Company;
	— connected with any member; or
	— a person in whom any member of the Company is a participator.
'Issued Capital'	means the whole of the Company's issued ordinary share capital for the time being.
'Third Party Notice'	means a written notice given by the Seller for the purposes of regulation [see x.3 [9A–147]] to the Company stating the number of Sale Shares subject to an offer, the name of the Independent Buyer and the Third Party Price.
'Unsold Shares Notice'	means a written notice given by the directors to the Seller stating the number of the Unsold Shares.
'Offer'	means an unconditional written offer to each of the members by an Independent Buyer to buy the Issued Capital on terms (including the price) which are the same for each share and each member.
'Offer Period'	means 28 days from the service of an Offer.
'Third Party Price'	means the price per share pursuant to regulation [see x.2 [9A–147]] offered by the Independent Buyer for the shares in the Third Party Notice.
'Minority Shareholders'	means all or any of the members except the Controlling Shareholder.
'Unsold Shares'	means Sale Shares in respect of which:
	— there is no Buyer within 14 days from any Offer Notice; or
	— the Buyer fails to complete the purchase within 28 days of the notification to Buyer under regulation [see 3.1 [9A–124]]

'Restricted Transfer'	means a transfer of shares which constitute a Controlling Interest by a Controlling Shareholder to an Independent Buyer.
'participator' and 'connected with'	have the meanings set out in Income and Corporation Taxes Act 1988, sections 417(1) and 839.

PART [X]: SALE TO THIRD PARTY

[9A–147] **x.1** The directors shall give an Unsold Shares Notice to the Seller without delay if:

— they do not within 14 days from the date of any Offer Notice find a Buyer of the Sale Shares;

— it appears that a Buyer of all of them will not be found; or

— if the purchase of any Sale Shares in respect of which Acceptances have been received is not completed within 28 days of the notification to Buyer under regulation 3.1 [see [9A–126]].

x.2 The Seller may for three months from the service of an Unsold Shares Notice seek an Independent Buyer to buy any or all of the Unsold Shares at a price not less than that specified by the Offer Notice.

x.3 Before transferring any Sale Shares to an Independent Buyer the Seller shall give a Third Party Notice to the directors who shall immediately offer the Sale Shares to the Company and the Relevant Members at the Third Party Price. The Third Party Price shall be treated as a Transfer Notice and regulations 2.6 to 2.10 [see [9A–093]] shall mutatis mutandis apply to it except that Offer Notices shall be issued immediately the directors have completed the provisional allocation of such Sale Shares amongst the Relevant Members.

x.4 If within 28 days of the date of service of the Third Party Notice the purchase of all the Sale Shares in it has not been completed (except as a result of the Seller's default) the Seller may during the next 28 days transfer those shares to the Independent Buyer at not less than the Third Party Price.

x.5 The directors shall register any transfer of shares made pursuant to regulation x.4 if (after considering such evidence as they reasonably require) they are satisfied that the shares are being transferred pursuant to a bona fide sale at the Third Party Price without any deduction, allowance, rebate or other payment to the Buyer. If they are not so satisfied they may refuse to register the transfer.

[9A–148] [1] This regulation enables a member, whose shares are not taken on the transfer notice procedure, to sell his or her shares to a third party and is intended to be added to the pre-emption regulations in the basic set in [9A–111]: see also [9A–135], note 1.

[9A–149] # 8 Articles: Additional pre-emption regulations for Controlling Shareholder to arrange sale of whole share capital to Independent Buyer[1]

ADDITIONAL DEFINITIONS

[9A–150] 'Minority Shareholders'	means all or any of the members except the Controlling Shareholder.

'Restricted   means a transfer of shares which constitute a
Transfer'   Controlling Interest by a Controlling Shareholder to an
                       Independent Buyer.

PART [X]: TRANSFER OF CONTROL

x.1 If a Controlling Shareholder wishes to make a Restricted Transfer to an Independent Buyer he shall procure that an Offer is made which is open for as long as is necessary to complete the procedures in this part of this regulation. [9A–151]

x.2 If during the Offer Period the Minority Shareholders make an unconditional offer to buy all the Controlling Shareholder's shares in the Company
— the Controlling Shareholder shall sell them to the Minority Shareholders on the terms of the Offer, and
— the Minority Shareholders then become Buyers and the Controlling Shareholder becomes a Seller.

x.3 If the Minority Shareholders do not make an unconditional offer to buy all the Controlling Shareholder's shares during the Offer Period and complete the purchase during the (*number*) days starting on the last day of the Offer Period
— the Controlling Shareholder may sell the whole of his shares on the terms of the Offer to the maker of the Offer who then becomes a Buyer,
— the Minority Shareholders shall be deemed to have given a Transfer Notice, and
— the Controlling Shareholder shall procure that the maker of the Offer completes the purchase of the whole of the Minority Shareholders' shares on the terms of the Offer.

x.4 Any share held by a person to whom a share is transferred as nominee under regulations [2] to [5] shall be deemed to comprise part of the transferor's holding.

[1] This regulation enables a controlling shareholder to override the transfer notice procedure on the sale of his or her shares to a third party if the same offer is extended to all the minority shareholders and is intended to be added to the pre-emption regulations in the basic set in [9A–111]: see also [9A–135], note 1. [9A–152]

9   Articles: Power for Seller whose shares are not bought under transfer notice to wind up Company[1] [9A–153]

x If the Seller is unable to sell the Sale Shares in accordance with regulation (*number*) he or she shall be entitled to convene a general meeting of the Company for the purpose of considering and if thought fit passing a resolution to wind up the Company and shall have such number of votes as exceeds by one vote 75% of the votes capable of being cast whether on a show of hands or on a poll in respect of that resolution. [9A–154]

[1] This regulation gives the would-be seller a powerful means of avoiding being locked into a company. The answer to the majority shareholders' objection to this power is that the price for the shares may be fixed by an independent person [9A–127]: the seller cannot use this power to hold out for an inflated price. [9A–155]

10 Articles: Additional set of regulations to create convertible Preference Shares[1]

PART 1: PRELIMINARY

[9A–157] **1** In this regulation the following terms shall have the following meanings.

'Redemption Dates'	means (*date*), (*date*), (*date*) and (*date*).
'Conversion Date'	means the date on which the conversion notice is received by the Company.
'Preference Shares'	means (*rate*)% [non-cumulative] redeemable preference £[1] shares with the rights in clause (*number*) of these articles.

[9A–158] **2** The share Company's capital is at the date of the adoption of this regulation £(...) ((...) pounds) divided into (*number*) ordinary £[1] shares and (*number*) Preference Shares. The Preference Shares shall have the rights given by the following sub-paragraphs of this regulation.

PART 2: AS TO DIVIDENDS

[9A–159] **3.1** The Company's distributable profits (in so far as they are sufficient) shall be applied:
— first in the payment to the holders of the Preference Shares on each [30 June] and [31 December] of a [non-]cumulative preferential dividend at a rate of (*rate*)% pa on the capital paid up on them (exclusive of associated tax credits);
— if that dividend and all arrears [and accumulations] of it have been paid in full the Company's profits available for distribution and resolved to be distributed shall be distributable by way of dividend to the holders of the ordinary shares.

3.2 If in any year a Preference Share is redeemed or converted into an ordinary share the dividend which would otherwise have been payable on that share shall be payable in respect of the period during that year before redemption or conversion calculated on a day-to-day basis.

PART 3: AS TO DISTRIBUTION ON WINDING UP

[9A–160] **4** The Company's surplus assets shall be applied:
— first in payment to the holders of the Preference Shares of the capital paid up on them;
— secondly in payment of any amounts due to the holders of the Preference Shares under paragraph (*number*) of this regulation whether or not a dividend has been declared or earned in respect of such amounts;
— thirdly in payment to the holders of ordinary shares of the capital paid up on them; and
— fourthly the residue (if any) shall be divided among the holders of ordinary shares in proportion to the amount paid up at the commencement of the winding up on the ordinary shares respectively held by them.

PART 4: AS TO FURTHER PARTICIPATION

5 Except as mentioned above the Preference Shares shall not confer on their holders any right to participate in the Company's profits or assets.

PART 5: AS TO MEETINGS AND VOTES

6 The holders of the Preference Shares shall not be entitled to attend at any meeting of the Company or vote on any resolution of the Company unless:
—   at the date of the notice convening the meeting the dividend on the Preference Shares is one month in arrears;
—   the Company has failed to redeem any Preference Share on the due date;
—   the resolution is a special or extraordinary resolution; or
—   the Company is in breach of any of the provisions set out in paragraph (*number*) of these articles.

PART 6: AS TO REDEMPTION

7.1 Subject to the Act the Company shall redeem the Preference Shares [at par] on the Redemption Dates as follows:
(*date*) (*number*) shares [at par];
(*date*) (*number*) shares [at £(*amount*) per share];
(*date*) (*number*) shares [at £(*amount*) per share]; and
(*date*) (*number*) shares [at £(*amount*) per share].

7.2 Not less than 14 days before each Redemption Date the Company shall serve on each holder of a Preference Share a notice stating the number of shares of that holder due to be redeemed on the relevant Redemption Date, [the number of additional shares to be redeemed] and the price payable and requiring him or her to lodge with the Company the certificate in respect of those shares.

7.3 Each Preference Share shall be redeemed on the date on which the Company (after receipt of the relevant share certificate) pays to its holder in full the amount payable for its redemption.

7.4 Immediately after the redemption the Company shall issue to each holder a certificate for the balance (if any) of the Preference Shares comprised in the certificate lodged with it.

[*add if the Company has the option to redeem additional shares*]

7.5 The Company may on any of the Redemption Dates redeem any Preference Shares in addition to those which it is obliged to redeem on that Redemption Date.

7.6 On the redemption of any Preference Shares other than those compulsorily redeemed, the directors shall ensure, as far as is possible, that the number redeemed is divided between the holders [equally (*or*) in the same proportions that their holdings bear to each other (*or*) in such proportions as the directors think fit].

PART 7: AS TO CONVERSION

[9A–164] **8.1** The holder of a Preference Share shall have the right [exercisable on or before (*date*)] to convert all or any of his or her Preference Shares into ordinary shares at [par (*or*) the rate of [three] ordinary shares for [five] Preference Shares]:

— at any time if any Preference Share registered in his or her name has not been redeemed at the due date whether or not the Company is permitted by the Companies Acts to make the redemption;

— at any time if any dividend on any Preference Share registered in his or her name is not paid on the due date;

— at any time if the Company fails to observe any of the conditions set out in clause (*number*); or

— he or she so elects by a notice to that effect served on the Company in the month preceding (*date*).

8.2 The holder of a Preference Share shall exercise the right to convert by giving to the Company written notice of conversion stating the number of Preference Shares in respect of which the right is exercised and lodging with the Company the certificate in respect of those shares.

8.3 Conversion shall be effective on the Conversion Date.

8.4 Immediately after the Conversion Date the Company shall issue to the holder of the preference shares a certificate for the ordinary shares resulting from the conversion and (if applicable) a certificate for the balance of the Preference Shares comprised in the certificate lodged under paragraph 8.2 of this regulation.

PART 8: AS TO OTHER CONDITIONS[2]

[9A–165] **9.0** For as long as any of the Preference Shares remains unredeemed or unconverted:

9.1 the Company shall not be entitled to create any share ranking in any respect in priority to or pari passu with the Preference Shares;

9.2 the Company shall provide to the holders of the Preference Shares copies of the Company's management accounts as soon as they are prepared and all such information as the holders reasonably require about the Company and its accounts and business; and

9.3 the Company shall not without the sanction of a special resolution of the holders of the Preference Shares do any of the following:

— discontinue or dispose of all or any part of its business;

— acquire any business;

— acquire or dispose of any shares in any Company;

— make any investment whose capital value (whenever payable) exceeds £(…) ((…) pounds);

— exercise its borrowing powers in any way which causes or might cause its total borrowings to exceed £(…) ((…) pounds); or

— dismiss or engage or alter the terms of employment of any director or any manager whose emoluments are or exceed £(…) ((…) pounds) p.a.

[9A–166]   [1]   This set of regulations can be added to the end of the articles [9A–056], but would normally appear in the capital section. It may be convenient, however, where a separate class and possible other regulations is required by an outside investor for a limited time, to place them all at the end of the articles so that they can be readily distinguished from the regulations affecting the 'proprietors' and deleted when superseded without affecting the clause numbering.

2   Preference shareholders commonly have no more rights than those set out in the regulations in [9A–159] and [9A–160]. However, where the preference shareholder is a substantial financial backer of the company, he may require correspondingly substantial reserve powers, as in this part of this set of regulations.

11   Minimal articles for wholly owned subsidiary or one person company[1]

[9A–167]

PRELIMINARY AND INTERPRETATION

1 Except as mentioned in these articles the regulations contained in or made applicable by the model articles ('model articles') in Schedule 1 to The Companies (Model Articles) Regulations 2008 shall apply to the Company.

[9A–168]

NUMBER OF DIRECTORS[2]

2 There may be a sole director and the maximum number of directors shall be [four].

[9A–169]

POWERS OF DIRECTORS[3]

3 Regulation 4 of the model articles shall not apply to the Company.]

[9A–170]

4 The directors shall not without the previous sanction of [an ordinary (*or*) a special] resolution of the Company (and shall procure that the directors of any subsidiary of the Company will not without the previous sanction of a special resolution of the Company carry out any such transaction in relation to the subsidiary):

—   sell or dispose of the Company's business or the shares of any of the Company's subsidiaries or any part of the business or shares or any interest in land or buildings where a substantial part of the Company's business is for the time being carried on;

—   acquire any business;

—   acquire or dispose of any shares in any company;

—   make any investment whose capital value (whenever payable) exceeds £(…) ((…) pounds);

—   exercise its borrowing powers in any way which causes or might cause its total borrowings to exceed £(…) ((…) pounds); or

—   dismiss or engage or alter the terms of employment of any director or any manager whose emoluments are or exceed £(…) ((…) pounds) p.a.

APPOINTMENT AND RETIREMENT OF DIRECTORS

5 The Company may by a resolution passed by a majority of not less than [55]%[4] remove any director before the expiration of his or her period of office, and may by an ordinary resolution appoint another director in his or her place. A person so appointed shall be subject to retirement at the same time as if he or she had become a director on the day on which the director in whose place he or she is appointed was last elected a director[5].

[9A–171]

[9A–172]   **6** Any [Controlling Shareholder (*or*) member or members holding over [50%] of the Company's issued share capital] may at any time by written notice to the Company do all or any of the following:
—   vary the number of directors of the Company;
—   appoint one or more additional directors; and
—   remove one or more directors from office.

7 Regulation 18 of the model articles is altered by the addition of the following sub-paragraph (g).
(g)   that person receives notice signed by all the other directors stating that that person should cease to be a director.[6]

PROCEEDINGS OF DIRECTORS

[9A–172A]   **8** Regulation 8 of the model articles does not apply to the Company.[7]

[9A–173]   **9** For so long as any member of the Company [holds over 50% of the issued shares in the company's capital (*or*) is the Controlling Shareholder] he or she shall be the chairman of the directors and shall have such number of votes as enables him or her to carry or defeat any proposal for a resolution of the directors.

[9A–174]   **10** The quorum at meetings of the directors shall be two holding together over 50% of the Company's issued share capital, and regulation 10 of the model articles shall be construed accordingly.

[9A–175]   **11** If at any meeting of the directors called by not less than [four] days' written notice a quorum is not present within half an hour of the time appointed for the meeting, the director present, if he holds not less than 50% of the issued share capital of the Company, shall be a quorum.

[9A–176]
1   See notes to the articles in precedent 4 [9A–056]. It is envisaged that this precedent will be used for wholly owned subsidiaries and companies wholly or substantially owned by one person, in which it is of prime importance to the principal shareholders to control the boards by the appointment and removal and votes of directors, and there is little or no need for special regulations concerned with the issue and transfer of shares.
2   See precedent 4, note 8 [9A–110].
3   Regulation 8 of the model articles for private companies provides for majority decision without a meeting, which in many cases may be sufficient and render this article unnecessary. Regulation 8 does however provide for more extensive powers and less consultation than some may find acceptable, in which case the whole of part of it could be excluded by the words in square brackets.
     See precedent 4, note 9 [9A–110].
4   See precedent 4, note 26 [9A–110].
5   See precedent 4, note 27 [9A–110].
6   This sub-paragraph was in the original draft of each of the model articles but omitted from subsequent drafts and the final versions.
7   This regulation (the exclusion of regulation 8 of the model articles) is likely to be desirable in the case of a wholly owned subsidiary with senior employees as some or all of the directors, unless the parent company or controlling shareholder retains and can exercise control under such a regulation as 9 above. The flexibility and informality of regulation 8 (unanimous decision) in the model articles may be very useful for companies in which all the directors are shareholders, effectively for quasi-partnership companies, but undesirable where management is separated from ownership.

OTHER AGREEMENTS

12 Agreement for sale of business of sole trader to limited company in consideration for allotment of shares — short form[1]

[9A–177]

DATE AND PARTIES

THIS AGREEMENT is made on (*date*) between (*name*) of (*address*) ('(*Party-A*)') and (*name*) Ltd company (*number*) whose registered office is at (*address*) ('(*Party-B*)').

[9A–178]

DEFINITIONS

1 In this deed the following terms shall have the following meanings.

[9A–179]

'Formation Agreement'	means an agreement dated (*date*) and made between the (*Party-A*) and (*name*) for the formation of the (*Party-B*) and the transfer of the Business to it.
'Sale Assets'	means all the (*Party-A*)'s assets used by [him] in connection with the Business at the Effective Date.
'Business'	means the business carried on by (*Party-B*) of the [manufacture and supply of (*description*) products] under the (*name*).
'Effective Date'	means the date of this deed (*or*) (*date*).
'Liabilities'	means the (*Party-A*)'s debts, liabilities and other obligations of in respect of the Business outstanding on the Effective Date.
'in agreed terms'	in relation to any document means in the form of the draft annexed to this (*document*) or as agreed in writing between the parties.
'clause' and 'schedule'	mean respectively clauses or schedules in this deed unless the context shows a contrary meaning.
'comply with'	includes 'observe and perform'.
'parties'	means the parties to this deed.

SALE

2 The (*Party-A*) agrees to sell [with full title guarantee][9] and the (*Party-B*) agrees to buy the Business and the Sale Assets [free from all encumbrances].

[9A–180]

LIABILITIES

3 The (*Party-B*) shall discharge all the Liabilities and shall at all times following [today (*or*) the Effective Date] compensate the (*Party-A*) in full on demand for all liability in respect of the Liabilities.

[9A–181]

TITLE

4 The (*Party-A*) warrants that [he] is the beneficial owner of the [assets of the] (*subject matter*) free from any incumbrance, charge, lien or claims in favour of

[9A–182]

or by any other person and the (*Party-B*) shall accept without investigation or objection such title as the (*Party-A*) has to them.

CONSIDERATION

[9A–183] **5** The purchase price payable by the (*Party-B*) for the transaction entered into by this [*document*] is £(...) ((...) pounds) which shall be paid:
— as to £(...) ((...) pounds) in cash; and
— as to £(...) ((...) pounds) by the allotment to the (*Party-A*) or [his] nominees of (*number*) of the ordinary [and (*number*) preference] shares in the (*Party-B*) credited as fully paid.

FURTHER ASSURANCE

[9A–184] **6.1** Each of the parties shall execute all documents and do all things which the other[s] [reasonably] require[s] to vest in the other[s] the full right title and interest in the (*subject matter*) and to carry this (*document*) into effect.

[9A–185] **6.2** The (*Party-A*) irrevocably appoints the (*Party-B*) as [his] attorney to execute any document or do anything which is required for any of the purposes of this (*document*) or the exercise or enforcement of any of the (*Party-B*)'s rights and remedies under it.

NON-COMPETITION

[9A–186] **7** The (*Party-B*) shall not during this (*document*) (*or*) and for [one] year after [its termination for any reason (*or*) completion] directly or indirectly carry on alone or in partnership or as the agent or servant of any other person within [one mile as the crow flies] from the Property any business competitive with or similar to the Business.

COSTS

[9A–187] **8** The (*Party-B*) shall pay all the costs of and incidental to the preparation and execution of this (*document*) and any further documents necessary to carry it into effect.

[executed as a deed]

[9A–188] ¹ No stamp: see [13–065], note 1. See also [13–001], [13–039] and [13–066] in Sale of Businesses. This is the agreement envisaged by clause [9A–043]. A proposed company has no capacity before its incorporation to enter into a contract. A contract which purports to be made by or on behalf of a company before the incorporation has effect, subject to any agreement to the contrary, as if made by the person purporting to act for the company or as assent for it and he is personally liable on it: CA 2006, s 51. Although it is doubtful whether a trust can exist for a non-existent object, it is common practice for the promoters to contract as trustees for the proposed company, and for the contract to provide for their release upon the company entering into a contract in like terms: for a novation agreement, see [9A–189].

If regulations yet to be produced under CA 2006, s 555 have the same effect (but almost inevitably with more words) as CA 1985, s 88, where shares are issued otherwise than for cash, the company must within one month of the allotment deliver to the registrar a copy of the contract for sale, services or other consideration for which the shares were allotted. If the contract is not reduced to writing, prescribed particulars must be filed with the retun of allotments. This form contains more financial details of the transaction than most companies would want to appear on a public register, and therefore a written agreement may be preferred. Where the agreement is made solely for this purpose, such as on the transfer of a sole trader's business to a 'one member company', this agreement may be reduced to an absolute minimum by omitting the whole of clauses 6 to 8.

13 Adoption by private company of pre-incorporation contract[1]

Suggested terms for parties:

(*Party-A*)	'Supplier' *or* 'Contractor'
(*Party-B*)	'Promoter'
(*Party C*)	'Company'

DATE AND PARTIES

THIS AGREEMENT is made on (*date*) between (*name*) of (*address*) ('(*Party-A*)'[)] the (*Party-A*),[2] (*name*) of (*address*) ('(*Party-B*)') and (*name*) Ltd company (*number*) whose registered office is at (*address*) ('(*Party-C*)'). [9A–190]

SUPPLEMENTARY

1 This deed is supplemental to an agreement '[Sale] Agreement' dated (*date*) and made between (*Party-A*) and (*Party-B*). [9A–191]

BACKGROUND

2 The (*Party-C*) (being the company the intended incorporation of which is referred to in the Sale Agreement) was incorporated on (*date*). [9A–192]

ADOPTION

3 The [Sale] Agreement is adopted by the (*Party-C*) and shall be of the same effect as if the (*Party-C*) had been in existence at the date of the [Sale] Agreement and had been a party to it in the place of the (*Party-B*) [with the alterations contained in clause (*number*)]. [9A–193]

ALTERATIONS TO SALE AGREEMENT

4 The [Sale] Agreement shall be altered as follows with effect from [(*date*) (*or*) the date of this (*document*)]: [9A–194]
— in clause (*number*) £(…)((…) pounds) shall be substituted for £(…)((…) pounds);
— in clause (*number*) after '(*set out*)' shall be inserted '(*set out*)';
— clauses (*number*) and (*number*) shall be deleted and replaced by the [following clauses (*or*) clauses in [the] schedule (*number*)]; and
— the following clauses shall be added to it.

RELEASE

5 The (*Party-B*) is released from all liability under the Sale Agreement. [9A–195]

THE SCHEDULE

[*new clauses inserted in deed*] [9A–196]

[*executed as a deed*]

---

[1]   No stamp (if the adopted agreement bore proper ad valorem stamp duty, if payable) and no increase in price is made in the adoption agreement. The sale agreement could be that in [9A–177], if the latter were made before the incorporation of the company. Whilst, following normal practice, this is called an adoption agreement it operates as and is a novation of the original contract. As to pre-incorporation contracts generally see [9A–188], note 1. [9A–197]

² In this example it is assumed that the vendor is one of the promoters and that the trustees contracting on behalf of the proposed company are both (or all of) the promoters but it may be used where the other contracting party is a stranger to the company.

[9A–198] ## 14 Assurance of real or leasehold property bought by a trustee on behalf of intended company[1]

Use Land Registry form TR1. Subject to the notes below, no special terms need to be included solely because of the nature of the transaction.

Transfer of whole   Land Registry

of registered title(s)

(if you need more room than is provided for in a panel, use continuation sheet CS and attach to this form)

[9A–199] **1** Stamp Duty[3]

Place 'X' in the appropriate box or boxes and complete the appropriate certificate.

[ ] It is certified that this instrument falls within category [ ] in the Schedule to the Stamp Duty (Exempt Instruments) Regulations 1987

[ ] It is certified that the transaction effected does not form part of a larger transaction or of a series of transactions in respect of which the amount or value or the aggregate amount or value of the consideration exceeds the sum of £(...)

[ ] It is certified that this is an instrument on which stamp duty is not chargeable by virtue of the provisions of section 92 of the Finance Act 2001

[9A–200] **2** Title number(s) of the Property (*leave blank if not yet registered*)

[9A–201] **3** Property[4]

In the case of unregistered land insert after the address or description: (*address or description*)

being the whole of the land described in a [conveyance *or as the case may be*] dated (*date*) made between (*parties*) ('the Conveyance').

If the land is registered, Land Registry form FR1 should be used accompanied by Land Registry form DL.

[9A–202] **4** Date

[9A–203] **5** Transferor (*give full names and Company's Registered Number if any*) *Insert name and capacity of the transferor where he is not the registered proprietor*[6]

[9A–204] **6** Transferee for entry on the register (*give full names and Company's Registered Number if any. For Scottish Co Reg Nos, use an SC prefix and for limited liability partnerships use an OC prefix before the registered number, if any. For foreign companies give territory in which incorporated.*)

Unless otherwise arranged with Land Registry headquarters, a certified copy of the Transferee's constitution (in English or Welsh) will be required if it is a body corporate but is not a company registered in England and Wales or Scotland under the Companies Acts.

7 Transferee's intended address(es) for service in the UK (*including postcode*) for entry on the register[7]

8 The Transferor transfers the property to the Transferee.

9 Consideration (*Place 'X' in the appropriate box. State clearly the currency unit if other than sterling. If none of the boxes applies, insert an appropriate memorandum in the additional provisions panel.*)

[ ] The Transferor has received from the Transferee for the Property the sum of (*in words and figures*)

[ ] (*insert other receipt as appropriate*)

[ ] The Transfer is not for money or anything which has a monetary value

10 The Transferor transfers with (*place 'X' in the appropriate box and add any modifications*)

[ ] Full title guarantee   [ ] limited title guarantee[9]

11 Declaration of trust *Where there is more than one Transferee, place 'X' in the appropriate box.*

[ ] The Transferees are to hold the Property on trust for themselves as joint tenants.

[ ] The Transferees are to hold the Property on trust for themselves as tenants in common in equal shares.

[ ] The Transferees are to hold the Property (*complete as necessary*)

12 Additional Provision(s) *Insert here any required or permitted statement, certificate or application and any agreed covenants, declarations, etc.*

DEFINITIONS AND INTERPRETATION

12.1:1 In this transfer the following terms shall have the following meanings.

'Documents'[12]   means the following documents:

Date	Document	Parties
(*insert details*)	(*insert details*)	(insert details)

12.1:2 In this (*document*):
— words expressed in any gender shall where the context so requires or permits include any other gender;
— words importing persons shall include bodies corporate and partnerships and other incorporated bodies and vice versa;
— words expressed in the singular shall where the context so requires or permits include the plural; and
— where any party is more than one person:
    — that party's obligations in this (*document*) shall take effect as joint and several obligations;
    — anything in this (*document*) which applies to that party shall apply to all of those persons collectively and each of them separately;
    — the benefits contained in this (*document*) in favour of that party shall take effect as conferred in favour of all of those persons collectively and each of them separately; and

— the receipt of the survivor of joint holders of this (*document*) shall be a good discharge to the (*Party-A*).

STATEMENTS

[9A–211] **12.2** (*details*)

INCUMBRANCES

[*Unregistered land*]

[9A–212] **12.3** The Property is transferred subject to [and with the benefit of] the matters contained or referred to in the [Conveyance [and (*or*) or] the Documents (*or*) insert details].

INDEMNITY COVENANT

[9A–213] [*Registered land*]

12.4 The Transferee[s] [jointly and severally] covenant[s] with the Transferor to observe and perform the covenants and conditions contained or referred to in the property [proprietorship] and charges registers of the title[s] above referred to and to compensate the Transferor and his successors in title in full on demand for all liability resulting from any failure by the Transferee[s] to observe or perform any of them but the Transferee[s] shall not be personally liable for any breach or non-observance committed after [[he] has (*or*) they have] parted with all interest in the Property.

[*Unregistered land*]

[9A–214] **12.4** The Transferee[s] [jointly and severally] covenant[s] with the Transferor to observe and perform the covenants and conditions contained or referred to in [the Conveyance [and (*or*) or] the Documents] and to compensate the Transferor and his successors in title in full on demand for all liability resulting from any failure by the Transferee[s] to observe or perform any of them but the Transferee[s] shall not be personally liable for any breach or non-observance committed after [[he] has (*or*) they have] parted with all interest in the Property.

ADDITIONAL PARTIES

[9A–215] **12.5** I (*name*) of (*address*) as (*insert capacity in relation to the transfer*) [consent to and concur in this transfer *or as the case may be*].

COVENANTS WITH THE ADDITIONAL PARTIES

[9A–216] **12.6** (*insert details*)

APPLICATIONS TO THE REGISTRAR

[9A–217] **12.7.1** (*name*) applies to the registrar for entry of the following restriction[s] on the register.

(*set out restriction*)

[9A–218] **12.7.2** The parties apply to the registrar to cancel the restriction entered in the proprietorship register of the title referred to in panel 2 on (*date*).

[*Acknowledgement for production of deeds*]

12.8 The Transferor acknowledges the right of the Transferee to production of the following documents and to delivery of copies of them [and undertakes for their safe custody].

Date	Document	Parties
(*insert details*)	(*insert details*)	(insert details)]

13 *The Transferors and all other parties should execute this transfer as a deed using the space below. Forms of execution are given in Schedule 9 to the Land Registration Rules 2003. If the transfer contains transferees' covenants or declarations or contains an application by them (eg for a restriction), it must also be executed by the Transferees.*

Notes

PANEL 1 STAMP DUTY

Tick the first box and insert the letter F in the second box.

PANEL 9 CONSIDERATION

Insert

[   ] The (Transferor) acknowledges that since its incorporation the (Transferee) has reimbursed to [him] the purchase price of Property and all costs and expenses incurred by the (Transferor) before the date of this (*document*) in respect of its purchase by the (Transferor).

PANEL 10 TITLE GUARANTEE

Tick the limited title guarantee box.

PANEL 12 ADDITIONAL PROVISIONS

Add the following

This transfer is made to give effect to a declaration of trust made by the Transferor in favour of the Transferee before its incorporation.

[1]   No stamp duty. See Notes on stamp Duty in the 19th edition. As to the use of Form TR1 see Sale of Land precedent [25–118]. As to pre-incorporation contracts see [9A–188], note 1.

15   Renounceable allotment letter on bonus issue including forms of renunciation and application for registration[1]

RENOUNCEABLE ALLOTMENT LETTER

(*name*) Ltd

company (*number*)

The Companies Act 2006

company limited by shares

(*date*)

(*name and address of allottee*)

Dear Sir/Madam

In accordance with the resolutions passed at the general meeting of the Company held on (*date*) the directors have allotted (*number*) ordinary £[1] shares credited as fully paid up by way of capitalisation of [revenue [and capital] reserves (*or*) the amount standing to the credit of its share premium account (*or*) the Capital reserve fund] to members on the register at that date, in the proportion of (*number*) new shares for every (*number*) existing share.

The number of ordinary shares held by you at that date was (*number*) and accordingly the number of new ordinary shares allotted to you is (*number*). If you wish the new ordinary shares to be registered in your name in the Company's books and the share certificate to be issued to you in due course, you need take no action on the receipt of this letter and should not sign the attached form of renunciation.

If, however, you wish to dispose of all or some of those shares, this letter should be lodged at this office on or before (*date*) with the attached form of renunciation signed and completed by you and the registration application form annexed to it signed and completed by the renouncee. The signed renunciation and registration application forms shall be conclusive evidence of the title of the party (or parties) surrendering it to deal with them and to receive the share certificate.

Yours faithfully,

(*signed*)

Company Secretary

FORM OF RENUNCIATION

[9A–228]   To the Company Secretary of (*name*) Ltd

I renounce my right to [(*number*) of] the (*number*) shares in the [annexed (*or*) above] allotment letter in favour of the person signing the registration application form set out below.

Dated (*date*)

(*signature*)

(*allottee*)

REGISTRATION APPLICATION FORM

[9A–229]   To: the Company Secretary of (*name*) Ltd

(*name*) of (*address*)

—   confirms acceptance of the shares subject to the company's memorandum and articles of association; and

—   requests you to cause those shares to be registered in its name.

Dated (*date*)

(*signature*)

(*renouncee*)

[9A–230]   ¹   No stamp. As to bonus issues generally see [9A–417], note 1.

16 Renounceable provisional allotment letter on rights issue including forms of renunciation, splitting and applications for additional shares and registration

RENOUNCEABLE ALLOTMENT LETTER

(*name*) Ltd

company (*number*)

The Companies Act 2006

company limited by shares

(*date*)

(*name and address of allottee*)

Dear Sir/Madam

As you are aware from the chairman's report issued with the company's accounts for the year to (*date*), the expansion programme for the company's business entails capital expenditure of around £(...) ((...) pounds) and additional working capital of around £(...) ((...) pounds), part of which may be raised by increased bank borrowing but £(...) ((...) pounds) of which was proposed to be raised by the issue of additional equity capital by way of rights issue to members of the Company.

At the [annual (*or*) extraordinary] general meeting of the Company held on (*date*), it was resolved to increase the Company's capital to £(...) ((...) pounds) by the creation of (*number*) new ordinary £[1] shares and to authorise the directors to offer to the Company's members on its register of members on (*date*) (*number*) ordinary £[1] shares (being the (*number*) ordinary £[1] shares then unissued and (*number*) of the new ordinary £[1] shares) all at £[1.50] per share including a premium of [50]p per share (*or*) at par in the proportion of [1] share to be allotted for every [5] shares registered in the respective names of each member at that date or at the close of business on (*date*).

Pursuant to that resolution the directors have made a provisional allotment of (*number*) ordinary £[1] shares less those represented by fractions of a share. The number of shares registered in your name at that date is stated in column 1 below, and the number of shares provisionally allotted to you and the amount to be paid by you for them are stated respectively in columns 2 and 3 below. Fractions arising in the course of the provisional allotment will be dealt with as explained below.

1	2	3
Existing holding of ordinary £[1] shares	Ordinary £[1] shares provisionally allotted	Amount payable
(*amount*)	(*amount*)	(*amount*)

You may accept the provisional allotment in respect of all or some of the shares mentioned in column 2 [and you may renounce your right to all or some of them to one or more persons [who is or are present members or employees of the Company or who is or are your spouse or child or remoter issue or the trustee of or for all or any of them and yourself or who is a

person to whom under clause (*number*) of the Company's articles of association you are entitled to transfer a share]. The directors reserve the right to
refuse, without giving any reason therefor, to accept the renunciation of any
shares to and the application for additional shares by any person of whom
they do not approve]. Acceptances of the provisional allotment must be made
by lodging at the Company's registered office before 3 pm on (*date*) ('time for
acceptance') the following:

1   this provisional allotment letter;

2   the attached form of renunciation signed by you if the right to all or any
     of the shares is renounced;

3.0 the attached application form in which must appear:

3.1 if you accept all or any of the shares, your name and address as
     provisional allottee, the number of shares accepted by you and the
     amount payable calculated at £[1.50] per share;

3.2 if you renounce your right to all or any of the shares, the name(s) and
     address(es) of the renouncee(s) as renouncee(s), and the number(s) of
     shares renounced to the [or each] renouncee and the amount(s) payable
     by the [or each] renouncee calculated at £[1.50] per share;

3.3 the number of additional shares applied for by you and the [or each]
     renouncee in accordance with terms relating to additional shares

[9A–233]   **17   Agreement for allotment of bonus shares for filing under
Companies Act 2006**

[*Regulations are awaited to show what prescribed information will be required in
a return of allotments under CA 2006, s 555 and whether any contract or terms,
as provided for by CA 1985, s 88, will be required. Pending the regulation, this
precedent is deleted and not replaced.*]

[9A–234]   **18   Agreement by company for purchase of its own shares**

Suggested terms for parties:

(*Party-A*)   'Shareholder'
(*Party-B*)   'Company'

DATE AND PARTIES

[9A–235]   AN AGREEMENT dated (*date*) between (*name*) of (*address*) (*or*) (*name*) of
(*address*) and (*name*) of (*address*) ('(*Party-A*)') and (*name*) Ltd registered in
England and Wales with company (*number*) whose registered office is at
(*address*) ('(*Party-B*)').

DEFINITIONS

[9A–236]   **1** In this agreement the following terms shall have the following meanings.

'Deceased'   means (*name*) who died on (*date*).

'Probate'	means the probate of the Deceased's will which was on (*date*) granted to [(*name*) and (*name*) (*or*) the (*Party-A*)] in the [Principal Registry of the Family Division (*or*) (*place name*) District Probate Registry].
'Sale Shares'	means all the shares in the Company's capital registered in the [(*Party-A*)'s name (*or*) Deceased's] name at the date of [his] death.
'Will'	means the Deceased's will dated (*date*).
'clause' and 'schedule'	mean respectively clauses or schedules in this agreement unless the context shows a contrary meaning.
'comply with'	includes 'observe and perform'.
'parties'	means the parties to this agreement.

BACKGROUND

2 The (*Party-B*) is a company limited by shares incorporated in England under the Companies Acts on (*date*) as company (*number*) whose capital is now £(*amount*) divided into (*number*) [ordinary] shares of £(*amount*) each [and (*amount*) [*rate*]% preference shares of £(*amount*) each] of which [all (*or*) (*number*) of the ordinary shares [and [none (*or*) (*number*)] of the preference shares] have been issued and are fully paid.

[9A–237]

SALE

3 [Each of] the (*Party-A*)s shall sell with full title guarantee and the (*Party-B*) shall buy the Sale Shares free from all encumbrances on the Effective Date [for £(…) ((…) pounds) (*or*) the Price].

[9A–238]

COMPLETION

4 The sale and purchase shall be completed immediately after the making of this agreement at the office of (*name*) & Co of (*address*) and on completion:
— the (*Party-A*) shall deliver to the (*Party-B*) a transfer or transfers of the whole of the Sale Shares and the certificates relating to them; and
— the (*Party-B*) shall deliver to the (*Party-A*) a banker's draft for the sale price

[9A–239]

[*executed as a deed*]

---

[1] It is no longer necessary for a company to be authorised by its articles to purchase its own shares. The general authority is in CA 2006, s 690. Unless CA 2006, ss 709–723 (redemption or purchase by private company out of capital) are complied with, the purchase of a company's own shares must be financed out of distributable profits or the proceeds of a fresh issue of shares: CA 2006, s 692. An 'off-market' purchase must be authorised by a contract authorised by a special resolution: CA 2006, s 694. A private company may purchase its own shares out of capital with (at the risk of oversimplification) the approval of a special resolution and statement by the directors that at the time of the purchase and for the following year the company will be able to carry on business as a going concern and pay its debts as they fall due.

[9.240]

19 Option for allotment of shares[1]

[9A–241]

Suggested terms for parties:

(*Party-A*)   'Company'

| (*Party-B*) | 'Buyer' |
| (*Party-C*) | 'Member(s)' |

DATE AND PARTIES

[9A–242] AN AGREEMENT made on (*date*) between (*name*) Ltd registered in England and Wales with company (*number*) whose registered office is at (*address*) ('(*Party-A*)') [and (*or*),] (*name*) of (*address*) ('(*Party-B*)') [and (*name*) of (*address*), (*name*) of (*address*) and (*name*) of (*address*) ('(*Party-C*)')].

DEFINITIONS

[9A–243] **1** In this agreement the following terms shall have the following meanings.

'Option Notice'	means written notice from the (*Party-B*) to the (*Party-A*) exercising the option granted by this deed.
'Option Period'	means (*number*) years from [date of this agreement (*or*) (*date*)].
'Price'	means at [par (*or*) £(...) ((...) pounds) per share (*or*) the amount agreed between the (*Party-A*) and the (*Party-B*) or if not agreed within one month after the service of the Option Notice the price assessed under clause (*number*)].
'Price Date'	means the date on which the Price is agreed or assessed.
'Sale Shares'	means [(*number*) ordinary £[1] shares in the (*Party-A*)'s capital (*or*) so many shares in the Company's capital whether present or increased as at any time during the Term remains unissued (*or*) as ensures that after the exercise of the option the (*Party-B*) is the holder of [51]% of the (*Party-A*)'s then increased issued share capital].
'Shares'	means shares of any description of class in the (*Party-A*)'s capital.
'clause' and 'schedule'	mean respectively clauses or schedules in this agreement unless the context shows a contrary meaning.

RECEIPT

[9A–244] **2** The (*Party-A*) acknowledges the receipt of £(...) ((...) pounds) paid to [him] by the (*Party-B*) as consideration for the transaction entered into by this (*document*).

GRANT OF OPTION

[9A–245] **3** The (*Party-A*) grants to (*Party-B*) an option during the Option Period to subscribe for and be allotted the Option Shares at the Price.

EXERCISE OF OPTION

[9A–246] **4.1** The option shall be exercisable during the Option Period by an Option Notice in respect of all of the Sale Shares or from time to time in respect of any of them stating the number of shares in respect of which it is exercised and the price per share which the (*Party-B*) proposes.

4.2 An Option Notice may not be withdrawn by the (*Party-B*) except by written notice to the (*Party-A*) within fourteen days of the Price Date stating that [he] does not agree the Price.

[9A-247]

PRICE

5.1 If the price is not fixed in any other way it shall be assessed:

[9A-248]

— by [the Company's auditor (*or*) an accountant to be selected by the (*Party-A*) and the (*Party-B*) or in default of agreement within 14 days starting on the date of the Option Notice to be nominated by the President for the time being of the Institute of Chartered Accountants on the application of the first of them to apply to him];
— as a fair price for the Sale Shares [disregarding (*or*) having regard to] the absence of any dividend or other return to the shareholders and the fact that the shares to be valued represent a majority or a minority interest in the Company's share capital or when registered will result in any person's interest in the Company's share capital becoming a majority.

5.2 If the Price is fixed by any person under clause 5.1 he or she shall certify it to the Company in writing and shall act as an expert and not an arbitrator.

[9A-249]

ALLOTMENT

6 (*Party-B*) may require the shares to be allotted to himself or to [his] nominee.

[9A-250]

CAPITAL AND RIGHTS

7 The (*Party-C*) that for as long as any rights are exercisable by the (*Party-B*) under this deed they will or will ensure that:

[9A-251]

— the Company's unissued capital is more than the Sale Shares;
— not to make any alteration of any description in the (*Party-A*)'s capital structure or issue of any capital or alter of any right attached to any Share; and
— to waive all rights of pre-emption to the allotment of Shares.

[*executed as a deed*]

[1] As to stamp duty see [13–065], note 1.

[9A-252]

ADDITIONAL CLAUSES

CONSTITUTION

Name

Letter to registrar applying to change the name of an existing company[1]

(*date*)

[9A-253]

Dear Sir,

(*name-A*) Ltd company (*number*)—proposed change of name

We act for the Company, which has passed a special resolution to change its name to '(*name-B*)' Ltd and enclose:

1   a cheque for the registration fee of [   ]; [and]

2   a signed copy of the special resolution

(or, if the change is made under a provision in the articles)

2   a statement of the means by which the change was made;[2]

3   notice of the change[; and

4   a letter of consent from (*name*) Ltd].[3]

[*explanation of proposed new name if it is within the category which is permitted only with consent*[4]]

We apply for the entry of the new name on the register in the place of the existing name. [Please arrange for the altered certificate of incorporation to be issued on (*date.*)]

Yours etc

[1]   CA 2006, s 77 states: 'A company may change its name by special resolution ..., or by other means provided for by the company's articles'. Section 81 states: 'A change of a company's name has effect from the date on which the new certificate of incorporation is issued'. For a resolution see [9A–260]. It is assumed that regulations to be made will state the fee to be paid and set out the form of any statement and notice to be sent to the registrar.

     By the IA 1986, s 216, if a company goes into insolvent liquidation, the name by which it was known at any time in the previous year and any name so similar as to suggest an association with the company becomes a 'prohibited name'. No person who was a director or shadow director in the same period may be involved in a company with a prohibited name for five years, which may be reduced by court order. *Penrose v Official Receiver* [1996] 2 All ER 96, [1996] 1 BCLC 389 and *Re Lightning Electrical Contractors Ltd* [1996] 2 BCLC 302 illustrate the flexible approach which the court are prepared to take.

[2]   For a specimen provision see [9A–109].

[3]   See CA 2006, s 66(1) and [9A–259].

[4]   See CA 2006, ss 54, 55.

Letter to registrar applying for two Companies to change their names one taking the name of the other

Dear Sir,

(*name-A*) Ltd company (*number*) and (*name-B*) Ltd company (*number*)

Changes of name

We act for (*name-A*) Ltd company (*number*) ('Old Company') which is in the course of being reconstructed, and [its wholly owned subsidiary] (*name-B*) Ltd company (*number*) ('New Company') [which is owned by the same shareholders], and enclose:

1   cheque for your fees of [   ];

2   signed copy of a special resolution of the Old Company to change its name to (*name*);

3   signed copy of a special resolution of the New Company to change its name to (*name*).

(*or, if the change is made under a provision in the articles*)

2   a statement of the means by which the change was made by the Old Company;[1]

3   a statement of the means by which the change was made by the New Company;[1] and

4   notice of the change.

It is intended that the Old Company will transfer to the New Company its business of (*description of business*), and that the New Company should be called '(*name-A*)'. It is also intended that immediately after the change of name of the New Company and the transfer of the business, the Old Company should be wound up voluntarily by its members (*or*) should change its name to '(*name-C*)'.

We apply for the entry of the new names on the register in the place of the existing names. [Please arrange for the certificates of incorporation on change of name to be issued on (*date*).]

Yours etc

1   CA 2006, s 79(1)(b).   [9A–256]

Letter to registrar consenting to use of name and illustrating particulars   [9A–257]
required to be stated in business letters[1]

(*name*) Ltd   [9A–258]

[an investment company (*or*) a charity]

(registered office)

(*address*)

Registered in England

Registered no (*number*)

[Directors (*name*), (*name*) etc]

[Paid up capital £10,000]

Dear Sir,

I am instructed by the board of directors of this company to write this letter to you.

This company passed [on (*date*) (*or*) today] a special resolution in accordance with s 78 of the Companies Act 2006 [*or describe other means by which the change was made*] to change its name to '(*name*) Ltd'.

Therefore the company consents to the use of any name incorporating the words '(*name-A*)' including the name '(*name-A*) Ltd' [on the formation of a new company by (*name*) & Co, solicitors of (*address*) (*or*) the change of name to '(*name-A*) Ltd' proposed to be made by company number (*number*) now known as '(*name-B*) Ltd'].

Yours etc

company secretary

1   This letter may be required, where solicitors or other agents form and hold a stock of   [9A–259]
     companies with a name, which they will wish to re-use on the formation of another company.
     It also illustrates the particulars which must be included in the business letters and certain
     other documents issued by the company. By CA 2006, s 82 regulations may be issued (but at
     the time of publication are still awaited), requiring companies to display specified information
     in specified locations and in specified description of documents. On the assumption that this

will substantially follow the CA 1985, ss 349 and 351, these will include its name, address of its registered office, the place and number of registration and (if the company refers to the amount of its capital) the amount stated must be the paid up share capital. Again it is assumed that a company will not need to show the names of its directors; but if it does do so it will be required to show the first names (or initials) and surname of every director and the corporate name of every corporate director, and (if the company is an investment company) that fact will have to be stated. If the company is a charity, that fact must be stated: Charities Act 1993, s 68. Every company must have a registered office to which communications and notices may be addressed: CA 2006, s 86. It is not necessarily at the works or business address, but in these cases adequate arrangements must be made for the onward transmission of correspondence, otherwise, for example, a writ may be served and judgment obtained without the company having actual knowledge. Failure to use the correct name in certain circumstances no longer makes the officer or other person in default personally liable.

Members' resolution: to change name[1]

[9A–260] **x** The Company's name be changed to '*(name)* Ltd' [if, but only if, the sale of the Company's business provided for in the agreement dated *(date)* of which a copy was produced to the meeting is completed].

[9A–261] [1] See [9A–259], note 1. Where the change of a name is conditional on the occurrence of an event, the notice given to the registrar must state that fact and whether the event has occurred: CA 2006, s 78(2), (3).

Standard heading for company documents — company limited by shares — name, number, Companies Act etc

[9A–262] *(name)* Ltd

company *(number)*

The Companies Act 2006

company limited by shares

Standard heading for company documents — company limited by shares — number, Companies Act etc but not name

[9A–263] company *(number)*

The Companies Act 2006

company limited by shares

Articles of association

Members' resolution: to alter articles (general)[1]

[9A–264] **x.0** The Company's articles of association be altered as follows:

x.1 in regulations *(number)* and *(number)*[2] the word 'special' is deleted and there is substituted for it the word 'ordinary';

x.2 the whole of regulation 4 is deleted and there is substituted for it a regulation 4 in the form of the draft [produced to the meeting initialled by the chairman and attached to the notice of it (*or*) annexed to this resolution];[3]

x.3 by the insertion after regulation [11(5) in the model articles] of the following new regulation:
'(6) For as long as *(name)* is a director of the Company, [he] shall be chairman of the directors and shall have [3] votes on every resolution of the directors'.

[9A–265] [1] Special resolution: CA 2006, s 21. A copy of the articles as altered must be forwarded to the registrar with the copy special resolution: CA 2006, s 26.

² These could be, eg, regulations 15(3) (conflicts of interest) or 42 (issuer of different classes of shares).
³ The alternative wording is for use if the resolution is passed in writing instead of at a meeting: see [9A–287].

Members' resolution: to delete an object[1]

x Article x of the Company's articles of association be deleted. [9A–266]

¹ A company may, but is not required to, state its objects: see [9A–060] and the note to it. [9A–267] Unless the objects clause is entrenched (see [9A–061] and the notes to it) it is simply an article (or regulation or paragraph) in the articles of association and may be altered in the same way as any other article, ie by a special resolution: CA 2006, s 21. It must be notified to the registrar and is not effective until entry of the notice is made on the register.

Members' resolution: to alter objects[1]

x Article x of the Company's articles of association be deleted and that there [9A–268] is inserted in its place the following article:
'x   The object of the Company is to carry on the business of [manufacturing, repairing and dealing] (*subject matter*) of all descriptions.'

¹ See the note in [9A–267]. [9A–269]

Members' resolution: to adopt new objects clause[1]

x The Company's objects be varied by deleting the whole of paragraph x of its [9A–270] articles of association and substituting for it a new paragraph x in the form of the draft [produced to the meeting initialled by the chairman and attached to the notice of it (*or*) annexed to this resolution].²

¹ See [9A–267], note 1. [9A–271]
² The alternative wording is for use if the resolution is passed in writing instead of at a meeting: see [9A–287].

Members' resolution: to adopt new articles[1]

x The Company's existing articles of association shall cease to apply to it² and [9A–272] [the Company adopts in substitution for them the new articles of association in the form of the draft [produced to the meeting initialled by the chairman and attached to the notice of it (*or*) annexed to this resolution] (*or*) the Company, being a private company, is governed henceforth by the regulations contained in the model articles in Schedule 1 to the Companies (Model Articles) Regulations 2007.³

¹ Special resolution: CA 2006, s 21(1). [9A–273]
² If the existing articles are cancelled and not replaced, the probable effect of the CA 2006, s 20, is that the relevant model articles will apply automatically, but it will be the model (or version of Table A) in force at the date of the company's incorporation, not that in force when the articles are cancelled.
³ The three sets of model regulations contained in the Companies (Model Articles) Regulations 2008, SI 2008/3229 are: Sch 1 (private company limited by shares), Sch 2 (private company limited by guarantee) and Sch 3 (public companies).

Registered office

Special resolution: Welsh companies[1]

The Company's registered office be stated in its register to be situated in [9A–274] Wales.

(*or*)

The Company's registered office be stated in its register to be situated in England and Wales.

[9A–275]   [1]   A company whose registered office is in Wales and as to which it is stated in the register that its registered office is situated in England and Wales, may by special resolution request that the register be altered to state that it is in Wales, and conversely if it is stated to be in Wales: CA 2006, s 88.

Directors' resolution: to move registered office[1]

[9A–276]   The Company's registered office be moved to (*address*).

[9A–277]   [1]   Notice of all changes must be given to the registrar, but, although the change takes effect on being registered, documents may be served on it for 14 days beginning with the date of registration: CA 2006, s 87.

Directors' resolution: to keep statutory registers at registered office[1]

[9A–278]   x The Company's statutory registers be kept at [the registered office (*or*) (*address*)].

[9A–279]   [1]   The first alternative in this resolution is merely declaratory, since its registers must be kept available for inspection at its registered office or a place to be specified by regulations: CA 2006, s 114(1). The company must give notice to the register of any change in the place: CA 2006, s 114 (2). The regulations about the place at which a company's records must be kept for inspection will, by CA 2006, s1136, apply to:
s 114 (register of members);
s 162 (register of directors);
s 228 (directors' service contracts);
s 237 (directors' indemnities);
s 275 (register of secretaries);
s 358 (records of resolutions etc);
s 702 (contracts relating to purchase of own shares);
s 720 (documents relating to redemption or purchase of own shares out of capital by private company);
s 743 (register of debenture holders);
s 805 (report to members of outcome of investigation by public company into interests in its shares);
s 809 (register of interests in shares disclosed to public company);
s 877 (instruments creating charges and register of charges: England and Wales);
s 892 (instruments creating charges and register of charges: Scotland).

NOTICES, MEETINGS AND WRITTEN RESOLUTIONS

Basic notices of general meetings

Notice of general meeting[1]

[9A–280]   (*name*) Ltd

company (*number*)

The Companies Act 2006

company limited by shares

NOTICE IS GIVEN that a general meeting of the Company will be held at (*address*) on [Monday] (*date*) at (*time*) am/pm for the purpose of considering and if thought fit passing the following resolution[s] which will be proposed as to resolutions 1 and 2 as ordinary resolutions and as to resolution 3 as a special resolution.

(*resolutions*)

(*or*) for the purpose of considering (*matters to be considered*) and passing such resolutions in relation to them as is thought fit.

Dated (*date*)

By order of the Board

(*signature*)

(Company Secretary)

Notes:

1 (*optional*) The holders of the Preference Shares shall not be entitled to attend at any meeting of the Company or vote on any resolution of the Company unless:

— at the date of the notice convening the meeting the dividend on the Preference Shares is one month in arrears;

— the Company has failed to redeem any Preference Share on the due date;

— the resolution is a special resolution; or

— the Company is in breach of any of the provisions set out in paragraph (*number*) of these articles.

2 A member entitled to attend and vote at the meeting is entitled to appoint a proxy to attend and vote in his or her place. A proxy need not be a member of the Company.[2]

3 (*optional*) Documents relating to the above meeting may be sent to the company by email to (*e-address*).[3]

4 (*optional*) We the undersigned being all the members or representatives of members of the Company having a right to attend and vote at the meeting consent to the convening of the annual general meeting for the date and place above mentioned and the transaction at it of the business above set out.

---

[1] A general meeting may be called on 14 days' notice, whether to consider an ordinary or a special resolution: CA 2006, s 301. For the electronic communication of notices see [9A–020]. The notice of a special resolution must include the text of the resolution: CA 2006, s 283(6). See also *Re Moorgate Mercantile Holdings Ltd* [1980] 1 All ER 40, [1980] 1 WLR 227, in which it was held that no departure from the substance of the text is permitted. It is prudent to set out the resolution in full in all cases. The requisitionists of a general meeting (see [9A–308]) may, if the directors do not do so within 21 days from the request, themselves convene the meeting. In this case the notice should be signed by the requisitionists instead of the company secretary and the following should be added in the place of the words 'By order of the Board':

'This meeting is being convened by us who have signed below pursuant to the powers conferred by s 305 of the 2006 Act.'

Companies must keep records comprising copies of all resolutions of members passed other than at general meetings, minutes of all proceedings of all general meetings and details of the decisions of a sole member: CA 2006, s 355. Any minute purporting to be signed by the chairman of the meeting at which the proceedings were held or the following meeting shall be evidence of the proceedings: CA 2006, s 356(4). There is no general principle of law that motions need a seconder as well as proposer: *Re Horbury Bridge Coal, Iron and Wagon Co* (1879) 11 Ch D 109, CA. The auditors are entitled to receive all notices and other communications to which the members are entitled and to attend general meetings: CA 2006, s 502.

[2] This statement must appear if the company has a share capital: CA 2006, s 325. Also see [9A–319].

[9A–281]

³ It is not compulsory to offer an electronic means of agreeing to the resolution. If the company gives an electronic address in the notice convening a meeting, it is deemed to have agreed that any document relating to the meeting (e g proxies) may be sent by electronic means to that address: CA 2006, s 333.

Notice of annual general meeting[1]

(*name*) Ltd

company (*number*)

The Companies Act 2006

company limited by shares

NOTICE IS GIVEN that the Company's [third] annual general meeting will be held at (*address*) on [Monday] the (*date*) at (*time*) am/pm when there will be transacted the following ordinary business:[2]

1   to receive and consider the report of the directors and the statement of accounts and balance sheet of the Company for the year ended (*date*) with the auditors' report on it;

2   to declare a dividend;[3]

3   to elect directors in the place of those retiring;[4]

[4   to elect (*name*) as an additional director;]

5   to[[re]elect auditors for the ensuing year[5] (*or*) elect auditors other than the retiring auditors];

6   to fix the remuneration of the auditors;

And the following special business.

To consider and, if thought fit, pass the following resolutions as ordinary resolutions:

(*set out resolutions*)

[*add where special notice of a resolution has been given to the Company*[6]]

AND NOTICE IS ALSO GIVEN that notice has been received by the Company of the intention to move at the [meeting (*or*) meeting convened by the accompanying notice to be held on (*date*)[7]] the following resolution [and that there have been received representations, of which a copy is enclosed]:

(*set out resolutions*)

Dated (*date*)

By order of the Board

(*signature*)

Notes:

The registers of members will be closed from the (*date*) to (*date*) inclusive, and no transfers will be registered during that time.

A member entitled to attend and vote at the meeting is entitled to appoint a proxy to attend and vote in his or her place. A proxy need not be a member of the Company.[8]

We the undersigned being all the members or representatives of members of the Company having a right to attend and vote at the meeting consent to the convening of the annual general meeting for the date and place above mentioned and the transaction at it of the business above set out.

(*signatures*)

[1] Every public company must hold an annual general meeting in each period of six months beginning with the day after its accounting reference date. Twenty-one days' notice in writing must be given (CA 2006, s 307(2)) unless, in the case of a private company, all the members holding not less than 95% of the shares giving a right to attend and vote agree to accept shorter notice (CA 2006, s 307(5), (6)). A public company's AGM may be held on short notice only if all the members entitled to attend and vote agree (CA 2006, s 337(2)).

[2] Neither the CA 2006 nor the model articles for public companies specify the business to be done at an annual general meeting, except that CA 2006, s 437 requires the directors of a public company to lay copies of its annual accounts and reports before the company in general meeting, defined in sub-s (3) as an accounts meeting, which may of course also be its AGM. This merely requires consideration (if that), and it is unnecessary (unless the articles provide otherwise) to adopt, approve or pass any resolution about them. The articles of association may specify what is the normal business of the AGM (eg items 1, 2, 3, 5 and 6 of this precedent are taken from regulation 52 of the 1948 Table A), in which case there is no need to set out the general business in the notice, although it has been common practice to do so.

[3] The CA 2006 does not state who has power to declare dividends, and the question is usually governed by the articles of association. The model articles for companies limited by shares contain procedures for paying dividends. Regulation 70 of the public company model articles states that the dividends may be declared by the general meeting but not of any amount exceeding that recommended by the directors, and that they may pay interim dividends. Regulation 28 of the private company model articles in sub-para (1) gives the directors power pay dividends and by (2) permits the shareholders by ordinary resolution to pay dividends as recommended by the directors. As to what distributions (the word 'dividend' is not used in the relevant part of the CA 2006) may be distributed, see the CA 2006, Pt 23, ss 829–853. An auditors' statement (required under ss 837(4) and 839(6) if the accounts have been qualified) must be available before the distribution is made. This is not a procedural matter which the members may waive: *Precision Dippings Ltd v Precision Dippings Marketing Ltd* [1986] Ch 447. For resolutions, see [9A–503]–[9A–507].

[4] This note assumes that regulation 20 of the model articles for public companies applies unaltered. All the directors retire at the first AGM of the company and thereafter they retire by thirds in rotation. Retiring directors are eligible for re-election. All three sets of the model articles provide for directors to be appointed by an ordinary resolution or a decision of the directors.

[5] An auditor must be appointed for each financial year of a company, unless the directors reasonably resolve otherwise on the ground that audited accounts are unlikely to be required: CA 2006, s 485 (private companies) and s 488 (public companies). In the case of a public company, the appointment must be made before the end of the accounts meeting at which the accounts and reports are laid: CA 2006, s 489(2). The auditor of a private company ceases to hold office at the end of the next period for appointing auditors and may be re-appointed or deemed to be re-appointed: CA 2006, s 487. Auditors of a public company hold office until the end of the next accounts meeting, unless reappointed: CA 2006, s 492. For a resolution to re-elect, see [9A–556], and to elect a different auditor, see [9A–560].

[6] See CA 2006, s 312 and [9A–317].

[7] This notice need not be set out in the notice convening the meeting, but should be given at the same time and in the same manner as the latter.

[8] See [9A–281], note 2.

Notice of adjourned general meeting[1]

(*name*) Ltd

company (*number*)

The Companies Act 2006

company limited by shares

NOTICE IS GIVEN that the general meeting of the Company, convened for (*date*) last, has been adjourned to [Friday] (*date*) next at (*time*) am/pm and will be held at (*place name*).

(*Set out business to be transacted at adjourned meeting as in notice of original meeting*)

Dated (*date*)

By order of the Board

(*signature*)

secretary

Note

A member entitled to attend and vote at the meeting is entitled to appoint a proxy to attend and vote in his or her place. A proxy need not be a member of the Company.

[9A–285]   [1]   Regulation 32 of the model articles for public companies provides that, where a meeting is adjourned beyond fourteen days, at least seven days' clear notice must be given of it. Regulation 32(7) says that no business may be transacted at the adjourned meeting which could not be transacted at the meeting if it had not been adjourned. While this is very wide, it may still be that, if the notice of the adjourned meeting (or a letter or informal note about it, if the adjournment is for less than 14 days) specifies the business of the meeting, the adjourned meeting may not be able to consider any business not in the notice etc: *Robert Batcheller & Sons Ltd v Batcheller* [1945] Ch 169, [1945] 1 All ER 522.

Written resolutions

Basic form of members' written resolution[1]

[9A–286]   (*name*) Ltd

company (*number*)

The Companies Act 2006

company limited by shares

RESOLUTION of the members passed on (*date*) in accordance with s 288 of the Companies Act 2006.

Resolved as [an ordinary (*or*) a special] resolution

(*resolution*)

(*resolution*)

(*resolution*)

(*signatures*)

(*all or requisite majority of the members*)

STATEMENT[2]

(as required by s 291(4) of the Companies Act 2006)

From the directors of the Company to every person entitled to vote on the above resolution.

1   If you agree to the above resolution please signify your agreement by signing where indicated above and returning it to the company in person or by post to (*address*).

2   This statement and the above resolution were sent or submitted to members on (*date*) and, if the resolution(s) is/are not passed on or before (*date*), the resolution will lapse.

¹ The CA 2006 may have removed the misguided rigmarole introduced by the CA 1989 (as mitigated by the Deregulation Order of 1996), but has instead given us thirteen sections (ss 288–300) of procedures and restrictions in the name of simplification. The CA 2006 expressly provides for private companies to pass resolutions in writing but makes no provision for public companies to do so. There is no need for the articles to contain a power to pass resolutions in writing, but if they do, any provision in the articles is void if it would prevent any resolution required or provided for by any enactment from being passed in writing: CA 2006, s 300. There is, therefore, no restriction on the kind of resolution which may be passed in writing, but by s 288(2) a written resolution may not be passed to remove a director from office before the expiry of his term of office under s 168 (but this restriction would not apply to a removal under the power in [9A–081]) or to remove an auditor from office under s 510.

Every person, who would have been entitled to vote on the resolution, at the time at which the first copy of the resolution is sent or submitted to the member, is an eligible member: CA 2006, s 289. If the directors propose (sic) a written resolution, the company must send a copy to every eligible member at so far as is practicable the same time or by submitting it or copies of it to them in turn, and may do so in hard copy, by email or by website.

A written resolution is passed when the required majority of eligible members have signified their agreement to it: CA 2006, s 296(4).

All the shareholders acting together can do anything intra vires the company, notwithstanding the lack of any notice, meeting or written and signed document: *Cane v Jones* [1981] 1 All ER 533, [1980] 1 WLR 1451, applying Buckley J in *Re Duomatic Ltd* [1969] 2 Ch. 365 at 373, [1969] 1 All ER 161 at 168. In the light of this decision there should be little doubt that resolutions of the company, if unanimous, can be passed in any way, written (whether hard copy or electronic) or oral, that the parties agree.

² This is the statement required by CA 2006, s 291(4). Note that sub-section (7) states: 'The validity of the resolution, if passed, is not affected by a failure to comply with this section'. Perhaps parliamentary draftsmen do have a sense of humour. If all, or a sufficient majority of the members sign the resolutions, which in practice is commonly done on or very soon after the day of issue, this statement may be omitted.

Basic form of members' written resolutions with choices which to agree¹

(*name*) Ltd

company (*number*)

The Companies Act 2006

company limited by shares

RESOLUTION of the members passed in accordance with s 288 of the Companies Act 2006.

Resolved as ordinary resolution

		for	against	abstain
1	(resolution)	☐	☐	☐
2	(resolution)	☐	☐	☐

(*as a special resolution*)

		for	against	abstain
3	(resolution)	☐	☐	☐

Please tick the appropriate boxes

(*signed*)

(all or requisite majority of the members)

¹ See [9A–286] and the notes to it. Unlike the preceding form, this is to be accompanied by a separate statement in accordance with CA 2006, s 291(4): see [9A–290].

Statement to accompany proposed written resplutions¹

(date)

From

(name) Ltd company *(number)* of *(address)*

to

All the members of the company who at the above date would be eligible to vote on the following resolutions if they were proposed at a general meeting of the Company.

STATEMENT

(as required by s 291(4) of the Companies Act 2006)

The directors propose that the resolutions set out the enclosed written resolution form be passed, if the members agree, by written resolutions. [*Add any necessary explanations of the resolutions and the reason for proposing them in writing.*]²

1   If you agree to the above resolutions please signify your agreement by ticking the appropriate boxes and then signing and returning the form to the company in person or by post to *(address)*.

[*If necessary add the following.*³] You may also signify your agreement to the resolutions or one or more of them by sending an email to the company at *(e-address)* in which you type one of the following:

(either) 'I agree to all the resolutions'

(or) 'I agree to resolution(s) [ ] and [ ] in the form of resolutions dated *(date)*.' inserting the number of the resolutions to which you agree.

(or) 'I do not agree to resolution(s) [ ] and [ ] in the form of resolutions dated *(date)*.' inserting the number of the resolutions to which you do not agree.

You may also add

(either) 'I abstain from voting on all the resolutions in the form of resolutions dated *(date)*.'

(or) 'I abstain from voting on resolution(s) [ ] and [ ] in the form of resolutions dated *(date)*.' inserting the number of the resolutions on which you abstain from voting.

2   This statement and the above resolutions were sent or submitted to members on *(date)* and, if the resolution(s) is/are not passed on or before *(date)*, the resolution[s] will lapse.

Dated *(date)*

(signature)

(Company Secretary)

¹ See [9A–286]. In all straightforward cases it should be sufficient to either incorporate the statement required by CA 2006, s 291(4) in the written resolution or to omit it entirely (in view of s 291(7)). A separate statement might be useful if, say, explanations are necessary.

2   There is no statutory requirement to give any explanations at all, but the statement in the two
     numbered paragraphs or statements to that effect are required.

3   If the company gives an electronic address in any document containing or accompanying the
     proposed resolution, it is deemed to have agreed that any document relating to the meeting
     may be sent by electronic means to that address: CA 2006, s 298. It may well be administra-
     tively cumbersome to issue the statement and proposed resolutions on paper and invite replies
     electronically. Therefore it may be more practical to deal with the resolutions wholly on paper
     or wholly electronically. If the statement and proposed resolutions are sent by email they
     should be sent as one email, preferably with the documents in the body of the email rather
     than as attachment, and statement 1 should read as follows.

    1 If you agree to all or any resolutions in the email to which this is a reply, your
    signification of your agreement must be by email using the reply facility (ie not as a new
    email). If you agree to all the resolutions, please type in your email whichever of the
    following applies 'I agree to all the resolutions'. If you agree to only one or more of them,
    please type 'I agree to resolution(s) [ ] and [..].)' inserting the number of the resolutions to
    which you agree.

    (*or*) 'I do not agree to resolution(s) [ ] and [ ] in the form of resolutions dated (*date*).'
    inserting the number of the resolutions to which you do not agree.

    You may also add

    (*either*) 'I abstain from voting on all the resolutions in the form of resolutions dated
    (*date*).'

    (*or*) 'I abstain from voting on resolution(s) [ ] and [ ] in the form of resolutions dated
    (*date*).' inserting the number of the resolutions on which you abstain from voting.

    Note that a written resolution may also be notified and passed by publication on a website:
CA 2006, s 299 on which it may be easier to provide for the tick boxes in the form than in an
email or its attachment.

Basic form of members' written resolution circulated at request of members[1]

[*Use either* [9A–286] *or* [9A–288] *and add the following to the accompanying*   [9A–292]
statement.]

The [resolution is (or) resolutions are] circulated at the request of members
[representing x% of the total voting rights of members entitled to vote on the
resolution[s]], who have provided the [following (or) enclosed] statement.

1   Members representing not less than 5% (or such lower percentages as is specified in the   [9A–293]
     articles) of the total voting rights of members entitled to vote on the resolution may require
     the resolutions and a statement of not over 1,000 words on the subject of the resolution to be
     circulated: CA 2006, s 292. The expenses of the circulation must be paid by the members
     requesting it, unless the company agrees to pay them: CA 2006, s 295.

Basic form of directors' written resolution[1]

(*name*) Ltd   [9A–294]

company (*number*)

The Companies Act 2006

company limited by shares

RESOLUTIONS of the directors passed on (*date*) under regulation [(*number*)
in the Company's articles of association (*or*) 7 of the model articles in
Schedule 3 to the Companies (Model Articles) Regulations 2007 incorporated
in the Company's articles of association].

(*resolution*)

(*resolution*)

(*signed*)

(*resolution*)

(by all the directors)

[9A–295] [1] The model articles for private companies (both share and guarantee), but not those for public companies, provide for unanimous decisions of the directors, which, by regulation 7(2)(b) may but need not take the form of a resolution in writing. This and regulation 8 (majority decisions without directors' meeting) probably have more or less the same effect in practice as *HL Bolton (Engineering) Co Ltd v TJ Graham & Sons Ltd* [1957] 1 QB 159, [1956] 3 All ER 624, CA, which held that it may be deemed, according to the intentions of the directors, that meetings have been held, although in fact no formal meetings were held.

Additional clauses in notices of meetings

Statement in notices of meetings of right to appoint proxies[1]

[9A–296] x A member entitled to attend and vote at the meeting is entitled to appoint a proxy to attend and vote in his or her place. A proxy need not be a member of the Company.

[9A–297] [1] This statement must appear in every notice calling a meeting of a company: CA 2006, s 325. A member of a company having a share capital may appoint more than one proxy: CA 2006, s 324(2). For forms of proxy, see [9A–319].

Consent by all members to short notice of annual general meeting—endorsed on notice[1]

[9A–298] x We the undersigned being all the members or representatives of members[2] of the Company having a right to attend and vote at the meeting consent to the convening of the annual general meeting for the date and place above mentioned and the transaction at it of the business above set out.

(signatures)

[9A–299] [1] CA 2006, s 337, which applies only to public companies. Private companies are not required to hold an annual general meeting. Even if a private company's articles provide for such meetings (e g by adopting public company articles as in [9A–055]), it would, anomalously, if it were prevented by CA 2006, s 307 from requiring unanimous consent.
[2] A representative appointed by a corporation has the same powers on behalf of the corporation as if the latter were an individual: CA 2006, s 323.

Consent by members with [95]% of votes to short notice of meeting — endorsed on notice[1]

[9A–300] x We the undersigned being members or representatives of members[2] of the Company holding not less than [95]% of the nominal value of the shares giving a right to attend and vote at the meeting consent to the convening of the extraordinary meeting for the date and place above mentioned and the passing at it of the resolution(s) above set out.

(signatures)

[9A–301] [1] CA 2006, s 207. The requisite percentage of the nominal value of shares with a right to attend and vote at the meetings or, if there is no share capital, the voting rights at that meeting is 95% in the case of a public company or, in respect of a private company, 90% or such larger percentage not exceeding 95% as is specified in the articles: see [9A–029].
[2] See [9A–299], note 2.

Register of members closed from *(date)* to *(date)* — endorsed on notice of meeting

[9A–302] x The registers of members will be closed from the *(date)* to *(date)* inclusive, and no transfers will be registered during that time.

Calling of meetings by directors

Directors' resolution: to convene AGM[1]

x The annual general meeting for (*date*) be convened to be held at (*time*) [9A–303]
am/pm on (*day*) (*date*) at the Company's registered office.

[1] For notice of AGM see [9A–282]. [9A–304]

Directors' resolution: to convene general meeting to change name and increase capital

x A general meeting of the Company be convened to be held at (*time*) am/pm [9A–305]
on (*day*) (*date*) at [the Company's registered office (*or*) (*address*)] to change the
Company's name to '(*name*) Ltd' and increase its capital to £(...) ((...)
pounds) by the creation of (*number*) ordinary £[1] shares.

Directors' resolution: to convene general meeting to consider resolutions

x A general meeting of the Company be convened to be held at (*time*) am/pm [9A–306]
on (*day*) (*date*) at [the Company's registered office (*or*) (*address*)] to consider
and if thought fit pass the following resolutions: (*resolutions*).

Calling of meetings by members or auditors

Request by shareholders for general meeting[1]

To the directors of (*name*) Ltd [9A–307]

We, the undersigned, being holders [of [more than] one-tenth of such of the
paid up Company's capital as at the date of this notice carries the right of
voting at general meetings of the Company (*or*) representing [more than]
one-tenth of the total voting rights of all the Company's members having at
the date of this notice a right to vote at the Company's general meetings]
require you to proceed forthwith to convene a general meeting of the
Company for the purpose of considering (*objects of meeting*) and for the
purpose of [passing such resolutions in relation to them as may be thought fit
(*or*) considering and if thought fit passing the following resolutions[s]].

(*resolution*)

(*resolution*)

Dated (*date*)

(*signed*)

(*all the requisitionists*)

[1] CA 2006, s 303. Members with one-tenth of voting shares (disregarding treasury shares) or, if [9A–308]
there is no share capital, one-tenth of the votes, may require the directors to call a general
meeting of the company. The request must state the objects of the meeting and may, but is not
required to, set out the resolutions. A request may be in hard copy or electronic form and must
be authenticated by persons making it.
  For authentication and service see preliminary note [9A–025].
  If the directors fail to convene the meeting within 21 days, to be held within 28 days after
the notice, the members who have requisitioned the meeting or some of them representing not
less than half of their votes may convene the meeting, but the meeting must be held not later
than three months after the deposit of the request: CA 2006, s 305. See [9A–281], note 1.

Requisition by auditor for general meeting[1]

To the directors of (*name*) Ltd [9A–309]

[I (*or*) We] (*name*) & Co of (*address*) refer to [my (*or*) our] notice of resignation as the Company's auditor[s] and require you to proceed forthwith to convene a general meeting of the company for the purpose of considering receiving and considering [my (*or*) our] explanation of the circumstances of [my (*or*) our] resignation.

Dated (*date*)

(*signed*)

(*auditor*[s])

[9A–310]   [1]   CA 2006, s 518. An auditor, whose resignation is accompanied by a statement which he considers should be brought to the members' attention, is entitled to requisition the calling of a general meeting. He may also, in this requisition or separately (see [9A–305]) require the directors to circulate to the members a written statement of the circumstances connected with his resignation. See also [9A–564].

Curiously, but quite irrelevantly, it is only in s 518 that the CA 2006 retains the word 'requisition' which it has replaced elsewhere with "request".

Request by members for circulation of statement[1]

[9A–311]   To the directors of (*name*) Ltd

We, the undersigned, being members of the Company representing [not less than] one-twentieth of the total voting rights having at the date of this request a right to vote at the [next] general meeting [to be held on (*date*)] (*or*) not less than 100 members holding shares in the Company on which there has been paid up an average amount per member of not less than £100] give you notice that we require you to circulate to the Company's members entitled to receive notice of that meeting notice copies of the attached statement.

(*signed*)

(*all the requisitionists*)

[9A–312]   [1]   Members having 1/20th of the votes (excluding votes allocated to treasury shares) or not less than 100 members holding shares on which an average of £100 per head has been paid up may under s 314 of the CA 2006, require a company to circulate to members entitled to attend a general meeting a statement of not over 1,000 words with respect to a proposed resolution or other matter to be dealt with at the meeting. A request must be in hard copy or electronic form, identify the statement to be circulated, be authenticated and received by the company at least one week before the meeting.

For authentication and service see preliminary note [9A–025].

Request by members of a public company for circulation of resolution[1]

[9A–313]   To the directors of (*name*) Ltd

We, the undersigned, being members of the Company representing [not less than] one-twentieth of the total voting rights having at the date of this request a right to vote at the [next] annual general meeting [to be held on (*date*)] (*or*) not less than 100 members holding shares in the Company on which there has been paid up an average amount per member of not less than £100] give you notice:

—   that we or one of us intends to move at the annual general meeting the resolution set out in the schedule below; and

—   that we require you to give to the Company's members entitled to receive notice of that meeting notice of that resolution.

THE SCHEDULE

(*resolution*)

(*resolution*)

Dated (*date*)

(*signed*)

(*all the requisitionists*)

<hr>

[1]   Members having 1/20th of the votes (excluding votes allocated to treasury shares) or not less than 100 members holding shares on which an average of £100 per head has been paid up may under s 338 of the CA 2006, require the company to send notice of a resolution with the notice of the next AGM. A request must be in hard copy or electronic form, identify the statement to be circulated, be authenticated and received by the company at least six weeks before the meeting or if later the time at which notice is given. This section does not provide for the circulation of a statement, as to which see [9A–311].   **[9A–314]**

For authentication and service see preliminary note [9A–025].

Requisition by auditor for circulation of resolution and statement[1]

To the directors of (*name*) Ltd.   **[9A–315]**

[I (*or*) We] (*name*) & Co of (*address*) refer to [my (*or*) our] notice of resignation as the Company's auditor[s] and require you to circulate to the Company's members before the general meeting [convened on [my (*or*) our] requisition[2]] [to be held on (*date*)] (*or*) at which [my (*or*) our] term of office would otherwise have expired or at which it is proposed to fill the vacancy caused by [my (*or*) our] resignation the accompanying statement of the circumstances connected with [my (*or*) our] resignation.

Dated (*date*)

(*signed*)

(*auditor*[s])

<hr>

[1]   See [9A–310], note 1.   **[9A–316]**
[2]   If the words in these brackets are used, this form should be adapted as an additional paragraph to [9A–309].

Special notice of resolutions

Special notice to Company of intended resolution: general form[1]

To the directors of (*name*) Ltd   **[9A–317]**

I being a member of the Company intend to move the resolution set out below at the [next] [annual] general [meeting to be held [on (*date*)]].

(*resolution*)

Dated (*date*)

(*signed*)

(*a member*)

<hr>

[1]   CA 2006, s 312. Resolutions on certain matters, set out below, are not effective unless, not less than 28 days before the meeting, notice (known as special notice) has been given to the company of the intention to move it, and the company has given notice of it to the members. The notice to the members must be with the notice of the meeting or, if that is not practicable, by newspaper advertisement or as otherwise provided by the articles, in either case not less than 14 days before the meeting. The 28-day time limit is relaxed if, after the special notice has been given a meeting is convened and held within that period, so that the proper period of notice is deemed to have been given if any such resolution is proposed at that meeting.   **[9A–318]**

The resolutions requiring special notice and the corresponding forms in this book are:
— to remove a director from office ([9A–542]);
— removing auditors before expiry of term of office ([9A–566]); and
— to appoint as auditor a person other than the retiring auditor or to fill a vacancy ([9A–560]).

Proxies and representatives

Appointment of proxy[1]

[9A–319]   (*name*) Ltd

PROXY FOR USE BY THE HOLDERS OF [ORDINARY] SHARES

I/We, (...) [shareholder[s]] of (...) (*address*) being [a] member[s] of the Company, appoint (...) [proxy] of (...) (*address*) or failing him/her (...) (*second proxy*) of (...) (*address*) or failing him or her the chairman of the meeting at the [annual] general meeting of the Company to be held on (*date*) next or at any adjournment of it to be my/our proxy and to vote[2] in my/our name[s] and on my/our behalf on any matter proposed:

*   either in such manner as the proxy thinks fit;

*   or as is indicated below;

*   Please delete as appropriate.

And if expedient to demand a poll[3]

Resolution 1 For/Against

Resolution 2 For/Against

Resolution 3 For/Against

Resolution 4 For/Against

Please delete 'For' or 'Against' as the case may be. In default of instruction the proxy will be used for each resolution.

Dated (*date*)

(*signed*)

To be valid this proxy must be completed, signed and lodged[4] (with any power of attorney or other authority under which it is signed, or a notarially certified copy of it) with the Company's registrars, (*name*) plc of (*address*)[5] not later than (*time*) am/pm on (*date*). A corporate shareholder must either affix its common seal to this proxy or sign it by a duly authorised officer.

[9A–320]   1   None of the three model articles of a company contains a form of proxy to be used but all, in substantially the same terms as each other (for a difference see note 5 below and [9A–321] and the notes to it), state what must be stated in a proxy notice and how they are to be used regs 43 and 44 (private – shares), 30 and 31 (private – guarantee) and 37 and 38 (public). A proxy notice must:
(a) state the name and address of the member appointing the proxy;
(b) identify the person appointed to be that member's proxy and the general meeting in relation to which that person is appointed;
(c) be executed by or on behalf of the member appointing the proxy; and
(d) be delivered to the company in accordance with the articles and any instructions contained in the notice of the general meeting to which they relate.
For service see preliminary note [9A–025].

2   There is nothing in the CA 2006 which prohibits a proxy from voting on a poll.

³   A proxy has a statutory right to demand a poll: see CA 2006, s 329. The inclusion of these
    words is unnecessary, though they may be useful as a reminder to the proxy of his right.
⁴   Not less than 48 hours before the time of the meeting or an adjourned meeting, or 24 hours
    before a poll: see CA 2006, s 327.
⁵   This is called the 'proxy notification address' in regulation 38 of the model articles for public
    companies, but the definition is omitted from the other models.

Notice of cancellation of proxy¹

from (*name*) of (*address*)   [9A–321]

to (*name*) Ltd

company (*number*) ('Company')

[and (*name*) of (*address*) ('Proxy')]

Companies Act 2006, section 375

I revoke the appointment signed by me on (*date*) of the Proxy as my proxy at
the meeting of the Company to be held on (*date*) and any adjournment of it.

1   All three model forms provide for a proxy to be revoked, in the case of a public company by   [9A–322]
    the delivery of a notice to the proxy notification address (see [9A–320], note 5) and in the case
    of private companies by delivering it before the start of the meeting, presumably to the
    company. Although not expressly required by the CA 2006 or in the model articles, and so not
    be necessary for the efficacy of the revocation, it seems on general principles that notice of
    revocation ought to be given also to the person to whom the proxy was given. The revocation
    does not affect things done by the proxy unless is was received by the company before the start
    of the meeting: CA 2006, s 330.

Certificate of authority of representative of Company at meeting of another¹

from (*name*) Ltd   [9A–323]

company (*number*) ('Appointer')

to (*name*) Ltd

company (*number*) ('Company')

Companies Act 2006, section 321

I certify that the Appointer has by a resolution of its directors authorised
(*name-A*) [(*or*) (*name-B*) if (*name-A*) is absent from or present in some other
capacity at the meeting] to act as its representative at [any meeting of the
Company's members (*or*) the annual (*or*) general meeting convened to be held
on (*date*)].

Dated (*date*)

(*signed*)

Company Secretary of the Appointer

¹   Any corporation may, if a member of a company, by a resolution of its directors or other   [9A–324]
    governing body authorise any person to be its representative at any meeting or class meeting
    of the company: CA 2006, s 323. This power effectively enables the corporation to attend,
    speak and vote at the meeting in person instead of appointing a proxy. For a resolution, see
    [9A–327].

Conduct of meetings

Directors' resolution: to fix quorum and dates of meetings¹

x The quorum at directors' meetings be three and a directors' meeting be held   [9A–325]
at noon on the [second Friday] of every month at (*address*).

[9A–326]   ¹   The model articles enable the directors to make further rules for decision making: regulation 15 (private) and 18 (public).

Directors' resolution: to appoint representative at meetings of another company¹

[9A–327]   **x** (*name*) (*or*) whoever of (*name*) and (*name*) is able to attend be appointed to act as the Company's representative at any meeting of the [members (*or*) creditors (*or*) annual (*or*) extraordinary general (*or*) creditors' meeting convened to be held on (*date*) of (*Party-B*)].

[9A–328]   ¹   See [9A–324], note 1.

Directors' resolution: to rescind earlier resolution

[9A–329]   **x** [The resolution (*or*) resolution no (*number*)] passed on (*date*) [to close the Company's account with (*name*) Bank plc of (*address*)] be rescinded.

Meeting closed — no other business

[9A–330]   **x** There being no other business, the meeting was declared closed.

Polls

Demand for a poll¹

[9A–331]   To the chairman of (*name*) Ltd

We, the undersigned, being [(*number*) shareholders (*or*) the holder of (*number*) shares in the Company], demand that a poll be held on the following resolution which you declared duly carried on a show of hands:

(*resolution*)

Dated (*date*)

(*signed*)

(*Shareholders*)

[9A–332]   ¹   Unless the articles require it, there is no need for the demand for a poll to be in writing: *R v Dover Corpn* [1903] 1 KB 668. There is no need in any of the model articles. They all provide that a poll may be demanded in advance of a meeting or before a show of hands on the resolution or immediately after the result is declared, and may be demanded by the chairman, the directors, and two persons having a right to vote or any person representing not less than 10% of the votes entitled to be cast on the resolution. As to the chairman's duty to use his right to ascertain the sense of the meeting with regard to the matter before it, see *Second Consolidated Trust Ltd v Ceylon Amalgamated Tea and Rubber Estates Ltd* [1943] 2 All ER 567; in *Byng v London Life Assurance Ltd* [1990] Ch 170, [1989] 1 All ER 560, CA, the chairman's decision to adjourn a meeting was in the circumstances unreasonable.

Notice of poll¹

[9A–333]   (*name*) Ltd

Notice is given that a poll will be held on the following resolution at (*address*) on (*day*) (*date*) between the (*time*) am/pm and (*time*) am/pm.

(*resolution*)

Dated (*date*)

By order of the board

(*signed*)

Company Secretary

1 Under both model articles for private companies, a poll must be taken immediately, but regulation 36(1) of the model for public companies provides that it will be taken as and when the chairman directs.

Polling paper[1]

(*name*) Ltd   [9A–335]

(*copy of proposed resolution*)

*I cast (...) votes for the resolution [1]

*I cast (...) votes against the resolution [1]

[*if appropriate for additional resolutions*] *Strike out or complete as desired[2]

(*Signature of shareholder*)

Number of shares held (...)

1 The most practical means of conducting a poll is by the issue of polling papers. Unless the   [9A–336]
   articles contain express provisions to that end, only persons present in person or by proxy may
   vote on a poll, and provision in the articles that a poll is to be taken 'in such manner as the
   chairman directs' does not of itself authorise the issue of polling papers to be deposited by
   voters at the office of the company or some other place: *McMillan v Le Roi Mining Co Ltd*
   [1906] 1 Ch 331. The absence of a member when the poll was demanded does not prevent him
   from voting when it is taken: *Campbell v Maund* (1836) 5 Ad & El 865, [1835–42] All ER Rep
   648. Alternatively two separate sheets of paper may be headed 'For' and 'Against' respectively
   and signed by the members or their proxies who state the number of votes cast.
2 On a poll taken at a meeting of a company or a meeting of any class of members of a
   company, a member entitled to more than one vote need not, if he votes, use all his votes or
   cast all the votes he uses in the same way: CA 2006, s 322.

Statement recording votes on a poll[1]

[9A–337]

Name of member	No. of Shares		Votes to which entitled	Votes given			
	Pref.	Ord.		Resolution 1		Resolution 2	
				For	Against	For	Against

1 It is not unusual when a poll is to be taken to prepare a statement substantially in the above   [9A–338]
   form. The names and shareholdings are filled in from the register of members, which is the
   only evidence by which the rights of members to vote at general meetings can be ascertained:
   Pender v Lushington (1877) 6 Ch D 70 and CA 2006, s 127.

Minutes and copy resolutions[1]

1 Minutes of directors' meetings must be recorded and kept for at least ten years: CA 2006,   [9A–339]
   s 248. Regulation 14 of the model articles for private companies requires the company to
   make and retain for ten years a written record of every unanimous or majority decision of the
   directors, apparently in compliance with s 248, but it is not immediately obvious (a) that a
   directors' decision without a meeting is a meeting for the purposes of s 248 and therefore (b)
   whether (and if so how) that section can apply to decisions by directors not made at a
   meeting. CA 2006, s 355 requires a company to keep and retain for ten years records of all
   resolutions passed otherwise than at a general meeting as well as minutes of all proceedings of

general meeting and s 357 makes a corresponding provision for the decisions of a sole director, but there appears to be no similar provision for decisions of directors made otherwise than at a meeting: if this is right, s 248 may be toothless. As to decisions made informally, see [9A–287] note 1.

Minutes of first meeting of directors after incorporation

[9A–340]
(*name*) Ltd

company (*number*)

MINUTES of the first meeting of the directors

PRESENT: (*names*)

IN ATTENDANCE: (*names*)

PLACE:

DATE:

TIME:

DOCUMENTS PRODUCED:

The following documents were produced to the meeting:
— the Company's certificate of incorporation on (*date*) as company number (*number*);
— a copy of the Company's memorandum and articles of association;
— 'Appointment Resolution'
a written resolution passed on (*date*) by the subscribers appointing (*name*) and (*name*) as directors;
— 'Resignations'
signed but undated resignations by (*name*) and (*name*) as directors and secretary;
— 'Transfers'
signed and stamped but undated transfers by (*name*) and (*name*) of [the right to subscribe for] the subscriber shares;
— 'Contracts Account'
an account setting out particulars of assets acquired, contracts entered into, moneys expended, liabilities incurred by (*name*) and (*name*) to the intent that they should be adopted and acquired by the Company after its incorporation;[1]
— (*name*) Bank plc's printed mandate and specimen signature form;
— applications by (*name-A*) for (*number*) shares and (*name-B*) for (*number*) shares;
— 'Sale Agreement'
an agreement intended to be made between (*name-A*) and the Company for the acquisition by the Company of (*name-A*)'s business of (*description*);
— 'Debenture-A'
a debenture intended to be given by the Company to (*name-A*);
— 'Debenture-B'
a debenture intended to be given by the Company to (*name-B*);
— 'Service Agreement-A' a service agreement intended to be made between (*name-A*); and
— 'Service Agreement-B' a service agreement intended to be made between (*name-B*).

[9A–341] **Reported**

A The Company had been incorporated by its subscribers (*name*) and (*name*) on (*date*) with number (*number*) and with the memorandum and articles of association a copy of which with the certificate of incorporation were produced to the meeting.

B The subscribers had appointed themselves to be the Company's first directors and (*name*) to be its secretary [and that they had lodged the Appointment Resolution and the Resignations with the Company].[2]

C The Company's registered office as filed with the registrar by the promoters is (*address*).

D The two subscribers had each undertaken to subscribe for one share in the Company's capital [and had lodged the Transfers with the Company duly stamped].[3]

Declarations of interests

[9A–342]

E (*Name*) and (*name*) declared their interests in the subject matter of resolutions (*number*), (*number*) and (*number*) [to be considered at the meeting].

Resolutions: Appointments of directors etc

[9A–343]

1 (*name*) and (*name*) be appointed additional directors of the Company until the next annual general meeting.

2 The [written] resignations [produced [to the meeting (*or*) with these resolutions]] of (*name*) and (*name*) as directors and of (*name*) as the Company's secretary be accepted with [immediate effect (*or*) effect from (*date*)].

[9A–344]

3 (*name*) be appointed chairman of the board of directors.

[9A–345]

4 (*name*) be appointed the Company's secretary.

[9A–346]

5 (*name*) & Co be appointed the Company's auditors.

[9A–347]

6 (*name*) Bank Ltd at its branch at (*address*) be appointed the Company's bank. (Attached to these minutes is the copy of the resolution and mandate form required by the bank.)

[9A–348]

7 (*name*) & Co be appointed the Company's solicitors.

[9A–349]

Registration etc formalities

[9A–350]

8 The Company's registered office be moved to (*address*).

9 The Company's statutory registers be kept at [the registered office (*or*) (*address*)].

[9A–351]

10 The Company's accounting reference date be (*date*).

[9A–352]

Seal[4]

[9A–353]

11 The seal impressed on these minutes be adopted as the Company's seal.

12 The transfer[s] from (*name*) to (*name*) [and from (*name*) to (*name*)], each of [the right to subscribe for] one share in the Company's capital, be accepted [the share[s] having been subscribed for in the memorandum of association but not having been issued and [the (*or*) each] transferee assuming the liability to pay the subscription price of £[1] to the Company.

[9A–354]

[9A-355] **13** The following shares [including the subscriber shares] be allotted for cash at par and that the allottees be entered in the register of members and that share certificates be executed by the Company and issued to them as follows:

	Shares		
Allottee	Number	From	To[2]
(*name*)	[500]	1	[500]
(*name*)	[300]	[501]	[800]
(*name*)	[200]	[801]	[1,000]
(*totals*)	[1,000]	1	[1,000]

and that [the Company's seal be affixed to the share certificates (*or*) the share certificates be signed by a director and the company secretary or any two directors[4]] and the certificates be delivered to the respective allottees.

[9A-356] **Business**

14 (*name*) and (*name*) declared their interests in the matter as Sellers. The Company adopts and acquires from them the whole of the assets acquired and the contracts entered into by them all of which are listed in the account produced to the meeting and annexed to these minutes and in consideration for them [pays to them in cash (*or*) acknowledges that it is indebted to them by way of [unsecured and interest-free] loans for such amounts as have been expended by them respectively in respect of those assets and are shown in the account] and undertakes to adopt and accept all liability for all of such contracts as have not been performed and to compensate (*name*) and (*name*) in full on demand for all liabilities in respect of them.

[9A-357] **15** (*Name-A*) and (*name-B*) declared their interests as seller and lender respectively in the matters dealt with in this resolution. The Company (having received from (*name-B*) an application for (*number*) shares to be issued at the price of £(…) ((…) pounds) per share and a cheque for the total price of £(…) ((…) pounds)):

— acquires from (*name-A*) the business of a (*description*) carried on by [him] and for that purpose enter into the [Sale Agreement (or) agreement produced to the meeting marked '(*name*)-1' ('Sale Agreement')];

— that the Sale Agreement be signed by (*name*) on behalf of the Company;

— the following shares [including the subscriber shares] be allotted as follows:

    (a)   to (*name-A*) (*number*) £[1] shares credited as fully paid pursuant to the Sale Agreement and in [part] consideration for the transfer of the business to the Company under it; and

    (b)   to (*name-B*) (*number*) £[1] shares credited as fully paid for cash at [the issue price of £[2] per share (*or*) par];

— the Company's seal be affixed to the share certificates and the certificates be delivered to the respective allottees;

— the Company acknowledges its indebtedness to (*name-A*) and (*name-B*) in respect of the [unsecured interest free] loans made as follows:

    (a)   by (*name-A*) for £(…) ((…) pounds) representing the balance of the consideration payable to [him] under the sale agreement, and

(b) by (*name-B*) for £(...) ((...) pounds) paid to the Company in cash; and

— the Company issues to (name-A) and (name-B) as security for the loans debentures in the form of the documents produced to the meeting and marked respectively '(name)-2' and '(name)-3' and accordingly that the Company's seal be affixed to the debentures.

Service agreements
[9A–358]

16 (*name*) and (*name*) declared their interests in the matter. Service agreements be offered to (*name*) and (*name*) in the form of the documents produced to the meeting and marked respectively '(*initials*)' and '(*initials*)' and (*name*) be authorised to sign them on behalf of the Company.

Conclusion
[9A–359]

17 There being no other business, the meeting was declared closed.

Signed[5]
[9A–360]

(*name*)

[9A–361]

[1] This account presupposes not a pre-existing business conducted in partnership, but such preliminary business activities and trade as the promoters need to conduct pending the incorporation of the company. As to pre-incorporation contracts, see [9A–188], note 1 and [9A–189].

[2] The promoters of a company, even if formed to be sold 'off the shelf', must appoint a director and, if the company is public must, or if private may, appoint a secretary: [9A–053], note 1. Therefore provision must be made for resignations and new appointments: for the latter resolution without a formal meetings, use [9A–294].

[3] Where the company is bought ready made or if formed by nominees, the consideration to be inserted in the stock transfer form may be expressed thus: 'In consideration of the transferee undertaking the transferor's obligation as subscriber for one share to pay £1 to the company.' The subscribers become members automatically on the incorporation of the company (CA 2006, s 16(2)) even if no shares are formally allotted to them, and therefore their particulars should appear in the register of members. A private company may have only one member and hence only one subscriber: see [9A–051], note 2

[4] A company may, but need not, have a seal: CA 2006, s 45(1). As to execution of documents under seal by a company see Formal Parts [4–037] and the note to it. If it has a seal, its name must be engraved in legible characters on it: CA 2006, s 45(2).

[5] As to the signing of minutes, see [9A–281], note 1.

Basic form of copy resolution passed at a meeting required to be lodged with the registrar[1]

(*name*) Ltd
[9A–362]

company (*number*)

The Companies Act 2006

company limited by shares

[Special (*or*) ordinary] resolution[s] of (*name*) Ltd

Passed on (*date*)

At a[n] [annual] general meeting of the Company's members duly convened and held at (*address*) the following [special (*or*) ordinary] resolution[s] [was (*or*) were] duly passed.

(*resolution*)

(*resolution*)

Dated (*date*)

(*signed*)

Company Secretary

[9A–363]   1   By the CA 2006, s 30 there must be forwarded to the registrar, within 15 days after it is passed or made, a copy of every resolution or agreement affecting a company's constitution, or if not in writing a memorandum of its terms. It is not necessary to use this or any other particular form: it seems that the present practice at Companies House is to accept anything which purports to be a photocopy of the resolution.

Basic form of copy written resolution required to be lodged with the registrar[1]

[9A–364]   (*name*) Ltd

company (*number*)

The Companies Act 2006

company limited by shares

[Special (*or*) ordinary] resolution[s] of (*name*) Ltd Passed on (*date*)

By [a] resolution[s] in writing passed in accordance with s 288 of the Companies Act 2006 the following [special (*or*) ordinary] resolution[s] [was (*or*) were] duly passed.

(resolution)

(resolution)

Dated (date)

(*signed*)

Company Secretary

[9A–365]   1   See [9A–363], note 1 and, as to written resolutions, [9A–286] and [9A–288] and the notes to them.

CAPITAL

Additional regulations for articles of association

Articles: creation of shares to which pre-emption provisions do not apply

[9A–366]   x The amount of capital which, on the date on which these articles are adopted, may be issued by the Company is £(...) ((...) pounds) divided into (*number*) ordinary £[1] shares all of which have been issued and (*number*) Restricted Shares none of which have been issued.[1]

[9A–367]   1   The pre-emption provisions of the CA 2006, s 560 do not apply to 'equity securities' as defined in s 560, ie ordinary shares (or the right to subscribe for them) which means 'shares other than shares which as respects dividends and capital carry a right to participate only up to a specified amount in a distribution'. For a definition of 'Restricted Shares' see [9A–057] and the note to it. As to 'authorised capital' see [9A–110], note 42. This article and that in [9A–368] envisage either new articles describing shares to be allotted or a change in class rights.

Articles: division of ordinary shares into 'A' and 'B' shares ranking pari passu except for directorships etc

x.0 The share capital issued at the date on which these articles are adopted is £[100] divided into two classes of which shares numbered [1] to [70] inclusive shall be 'A' shares and shares numbered [71] to [100] inclusive shall be 'B' shares.[1]

[9A–368]

(*or*)

x.1 The share capital issued at the date on which these articles are adopted is £2 divided into two classes of which share numbered 1 shall be an 'A' share and share numbered 2 shall be a 'B' share.

x.2 Unless otherwise agreed by a special resolution any share in the Company's capital allotted to the holder of an 'A' share shall on allotment become an 'A' share and any share allotted to the holder of a 'B' share shall on allotment become a 'B' share.

x.3 If all or any of the 'A' shares are transferred to one or more holders of a 'B' share the 'A' shares so transferred shall on the approval by the directors of the transfers be converted automatically into 'B' shares, and correspondingly if all or any of the 'B' shares are transferred to one or more holders of an 'A' share.

x.4 The 'A' shares and the 'B' shares shall rank pari passu except as mentioned in clauses x.3, x.4, (*number*), (*number*), (*number*), (*number*), (*number*), (*number*) and (*number*) of these articles.

[1] See the note to the preceding form [9A–366].

[9A–369]

This regulation envisages that two individuals or groups are members with certain rights as a class relating to voting, share transfers and directorships as set out in the specified regulations, such as those in the following forms:
— x.2 above (allocation to share class on allotment);
— x.3 above (change of class on transfer);
— [9A–134] (Part 6) (transfer to another holder of same class);
— [9A–370] (quorum at general meetings);
— [9A–372] (number of votes on a poll);
— [9A–374] (appointment and removal of directors); and
— [9A–376] (quorum at directors' meetings).

The regulation can be adopted for three or more shareholders or for a 50/50 relationship. In the latter case regulations [9A–094] and [9A–069] may be required to exclude the chairman's casting vote and the regulation giving weighted voting [9A–372] must be excluded.

Articles: quorum at members' meetings to include each of 'A' and 'B' shareholder[1]

x In regulation [36 (*if a private company*) (*or*) 29 (*if public*)] of the [model articles (*or*) model articles in Schedule [1 (private) (*or*) 3 (public)] to the Companies (Model Articles) Regulations 2007, the words 'as provided under the Companies Acts' are deleted and replaced by the words 'two persons entitled to vote of whom not less than one is the holder of an "A" share and not less than one is the holder of a "B" share'.

[9A–370]

[1] By this regulation a quorum will be at least one 'A' shareholder and at least one 'B' shareholder. See also [9A–110], note 10.

[9A–371]

Articles: on poll 'A' shares [one] vote and 'B' shares [ten] votes

x In a poll the number of votes which may be cast on each 'A' share is [one] and the number which may be cast on each 'B' share is [ten].[1]

[9A–372]

[9A–373] ¹ By this regulation and assuming, for example, 70 'A' shares and 30 'B' shares, the holders of the 'A' shares would enjoy 70% of the profits distributed as dividends, whilst the holders of the 'B' shares would have over 75% of the votes (300 out of 370). The rights of the holders of the 'A' shares would be protected by the CA 2006, s 630, against a special resolution to change these rights.

Articles: no directors except as appointed by holders of 'A' and 'B' shares ([2] each)

[9A–374] **x.1** The Company shall not have any directors except directors appointed under this clause.¹

x.2 The holders of the 'A' shares may at any time by a written notice to the Company appoint not more than [two] persons to be directors of the Company and remove and replace any director so appointed.

x.3 The holders of the 'B' shares may at any time by a written notice to the Company appoint not more than [two] persons to be directors of the Company and remove and replace any director so appointed.

[9A–375] ¹ Use these regulations only if the regulation in [9A–368] applies.

Articles: quorum at directors' meetings to include each of 'A' and 'B' shareholder¹

[9A–376] **x** In regulation [10 (*if a private company*) (*or*) 9 (*if public*)] of the [model articles (*or*) model articles in Schedule [1 (private) (*or*) 3 (public)] to the Companies (Model Articles) Regulations 2007, after the words 'be less than two' there shall be added the words 'of whom one is or is appointed by the holder of an "A" share and one is or is appointed by the holder of a "B" share'.

[9A–377] ¹ Omit if the regulation in [9A–368] is omitted.

Create and alter capital

Members' resolution: to increase capital¹

[9A–378] **x** The [amount of capital which may be issued by the Company (*or*) Company's capital²] be increased to £(...) ((...) pounds) by the creation of (*number*) ordinary £[1] shares (*or*) (*number*) 'A' ordinary £[1] shares having no voting rights but otherwise ranking pari passu with the existing shares in the Company's capital [and this increase is made for the purpose of acquiring [(*number*) shares in (*or*) the undertaking of] an existing company named (*name*) Ltd number (*number*)].

[9A–379] ¹ This resolution will be necessary only if the company has in its articles a provision such as that in [9A–096], because the concept of authorised capital does not exist in the CA 2006. It may also be required if the transitional provisions expected to be introduced preserve the authorised capital of existing companies. See [9A–110], note 42.
² The first alternative tracks the wording in [9A–096], while the second is the historically 'normal' wording on the assumption, which may be incorrect, that the transitional provisions will preserve the authorised capital of existing companies.

Members' resolution: to increase capital and authorise rights issue¹

[9A–380] **x** £(...) ((...) pounds) be raised by the issue of (*number*) ordinary £[1] shares [(being as to (*number*) shares part of those created by the preceding resolution)²] to be offered to the Company's existing members at the price of [£1.50] per share including a premium of [50p] per share (*or*) at par in the proportion of [1] share for every [5] shares registered in the respective names of each member in the Company's books at the close of business on (*date*) and the directors be authorised [for [one month] from the date of this resolution] to proceed with the offer by way of the issue of renounceable provisional letters of allotment and to deal with the issue generally, fractions arising and provisional allotments not accepted in such manner as they think fit.

1   The directors of a private company with only one class of shares may allot shares and give rights to subscribe for or convert securities into shares, except to the extent that they are prohibited from doing so by the articles: CA 2006, s 550. If the directors are already authorised to issue the shares, for example, under that section, under the articles [9A–101] or by resolution [9A–398], this may not be a matter which will ordinarily and necessarily require a resolution of the members, but because it is a matter of such importance to the company, it is commonly desired that the directors be given by an ordinary resolution of the members specific authority to do what may be strictly within their powers. See also the directors' resolution in [9A–418].   [9A–381]

2   See [9A–367], note 1.

Members' resolution: sub-divide shares[1]

x Each of the existing £[1] shares in the Company's capital be divided into four shares of 25p each.   [9A–382]

1   CA 2006, s 619. An ordinary resolution suffices and the power may be excluded by the articles. Notice of the sub-division and a statement of capital must be lodged with the registrar within one month after the resolution: CA 2006, s 619.   [9A–383]

Members' resolution: to sub-divide shares into shares of different classes[1]

x Each of the existing £[1] shares in the Company's capital be divided into [ten] shares of [10]p each [two] of which are 'Dividend Shares' and [eight] of which are 'Voting Shares' all of which shall rank pari passu with each other except that: [9A–384]

—   the holders of the Dividend Shares are entitled to all dividends declared by the Company [but are not entitled to [receive notice of,] attend or vote at any general meeting of the Company [except a meeting at which it is intended to propose a resolution to alter the Company's memorandum or articles of association or to wind up the Company]]; and

—   the holders of the Voting Shares are entitled to receive notice of attend and vote at all general meetings of the Company but are not entitled to receive any dividends declared by the Company.

1   See [9A–383], note 1.   [9A–385]

For an alternative means of giving different rights, see [9A–369], note 1. Shares in both of these classes would rank equally in the winding up of the company. The holders of the dividend shares are in a vulnerable position, but an arrangement such as this might suit widow[er]s, family trusts and others who require dividend income, whilst those members of the family who are employed by and manage the company retain control.

This is also a change of class rights. An ordinary members' resolution suffices, but, unless the articles provide for the change, it may be made only with the consent of the holders of shares of that class, either by the written consent of three quarters of them in nominal value or a special resolution of a separate meeting of the class. For a consent to a change of rights see [9A–392] and for a class resolution see [9A–394]

In addition to notice of the sub-division, notice of the change of rights must be delivered to the registrar within one month of the change: CA 2006, s 637.

Members' resolution: to consolidate shares[1]

x The [10,000] existing shares of [25]p each in the Company's capital be consolidated and divided into [2,500] £[1] shares.   [9A–386]

1   See [9A–383], note 1.   [9A–387]

Members' resolution: to convert shares into deferred shares[1]

[9A–388] x The existing £[1] shares numbered (*number*) to (*number*) the Company's capital registered in its books at the close of business on (*date*) be converted into (*number*) deferred £[1] shares to rank pari passu with the ordinary shares except that:

— no dividend be paid on the deferred shares until the net pre-tax profits disclosed in the Company's audited accounts exceed £(…) ((…) pounds) for two consecutive years;

— that on the Company's winding up no payment in respect of surplus assets be made to the holders of the deferred shares until there has been paid to the holders of the ordinary shares £[1] per share.

[9A–389] [1] This is a change of class rights: see [9A–285], note 1.

Members' resolution: to alter the rights of preference shares[1]

[9A–390] x That the rate of conversion of the preference shares into ordinary shares be altered to be [two] ordinary shares for [five] preference shares [and that regulation [8.1 [9A–164]] in the Company's articles of association be altered accordingly].

[9A–391] [1] This is a change of class rights: see [9A–285], note 1.

Written consent by members of a class to a variation of rights[1]

[9A–392] (*name*) Ltd

company (*number*)

The Companies Act 2006

company limited by shares

The shareholder named below as the holder of the shares mentioned below in the capital of the Company consents to the passing by the Company of the resolution of which a copy is set out below and to the variation[s] of the rights attached or belonging to the above shares resulting from the passing of that resolution.

shareholder's name	
class of shares	
number of shares	

(*resolution*)

(*insert or attach copy resolution*)

(*date*)

(*signed*)

[9A–393] [1] Unless the articles of association provide otherwise, the rights of a class of shareholders may be varied only if either the holders of three-quarters in nominal value of them consent in writing or it is sanctioned by a special resolution of a separate meeting of the members of the class: CA 2006, s 630. Where the number of class members is small, written consent, as in this precedent, may be simpler than holding a meeting: for a specimen resolution see [9A–394]. Holders of not less that 15% of the issued shares of the class, who did not consent to or vote in favour of the change, may apply to the court to have the changed cancelled: CA 2006, s 633. A variation of the rights right may have a commercial impact on another class, but does not necessarily alter the rights of the latter. In *Greenhalgh v Arderne Cinemas Ltd* [1945] 2 All ER

719; affd [1946] 1 All ER 512, CA, the sub-division of a class of 50p ordinary shares into 10p shares did not alter the rights of the existing 10p shares, even though it resulted in a shift in the balance of voting power: Lord Greene MR observed that former 10p share remained what it had been and still had the right to one vote pari passu with the other issued shares including the new 10p shares.

Resolution by members of a class to consent to a variation of rights[1]

The holders of the [convertible preference] shares in the Company's capital consent to the variation[s] of the rights attached or belonging to the above shares resulting from the passing of the resolution of the Company (of which a copy is set out in the notice convening this meeting and is produced to this meeting signed by the chairman for the purpose of identification) at its general meeting held immediately before this meeting.

[9A–394]

1 See [9A–393], note 1.

[9A–395]

Members' resolution to redenominate the company's share capital[1]

Each share in the Company's capital with a nominal value in pounds sterling is redenominated into a share with a nominal value in Euros converted at the spot rate (bid) on the UK Forex market on *(date)*.

[9A–396]

1 Shares in a limited company having a share capital may be denominated in any currency, and different classes of shares may be denominated in different currencies: CA 2006, s 542(3). By s 622 a company may by an ordinary resolution redenominate its capital in another currency. This section does not require the nominal value to be stated in either currency, but that the conversion is made at a spot rate specified in the resolution on either a date specified in the resolution or an average of rates on consecutive days of a period also specified in the resolution. The date or period must be within a period of 28 days ending on the resolution. Notice of the resolution must be given to the registrar under s 625. See [9A–480] for a resolution to reduce capital in connection with redenomination.

[9A–397]

Authority to directors to allot shares

Members' resolution: to allot shares — general[1]

x The directors are authorised generally and without conditions for [a period expiring five years from the date of this resolution *(or)* an indefinite term] to allot up to [*(number)* ordinary £[1] shares *(or)* £(...) ((...) pounds) nominal value *(or)* the unissued amount of the Company's capital which, at the date of this resolution, may be issued under regulation [32] of its articles of association[2]] or to allot those shares after that period but pursuant to an offer or agreement made during it.

[9A–398]

1 The directors of a private company with only one class of shares may allot shares and give rights to subscribe for or convert securities into shares, except to the extent that they are prohibited from doing so by the articles: CA 2006, s 550. Otherwise directors may exercise a power to allot shares only in accordance with CA 2006, s 551, under which they must be authorised either by the articles or by an ordinary resolution, and this is so even if it alters the articles (s 551(8)). The resolution must be forwarded to the registrar: CA 2006, s 30 and s 551(9). The authority may be for a particular exercise or general, conditional or unconditional, but must state the maximum amount which may be allotted and the period within which the authority must be exercised, which may not be more than five years from the resolution giving the authority or the incorporation of the company if the authority is contained in the original articles. A copy of the resolution must be filed at Companies House [9A–363], note 1.
2 This alternative will apply only if the company has an authorised capital or something akin to it: see [9A–096] and [9A–378] and the notes to them.

[9A–399]

119

Members' resolution: to allot shares — particular[1]

[9A–400] **x** The directors are authorised [for one week from] the date of this resolution to allot (*number*) ordinary £[1] shares in the Company [pursuant to an agreement made on (*date*) between (*name*) and (*name*)].[2]

[9A–401] [1] See [9A–399], note 1.
[2] For example, [9A–177].

Members' resolution: renewal or variation of authority to allot shares[1]

[9A–402] **x** The authority to the directors to allot (*number*) ordinary £[1] shares given by [clause (*number*) of the articles of association (*or*) a resolution passed on (*date*)] be extended [in respect of the (*number*) shares not yet allotted] until [(*date*) (*or*) the expiry of five years from the date of this resolution] [and varied by increasing the maximum amount of capital to which it applies to (*number*) ordinary £[1] shares].

[9A–403] [1] Ordinary resolution notwithstanding that it may alter the articles: CA 2006, s 551(8). The maximum amount must be stated or restated (s 551(5)).

Members' resolution: disapplication of pre-emption rights on allotment of shares[1]

[9A–404] **x** The directors are authorised to make the allotments authorised by a resolution passed [the date of this resolution (*or*) on (*date*)] as if the pre-emption provisions of section 561 of the Companies Act 2006 did not apply to them.

[9A–405] [1] CA 2006, ss 560–576: disapplication under s 569, 560 or 571. By s 561 a company may not allot equity securities unless it has offered them to holders of ordinary shares in proportion to their existing holdings in accordance with the other provisions of these sections. Note that, whereas the authority to allot under s 551 ([9A–398] or [9A–400]) applies in effect to any shares in the company, the pre-emption provisions apply only to 'equity securities'. Equity security is defined by CA 2006, s 560 as meaning an ordinary share or the right to subscribe for or convert to any security into an ordinary share, and an ordinary share means any share except shares with limited rights to participate in dividends and capital. The pre-emption provisions do not apply to bonus shares (s 564), issues for a non-cash consideration (s 565) or shares in an employee share scheme (s 566). It seems that any limit, however trivial or excessive, might suffice to remove a share from the definition: see [9A–366].
There are three forms of disapplication.
1 The articles or a special resolution of a private company with only one class of shares may authorise the directors to allot shares as if s 561 did not apply or applied to the allotment with such modifications as the directors determine: CA 2006, s 569.
2 Where the directors are already generally authorised to allot shares under s 551, they may also be authorised by the articles or a special resolution to allot shares as if s 561 did not apply or applied to the allotment with such modifications as they determine: CA 2006, s 570.
3 Where the directors are already authorised to allot shares under s 551 whether generally or not, the company may by special resolution resolve that s 561 does not apply to a specific allotment or applies to an allotment with such modifications as is specified in the resolution: CA 2006, s 571. Additional conditions apply to this disapplication, which are that the resolution has been recommended by the directors and they have made a written statements their reasons for the recommendation, the amount to be paid to the company for the allotment and their justification for the amount.

Members' resolution: combined authority to directors to allot shares and disapplication of pre-emption rights until next AGM[1]

[9A–406] **x** The directors are authorised generally and without conditions for a period expiring on the date of the Company's next [annual] general meeting after the date of this resolution to allot up to a maximum of [one-tenth of] the amount at the date of this resolution unissued [if the amount which may be issued under regulation [22] of its articles of association (or) in the Company's capital[2]] and that in the exercise of that authority they may make allotments of shares as if the pre-emption provisions of section 551 of the Companies Act 2006 did not apply to the allotments.

[1]   This must be a special resolution; some companies have formed the habit of proposing resolutions of this type at each annual general meeting.

[2]   See [9A–399], note 2.

[9A–407]

Application and payment for shares

Application for shares[1]

To the company secretary of (*name*) Ltd

(*address*)

(*name*) of (*address*)

1 applies for the allotment to [him] of (number) ordinary £[1] shares in the Company's capital at the total price of £(...) ((...) pounds) of which the whole (or) (amount)p per share is payable on application; and

2 encloses a cheque for £(...) ((...) pounds) being the amount payable on application.

Dated (*date*)

(*signed*)

[1]   Formal application is not normally required on the issue of shares in small private companies.

[9A–408]

[9A–409]

Directors' resolution: to make a call on part paid shares[1]

A [further (*or*) final] call of (*amount*)p per share be made on all the [ordinary] £[1] shares in the Company's capital payable [at the Company's registered office (*or*) (*name*) Bank plc at (*address*)] on [(*date*) (*or*) by the following instalments:
> £(...) ((...) pounds) on (*date*);
> £(...) ((...) pounds) on (*date*);
> £(...) ((...) pounds) on (*date*); and
> £(...) ((...) pounds) on (*date*)].

[1]   For an appropriate letter to members, see [9A–412]. Note that regulation 20 of the model articles for a private company limited by shares in Schedule 1 to the Companies (Model Articles) Regulations 2007 expressly states that all shares must be fully paid. Therefore a private company wishing to issue part paid shares must either alter its articles to obtain the necessary powers or, as in the articles in [9A–056] adopt instead the public company articles.

[9A–410]

[9A–411]

Call on partly paid shares[1]

(*name*) Ltd

company (*number*)

The Companies Act 2006

company limited by shares

(*date*)

Dear Sir/Madam

[9A–412]

The directors resolved [today (*or*) on (*date*)] to make a [further (*or*) final] call of (*amount*)p per share on all the [ordinary] £[1] shares in the Company's capital, payable on (*date*) next.

You are registered as the holder of (*number*) shares and the amount due from you is £(…) ((…) pounds), and you are required to pay this amount to [me (*or*) to the Company's (*name*) Bank plc at (*address*)] [on or before that date (*or*) by the following instalments:

> £(…) ((…) pounds) on (*date*); and
>
> £(…) ((…) pounds) on (*date*)].

On making [the (*or*) each] payment your share certificate[s] should be forwarded to me for a memorandum of payment to be endorsed [or where the shares become fully paid] to be cancelled and for a new certificate to be issued. No transfers of shares will be registered until the call made by this letter has been paid in full.

By order of the board.

(*signature*)

Company Secretary

[9A–413] [1] The terms of the issue of shares will normally state the amounts to be paid on application. The balance, if the whole is not paid on application, will be payable in accordance with the articles either by the instalments fixed by the terms of issue or by calls made by the directors. Regulation 53 of the public company model articles provides that at least 14 days' notice of the payment must be given. The directors may call different amounts from different members: CA 2006, s 581. The directors may charge interest on arrears at the rate fixed by the allotment or notice of call or, if none has been fixed, 5% pa: public company model articles, regulation 56.

Issue and allotment of shares

Directors' resolution: to allot shares including subscriber shares for cash[1]

[9A–414] **x** The following shares [including the subscriber shares] be allotted for cash at par and that the allottees be entered in the register of members and that share certificates be executed by the Company and issued to them as follows:

Allottee	Shares		
	Number	From	To[2]
(*name*)	[500]	1	[500]
(*name*)	[300]	[501]	[800]
(*name*)	[200]	[801]	[1,000]
(*totals*)	[1,000]	1	[1,000]

and that [the Company's seal be affixed to the share certificates (*or*) the share certificates be signed by a director and the company secretary or any two directors[3]] and the certificates be delivered to the respective allottees.

[9A–415] [1] A return of allotments must be filed with the registrar within one month: CA 2006, s 554.
[2] See [9A–496], note 1.
[3] Sealing is not necessary: see CA 2006, s 45(1) and [9A–361], note 4.

Members' resolution: to capitalise reserves[1]

[9A–416] **x** £(…) ((…) pounds) representing [as to £(…) ((…) pounds)] part of the amount standing to the credit of the Company's [revenue] reserve account [and as to £(...) ((...) pounds) part of the amount standing to the credit of its [capital reserve account (*or*) share premium account (*or*) capital redemption reserve]] be capitalised and be applied in paying in full at par for (*number*) ordinary £[1] shares to be distributed as fully paid amongst the persons who were registered as the holders of the ordinary £[1] [shares (*or*) stock] in the Company's capital at the closing of the Company's books on (*date*) at the rate of (*number*) fully paid ordinary shares for every 1 of the £[1] shares (*or*) for every £[1] of the stock held by such persons respectively [and any fractions of shares arising in the course of such distribution of shares be disregarded and the whole shares representing fractions be disposed of in such manner as the directors think fit[2]].

[1] The CA 2006 does not make any distinction between revenue and capital reserves although it does distinguish between distributable and non-distributable profits (Part 23I). However, a 'distribution' does not include an issue of bonus shares (s 829(2)), and so any non-distributable profits may be used. This is reflected in the power given in the model articles of association, by regulations 34(1)(a) (private) and 78(1)(a) (public). The directors' resolution to recommend the issue is [9A-420]. For a so-called capitalisation of a loan account see [9A-426].   **[9A-417]**

[2] As to fractions, see [9A-051], note 10.

Directors' resolution: to make a rights issue[1]

x Pursuant to the resolution to make a rights issue passed at the Company's annual (*or*) general meeting held on (*date*):   **[9A-418]**
— there be allotted provisionally (*number*) ordinary £[1] shares (less the fractions of shares which arise) as set out in the schedule of members and proposed allotments produced to the meeting (*or*) where the number of members is small as follows:

Names of members	Holding of ordinary shares	Number of shares provisionally allotted	Fractions of shares provisionally allotted
(*name*)	(*number*)	(*number*)	(*fraction*)
(*name*)	(*number*)	(*number*)	(*fraction*)
(*name*)	(*number*)	(*number*)	(*fraction*)
(*etc*)	(*etc*)	(*etc*)	(*etc*)
	(*total*)	(*total*)	(*total*)

— the draft [renounceable] provisional allotment letter[2] produced to the meeting, which sets out in detail the terms and procedures of the rights issue, be approved;
— the dates for acceptance and the issue of definitive certificates in the draft letter be respectively (*date*) and (*date*); and
— the secretary be directed to prepare and send copies of the draft letter to the Company's members named [in the schedule (*or*) above] in respect of the holdings and provisional allotments set opposite their respective names.

[1] See members' resolution in [9A-380], which, if necessary, could be drawn as a directors' resolution.   **[9A-419]**

[2] See [9A-231].

Directors' resolution: to recommend capitalisation of profits[1]

x There be recommended to a general meeting of the Company to be convened for that purpose that £(...) ((...) pounds) of the Company's reserves   **[9A-420]** be capitalised by the issue of (*number*) ordinary £[1] shares to the Company's existing members in the ratio of [9] new shares for every [100] existing shares held by each of them.

[9A–421]   [1]   See [9A–417], note 1.

Directors' resolution: to issue bonus shares detailed in resolution[1]

[9A–422]   x Pursuant to the capitalisation resolutions passed on [(*date*) (*or*) the date of this resolution] (*number*) new ordinary £[1] shares be allotted credited as fully paid to the Company's members at the close of business on (*date*) in the ratio of (*number*) new shares for every (*number*) existing shares held by them respectively and that the names of the allottees be entered in the register of members in respect of those shares and that share certificates be executed[2] and issued to them as follows:

	Shares		
Allottee	Number	From	To[3]
(*name*)	[500]	1	[500]
(*name*)	[300]	[501]	[800]
(*name*)	[200]	[801]	[1,000]
(*totals*)	[1,000]	1	[1,000]

[9A–423]   [1]   See [9A–416].
[2]   See [9A–415], note 3.
[3]   See [9A–496], note 1.

Directors' resolution: to issue bonus shares by renounceable allotment letters[1]

[9A–424]   x Pursuant to the capitalisation resolutions passed on [(*date*) (*or*) the date of this resolution] there be issued renounceable allotment letters for (*number*) new ordinary shares credited as fully paid to the Company's members at the close of business on (*date*) in the ratio of (*number*) new shares for every (*number*) existing share held by them respectively such letters to be renounceable on or before (*date*).

[9A–425]   [1]   See [9A–604].

Directors' resolution: to issue shares in settlement of loan account[1]

[9A–426]   x £(...) ((...) pounds) representing [part (*or*) the whole] of the Company's indebtedness to the persons named below on loan account be repaid and applied in paying in full at par for (*number*) ordinary £[1] shares, the loan to be repaid, the shares to be [allotted and the respective allottees to be entered in the register of members and share certificates to be executed[2] and delivered to them (*or*) by renounceable allotment letters] as follows:

Name of creditor and allottee	Amount of loan repayed	Shares allotted		
		Number	From	To[3]
(*name*)	£[25,000]	[25,000]	[50,001]	[75,000]
(*name*)	£[12,500]	[12,500]	[75,001]	[89,500]

Name of creditor and allottee	Amount of loan repayed	Shares allotted		
		Number	From	To³
(*name*)	£[10,000]	[10,000]	[89,501]	[99,500]
(*totals*)	£[47,500]	[47,500]	[50,001]	[99,500]

¹ If the directors have the necessary powers relating to the issue of shares (eg [9A–423]) a directors' resolution is sufficient. Whilst in practical terms this may be regarded as a capitalisation of the loan accounts, in contrast with a capitalisation of reserves by the issue of 'bonus' shares (see [9A–416] and [9A–422]), it takes effect as an allotment of shares for cash. Therefore a return of allotments must be made under CA 2006, s 555. **[9A–427]**

² See [9A–415], note 3.

³ See [9A–496], note 1.

Directors' resolution: to issue shares for acquisition of shares or business of another company¹

[For the purpose of acquiring [(*number*) shares in (*or*) not less than 90% of the issued share capital (*or*) the whole of the undertaking] of (*name*) Ltd)] (*number*) £[1] shares in the Customer's capital be allotted and that the allottees be entered in the register of members [and that share certificates be sealed and delivered to them] as follows: **[9A–428]**

Allottee		Shares		
	No	From		To
(*name*)	[6,500]	[10,001]		[16,500]
(*name*)	[6,500]	[16,501]		[23,000]
(*name*)	[4,500]	[23,001]		[27,500]

¹ See Declarations [3–233]. **[9A–429]**

Forfeiture and lien

Directors' resolution: to demand payment of debt before exercise of lien¹

x A notice be sent to (*name*) of (*address*) requiring [him] to pay £(...) ((...) pounds) owing by [him] to the Company in respect of (*nature of debt*) and notifying [him] that, if the amount is not paid within 14 days from the service of the notice, the Company will exercise the lien which it has over the (*number*) ordinary £[1] shares registered in [his] name by selling them. **[9A–430]**

¹ For a notice relating to liens, see [9A–437]. **[9A–431]**

Directors' resolution: to demand payment of unpaid call before forfeiture¹

x A notice be sent to (*name*) of (*address*) requiring [him] to pay £(...) ((...) pounds) payable by [him] in respect of the call made on (*date*) and notifying [him] that if that amount is not paid within 14 days from the service of the notice, the (*number*) ordinary £[1] shares registered in [his] name will be forfeited. **[9A–432]**

¹ For a notice relating to forfeiture, see [9A–439]. **[9A–433]**

Directors' resolution: to forfeit shares

[9A–434]   **x** (*name*) not having paid £(...) ((...) pounds) by (*date*) as required by the notice served on [him] on (*date*) pursuant to the resolution in that behalf on (*date*) that the (*number*) ordinary £[1] shares in the Company's capital registered in [his] name are forfeited.

Directors' resolution: to sell shares in exercise of lien

[9A–435]   **x** The (*number*) £[1] ordinary shares in the Company's capital numbered (*number*) to (*number*) registered in (*name*)'s name in respect of which the Company exercises its lien be sold to (*name*) of (*address*) for £(...) ((...) pounds) each making a total of £(...) ((...) pounds) and that a certificate for those shares be issued to (*name*) [credited with [50p] paid up per share] and the proceeds be applied in settlement of the debt of £(...) ((...) pounds) owing by (*name*) to the Company.

Directors' resolution: to sell forfeited shares

[9A–436]   **x** The (*number*) £[1] ordinary shares in the Company's capital numbered (*number*) to (*number*) registered in (*name*)'s name and now forfeited by the Company be sold to (*name*) of (*address*) for £(...) ((...) pounds) each making a total of £(...) ((...) pounds) and that a certificate for those shares be issued to (*name*) [credited with [50p] paid up per share].

Lien on shares notice to member[1]

[9A–437]   (*name*) Ltd

company (*number*)

The Companies Act 2006

company limited by shares

To (*name*) of (*address*) I give to you notice that:

—   you are indebted to the Company for £(...) ((...) pounds) in respect of (*nature of debt*);

—   payment must be made to the Company at its registered office within 14 days of the giving of this notice;

—   if the payment is not made the Company will exercise its lien over the (*number*) shares in its capital registered in your name and will sell those shares; and

—   the proceeds of sale will be applied in or towards the discharge of the debt and the balance (if any) will be paid to you.

Dated (*date*)

By order of the board

(*signed*)

Company Secretary

[9A–438]   [1]   Regulations 51 and 52 of the public company model articles apply only to part paid shares, but it is common practice to provide in the case of private companies for the lien to extend to all shares: see [9A–099]. For the directors' resolution see [9A–430].

Forfeiture of shares: notice to member[1]

(*name*) Ltd

company (*number*)

The Companies Act 2006

company limited by shares

To (*name*) of (*address*)

I give to you notice to pay [to me (*or*) to the Company's bank (*name*) Bank plc at (*address*)] on or before (*date*)[2] £(…) ((…) pounds) being the [first instalment of the] call of (*amount*)p per share made on you on (*date*) in respect of the (*number*) £[1] shares in the Company's capital registered in your name. If that amount is not paid by you as required by this notice the shares in respect of which the call was made will be liable to be forfeited.

Dated (*date*)

By order of the board

(*signed*)

Company Secretary

[1] This notice as drawn is given under regulation 52 of the public company model articles. The procedures for forfeiture contained in the articles must be strictly observed. For the necessary directors' resolutions see [9A–432] and [9A–434].
[2] Not less than 14 days after the service of the notice.

Forfeiture of shares: statutory declaration as to forfeiture[1]

I, (*name*) of (*address*) do solemnly and sincerely declare as follows.

1 In this declaration the following terms shall have the following meanings.

'Company'   means (*name*) [Ltd (*or*) plc] company (*number*).

'Shares'   means (*number*) fully paid [£1] [ordinary (*or*) preference] shares in the Company numbered (*number*) to (*number*) inclusive formerly registered in the Company's books in the name of (*name*).

2 I am and at all material times have been [a director (*or*) the company secretary] of the Company.

3 On (*date*) the Shares were forfeited in accordance with the Company's articles of association.

4 [The facts stated in this declaration are in my own knowledge [except where I have stated the documents or other source of my knowledge].

4 I make this solemn declaration conscientiously believing it to be true and by virtue of the provisions of the Statutory Declarations Act 1835.

DECLARED on (*date*) at (*place name*) before me

(*signature of declarant*)

(*signature of commissioner etc*)

a commissioner for oaths (or) a justice of the peace for

(*name of county*) (or) solicitor

[9A–443]   1   Regulation 52(5) of the public company model articles states that a statutory declaration that the declarant is a director or the secretary of the company and that a share has been duly forfeited shall be conclusive evidence of the facts stated in it against all persons claiming to be entitled to the share. It is submitted that it is unnecessary to set out in the declaration the facts leading to the forfeiture.

Notices under transfer pre-emptions

Intention to transfer shares — notice by member under pre-emption clause in articles of association[1]

[9A–444]   To the directors of (*name*) Ltd

I give to you notice that it is my intention to transfer to (*name*) of (*address*) the whole (*or*) (*number*) of my holding of (number) shares in the Company [to (*name*) capital [at the price of £(...) ((...) pounds) per share (*or*) as a gift]].

Dated (*date*)

(*signed*)

(*proposed Seller*)

[9A–445]   1   This is the Transfer Notice in [9A–111].

Intention to transfer shares — notice by personal representatives of deceased member under pre-emption clause in articles of association[1]

[9A–446]   To the directors of (*name*) Ltd

As [solicitors for] (*name*) and (*name*) the personal representatives of (*name*) deceased who died on (*date*) and whose will was proved by [us (*or*) them] on (*date*) in the [Principal Registry of the Family Division (*or*) the (*name*) District Probate Registry] we give to you notice that [we (*or*) (*name*)] and (*name*) intend to transfer to [(*name*) of (*address*) [and (*name*) of (*address*) equally] (*or*) to (*name*) of (*address*)] (*number*) shares and to (*name*) of (*address*) (*number*) shares representing together [the whole (*or*) (*number*)] of the late (*name*)'s holding of (*number*) shares in the Company's capital [at the price of £(...) ((...) pounds) per share (*or*) in satisfaction of legacies given by [his] will].

Dated (*date*)

(*signed*)

(*personal representatives or their solicitors*)

[9A–447]   1   This notice may be adapted in the case of a bankrupt member.

Notice to transfer shares — by directors to former member or personal representatives of deceased member under pre-emption clause in articles of association[1]

[9A–448]   (*name*) Ltd

(*address*)

To (*name*) of (*address*) [and (*name*) of (*address*)]

I give to you notice that clause (*number*) of the Company's articles of association takes effect forthwith and that on the service of this notice you are deemed to have served on the Company's directors a Transfer Notice within the meaning of clause (*number*) of its articles of association in respect of the whole of the shares held by [you (*or*) (*name*) [deceased]].

Dated (*date*)

By order of the directors

(*signed*)

Company Secretary

¹ This is the letter to be written by the directors under [9A–114], regulation 2.1, or [9A–139], regulation 3. This form may also be adapted for use in the case of a bankrupt member.

Number and price of shares — offer by independent buyer to members and acceptance of offer under pre-emption clause in articles of association¹

(*name-A*) Ltd

(*address*)

To (*name*) of (*address*)

(*name-B*) Ltd ('Company')

(*name*) [and (*name*)], who [owns (*or*) between them own] (*amount*)% of the Company's share capital, [has (*or*) have] provisionally agreed terms for the sale of [[his] (*or*) their] shares to my company, (*name-A*) Ltd at £(...) ((...) pounds) per share. In accordance with clause [x.1 see [9A–151]] of the Company's articles of association (*name-A*) Ltd offers to buy all the (*number*) shares in the Company registered in your name at the same price.

You [and the Company's other minority shareholders] may offer during the same period to buy all the shares in the Company owned by (*name*) [and (*name*)] at the same price. The offer must be made in 28 days from the date of this letter and completed in the following 7 days and may be made by signing the form at the end of this offer and sending it to the Company's registered office. If all the shares in the Company owned by (*name*) [and (*name*)] are not purchased in that time, my company's offer in this letter shall take effect in accordance with the Company's articles.

The making of offers to buy all the shares in the Company owned by (*name*) [and (*name*)] in 28 days from the date of this letter will create a contract for you [and the Company's other minority shareholders] to buy those shares at the above price. The failure to offer to buy those shares in that time and complete the purchase in the following 14 days will create a contract for you to sell your shares in the Company to my company at the above price. Instead of offering to buy shares in the Company owned by (*name*) [and (*name*)] you may accept now my company's offer in this letter, which you may do by returning to me within 28 days from the date of this letter at the Company's registered office the acceptance at the end of this notice completed and signed by you. Your acceptance will create a contract for you to sell your shares in the Company to my company at the above price.

Acceptances of offers sent to the Company's registered office in response to this offer will be forwarded to my company or (*name*) [and (*name*) of (*address*)] as appropriate.

Dated (*date*)

By order of the directors

(*Signature*)

Company Secretary of (*name-A*) Ltd

(*on copy offer*)

To the directors of (*name-A*) Ltd

either:

ACCEPTANCE OF (*name-A*) LTD's OFFER TO BUY SHARES IN (*name-B*) LTD.

I (*name*) of (*address*) being the registered holder of (*number*) shares in (*name-B*) Ltd's capital accept the offer in the offer to buy them at the price stated in it.

or:

OFFER TO BUY SHARES IN (*name-B*) LTD

I (*name*) of (*address*) being the registered holder of shares in (*name-B*) Ltd's capital offer to buy the whole (*or*) (*number*) of the shares in (*name-B*) Ltd from (*name*) [and (*name*)] at the price stated in the notice.

Dated (*date*)

(*signed*)

(*member*)

[9A–451]   1   This is the Offer Notice in the circumstances of [9A–149]–[9A–169], and the member's alternatives of offering to buy the controlling shareholder's shares or accepting the offer. Inaction will simply result in the member's shares being bought under a deemed transfer notice under [9A–147], regulation x.3.

Price of shares as assessed — notice by directors to Seller under pre-emption clause in articles of association[1]

[9A–452]   (*name*) Ltd

company (*number*)

The Companies Act 2006

company limited by shares

To (*name*) of (*address*)

I give to you notice that the price of the (*number*) shares in your transfer notice of (*date*) fixed by (*name*) & Co, pursuant to the Company's articles of association is £(...) ((...) pounds) per share.

Dated (*date*)

By order of the directors

(*signed*)

Company Secretary

[9A–453]   1   This is the notification of the price in [9A–111], regulation 2.4. The articles do not require the company to inform the member of his right to withdraw the transfer notice.

Withdrawal of notice of intention to transfer shares — under pre-emption clause in articles of association[1]

To the directors of (*name*) Ltd I have received the valuation dated (*date*) of **[9A–454]** (*name*) & Co of the shares in my notice of (*date*) to you, and withdraw that notice.

Dated (*date*)

(*signed*)

(*proposed Seller*)

[1]   See [9A–111], regulation 2.5.   **[9A–455]**

Number and price of shares provisionally allocated — notice by directors to members and acceptance under pre-emption clause in articles of association[1]

(*name*) Ltd   **[9A–456]**

company (*number*)

The Companies Act 2006

company limited by shares

To (*name*) of (*address*)

I give to you notice that the Company has received notice from (*name*) of [his] intention to transfer (*number*) (*description*) £[1] shares in the Company's capital. The price of those shares fixed by (*name*) & Co, pursuant to the Company's articles of association is £(...) ((...) pounds) per share.

The directors have provisionally allocated (*number*) of them to you, but you may apply to buy shares in addition to those provisionally allocated. If you wish to buy some or all of the shares at that price please notify me of the fact by returning to me within 14 days from the date of this notice at the Company's registered office the offer at the foot of this notice completed and signed by you.

If you sign and return the acceptance at the end of this letter without completing the number of shares you wish to buy, the number provisionally allocated will be treated as the number in your acceptance. Your acceptance will create a contract for you to buy the number of shares (if any) actually allocated to you by the directors: this will not be more than the number in your acceptance.

Dated (*date*)

By order of the directors

(*Signature*)

Company Secretary

To the directors of (*name*) Ltd

ACCEPTANCE OF OFFER OF SHARES   **[9A–457]**

I (*name*) of (*address*) being the registered holder of (*number*) shares in the Company's capital am willing to buy the whole (*or*) (*number*) of the shares comprised in the notice at the price stated in it.

Dated (*date*)

(*signed*)

(*member*)

¹ This is the Offer Notice in [9A–111], regulation 2.8 and the member's acceptance at the foot is the Acceptance under that form.

Number of shares to be transferred to members — notice by directors and request for price under pre-emption clause in articles of association¹

(*name*) Ltd

company (*number*)

The Companies Act 2006

company limited by shares

To (name) of (address)

I am directed to inform you that the directors have completed the division of the shares comprised in the notice of (name) and that [the whole (*or*) none (*or*) (*number*)] of the (*number*) shares, which you expressed your willingness to buy, are available to be bought by you. Please send to me without delay remittance for £(...) ((...) pounds) representing the price of £(...) ((...) pounds) and stamp duty of £(...) ((...) pounds). The certificate for the shares bought by you will be posted to you in due course.

Dated (*date*)

By order of the directors

(*signature*)

Company Secretary

¹ This notice is the notification of the number of shares allocated to the buyer and request for payment under [9A–111], regulation 3.1. It cannot exceed the number in the buyer's acceptance.

Division of shares — notice to Seller requesting share certificates and transfers under pre-emption clause in articles of association¹

(*name*) Ltd

company (*number*)

The Companies Act 2006

company limited by shares

To (*name*) of (*address*)

I give to you notice that offers have been received by the directors for the purchase of the whole of the (*number*) shares comprised in your Transfer Notice dated (*date*). Please forward to me immediately your certificate[s] for those shares and return duly signed the enclosed share transfer forms. The purchase price [and the certificate for the balance of your shares] will be sent to you on the receipt of the certificate[s] and all the signed transfers. Please notify me if this or any share certificate is not available and I shall advise you what action needs to be taken.²

Dated (*date*)

By order of the directors

(*signature*)

Company Secretary

1 This notice is the notification to the seller of the number of shares sold and request for the
   share certificate and transfer under [9A–111], regulation 3.1.
2 See Guarantees and Indemnities [11–064].

Offers have not been received for the whole of the shares — notice to Seller
that Seller released from obligation, but if so wishes may sell shares under
pre-emption clause in articles of association[1]

(*name*) Ltd

company (*number*)

The Companies Act 2006

company limited by shares

To (*name*) of (*address*)

I give to you notice that no offers have been received by the directors for the
purchase of (*number*) of the (*number*) shares comprised in your Transfer
Notice dated (*date*). Therefore you are released from that notice. If however
you are willing to sell the (*number*) shares at the price fixed by the auditors,
please forward immediately your certificate[s] for those shares and return duly
signed the enclosed share transfer forms. The purchase price [and the certificate for the balance of your shares] will be sent to you on the receipt of the
certificate[s] and all the signed transfers. Please notify me if this or any share
certificate is not available and I shall advise you what action needs to be
taken.[2]

Dated (*date*)

By order of the directors

(*signature*)

Company Secretary

1 Under the second version of [9A–111], regulation 3.2, the seller cannot be compelled to sell
   some only of the shares comprised in his transfer notice. However this notice should be used
   to ascertain whether he is willing nevertheless to sell part only of those shares.
2 See Guarantees and Indemnities [11–064].

Notice of unsold shares — by directors to former member under pre-emption
clause in articles of association[1]

(*name*) Ltd

company (*number*)

The Companies Act 2006

company limited by shares

To (*name*) of (*address*)

I give to you notice that [no buyer has been (*or*) it appears that no buyer will
be found for your shares (*or*) the intended purchase of your shares has not

been completed in the time specified in the Company's articles of association].
You may therefore for three months from the date of this notice seek a buyer
for your shares under regulation [x.2 see [9A–147]] of the articles.

Dated (*date*)

By order of the directors

(*signature*)

Company Secretary

[9A–466] [1] This is the Unsold Shares Notice under [9A–147], regulation x.1.

Transfers of shares

Director's resolution: to approve transfer[s] of subscriber share[s][1]

[9A–467] **x** The transfer[s] from (*name*) to (*name*) [and from (*name*) to (*name*)], each of
[the right to subscribe for] one share in the Company's capital, be accepted
[the share[s] having been subscribed for in the memorandum of association
but not having been issued and [the (*or*) each] transferee assuming the liability
to pay the subscription price of £[1] to the Company.

[9A–468] [1] This resolution assumes that one or more subscribers have undertaken in the memorandum to
take shares and that the company has been acquired before the subscriber share or shares have
been allotted. A private company needs only one member: see [9A–361], note 3.

Directors' resolution: to approve share transfers

[9A–469] **x** The following transfers be approved [(subject to the transfers being represented duly stamped)] and the transferees be entered in the register of
members [and that share certificates be signed and issued to the transferees[1]]
as follows:

Transferor's name	Shares			Transferee's name
	No	Form	To[2]	
(*name*)	1,000	1,001	2,000	(*name*)
(*name*)	500	501	1,000	(*name*)

[9A–470] [1] The words in these brackets will not be required if there is a separate resolution to seal and
issue the new certificates, which will usually be more convenient where the transferor is selling
only part of his holding and will be receiving a certificate for the balance of his holding or
where the certificate includes shares other than those comprised in the transfer or allotment.
See [9A–485].
[2] See [9A–496], note 1.

Directors' resolution: to refuse a transfer[1]

[9A–471] **x** The transfer by (*name*) to (*name*) of (*number*) £[1] ordinary shares be not
approved and notice be given accordingly to (*name*).

[9A–472] [1] None of the model articles or Table A in its various guises to date gives the directors power to
refuse transfers of part paid shares. Only Pt II of the 1948 Table A (repealed 22 December
1980) empowered them to refuse transfers of fully paid shares. When necessary an express
power should be incorporated in the articles: see [9A–106].

Directors' resolution: to transmit shares to personal representative[1]

x The [probate of the will (*or*) letters of administration to the estate] of (*name*) deceased (an office copy of which with a letter applying for registration was produced to the meeting) be noted and [the names of (name) and (name) as the personal representatives of (*name*) deceased be entered in the register of members as the holders of the shares now registered in the name of (*name*) (*or*) notice be given to (*name*) and (*name*) that clause (*number*) of the Company's articles of association shall take effect[2].]   **[9A–473]**

[1] If regulations 25 and 26 of the model articles (private) or 65 and 66 (public) apply to the company, the person becoming entitled to the shares on the death or bankruptcy of the owner may be registered himself or nominate, by a transfer, some other person to be registered in respect of them.   **[9A–474]**

[2] See relevant event and transfer notice procedure [9A–111], regulation 2.1; or [9A–136] regulation x.3.

Waiver of pre-emption rights[1]

(*name*) Ltd   **[9A–475]**

company (*number*)

The Companies Act 2006

company limited by shares

We, the undersigned, being all the members of the Company consent to the transfer[s] of (*number*) £[1] shares in the Company's capital [from (*name*) to (*name*) (*or*) as set out in the schedule below] and waive all restrictions on transfer and rights of pre-emption affecting those shares.

Dated (*date*)

THE SCHEDULE

Proposed seller	No of shares	Proposed buyer
(*name*)	(*number*)	(*name*)
(*name*)	(*number*)	(*name*)
(*name*)	(*number*)	(*name*)

(*signature*)

(*all the members*)

[1] This document will be required when there is a sale of shares not in accordance with the articles of association.   **[9A–476]**

Reduction of capital[1]

[1] A private limited company may reduce its share capital by a special resolution supported by a solvency statement in prescribed form and a public or a private company by special resolution confirmed by the court: CA 2006, s 641(1). It may do so in any way and in particular it may: (a) extinguish or reduce the liability on any of its shares in respect of share capital not paid up, or (b) either with or without extinguishing or reducing liability on any of its shares— (i)cancel any paid-up share capital that is lost or unrepresented by available assets, or (ii)repay any paid-up share capital in excess of the company's wants.   **[9A–477]**

Members' resolution: to reduce share capital by cancellation of amount not paid up[1]

[9A–478]   x The Company's capital now consisting of £(...) ((...) pounds) divided into (*number*) £[1] shares on which there has been paid [50]p per share reduced to £(...) ((...) pounds) divided into (*number*) [50]p shares by extinguishing the liability on each of the shares by [50]p per share.

[9A–479]   [1]   See also [9A–477], note 1.

Members' resolution: to reduce share capital by cancellation of lost capital

[9A–480]   x The Company's capital now divided into (*number*) ordinary £[1] shares, (*number*) 'A' ordinary £[1] shares and (*number*) £[0.50p] 10% preference shares all of which are fully paid be reduced by £(...) ((...) pounds) and that the reduction be effected by cancelling capital which has been lost or is unrepresented by available assets to the extent of the whole of the (*number*) £[0.50p] 10% preference shares.

Members' resolution: to reduce share capital by return of capital in excess of requirements[1]

[9A–481]   x The Company's capital consisting of £(...) ((...) pounds) divided into (*number*) fully paid £[1] shares be reduced by returning to the shareholders [25]p per share being capital in excess of the Company's requirements so that each £[1] share is deemed to have been paid up to the extent and to have a nominal value of [75]p.

[9A–482]   [1]   This resolution may be followed by one subdividing the reduced shares into three of 25p each, which is a more usual nominal value than 75p: see [9A–382] and see also [9A–477], note 1.

Members' resolution: to reduce share capital in connection with a redenomination of shares[1]

[9A–483]   x The Company's the nominal value of each €x be reduced to €y and that the aggregate amount of the capital so reduced be transferred to a redenomination reserve.

[9A–484]   [1]   Special resolution: CA 2006, s 626. Where a company redenominates its capital, as to which see [9A–396], it may, not later than three months after the redenomination, reduce its capital by not more than 10% in order to adjunct the nominal value of its shares to a more suitable value (which must mean to reduce the number of decimal points). Notice of the reduction must be given to the registrar under s 627, and s 628 requires the amount reduced to be transferred to a redenomination reserve, which may be used for the allotment of bonus shares, as to which see [9A–416].

Directors' resolution: to cancel, seal and issue share certificates[1]

[9A–485]   x [Pursuant to the preceding resolution] the certificate for (*number*) shares in the name of (*name*) produced to the meeting be cancelled and the following share certificates be signed and issued to the respective members:

Member	Shares		
	No	From	To[2]
(*name*)	(*number*)	(*number*)	(*number*)
(*name*)	(*number*)	(*number*)	(*number*)
(*name*)	(*number*)	(*number*)	(*number*)

Purchase of own shares; financial assistance

Members' resolution: to approve agreement to buy own shares[1]

x The Company approves the terms of the proposed contract [in the form of   [9A–487]
the agreement produced with this resolution and for the purpose of identification signed by the chairman[2]] for the purchase by the Company from
[*(name)* *(or)* *(name)* and *(name)* (as the personal representatives of *(name)*
deceased)] of *(number)* ordinary £[1] shares in its capital at an aggregate price
of £(...) ((...) pounds) and the directors be authorised to take all such steps as
are necessary for the purpose of executing and performing that contract [and
the payment for the shares may be made out of capital[3]].

1   Unless expressly permitted, a company may not purchase its own shares: CA 2006, s 658. By   [9A–488]
    CA 2006, s 693 a company may purchase its own shares in pursuance of a contract approved
    in advance. Approval is that either the contract is authorised by a special resolution or is
    conditional on the authority of a special resolution: CA 2006, s 694. For an agreement see
    [9A–234], and for the relevant directors' resolution, see [9A–489]. A return of the purchase
    must be made to the registrar: CA 2006, s 707.
        If the company buys 'qualifying shares' (in effect quoted) out of distributable profits, the
    company may either hold them as treasury shares or dispose of or cancel them. Not more
    than 10% of the nominal value of the company's issued shares may be treasury shares.
    Treasury shares are registered in the company's name but the company must not exercise any
    rights in respect of them (including rights to dividends, attendance at meetings and voting).
    They may be sold for cash, transferred to an employees' share scheme or cancelled. See CA
    2006, Part 18, Chapter 6 (ss 724–732). These provisions are not applicable to private or to
    public unquoted companies, and nor are those of s 693 permitting the purchase of a
    company's own shares by a market purchase, ie on a recognised stock exchange.
2   The contract may, but need not, be in writing. A copy of it, or if it is not in writing, a
    memorandum of its terms, must be kept at the registered office of the company for ten years
    from the purchase: CA 2006, s 720(3).
3   A private company may, by a special resolution and unless prohibited in its articles, approve
    the purchase of its shares 'otherwise than out of its distributable profits or the proceeds of a
    fresh issue of shares' (ie out of capital as s 692(1) puts it): CA 2006, ss 709 to 723. A payment
    out of capital is permitted only to the extent that the purchase price exceeds any available
    profits and proceeds of any fresh issue of shares and may be made only if the following
    requirements of the following sections are met:
    — s 714 (directors' statement and auditor's report);
    — s 716 (approval by special resolution);
    — s 719 (public notice of proposed payment);
    — s 720 (directors' statement and auditor's report to be available for inspection).

Directors' resolution: for Company to buy its own shares from named persons[1]

x The Company buys for £(...) ((...) pounds) the *(number)* ordinary £[1]   [9A–489]
shares in the Company registered in the name[s] of [*(name)* *(or)* *(name)* and
(name) (as the personal representatives of *(name)* deceased)] in accordance
with the approval given by the Company's resolution on *(date)* and accordingly:

      —   the agreement produced to the meeting and intended to be made
           between [*(name)* *(or)* *(name)* and *(name)*] and the Company be
           approved and that *(name)* be authorised to sign it on behalf of the
           Company;

      —   the transfer produced to the meeting of *(number)* shares in the Com-
           pany from [*(name)* *(or)* *(name)* and *(name)*] to the Company be
           approved; and

— that the (*number*) shares transferred to the Company be cancelled and that £(...) ((...) pounds) be transferred to the Company's capital redemption reserve.[2]

[9A–490] [1] See shareholders' resolution [9A–487], and agreement [9A–234], and the notes to them.
[2] CA 2006, s 733.

Directors' resolution: for Company to buy its own shares comprised in transfer notice under pre-emption clause[1]

[9A–491] **x** The Company buys for £(...) ((...) pounds) [the whole of the (*or*) (*number*)] ordinary £[1] shares in the Company in the transfer notice [deemed to have been] given by [(*name*) (*or*) (*name*) and (*name*) (as the personal representatives of (*name*) deceased)].

[9A–492] [1] This is the resolution envisaged by [9A–111], regulation 2.6 [*articles: transfer notice*].

Members' resolution (private company): to approve financial assistance for purchase of shares[1]

[9A–493] **x** There be approved the proposed financial assistance by the Company for the acquisition of its own shares described below. In connection with the proposed sale by (*name*) to (*name*) Ltd of (*number*) shares in the Company at a price of £(...) ((...) pounds) the Company [will lend to (*name*) Ltd £(...) ((...) pounds) (*or*) will give a debenture to (*name*) Bank plc to secure an advance of £(...) ((...) pounds) to (*name*) Ltd (*or*) pay a dividend to (*name*) Ltd of £(...) ((...) pounds) (*or*) buy from (*name*) Ltd plant and machinery to the value of £(...) ((...) pounds)].

[9A–494] [1] Ordinary resolution and no special formalities or conditions. The so-called 'whitewash' provisions in CA 1985, ss 151 to 158 are repeated in CA 2006. There is no general prohibition of financial assistance but financial assistance by a public company, subject to exceptions such as the payment of dividends or reductions of capital, is permitted only if the principal purpose of the assistance is not to give it for the purpose of the transaction but it was given only an incidental part of a larger purpose: see CA 2006, Part 18, Chapter 2.

Shares — miscellaneous and dividends

Directors' resolution: to discontinue numbering of shares[1]

[9A–495] **x** The (*number*) [ordinary] £[1] shares in the Company's capital numbered [1] to (*number*) inclusive (which are fully paid up and rank pari passu for all purposes) shall henceforth bear no distinguishing numbers.

[9A–496] [1] Each share must be distinguished by its appropriate number, but they need not have distinguishing numbers if all the issued shares, or those of the particular class are fully paid up and rank pari passu: CA 2006, s 543.

Members' resolution: to exempt share transfer from pre-emption provisions in the articles[1]

[9A–497] **x** The provisions of the Company's articles of association restricting the right of members to transfer shares shall not apply to the transfer proposed to be made by (*name*) to (*name*) of (*number*) £[1] shares in the Company's capital and the directors be directed to approve the transfer when it is presented to them.

[9A–498] [1] See [9A–111], reg 6.

Directors' resolution: to receive renounced allotment letters[1]

x The following renunciations of allotment letters be accepted and that the renouncees be entered in the register of members [and that share certificates be signed and issued to the renouncees] as follows:

[9A–499]

Allottee	Shares			Renouncee
	No	From	To[2]	
(name)	*(number)*	*(number)*	*(number)*	*(name)*
(name)	*(number)*	*(number)*	*(number)*	*(name)*
(name)	*(number)*	*(number)*	*(number)*	*(name)*
(name)	*(number)*	*(number)*	*(number)*	*(name)*

[1]   For letter of allotment and renunciation see [9A–226].
[2]   See [9A–496], note 1.

[9A–500]

Directors' resolution: to issue certificates for shares not renounced

x The names of the following allottees, to whom the £[1] ordinary shares mentioned below were on *(date)* provisionally allotted and who have not renounced them before the last date for renunciation, be entered into the register of members in respect of the shares mentioned below and that share certificates be signed and delivered to them as follows:

[9A–501]

Allottee	Shares		
	No	From	To[1]
(name)	*(number)*	*(number)*	*(number)*
(name)	*(number)*	*(number)*	*(number)*
(name)	*(number)*	*(number)*	*(number)*
Total	*(number)*	*(number)*	*(number)*

[1]   See [9A–496], note 1.

[9A–502]

Dividends Members' resolution: to declare dividend[1]

x The dividend[s] of [(*amount*)p per share on the preference shares and] (*amount*)p per share on the ordinary shares recommended by the directors be sanctioned and that the directors be authorised to pay it (*or*) them.

[9A–503]

[1]   See [9A–283], note 3.

[9A–504]

Directors' resolution: to recommend a dividend[1]

x There be recommended to the [annual] general meeting to be held on *(date)* that a dividend of (*amount*)p be declared on each of the ordinary shares to be paid (if declared by that meeting) 14 days after the date of that meeting to the holders of them registered in the Company's books at the close of business on *(date)*.

[9A–505]

[1]   See [9A–283], note 3.

[9A–506]

Directors' resolution: to declare a dividend[1]

[9A–507]   **x** An [interim] dividend of (*amount*)p be paid on each of the ordinary shares to the holders of them registered in the Company's books at the close of business on (*date*).

[9A–508]   [1] See [9A–283], note 3. Note that the directors of a company governed by the model articles for a private company may pay dividends without distinction between interim and final, but that, if it is governed by the model articles for public companies, they may pay only interim dividends.

Dividend warrant[1]

[9A–509]   (*name*) Ltd

company (*number*)

The Companies Act 2006

company limited by shares

(*number*) ordinary £[1] shares

Notice of interim (*or*) final dividend for the [year] ended (*date*) payable on (*date*)

To (*name*) of (*address*)

A dividend at the rate of (*rate*)% on the Company's [ordinary] shares having been duly declared for the [year] ended (*date*) I forward to you the attached [warrant (*or*) cheque] for the amount in respect of the shares registered in your name:

Holding	Tax credit	Net amount of dividend
(*number*)	£(*amount*)	£(*amount*)

(*signature*)

Company Secretary

[9A–510]   [1] It is generally more practical for a small company with few members to issue ordinary cheques for dividends and typed or duplicated tax certificates than to print warrants.

Waiver of dividend[1]

[9A–511]   To the directors of (*name*) Ltd

I, (*name*) of (*address*) waive the [whole (*or*) one-half] of the dividend [declared on (*date*) (*or*) or to be declared in the year to (*date*)] in respect of [the whole (*or*) (*number*)] of my £[1] ordinary shares in the Company.

Dated (*date*)

[*executed as a deed*]

[9A–512]   [1] No special form of waiver is required but it should be as a deed as no consideration is given for it. The waiver may be made before or after the dividend had been declared at a general meeting (see [9A–283], note 3), but in the latter case it must be waived before the date on which payment is to be made. A dividend which has been effectively and unconditionally waived does not form part of the shareholder's income for income tax purposes.

DIRECTORS AND SECRETARY

Additional regulations for articles of association

Articles: (name) to be chairman whilst director[1]

x For so long as (*name*) is a director of the Company [he (*or*) she] shall be chairman of the board of directors. [9A–513]

[1] If either of this regulation or that in [9A–070] (they are alternatives) are used, omit the regulations in [9A–069] and [9A–094]. [9A–514]

Articles: may have sole director and no maximum number[1]

x Unless otherwise determining by [an ordinary (*or*) a special] resolution, there may be a sole director and there shall be no maximum number of directors. [9A–515]

[1] A private company may have a sole director (CA 2006, s 154), and at least one director of every company must be a natural person (CA 2006, s 155). [9A–516]

Appointment[1]

Notice of intention to propose a person for election as a director[2]

To the directors of (*name*) Ltd [9A–517]

I the undersigned being a member of the Company entitled to attend and vote at the [annual (*or*) extraordinary] general meeting convened to be held on (*date*) give to you notice of my intention to propose at that meeting that (*name*) be elected a director of the Company.

Dated (*date*)

(*signature*)

I the undersigned being the person named in the notice give to you notice that I am willing to be elected a director of the Company.

Dated (*date*)

(*signature*)

[1] As to election of directors generally see [9A–283], note 4, and as to special notice for removal see [9A–318], note 1, and [9A–543], note 1. [9A–518]
[2] This is required if the company is governed by Table A (reg 93 of the 1985 version, 93 if 1948), but will not be necessary if it is governed by one of the model articles, all of which provide that any person willing to be appointed as a director may be appointed by an ordinary resolution or a decision of the directors: regulation 16 (private, both share capital and guarantee) and regulation 19 (public).

Members' resolution: to appoint directors under a single resolution[1]

x The motions for the appointment of (*name*), (*name*), (*name*) and (*name*) as directors be made by a single resolution. [9A–519]

[1] Directors of a private company may be elected en bloc, but those of a public company must be voted for individually, unless there has first been passed, with no vote against it, a resolution that their election be voted on under one resolution: CA 2006, s 160. [9A–520]

Members' resolution: to re-elect a or the retiring director[s][1]

x (*name*) [or (*name*), (*name*) and (*name*)] who retire[s] at this meeting as [by rotation (*or*) having been appointed by the directors during the preceding year] be re-elected. [9A–521]

[9A–522]   ¹   At the first AGM of a company governed by the model articles for public companies, all the directors retire under regulation 20. Directors of such a company appointed by the directors, to fill a casual vacancy or as additional directors, retire at the first AGM after their appointment: regulation 20. There is no provision in the model articles for such directors to be re-elected automatically. For such a provision see [9A–080] and for a resolution not to fill a vacancy see [9A–538].

Members' resolution: to elect additional directors (*or*) to fill a casual vacancy

[9A–523]   **x** (*name*) [and (*name*)] be appointed as [an] additional director[s] of the Company (*or*) to fill a vacancy caused by the [death (*or*) resignation of (*name*)].

Directors' resolution: to fill a casual vacancy on the board¹

[9A–524]   **x** (*name*) be appointed a director of the Company until the next annual general meeting in the place of (*name*) who on (*date*) [retired (*or*) was removed from office (*or*) died].

[9A–525]   ¹   See [9A–283], note 4.

Directors' resolution: to appoint additional directors¹

[9A–526]   **x** (*name*) and (*name*) be appointed additional directors of the Company until the next annual general meeting.

[9A–527]   ¹   See [9A–283], note 4.

Directors' resolution: to appoint chairman of board

[9A–528]   **x** (*name*) be appointed chairman of the board of directors.

Directors' resolution: to appoint secretary¹

[9A–529]   **x** (*name*) be appointed the Company's secretary.

[9A–530]   ¹   A private company is not required to have a company secretary: CA 2006, s 270. See also [9A–091] and the note to it.

Notice by director of [revocation and] appointment of an alternate director¹

[9A–531]   To the directors of (*name*) Ltd

I [revoke the appointment of (*name-A*) as my alternate director and in [his] place] appoint (*name-B*) of (*address*) to be my alternate director. I request that approval to (*name-B*) so acting be given at the board meeting at which this letter is presented and that (*name-B*) be entitled to attend that [and (until further notice) all subsequent] board meeting[s].

Please confirm to me that if (*name-B*) attends any board meeting as an alternate director for more than one director of the Company, [he] shall be entitled to the votes of each director for whom [he] is acting as an alternate.

Dated (*date*)

(*signature*)

[9A–532]   ¹   A director may appoint an alternate to act in his absence if the articles contain power to do so. No such power is contained in the model articles for private companies, but there is in regulation 26 of those for public companies.

Remuneration

Members' resolution: to approve compensation for loss of office[1]

x The proposed payment to (*name*) of £(…) ((…) pounds) as compensation on [his] [retirement (*or*) resignation (*or*) dismissal] from office as a director be approved.

[1]   No payment by a company to any director of compensation for loss of office is lawful unless particulars of it are disclosed to the members and approved by the company: CA 2006, s 217. The payment of bona fide damages for breach of contract and of pensions and gratuities on retirement are exempted from that section: CA 2006, s 220(1).

[9A–533]

[9A–534]

Resignation, removal or non-appointment

Notice of resignation by director [and secretary][1]

x To the directors of (*name*) Ltd

I give you notice that I resign my office[s] as director [and company secretary] with effect from [the date of this notice (*or*) (*date*)] and that I have no claims against the Company for compensation for loss of office.

Dated (*date*)

(*signature*)

[1]   Notice of the resignation must be given to the registrar under CA 2006, s 167, whether or not a new director is appointed (this section applies also to becoming a director and changes in particulars). A director may be an office holder and is not necessarily an employee, even if he or she works full time for the company: *McLean v Secretary of State for Employment* (1992) 455 IRLB 14, EAT. If the director (or secretary) is an employee, this resignation will not bar a claim for unfair dismissal: Employment Rights Act 1996, s 94.

[9A–535]

[9A–536]

[9A–537]

Members' resolution: not to fill vacancy arising from retirement[1]

x The vacancies caused by the retirement [by rotation] of (*name*) and (*name*) be not filled.

[1]   Regulation 20 in the model articles for public companies does not provide for the automatic re-election of director retiring by rotation, so this resolution will not be required for a company which has adopted those articles and not altered that provision: for such a provision see [9A–080]. For the re-election of retiring directors see [9A–521].

[9A–538]

[9A–539]

Director's resolution: to accept resignation of secretary and directors[1]

x The [written] resignations [produced [to the meeting (*or*) with these resolutions]] of (*name*) and (*name*) as directors and of (*name*) as the Company's secretary be accepted with [immediate effect (*or*) effect from (*date*)].

[1]   A return of changes of directors and secretary must be made to the registrar within 14 days of the change under CA 2006, s 167 (directors) and s 276 (secretaries); and a change of directors (but not secretary) will not be effective against other persons unless it is duly notified to the registrar: CA 2006, s 1079.

[9A–540]

[9A–541]

Members' resolution requiring special notice: to remove director from office[1]

x (*name*) be removed from office as a director [and (*name*) is appointed a director in [his] place[2]].

[1]   A director may be removed from office at any time by an ordinary resolution of the members (CA 2006, s 168), but without prejudicing any claim for damages or compensation for the termination of that office or any terminating with it. Special notice must be given to the company, and a copy of it must be given forthwith to the director, who has a right to make

[9A–542]

[9A–543]

written representations to be sent to the members and , even if not a member, shall be entitled to be heard at the meeting: CA 2006, s 169. For special notice, see [9A–317].

2   Any person so appointed is deemed for the purpose of retirement to have been appointed when the director removed by the resolution was last appointed. If no person is elected under this resolution, the place may be filled as a casual vacancy by a general meeting [9A–523] or the directors ([9A–524]).

Notice by directors to remove a director[1]

[9A–544]   (*on the company's letter paper*)

to (*name*)

(*address*)

We, being all the directors of the Company other than you, give you notice that you cease to be a director of the Company with immediate effect.

(*date*)

(*signed*)

(*by all the directors other than the addressee*)

[9A–545]   1   All three model articles provide that a director may be removed by a notice signed by all the other directors: regulation 17(g) (private, both share capital and guarantee) and regulation 21 (public).

Interests

Declaration of interest by directors[1]

[9A–546]   (*name*) and (*name*) declared their interests in the subject matter of resolutions (*number*), (*number*) and (*number*) [to be considered at the meeting].

[9A–547]   1   This declaration is required under the CA 2006, s 182. See also [9A–110], note 22. The declaration may be made in writing if it complies with CA 2006, s 184. In the case of a sole director, CA 2006, s 186 requires that the declaration must be made in writing, which gives statutory effect to the decision of Lightman J in *Neptune (Vehicle Washing Equipment) Ltd v Fitzgerald* [1996] Ch 274, [1995] 1 BCLC 352, to the effect that s 317 of the CA 1985 required a sole director to disclose his interest. Busy directors were then relieved to be advised that, unless someone else is present, e g the company secretary, it is not necessary to make the declaration out loud!

Directors' resolution recording contract made between Company and its sole member[1]

[9A–548]   x It was noted that on (*date*) a contract was made between the Company and (*name*) and the terms of the contract are as follows.

(*terms of the contract*)

[9A–549]   1   A contract (except one made in the ordinary course of business) between a company and its sole member (see [9A–361], note 3) if he is also a director (or shadow director) must, if it is not in writing, be set out in a written memorandum or recorded in the minutes of the first meeting of the directors after the making of the contract: CA 2006, s 231. Despite the fine for non-compliance, the effect of this section is unclear as many companies to whom it applies have only one director and rarely, if ever, hold a director's meeting. See also [9A–339], note 1.

Members' resolution: to approve a substantial property transaction in which a director has an interest[1]

[9A–550]   x The [purchase (*or*) sale] by the [company (*or*) company's subsidiary (*name*)] of the freehold premises known as (*address*) for £[   ] ([   ] pounds) [from (*or*) to] (*name of company*), a company connected with (*name of director*) a director of the [company (*or*) company's holding company] be approved.

¹ Ordinary resolution: see CA 2006, s 190 which requires certain substantial acquisitions or disposals by a company (and in some cases by the company's holding company) of non-cash assets to have the prior approval of the company in general meeting. In *Micro Leisure v County Properties* 1999 SLT 1428 (a Scottish case) it was held that the value must be determined by the value to the director, so that it is the enhanced value which must be used in the case of the 'marriage value' under which two adjoining plots are worth more together than separately. **[9A–551]**

AUDITORS

Appointment

Directors' resolution: to appoint [first] auditors¹

x (*name*) & Co be appointed the Company's auditors. **[9A–552]**

¹ Unless the directors reasonably resolve otherwise on the ground that audited accounts are unlikely to be required, an auditor must be appointed for each financial year of the company: CA 2006, s 485(1), but the first auditor may be appointed by the directors: CA 2006, s 485(3). A small company (annual turnover not more than £5.6m and balance sheet total not more than £2.8m) is except form audit by CA 2006, s 477, as is a dormant company by s 480.
   Auditors (of a private company) may deemed to be reappointed automatically: CA 2006, s 487. **[9A–553]**

Directors' resolution: to fill a vacancy in the office of auditor¹

x (*name*) & Co be appointed the Company's auditors to fill a casual vacancy caused by the [retirement (*or*) resignation (*or*) ineligibility (*or in the case of a sole practitioner*) the death] of (*name*) [& Co]. **[9A–554]**

¹ The directors or company in general meeting may fill any casual vacancy in the office of auditor (CA 2006, s 475(3)), but the automatic re-appointment provisions of s 487 do not apply. **[9A–555]**

Members' resolution: to reappoint auditors and fixing remuneration¹

x (*name*) & Co be reappointed the Company's auditors at [a fee of £(...) ((...) pounds) (*or*) a fee to be fixed by the directors]. **[9A–556]**

¹ Auditors must be elected for each financial year of the company: CA 2006, s 485. The remuneration of auditors appointed by the company in general meeting must be fixed by the company by an ordinary resolution or by the directors if they made the appointment: CA 2006, s 492. **[9A–557]**

Members' resolution: to fill a vacancy in the office of auditor

x (*name*) & Co be appointed the Company's auditors to fill a casual vacancy caused by the [retirement (*or*) resignation (*or*) ineligibility (*or in the case of a sole practitioner*) the death] of (*name*) [& Co] [and that the directors be authorised to fix their fees]. **[9A–558]**

Members' resolution requiring special notice: to appoint as auditors persons other than the retiring auditors or to fill a vacancy¹ **[9A–559]**

x (*name*) & Co be appointed the Company's auditors in the place of (*name*) & Co [whose period of office comes to an end at the conclusion of this meeting (*or*) to fill the vacancy caused by the retirement (*or*) resignation (*or*) ineligibility (*or in the case of a sole practitioner*) the death of (*name*) [& Co]].² **[9A–560]**

[1]   CA 2006, s 515. As to appointment of auditors generally see [9A–283], note 5. A copy of the special notice [9A–317] must be given to the auditor proposed to be appointed or removed, retiring or (where the casual vacancy was caused by retirement) retired auditor, who is entitled to make written representations. Any auditor who has been removed is entitled to attend and speak at the meeting at which his appointment would have expired or at which the vacancy caused by his removal is to be filled: CA 2006, s 513.

[2]   As to eligibility to be an auditor, see CA 2006, s 1212ff. An auditor who to his knowledge becomes disqualified must vacate his office and give to the company notice that he has vacated it for that reason: s 1223.

Members' authorisation of auditor's liability limitation agreement[1]

[9A–562]   **x** A liability limitation agreement between the Company and (*name*) in the form of the draft produced to the meeting and for identification signed by the chairman be authorised and that the need for the approval of its terms be waived.

(*or*)

x The terms[2] of a liability limitation agreement between the Company and (*name*) in the form of the draft produced to the meeting and for identification signed by the chairman be agreed and the making of the agreement be authorised.

(*or*)

x The limitation agreement made on (*date*) between the Company and (*name*) of which a copy is produced to the meeting and for identification signed by the chairman be approved.

[9A–563]   [1]   An agreement to exempt an auditor's liability for negligence, default, breach of duty or breach of trust in relation to the company in the course of the audit of accounts or to indemnify him is void, except as permitted by s 533 (indemnity for costs of successfully defending proceedings), or ss 534 to 536 (liability limitation agreements): CA 2006, s 532. A liability limitation agreement may be authorised by a resolution of the company under CA 2006, s 536, and in the case of a private company, may be authorised in any of the three ways shown above. The option to waive approval is not available to a public company.

[2]   What CA 2006, s 536(2)(b) required is that the principal terms are approved, but it is submitted that these are necessarily agreed if the whole agreement is approved.

Resignation, removal or non-appointment

Notice of resignation by an auditor[1]

[9A–564]   To the directors of (*name*) Ltd

Gentlemen,

We give you notice that we resign our office as the Company's auditors with effect from [the date of this notice (*or*) (*date*)]. [There are no circumstances connected with our resignation which we consider ought to be brought to the notice of the Company's members or creditors. (*or*) The circumstances connected with our resignation which we consider ought to be brought to the notice of the Company's members or creditors are as follows:

(*circumstances*)]

Dated (*date*)

(*signature*)

[9A–565]   [1]   CA 2006, s 516. An auditor may resign by notice in writing deposited at the registered office of the company, but the notice will be ineffective unless it contains a statement that there are no circumstances, or setting out the circumstances as mentioned in the precedent. Where there are such circumstances, the auditor may requisition a meeting of the company to receive and consider such explanation of the circumstances as he may wish to make and he may also require the statement to be circulated, similarly to the representations mentioned in [9A–561], note 1: CA 2006, s 518. For requisitions, see [9A–309] and [9A–315]. Note that even after a resignation, where there are no such circumstances, there must be given to the retiring auditor special notice of the resolution of the company to fill the vacancy: [9A–560].

Members' resolution requiring special notice: to remove auditors before expiry of term of office[1]

x (*name*) & Co be removed from office as the Company's auditors [and that (*name*) & Co be appointed auditors in their place].

[9A–566]

[1] CA 2006, s 510. See also [9A–317], note 1 and [9A–561], note 1. A company may by ordinary resolution, of which special notice has been given, remove an auditor from office, but must within 14 days give notice to the registrar under s 512.

[9A–567]

Members' notice to prevent deemed reappointment of auditor[1]

notice

[9A–568]

to (*name*) Ltd

(*address*)

We, being members of the company representing at least 5% of the total voting rights of all members who would be entitled to vote on a resolution, give you notice under s 488 of the Companies Act 2006 that the auditor should not be reappointed.

(*date*)

(*signed*)

(*members*)

[1] See [9A–553], note 1, second paragraph. The notice may be in hard copy or electronic, must be authenticated and received by the company before the end of the accounting reference period immediately preceding the time when the deemed reappointment would take effect: CA 2006, s 488. For authentication and service see preliminary note [9A–025].

[9A–569]

ACCOUNTS

Financial year

Directors' resolution: to change accounting reference date[1]

x The accounting reference date of the [current (*or*) previous] and all subsequent accounting reference periods be altered to (*day and month*) and that the [current (*or*) previous] accounting reference period is to be treated as [shortened (*or*) extended] and to [have] come to an end on (*date*).

[9A–570]

[1] The initial accounting reference date of a company is the last day of the month in which the anniversary of its incorporation falls and its first accounting reference period (in English, its accounting year) is a period of not less than six months nor more than 18 from its incorporation: CA 2006, s 391(4), (5). By s 391(6) its subsequent ARPs are successive periods of twelve months ending on its ARD.

    Notices of alterations must be given under CA 2006, s 392. An extension of ARD of the current or previous period is not normally effective if given within five years of a previous extension or if the extension is for more than eighteen months. An extension in respect of a previous ARP cannot be made if the period for filing account for that period has expired. The main exception from the five year rule is if the purpose it to align the date with that of the company's subsidiary or holding company which is a company established in an EEA State.

[9A–571]

There is no restriction if the company wishes to shorten its ARP. The restrictions are also relieved if an administration order under the IA 1986 is in force.

Accounts

Directors' resolution: to approve annual accounts[1]

[9A–572] x The balance sheet as at (*date*), the profit and loss account to that date and the report of this board on them be approved and (*name*) be authorised to sign the report on behalf of the board.

[9A–573] [1] The directors' report must be approved by the board and signed on its behalf by a director or the secretary: CA 2006, s 419.

BANK AND OTHER APPOINTMENTS

Directors' resolution: to appoint bank

[9A–574] x (*name*) Bank Ltd at its branch at (*address*) be appointed the Company's bank. (Attached to these minutes is the copy of the resolution and mandate form required by the bank.)

Directors' resolution: to appoint solicitors

[9A–575] x (*name*) & Co be appointed the Company's solicitors.

CONDUCT OF BUSINESS

Execution of documents

Directors' resolution: to adopt seal[1]

[9A–576] x The seal impressed on these minutes be adopted as the Company's seal.

[9A–577] [1] A company need not have a seal: see [9A–361], note 4. Contracts may be made by a company under its common seal or on its behalf by a person acting with its express or implied authority, and formalities which apply to an individual apply to a company unless a contrary intention appears: CA 2006, s 43.

Directors' resolution: to execute a deed[1]

[9A–578] x The (*document*) [for the (*description of property transaction etc*)] produced to the meeting be approved and be executed as a deed by [affixing the Company's seal to it (*or*) the signature of any director and the company secretary or any two directors [but that it be not delivered until [it is dated (*or*) the transaction to which it relates is completed]].

[9A–579] [1] See [9A–577], note 1.

Directors' resolution: to execute several deeds[1]

[9A–580] x The (*Document-A*), the (*Document-B*), the (*Document-C*) and the (*Document-D*) (*or*) the (*Documents*) be approved and be executed as deeds by [affixing the Company's seal to them (*or*) the signature of any director and the company secretary or any two directors] [but that [they be not delivered until they are dated (*or*) the transaction to which they relate is completed]].

[9A–581] [1] See [9A–577], note 1.

Directors' resolution: to approve and authorise signing of document[1]

x The (*document*) for the (*description of transaction*) produced to the meeting (*or*) the (*document*) be approved and (*name*) be authorised to sign it on behalf of the Company. [9A–582]

[1] See [9A–577], note 1. [9A–583]

Borrowing

Directors' resolution: to borrow for purchase of property and execute mortgage of it — short form

x The Company borrows £(...) ((...) pounds) from (*name*) for the purpose of buying (*description of property*) on the terms of the [Offer Letter (*or*) offer in the letter produced to the meeting (*or*) with the resolutions] and executes the mortgage of (*description of property*) also produced. [9A–584]

Extract of minutes or written resolutions of directors of borrowing company to approve execution of security and guarantee documents

DOCUMENTS

The following documents ('Security Documents') were produced [to the meeting (*or*) with these resolutions]: [9A–585]

'Facility Letter-A'	means a copy of a letter dated (*date*) from (*name*) Bank plc ('Lender-A') to the Company offering overdraft and other facilities totalling (*amount*).
'Facility Letter-B'	means a copy of a letter dated (*date*) from (*name*) Ltd company (*number*) ('Lender-B') to the Company offering a loan facility of (*amount*) and other facilities to the Company.
'Debenture-A'	means a mortgage debenture intended to be made between the Company and the Lender-A to give to the Lender-A a first fixed charge over the Company's book debts and a floating charge over all the Company's undertaking and assets including goodwill and uncalled capital as security for all moneys and liabilities from time to time owing or incurred by the Company to the Lender-A.
'Debenture-B'	means a mortgage debenture intended to be made between the Company and the Lender-B to give to the Lender-B a first fixed charge over certain assets of the Company and a floating charge over all the Company's other undertaking and assets including goodwill and uncalled capital as security for all moneys and liabilities from time to time owing or incurred by the Company to the Lender-B.
'Specific Mortgage'	means a mortgage intended to be made between the Company and the Lender-A to give the Lender-A a first fixed charge over its freehold property known as (*description*) as further security for all moneys and liabilities from time to time owing or incurred by the Company to the Lender- A.

'Priority Deed'   means a deed of priorities between Lender-A, Lender-B and the Company.

'Guarantee'   means a guarantee to be given [joint and severally] by the Company [and (*name*) Ltd company (*number*) and (*name*) Ltd company (*number*) ('Co-Guarantors') each a guarantor of] the liabilities of (*name*) Ltd company (*number*) ('Parent (*or*) Subsidiary') [and each of the Co-Guarantors] to the Lender-A.

BACKGROUND

[9A–586]   **0.1** It was acknowledged that the Lender-A had agreed to make available and continue overdraft and other facilities to the Company as set out or referred to in the Facility Letter-A and the Lender-B had agreed to make available to the Company the facilities as set out or referred to in the Facility Letter-B.

0.2 It was noted that one effect of the Guarantee in conjunction with the Debenture-A and the Specific Mortgage will be to charge the whole of the Company's assets with the liabilities of the [Parent (*or*) Subsidiary] [and the Co-Guarantors] to the Lender-A.

0.3 The directors fully and carefully considered the terms of the Security Documents, the nature and scale of the liabilities undertaken pursuant to them and the commercial and financial consequences of executing them so far as they affect the Company, its trade, its financial position and its future trading and financial requirements.

RESOLUTIONS

[9A–587]   **1** No limits on the power of the Company or its directors to borrow money or give guarantees or create security will be exceeded by the execution of the Security Documents.

2 In the opinion of the directors the transactions effected by the Security Documents are in the best interests of the Company and entered into in good faith and for the purpose of carrying on the business of the Company and there are reasonable grounds for believing that the transactions will be for the benefit of the Company.

3 The following are reasonable grounds for believing that the Guarantee is for the benefit of the Company:
—   the Company, the [Parent (*or*) Subsidiary] and the Co-Guarantors are all part of a group which constitutes together one trading organisation and through it their commercial interests are common; and
—   the finances made available under the Facility Letter A are required to provide necessary working capital facilities for the Company and that those finances are not available except as part of a larger scheme of financial arrangements of which the Security Documents are part.

4 The Security Documents be approved.

5 The duplicate of each of the Facility Letters be signed by (*name*) on behalf of the Company and delivered to the Lender-A and the Lender-B with certified copies of these resolutions and payment of the respective arrangement fees be authorised.

6 Each of the Debenture-A, the Debenture-B, the Specific Mortgage, the Guarantee and the Priority Deed be executed by the Company (but with the intention that they will not be delivered until they are dated) [by the signatures of any two directors of the Company or one of them and the company secretary (*or*) under its common seal and that the affixing of the seal be witnessed by any two directors of the Company or one of them and the company secretary] as a deed.

7 Any director is authorised to agree amendments to the Security Documents and that any two directors or one director and the secretary is authorised to agree, negotiate and execute whether under hand or as a deed and deliver any other documents which are required in connection with the proposed transactions.

Extract of minutes or written resolutions of directors of company to borrow from parent company and execute debenture

BACKGROUND

(*name*) explained that [9A–588]
— although the Company was then [in credit (*or*) within its facility limit at its bank], cheques now drawn and transactions undertaken would [put into debit (*or*) take its borrowings beyond that limit],
— the Company's indebtedness to the bank is guaranteed by its holding company (*name*) Ltd ('Lender'),
— the Company is indebted to the Lender for £(...) ((...) pounds), and
— the Lender has agreed to continue with its support and to make to the Company an immediate further advance of £(...) ((...) pounds),
— but will do so only on condition that the Company issues to the Lender a debenture (in the form produced to the meeting) giving fixed and floating charges over all its assets present and future as security for not only money now to be advanced by the Lender but also for any money at any time in the future owing by the Lender to the Lender on any account including money paid by the Lender to the bank under the guarantee and interest at (*rate*)% pa over the (*name*) Bank plc base rate from time to time in force.

RESOLVED

The debenture by the Company in favour of the Lender produced [to the meeting (*or*) with the resolutions] be approved and executed as a deed by the Company (but with the intention that it will not be delivered until it is dated) [by the signatures of any two directors of the Company or one of them and the company secretary (*or*) under its common seal and that the affixing of the seal be witnessed by any two directors of the Company or one of them and the company secretary]. [9A–589]

Members' resolution: to ratify borrowing ultra vires the directors[1]

x The borrowing by the Company of £(...) ((...) pounds) from (*name*) Ltd made by the directors on (*date*) and the sealing and issue in respect of it a debenture giving a floating charge over all the Company's undertaking and assets present and future (including uncalled capital), bearing interest at (*rate*)% pa and repayable on (*date*) (which borrowing and issues of debenture were ultra vires the directors) be approved, ratified and confirmed. [9A–590]

¹ An act of the directors, which is outside their powers, but within those of the company, may be ratified by the company: *Irvine v Union Bank of Australia* (1877) 2 App Cas 366, CA; and *Bamford v Bamford* [1970] Ch 212, [1969] 1 All ER 969, CA. The third party may be protected by the rule in *Royal British Bank v Turquand* (1856) 6 E & B 327 and s 39 of the CA 2006].

Acquisition or disposal of business

Directors' resolution: to adopt contracts entered into by directors or promoters — declaration of interest¹

[9A-592] **x** (*name*) and (*name*) declared their interests in the matter as Sellers. The Company adopts and acquires from them the whole of the assets acquired and the contracts entered into by them all of which are listed in the account produced to the meeting and annexed to these minutes and in consideration for them [pays to them in cash (*or*) acknowledges that it is indebted to them by way of [unsecured and interest-free] loans for such amounts as have been expended by them respectively in respect of those assets and are shown in the account] and undertakes to adopt and accept all liability for all of such contracts as have not been performed and to compensate (*name*) and (*name*) in full on demand for all liabilities in respect of them.

[9A-593] ¹ See [9A–177] and [9A–189] and the notes to them.

Directors' resolution: to acquire business from director for shares and loan and allot other shares for cash¹

[9A-594] **x** (*Name-A*) and (*name-B*) declared their interests as seller and lender respectively in the matters dealt with in this resolution. The Company (having received from (*name-B*) an application for (*number*) shares to be issued at the price of £(…) ((…) pounds) per share and a cheque for the total price of £(…) ((…) pounds)):

— acquires from (*name-A*) the business of a (*description*) carried on by [him] and for that purpose enter into the [Sale Agreement (or) agreement produced to the meeting marked '(*name*)-1' ('Sale Agreement')];

— that the Sale Agreement be signed by (*name*) on behalf of the Company;

— the following shares [including the subscriber shares] be allotted as follows:

    (a) to (*name-A*) (*number*) £[1] shares credited as fully paid pursuant to the Sale Agreement and in [part] consideration for the transfer of the business to the Company under it; and

    (b) to (*name-B*) (*number*) £[1] shares credited as fully paid for cash at [the issue price of £[2] per share (*or*) par];

— the Company's seal be affixed to the share certificates and the certificates be delivered to the respective allottees;

— the Company acknowledges its indebtedness to (*name-A*) and (*name-B*) in respect of the [unsecured interest free] loans made as follows:

    (a) by (*name-A*) for £(…) ((…) pounds) representing the balance of the consideration payable to [him] under the sale agreement, and

    (b) by (*name-B*) for £(…) ((…) pounds) paid to the Company in cash; and

— the Company issues to (*name-A*) and (*name-B*) as security for the loans debentures in the form of the documents produced to the meeting and marked respectively '(*name*)-2' and '(*name*)-3' and accordingly that the Company's seal be affixed to the debentures.

¹ See [9A–188], note 1. For other allotments of shares, see [9A–414] to [9A–428]. [9A–595]

Members' resolution: to authorise sale of undertaking¹

x The directors be authorised to sell all the undertaking, property and assets [9A–596] of [the Company (*or*) its (*description*) division] subject to its liabilities, to (*name*) Ltd, for £(...) ((...) pounds) to be paid in cash or satisfied by the allotment of fully paid shares or debentures in (*name*) Ltd, or partly in the one way and partly in the other as the directors determine.

¹ This does not require a member's resolution unless the articles of association contain a [9A–597] restriction on the directors' powers such as is in [9A–063], although in practice the sharehold-ers' authority is often obtain for such an act as this. See also CA 2006, s 39 and all three versions of the model articles reg 2 (directors' general authority) and reg 3 (shareholders' reserve power). If, however, it is proposed to wind up the company then the sale in consideration of shares can only be carried out in compliance with the IA 1986, s 110.

Other

Directors' resolution: to agree service agreements with directors¹

x (*name*) and (*name*) declared their interests in the matter. Service agreements [9A–598] be offered to (*name*) and (*name*) in the form of the documents produced to the meeting and marked respectively '(*initials*)' and '(*initials*)' and (*name*) be authorised to sign them on behalf of the Company.

¹ See [9A–547], note 1. [9A–599]

WINDING UP

Note: This section applies to members' voluntary winding-up and not to an insolvent winding up.

Resolutions

Members' resolution: to wind up voluntarily by the members¹

x The Company be wound up voluntarily, and that (*name*) of (*address*) be [9A–600] appointed liquidator for the purposes of the winding up (and that (*name*)'s remuneration be fixed). The remuneration of the liquidator (*or*) of each of the liquidators for [his] (*or*) their services in the winding up be fixed (under rule 4.148A(2)(a) of the Insolvency Rules 1986) at an amount equal to (*rate*)% on the amount of the assets realised or distributed in the winding up during [his] (*or*) their period of office.

¹ A special resolution is required if the members wish to wind up the company voluntarily: IA [9A–601] 1986, s 84(1)(b). If the articles of association fix a period for the life of the company which has expired or some other occurrence on which the company is to be wound up and it has occurred, an ordinary resolution suffices: IA 1986, s 84(1)(a). The appointment of the liquidator and the fixing of his remuneration can be made by subsequent ordinary resolutions. This being a members' winding up it may be assumed that creditors are not vitally interested and there is no objection to combining all these matters in one resolution. A declaration of solvency (winding up in Sch 4 to the Insolvency Rules 1986, SI 1986/1925, form 4.70) must be made by a majority of the directors not more than five weeks before the date of the passing of the resolution and delivered to the registrar before that date: IA 1986, s 89. Within 14 days of the resolution notice must be published in the *London Gazette* (IA 1986, s 109) and within 15 days a copy of the resolution must be filed with the registrar (CA 2006, s 30).

Members' resolution: to fix remuneration of liquidator at a percentage of assets recovered[1]

[9A–602] x The remuneration of the liquidator (*or*) of each of the liquidators for [his] (*or*) their services in the winding up be fixed (under rule 4.148A(2)(a) of the Insolvency Rules 1986) at an amount equal to (*rate*)% on the amount of the assets realised or distributed in the winding up during [his] (*or*) their period of office.

[9A–603] ¹ The remuneration is fixed by the company in general meeting, and this resolution may be combined with the resolution appointing the liquidator. The remuneration must be either a percentage, as under this form, or on a time basis: Insolvency Rules 1986, SI 1986/1925, r 4.148A.

Members' resolution: to fix remuneration of liquidator at a monthly amount[1]

[9A–604] x There is paid to [the liquidator (*or*) each of the liquidators] by way of remuneration for [(his) (*or*) their] services in the winding up, be fixed (under rule 4.148A(2)(b) of the Insolvency Rules 1986) by reference to the time properly given by the insolvency practitioner (as liquidator) and his staff in attending to matters arising in the liquidation.

[9A–605] ¹ See [9A–601], note 1.

Members' resolution: to fix remuneration of liquidator at the rate provided for liquidations by the Official Receiver[1]

[9A–606] x The remuneration of the liquidator be in accordance with the scale laid down in Schedule 6 of the Insolvency Rules 1986.

[9A–607] ¹ This resolution may not be strictly necessary, because this method of remuneration applies automatically if the liquidator's remuneration is not fixed under [9A–602] or [9A–603]: Insolvency Regulations 1986, SI 1986/1925, r 4.148B.

Members' resolution: to fill vacancy in office of liquidator[1]

[9A–608] x (*Name*) of (*address*) be appointed to fill the vacancy caused by the [death (*or*) resignation] of (*name*) and that [he] be remunerated in the same manner as (*name*).

[9A–609] ¹ IA 1986, s 92. The meeting for this purpose may be convened by the continuing liquidator or liquidators or by any contributory, unless some special arrangement has been made with the creditors for the purpose of appointing new or additional liquidators. In the case of a members' winding up, such an arrangement will not usually be made, but, if made, the appointment of the new liquidator must follow the provisions of the special arrangement.

Members' resolution: to continue the powers of directors for certain purposes[1]

[9A–610] x Notwithstanding the appointment of liquidators of the Company, the Company's directors be authorised to continue to exercise their powers as directors for the purposes of (carrying on the Company's business so far as may be required for its beneficial winding up).

[9A–611] ¹ A continuation of the directors' powers in this manner may be authorised in general meeting under the IA 1986, s 91(2). For an alternative means of sanction, see [9A–618].

Members' resolution: to authorise liquidator to divide assets or specific assets in specie[1]

[9A–612] x The liquidator be authorised to divide in specie among the Company's members all or such of the Company's surplus assets as [he] thinks fit.

¹ There is no equivalent in the model articles to the winding up regulations in Table A (117 in 1985 and 135 in 1948) permitting the distribution of assets in specie, but even in the absence of any express provisions to this effect in the articles of association, it is thought that a liquidator of a company in voluntary liquidation has power to convey assets in specie to a member in satisfaction of his interest in the company, because the IA 1986, s 107 does not expressly provide that the assets shall be sold. **[9A–613]**

Notices and other documents

Notice to registrar of special resolution to wind up¹

company (*number*) **[9A–614]**

The Companies Act 2006

company limited by shares

To the registrar

At a general meeting of the above-named Company, duly convened and held at (*place name*), on (*date*), the following (*special*) resolution was duly passed.

(*resolution*)

Dated (*date*)

(*signed*)

(*Chairman*)

¹ 2006 Act, s 30. This must be passed within 15 days of the passing of the resolution that must be notified on the prescribed form under the IA 1986, s 109. Notice of an ordinary resolution to wind up must also be given. The notice should not go on to refer to the appointment of a liquidator since special official forms are provided for that purpose: (nos 600 or 600(a) as appropriate). **[9A–615]**

Advertisement in the London Gazette of special resolution to wind up¹

In the matter of the Insolvency Act 1986, and in the matter of (*name*) Ltd, in voluntary liquidation, members' winding up. **[9A–616]**

At a general meeting of the above-named company duly convened and held at (*place name*), on (*date*), the following special resolution was duly passed.

(special resolution)

Dated (*date*)

(*name of chairman*)

Chairman

¹ IA 1986, s 85. The time for insertion of this advertisement is 14 days after the passing of the resolution. **[9A–617]**

Sanction of liquidator to the continuance of directors' powers in certain respects¹

To the directors of (*name*) Ltd **[9A–618]**

As the Company's liquidator, I sanction in accordance with section 91(2) of the Insolvency Act 1986 the continuance of your powers as the Company's directors in the following respects and for the following purposes:

(*powers continued and purposes for which they are continued*)

Dated (*date*)

(*signed*)

Liquidator

[9A–619] ¹ The Act allows continuance of the powers either by resolution of the company in general meeting [9A–610] or by sanction of the liquidator, but the latter method will be much more convenient in practice provided the liquidator is willing to act, and it would not appear in any way improper for him to do so since the company will almost certainly be solvent.

Notice of meeting of Company at end of each year of the winding up¹

[9A–620] company (*number*)

The Companies Act 2006

company limited by shares

In the matter of (*name*) Ltd in voluntary liquidation, members' winding up, and in the matter of the Insolvency Act 1986.

Take notice that in pursuance of section 93 of the Act a general meeting of the above-named company will be held at (*address*) on (*date*) at (*time*) am/pm when also in pursuance of section 93 of the Act I shall lay before the meeting an account of my acts and dealings and of the conduct of the Company's winding up during the year from (*date*) to (*date*).

Dated (*date*)

(*signed*)

Liquidator

A member entitled to attend and vote at the meeting is entitled to appoint a proxy to attend and vote in his or her place. A proxy need not be a member of the Company.

[9A–621] ¹ The meeting must be called at the end of each year of the winding up or within three months of the end of such year or at such later date as the Department of Trade and Industry may allow (IA 1986, s 93).

Advertisement of final meeting of company under Insolvency Act 1986, section 94¹

[9A–622] company (*number*)

The Companies Act 2006

company limited by shares

In the matter of (name) Ltd, in voluntary liquidation, members' winding up, and in the matter of the Insolvency Act 1986.

Notice is given that in pursuance of section 94 of the Insolvency Act 1986 the final general meeting of the above-named company will be held at (*address*) (*date*) at (*time*) am/pm for the purposes of laying before such meeting the account of the winding up of the above-named company and of giving any explanation of it.

Dated (*date*)

(*signed*)

Liquidator

A member entitled to attend and vote at the meeting is entitled to appoint a proxy to attend and vote in his or her place. A proxy need not be a member of the Company.

[1]   The meeting must be called by advertisement in the *London Gazette* at least one month before   **[9A–623]**
        the meeting (IA 1986, s 94).

10 Employment

PRELIMINARY NOTE

COMPENSATION, WEEK'S PAY

[10–000A] Statutory maximum compensation: £66,200

	1 February 2007	1 February 2008	1 February 2009	1 October 2009	1 February 2010
compensatory award	£60,600	£63,000	£66,200	£66,200	tba
week's pay	£310	£330	£350	£380	£380

[10–000B] ### NATIONAL MINIMUM WAGE

	1 October 2006	1 October 2007	1 October 2008	1 October 2009
adult	£5.35	£5.52	£5.73	£5.80
18–21 year olds	£4.45	£4.60	£4.77	£4.83
16–17 year olds	£3.30	£3.40	£3.53	£3.57

PRECEDENTS

PART I: STATUTORY TERMS AND NOTICES, AND MANUAL

[10–009] ### 3 Written statement of terms of employment pursuant to the Employment Rights Act 1996, s 1 – full form incorporating contract terms[1]

[10–088] [13] For annual leave to which a worker is entitled, see 'Working Time Documents' [10–686] and [10.702], note 9. For an example of 'rolled-up' holiday pay see Additional clauses [10–714].

[36] There is a distinction between disclosing and using, and it is more difficult to prove use than disclosure: *Thomas Marshall (Exports) Ltd v Guinle* [1979] Ch 227, [1978] 3 All ER 193, in which, however, it was held that a company could refuse to accept wrongful repudiation of his contract by the managing director, who remained subject to his obligations under it, and an injunction was granted to restrain acts of competition by the managing director, which were in gross breach of his duty of good faith. It is prudent to warn an employee who is put in possession of secret knowledge that the information is to be regarded as confidential unless it is obvious that this must be so (*Triplex Safety Glass Co v Scorah* [1938] Ch 211, [1937] 4 All ER 693). For a review of the law see *Faccenda Chicken Ltd v Fowler* [1987] Ch 117, [1986]

ICR 691, CA: in particular a restrictive covenant will not protect information short of a trade secret which has become part of the employee's own skill and knowledge. For an extension of the *Faccenda* principle to a consultant, who had done research work for the claimant, see *Vestergaard Frandsen A/S v Bestnet Europe Ltd* [2007] EWHC 2455 (Ch), [2007] All ER (D) 391 (Oct) and [2009] EWHC 1456 (Ch), [2009] All ER (D) 57 (Oct).

4 Short written statement of terms of employment to be accompanied by employment manual[1]

[10–089]

[1] This precedent is intended to provide all the variables on one sheet of paper to be signed by the parties and to be issued with the employer's employment manual (see precedent [10–097]). It is a very practical way of combining the statutory statement and contract of employment, but, strictly speaking, it does not comply with the esoteric complexities of ss 1 to 3 of ERA 1996, as to which see [10–005], note 2. See also [10–563] note 1 (Statements of policy and contract terms).

[10–090]

PART II: EMPLOYMENT CONTRACTS

9 Contract for the employment of an executive director of company or senior manager — full form[1]

[10–230]

[1] Whilst directors are by that office not employees of a company, they may at the same time as holding that office be employed in an executive or some other capacity. The uncertainty whether they enjoy in all cases the same rights as other employees under the employment protection legislation appears to have been resolved by *Secretary of State for Trade and Industry v Bottrill* [1999] IRLR 326, (CA), in which an employee of the company in which he held the sole issued share and, therefore, was entitled to recover redundancy and other payments from the Secretary of State when the company went into voluntary liquidation, preferred the decision of the Court of Session in *Fleming v Secretary of State for Trade and Industry* [1997] IRLR 682 to that of the EAT in *Buchan and Ivey v Secretary of State for Employment* [1997] IRLR 80. *Bottrill* was applied by the EAT in *Swanney v Penn Hill Pharmacy Ltd* [2004] All ER (D) 443 (Nov). Directors must be appointed to that office and may be removed as provided for in the Companies Act 2006 and the company's articles of association: Companies Act 2006, ss 168, 169. The company must keep at a place of which notice has been given to the Registrar of Companies, a copy of directors' service contracts or memoranda of their terms if not reduced to writing. The copies must be available for inspection free of charge by the shareholders: Companies Act 2006, s 228.

[10–366]

[7] The 'accounting reference period' is an expression introduced by the Companies Act 1976, now s 391 of the 2006 Act. It is usually a year, but may be for a period of more or less than a year if the accounting reference date is changed.

PART III: TERMINATION OF EMPLOYMENT

19 Compromise agreement (full form)[1]

[10–528]

COMPENSATION PAYMENTS[4A]

7 The Company shall pay the following amounts to the Employee [on or not more than [seven] days after the date of this deed (*or, if later*) on the Effective Date]:

[10–536]

(a)   £[...] ([...] pounds) free of tax as compensation for loss of office;
(b)   £[...] ([...] pounds) for [*particulars*];
(c)   £[...] ([...] pounds) as a statutory redundancy payment; and
(d)   £[...] ([...] pounds) which the Employer will pay as a contribution to the Employee's pension scheme.

(*or*)

[10–562] [4a] In *Gibb v Maidstone and Tunbridge Wells NHS Trust* [2009] EWHC 862 (QB), [2009] IRLR 707 the former employer, as a public body, had to exercise its powers in the public interest and under the Wednesbury principle of reasonableness. The amount of the compensation in the compromise agreement had been irrationally generous and therefore the agreement was ultra vires.

PART IV: STATEMENTS OF POLICY[1]

[10–563] [1]In the absence of an express power, contractual terms of employment, like terms of other contracts, cannot be altered unilaterally. Other contract terms may be 'works rules' or policy or administrative provision and not contractual, in which case the employer may be able to alter them unilaterally. In *Haigh v Department for Work and Pensions* [2004] All ER (D) 367 (Dec), QBD, the employer's appraisal system, although linked to performance related pay, formed part of the administrative or regulatory element of the employment relationship, fell to be regarded as policy not contract and could be altered unilaterally by the employer. See also [10–735], note 1. As to changes in terms see *Harlow v Artemis International Corpn Ltd*, [2008] EWHC 1126 (QB), [2008] IRLR 629, in which a redundancy policy was treated as a contractual term.

[10–564] 20   Disciplinary rules and procedure[1]

[10–564A] **Note** By the Employment Act 2008, s 1, the unloved statutory resolution procedure, in the Employment Act 2002, ss 29–33, Schs 2–4, was revoked with effect from 6 April 2009 with savings for disciplinary or grievance cases started before that date, and by the Employment Act 2008, s 3, a new s 207A was introduced into the Trade Union and Labour Relations (Consolidation) Act 1992, with the effect that from that date, an award made by an employment tribunal to an employee may be increased by not more than 25% if the employer had unreasonably failed to comply with a relevant ACAS code of practice, or reduced by a like amount if the failure was on the part of the employee. ACAS has revised, and in April 2009 republished, its code of practice on disciplinary and grievance procedures. The effect broadly speaking is that the law reverts to what it was on 30 September 2004, when the now repealed provisions were brought into force. The main impact on precedents 20 [10–564] and 21 [10–608] is the replacement of a footnote and the insertion of new disciplinary and grievance procedures as follows.

An alternative means of resolving unfair dismissal disputes is the ACAS Arbitration Scheme, which was introduced from 21 May 2001, and was replaced with a revised scheme from 6 April 2004 by the ACAS Arbitration Scheme (Great Britain) Order 2004, SI 2004/753. See chapter 5 (Arbitration) note [5–005] and precedent 6 [5–050].

The headings 'A non-statutory disciplinary procedure[11]' and 'B discipline – procedures based on the statutory form' to [10–583] and [10–585] respectively and footnote 11 are deleted.

[10–584A]– *(Or, as alternatives for clauses 19 and 20, use the following clauses, which closely*
[10–584B]   *track the ACAS Code.)*

[10–584C] *Investigation*

19 The employer must carry out necessary investigations of potential disciplinary matters without unreasonable delay to establish the facts of the case. In some cases this will require the holding of an investigatory meeting with the employee before proceeding to any disciplinary hearing. In others, the investigatory stage will be the collation of evidence by the employer for use at any disciplinary hearing.

Notification of employee

20 If the employer decides that there is a disciplinary case to answer, it should notify the employee of this in writing. The notification must contain sufficient information about the alleged misconduct or poor performance and its possible consequences to enable the employee to prepare to answer the case at a disciplinary meeting. Whenever appropriate the employer may provide copies of any written evidence, which may include any witness statements, with the notification. The notification must also give details of the time and venue for the disciplinary meeting and advise the employee of his or her right to be accompanied at the meeting.

Disciplinary meeting

21 The meeting should be held without unreasonable delay whilst allowing the employee reasonable time to prepare his or her case.

22 At the meeting the employer must explain the complaint against the employee and go through the evidence that has been gathered. The employee must be allowed to set out his or her case and answer any allegations that have been made. The employee must also be given a reasonable opportunity to ask questions, present evidence, call relevant witnesses and raise points about any information provided by witnesses. The employer and the employee must give advance notice to the other of any intention to call relevant witnesses.

Decision

23 The decision may be given at the meeting, and, if it is, must be confirmed in writing. If no decision is made at the meeting, the employer must decide as soon as possible after the meeting whether or not disciplinary or any other action is justified and inform the employee accordingly in writing.

Appeal

24 Where an employee feels that disciplinary action taken against him or her is wrong or unjust, he or she they may appeal against the decision in writing. Appeals must be heard without unreasonable delay. Employees must let the employer know the grounds for the appeal.

25 The appeal must be dealt with, wherever possible, by a manager or director who has not previously been involved in the case.

Meetings and timings

26 The time and place of all meetings must be reasonable. So far as is practicable no more than one week should elapse between each stage of the procedure.

Representation[11]

27 The employee is entitled to be accompanied at any meeting by a trade union employee or official or another of the employer's workers, who may address the meeting and confer with the employee during it.

[10–607]   [11] Employees in the public sector facing an internal disciplinary proceedings such as one in which professional misconduct is alleged, which might end not just the particular employment but their professional careers, may be entitled to legal representation: *Kulkarni v Milton Keynes Hospital NHS Trust* [2009] EWCA Civ 789, [2009] IRLR 829.

[10–608]   # 21   Statutory disciplinary and grievance procedures[1]

Note The whole of the disciplinary and grievance procedure in precedent 21 [10-608]–[10–643] is replaced by the new grievance procedure below.

[10–609]   *Purpose*

1 The purpose of the grievance procedure is to enable employees to raise and discuss grievances with the employer and, if reasonably practical, to resolve them and if not to give an explanation which might assist the employee. The word 'grievance' is used to include any concern, problem or complaint in connection with the employee's work and relations with the employer and other employees.

[10–610]   *Notification*

2 If it is not possible to resolve a grievance informally, employees should raise the matter formally and without unreasonable delay with a manager who is not the subject of the grievance. This should be done in writing and should set out the nature of the grievance.

[10–611]   *Meeting*

3 Employers must arrange for a formal meeting to be held without unreasonable delay after a grievance is received, at which the employee must be allowed to explain his or her grievance and how he or she think it should be resolved. Consideration should be given to adjourning the meeting for any investigation that may be necessary.

[10–612]   *Decision*

4 Decisions whether or not any action should be taken may be made at the meeting. If made at the meeting, the decision must be confirmed in writing, and, if not made at the meeting, should be communicated to the employee, in writing, without unreasonable delay and, where appropriate, should set out what action the employer intends to take to resolve the grievance. The employee must be informed that they can appeal if they are not content with the action taken.

[10–613]   *Appeal*

5 Where an employee feels that his or her grievance has not been satisfactorily resolved he or she may appeal. He or she should let the employer know the grounds for the appeal without unreasonable delay and in writing. The appeal should be dealt with impartially and wherever possible by a manager who has not previously been involved in the case.

6 The outcome of the appeal should be communicated to the employee in writing without unreasonable delay.

Meetings and timings [10–614]

7 The time and place of all meetings must be reasonable. So far as is practicable no more than one week should elapse between each stage of the procedure.

Representation[2] [10–615]

8 The employee is entitled to be accompanied at any meeting by a trade union employee or official or another of the employer's workers, who may address the meeting and confer with the employee during it.

[1] This precedent tracks the ACAS Code of Practice closely. See [10–564A] note.	[10–616]–
[2] See [10–607], note 11.	[10–644]

22   Redundancy policy[1] [10–645]

[1] The basic legislation is in Pt X of ERA 1996 (ss 94–134), but see also the general unfair [10–655] dismissal and 'fairness' provisions. The consultation and notification provisions are mainly in the Trade Union and Labour Relations (Consolidation) Act 1992, s 188 and the Collective Redundancies and Transfer of Undertakings (Protection of Employment) (Amendment) Regulations 1995, SI 1995/2587.

[2] The former policy of dismissing first any employees over the normal retirement age is likely now to result in unfair dismissals on the grounds of age discrimination: see [10–088], note 28. The LIFO principle is not necessarily discriminatory: in *Rolls-Royce Plc v Unite* [2009] EWCA Civ 387, [2009] IRLR 576, it was held that the inclusion of a length of service criterion in a collective agreement was a proportionate means of achieving the legitimate aim of rewarding loyalty and achieving a stable workforce in the context of a fair process of redundancy selection. The selection procedure may be unfair if there was no consultation with the union or employees about the method of selection or if the person applying subjective criteria did not support his marking by reference to company documents or speaking to other managers: *E-ZEC Medical Transport Service Ltd v Gregory*, EAT [2008] All ER (D) 193 (Dec).

[3] As to part-time workers see [10–226], note 10.

23   Health and safety policy[1] [10–656]

H & S — SMOKING [10–672]

24 No smoking is permitted at any time in any part of (*Party-A*) premises[2].

[1] The Corporate Manslaughter and Corporate Homicide Act 2007 came into force on 6 April [10–673A] 2008 and is intended to make it easier to prosecute organisations. Formerly a body corporate could be prosecuted successfully only if there was sufficient evidence to find a senior employee guilty, but under this Act the courts may consider the management of the body by its senior mangers instead of focussing on the activities of one individual. No prosecution under this Act is reported in any of the series of law reports provided by the LexisNexis online service, but information about prosecutions may be found on the following website: http://www.corporateaccountability.org/manslaughter/cases/ongoing.htm (accessed 4 October 2009).

[2] Premises are smoke-free if they are used as a place of work by more than one person: Health Act 2006, s 2(2).

24A   Safeguarding Vulnerable Groups Act policy[1]

(*name*) Ltd — vulnerable persons policy

1 The company is a 'regulated activity provider' and is subject to the provisions of the Safeguarding Vulnerable Groups Act 2006 and associated legislation ('Legislation'). For this purpose we have three groups of person who work for the company, whether employees, workers or volunteers, who are:

   (a)   those who carry on a 'regulated activity', which, broadly, includes everybody who has direct contact with children and vulnerable adults;

   (b)   those who carry on a 'controlled activity', which, broadly, may give the opportunity for contact with children and vulnerable adults and includes those who have access to their records; and

   (c)   all other employees, workers or volunteers, ie those who do not fall into either of those categories.

2 The company:

   (a)   is entitled to know whether any person who works for it in any regulated or controlled activity is on either or both of the Children's Barred List and the Adults' Barred List maintained by the Independent Safeguarding Authority under the Vetting and Barring Scheme;

   (b)   will make, and from time to time renew, enquiries about those persons;

   (c)   will monitor those persons; and

   (d)   will keep records to show the status of each such person.

All records kept under this policy are subject to the employer's data protection policy[2].

3 It is a strict rule of the company that no person working for it may do anything which falls within a regulated activity in relation to (a) children if he or she is on the Children's Barred List and/or (b) adults if he or she is on the Adults' Barred List.

4 All information about any child or vulnerable adult for whom the company has or has had any responsibility or involvement is confidential. The duty of confidentiality in respect of this information extends to all who work for the company in any capacity whether or not they work in any regulated or controlled activity.

5 Any person who works for the company in a controlled activity and is on either or both of the Children's Barred List and the Adults' Barred List must comply with all safeguards imposed at any time in respect of that person's work.

6 A breach of the Legislation may be a criminal offence on the part of both the company and the person carrying on the activity.

7 Any breach of the Legislation or this policy by any person who works for the company in any capacity (whether or not the person has been prosecuted) will be treated as gross misconduct, entitling the company to terminate that person's employment or other contract summarily and without compensation. Any person who works for the company and who knows or has grounds for suspecting that any person is breach of the Legislation or this policy, must

report it to (*insert name of person responsible*) or, in their absence, (*state alternative person responsible*) at the company without delay. An unreasonable failure to make such a report will also be treated as gross misconduct, entitling the company to terminate that person's employment or other contract summarily and without compensation.

8 The company may at any time add to or alter this policy by written notice.

1   The employer should display this policy on notice boards at its place of work and its staff intranet, as well as proving it to all employees, workers and volunteers, which it may do either as part of the employment manual (see precedent 7, [10–097]) or a stand-alone policy statement.

   It is an offence under the Safeguarding Vulnerable Groups Act 2006 for (a) an employer to employ a person to work with children or vulnerable adults unless the latter is registered with the Independent Safeguarding Authority ('ISA') set up under the Act, and (b) an unregistered person to work with children or vulnerable adults. Under the Vetting and Barring Scheme (VBS), ISA establishes and maintains lists of persons barred from carrying out 'regulated activity', a 'Children's Barred List' and an 'Adults' Barred List'. These lists do not replace Criminal Record Bureau disclosure. Persons wanting to work with children and vulnerable adults will be able to register with, and be checked by, the VBS from July 2010, and from November 2010 all new employees and volunteers doing such work must be registered and it will be illegal to employ people to do such work if they are not registered with ISA.

[10–676B]

2See precedent 26, [10–680].

25   Equal opportunities policy

[10–677]

Note The Equality Bill 2009 published on 27 April 2009 is expected, if the government meets its target, to receive Royal Assent in Spring 2010. Its main aim is to being all forms of discrimination into one piece of legislation.

27A   Retirement policy and ancillary documents

[10–685A]

Note By the Employment Equality (Age) Regulations 2006, SI 2006/1031, the UK government implemented the age aspect of the Council Directive 2000/78/EC establishing a general framework for equal treatment in employment and occupation. For a general equal opportunities policy see [10–677] and the note to it. Employers could rely on that alone, but because of the detailed procedures to be followed on retirement it is desirable to prepare a retirement policy and either distribute it or make available to employees. See also [10–088], note 28. Employers must be particularly aware that the statutory procedures for dismissal on retirement differ from those applicable on other dismissals (see [10–608]), which do not normally apply to retirement dismissals, unless (a) the employee shows that retirement at the reticent age was not the reason for the dismissal or (b) there is no retirement age.

[10–685B]

The regulations provide that all notices and decisions made and notified to the employee under this procedure must be in writing and dated. If this requirement is not met (for example, if one letter is not dated) this will constitute a breach of procedure and could result in a finding of automatic unfair dismissal.

STATEMENT THAT NO RETIREMENT AGE[1]

[10–685C]

The [*Party-A*] has no retirement age for its employees.

RETIREMENT POLICY[2]

(*name*) Ltd — retirement policy

Normal retirement age

The normal retirement age for all employees is [65 years of age[3] (*or*) as set out in your contract]. The date of retirement is [your 65th birthday (*or*) the [first (*or*) last] of the month in which you reached age 65].

You have the right to apply not to retire at your normal retirement age.

Retirement procedure and timetable

stage 1 Notification from us to you of your date of retirement and right to request not to retire.
    Six to twelve months before each intended date of retirement[4].

stage 2 Your request to us not to retire at that date.
    Three and six months before the intended date of retirement.

stage 3 Acceptance of your request or a meeting to discuss it.
    Reasonable period (usually within [ten] working days) of your request in stage 2.

stage 4 Appeal

Details of procedure

stage 1 We will write to you to inform you of the date on which you are due to retire and that you have the right to make a request not to retire. If we do not do so, you will have a right to make a request not to retire at any time during the six-month period up to and ending with the dismissal.[5]

stage 1 If you agree to retire at or before the intended retirement date.
Your employment will end on the intended date of retirement we notified to you. You are not obliged to notify us that you agree to retire, but would appreciate it if you do so.

stage 2 If you do not wish to retire at the intended date of retirement, you must write to (*name*) with a request that your employment will continue beyond your intended date of retirement:
(a)   indefinitely;
(b)   for a stated period; or
(c)   until a stated date.
You may only make one request not to retire in relation to any one intended date of retirement. You may not make a request:
(a)   in relation to an intended date of retirement that falls six months or less after a date previously identified as the intended date of retirement; or
(b)   in circumstances where you and we have agreed that your retirement will take place on a date earlier than the date previously identified as the intended date of retirement.

stage 3 acceptance of request
If we accept your request[6] (or if you and we agree a compromise solution), we will write to you as soon as reasonably practicable after the meeting (usually

within [five] working days) (or, if there is no meeting, after our consideration of your request and any representations made by you) to notify you:

(a)   that your request (or a compromise solution) has been accepted;

(b)   of the period for which your employment will continue (that is, indefinitely or for an agreed period, and in the latter case, stating the date on which that agreed period will end); and

(c)   if we agree to allow you to work beyond retirement but for a shorter period than the one proposed by you in your request, of your right to appeal our decision.

stage 3 meeting
If we do not accept your request, we will hold a meeting with you to discuss your request.
You must take all reasonable steps to attend the meeting and have the right to be accompanied at it. If for any reason the meeting cannot be held within a reasonable period (for example, because you are absent from work due to ill health), we may make a decision without holding a meeting but, before doing so, will give you the opportunity to make [written][7] representations and will take those into account when making the decision.

stage 3 refusal of request
If we refuse your request, we will write to you as soon as reasonably practicable after the meeting (usually within [five] working days) (or, if there is no meeting, after our consideration of your request and any representations made by you) to notify you:

(a)   that your request has been refused;[8]

(b)   that we wish to retire you;

(c)   the date of your retirement; and

(d)   your right to appeal against our decision.

stage 3 acceptance of our decision
Your employment will end on the date specified in the notice. You are not obliged to notify us that you accept our decision, but would appreciate it if you do so.

stage 3 appeal
If you wish to appeal, you must write to (*name*) [within [ten] working days of (*or*) as soon as reasonably practicable after][9] receipt of the decision. Your appeal should set out the grounds of your appeal.
We will either:

(a)   agree with you (without holding a meeting) that your employment will continue for the period requested by you; or

(b)   hold a meeting with you within a reasonable period after receiving your appeal (usually within [ten] working days) to discuss it. You must take all reasonable steps to attend the meeting. You have the right to be accompanied at the appeal meeting. If for any reason the appeal meeting cannot be held within a reasonable period (for example, because you are absent from work due to ill health), we have the right to make a final decision without holding an appeal meeting but, before doing so, will give you the opportunity to make representations and will take those into account when making the decision.

stage 3 appeal successful
If an agreement is reached or your appeal is successful, we will write to you as soon as reasonably practicable after the appeal meeting (usually within [five]

working days) (or if it does not hold a meeting, after its consideration of the request and any representations made by you) to notify you:

(a)   that your appeal (or a compromise solution) has been accepted; and

(b)   of the period for which your employment will continue (that is, indefinitely or for an agreed period, and, in the latter case, stating the date on which that agreed period will end).

stage 3 appeal fails

If your appeal is unsuccessful, we will write to you as soon as reasonably practicable after the meeting to notify you (usually within [five] working days):

(a)   that your request has been refused;

(b)   that we wish to retire you; and

(c)   the date of your retirement.

all meetings — right to be accompanied[10]

You have the right to be accompanied at any meeting under this Policy by a work colleague employed by us. He or she may address the meeting and confer with you during the meeting but cannot answer questions on your behalf.

If your companion cannot attend on the date set for the meeting, we will postpone the meeting as long as you propose an alternative date that is convenient for you, your companion and us and that falls within seven days of the original meeting.

[1]   One response to the age regulations is simply to remove the retirement age. This clause could be inserted in the terms of employment or employee manual in the place of the existing statements of an employee's retirement age: see [10–065], [10–193], [10–336], [10–337], [10–374] and [10–716].

[2]   This policy, the following specimen letters and the notes to them are based substantially on the precedents in the Encyclopaedia of Forms and Precedents. The policy reflects the full statutory requirements for dismissal on grounds of retirement, as set out in the Employment Equality (Age) Regulations 2006, SI 2006/1031. Note also that any breach, however minor, of the statutory procedure could result in a claim for unfair dismissal or age discrimination or both.

[3]   If there are different retirement ages for different groups of employees, set out the 'normal retirement ages' here.

[4]   If notification is not provided in accordance with paragraph 2 the employer is under a continuing duty to notify the employee of their right to request not to retire until the 14th day before dismissal. This would bring into question whether the reason for dismissal is 'retirement' and so bring potential unfair dismissal and age discrimination liability. The notification obligation applies at any intended date of retirement, ie each time a retirement process is commenced in relation to an employee, unless the process has already been followed in relation to the retirement and the retirement is taking place either: (a) less than six months after a date previously identified as the intended date of retirement; or (b) in circumstances where it has been agreed with the employee that the retirement will take place before the intended date of retirement.

[5]   The employee can also bring an employment tribunal claim for eight weeks' pay (subject to a statutory cap on a week's pay). If any such request is made, it is important to follow the remainder of this policy to avoid a finding of automatically unfair dismissal.

[6]   If the request is accepted, the employee's terms and conditions should remain as before, except that any provision relating to retirement age will cease to apply or will be set at a later date. An offer of continued employment conditional on new terms and conditions could amount to unlawful age discrimination. However, if the employee requests new terms, for example, a flexible working pattern, and the request is granted, the contract can be varied and there should not be any age discrimination issues. Note, however, that the fact that an employee signs up to a new contract does not preclude the possibility of a claim on the basis that a term of the contract is unlawful discrimination.

[7]   The legislation does not require the representations to be put in writing although it may be helpful to the Company: writing may therefore be requested but cannot be insisted upon.

[8]   There is no requirement to provide reasons for the refusal of a request (and ACAS's advice to give reasons 'to enable the employee to leave with dignity ...' could backfire if they are too

honest), but it is advisable to do so to defend other claims, for example, 'normal' unfair dismissal or that the refusal is contrary to the Sex Discrimination Act 1975 or Race Relations Act 1976.

9   The employee must appeal 'as soon as reasonably practicable' after receiving the employer's decision. The employer can stipulate a preferred timeframe for the appeal, but the employer must also consider requests made outside that timeframe because, if the request has been made 'as soon as reasonably practicable', and the employer refuses to hear the appeal, the employer will be in breach of the procedure, which could result in an automatically unfair dismissal and an age discrimination complaint.

10   Work colleague includes employees and workers (i e consultants, freelancers, etc) working for the Company. The right does not extend to trade union officials who are not employed by the employer.

LETTER INFORMING EMPLOYEE OF INTENDED DATE OF RETIREMENT ON REACHING THE NORMAL RETIREMENT AGE[1]   [10–685F]

(*to be printed on the company's headed notepaper*)

(*date*)[2]

Dear (*employee*),

Notice of Retirement

Our records show that you are due to be (*age*) years old on (*date*). As you are aware, this is our normal retirement age [for your position]. You are therefore due to retire on (*date*) (your 'intended date of retirement'), being [the day on (*or*) the end of the month in] which you will turn (*age*).

You have the right to apply to continue working beyond your intended date of retirement. If you wish to exercise this right, you must write[3] to (*insert details*) no later than three months before your intended date of retirement. If you do not apply within this time, you will lose your right to apply and you will be retired on your intended date of retirement. [Your request[4] must:

—   confirm that you wish to work beyond your intended date of retirement;

—   state that your request is being made under the Employment Equality (Age) Regulations 2006 Schedule 6 paragraph 5; and

—   confirm the period for which you wish to continue working (that is indefinitely, for a fixed period, or until a certain date).]

We will consider any request that you make in accordance with our retirement policy[5] set out in [our employment handbook]. Please note that, whilst we will consider your request, [we may refuse it for any reason and] there is no guarantee that it will be granted, so you should be prepared for the possibility that you may retire on your intended date of retirement.

If you wish to retire on your intended date of retirement, you do not need to take any action. Your employment will end on (*intended date of retirement*).

Yours sincerely,

(*signature*)

For and on behalf of (*company*)

1   This letter complies with the employer's obligations under the Employment Equality (Age)   [10–685G]
   Regulations 2006, SI 2006/1031, Sch 6, para 2. The letter must be sent six to twelve months before the employee's 'normal' intended date of retirement. If notification is not provided in accordance with these regulations the employer is under a continuing duty to notify the employee of his right to request not to retire until the 14th day before dismissal. If notification

is not provided this would bring into question whether the reason for dismissal is 'retirement' and so bring potential unfair dismissal and age discrimination liability.

2   It is important that the letter is dated, as this is a requirement of the procedure. If the letter is not dated in error, this is technically a breach of the procedure and could result in an automatically unfair dismissal and age discrimination complaint.

3   A request must be in writing.

4   Consider whether to include the wording in square brackets, which sets out the employee's obligations. If this wording is included in the policy, there is unlikely to be scope for a challenge to the request on the grounds that it is technically invalid. However, if this information is going to be requested in any event, it is more time efficient, and better practice, to ask for the information upfront.

5   For a form of retirement policy see [10–685C].

[10–685H]   LETTER INFORMING EMPLOYEE OF RETIREMENT WHERE THE COMPANY HAS NO NORMAL RETIREMENT AGE[1]

(*to be printed on the company's headed notepaper*)

(*date*)[2]

Dear (*employee*),

Notice of Retirement

[Further to our conversation on (*date*),] I am writing to inform you that you are due to retire on (*date*) (your 'intended date of retirement').

You have the right to apply to continue working beyond your intended date of retirement. If you wish to exercise this right, you must write[3] to (*insert details*) no later than three months before your intended date of retirement. If you do not apply within this time, you will lose your right to apply and you will be retired on your intended date of retirement. [Your request[4] must:

(a)   confirm that you wish to work beyond your intended date of retirement;

(b)   state that your request is being made under the Employment Equality (Age) Regulations 2006 Schedule 6 paragraph 5; and

(c)   confirm the period for which you wish to continue working (that is indefinitely, for a fixed period, or until a certain date).]

We will consider any request that you make in accordance with our [retirement policy[5]] set out in [the our employment handbook]. Please be aware that, whilst we will consider your request, [we may refuse it for any reason and] there is no guarantee that it will be granted, so you should be prepared for the possibility that you may retire on your intended date of retirement.

If you wish to retire on your intended date of retirement, you do not need to take any action. Your employment will end on (*intended date of retirement*).

Yours sincerely,

(*signature*)

For and on behalf of (*company*)

[10–685I]   1   This letter complies with the employer's obligations under the Employment Equality (Age) Regulations 2006, SI 2006/1031. As to the procedure to be followed under the Regulations see [10–685C].

2   It is important that the letter is dated, as this is a requirement of the procedure. If the letter is not dated in error, this is technically a breach of the procedure and could result in an automatically unfair dismissal and age discrimination complaint.

3   A request not to retire must be in writing.

⁴ Consider whether to include the wording in square brackets, which sets out the employee's obligations. If this wording is included in the policy, there is unlikely to be scope for a challenge to the request on the grounds that it is technically invalid. However, if this information is going to be requested in any event, it is more time efficient, and better practice, to ask for the information upfront.

⁵ For a form of retirement policy see [10–685C].

LETTER REJECTING A REQUEST NOT TO RETIRE AND CONFIRMING INTENDED DATE OF RETIREMENT¹

[10–565J]

(*to be printed on the company's headed notepaper*)

(*date*)²

Dear (*employee*),

Confirmation of retirement

Following our meeting on (*date*) to discuss your request not to be retired, we have rejected your request not to retire [for the following reason[s]:³

(insert reasons given, e g needs of business, costs, succession planning, nature of role, etc)]

We will therefore retire you on your intended date of retirement, which is (*date*).

You have a right to appeal this decision. If you wish to appeal you must write to (insert details) [as soon as reasonably possible (or) within [ten] working days].⁴ You have the right to appeal against this decision. If you appeal you must set out the grounds on which you are making the appeal.

Yours sincerely,

(*signature*)

For and on behalf of (*company*)

¹ This letter complies with the employer's obligations under the Employment Equality (Age) Regulations 2006, SI 2006/1031, Sch 6, para 7(6), (7)(b). As to the procedure to be followed under the Regulations see [10–685C].

[10–685K]

² It is important that the letter is dated, as this is a requirement of the procedure: SI 2006/1031, Sch 6, para 7(8). If the letter is not dated in error, this is technically a breach of the procedure and could result in an automatically unfair dismissal and age discrimination complaint.

³ There is no requirement to provide reasons for the refusal of a request. However, the Advisory, Conciliation and Arbitration Service ('ACAS') advises employers to give reasons 'to enable the employee to leave with dignity and help maintain good workplace relationships with other employees' and it is advisable to defend other claims, e g that the refusal is contrary to the Sex Discrimination Act 1975 or Race Relations Act 1976 (7 Halsbury's Statutes (4th Edn) Civil Liberties and Human Rights). It is acceptable to state in the policy that reasons will be provided, but this should only be done if this can be done in all cases.

⁴ The legislation states that the employee must appeal 'as soon as reasonably practicable' after receiving the employer's decision. The employer can stipulate a preferred timeframe for the appeal, but the employer must also consider requests made outside that time because, if the request has been made 'as soon as reasonably practicable', and the employer refuses to hear the appeal, the employer will be in breach of the procedure which could result in an automatically unfair dismissal and an age discrimination complaint.

LETTER REJECTING AN APPEAL AND CONFIRMING INTENDED DATE OF RETIREMENT¹

[10–685L]

(*to be printed on the company's headed notepaper*)

(*date*)²

Dear (*employee*),

Confirmation of retirement

Following our meeting on (*date*) to discuss your appeal against our decision relating to your request not to be retired, we have rejected your appeal [for the following reason[s]:[3]

(*insert reasons given*, e g needs of business, costs, succession planning, nature of role, etc)]

We will therefore retire you on your intended date of retirement, which is (*date*).

Yours sincerely,

(*signature*)

For and on behalf of (*company*)

[10–685M]   [1]   This letter complies with the employer's obligations under the Employment Equality (Age) Regulations 2006, SI 2006/1031, Sch 6, para 8(8), (9)(b). As to the procedure to be followed under the Regulations see [10–685C].

      [2]   It is important that the letter is dated, as this is a requirement of the procedure: SI 2006/1031, Sch 6, para 8(10). If the letter is not dated in error, this is technically a breach of the procedure and could result in an automatically unfair dismissal and age discrimination complaint.

      [3]   There is no requirement to provide reasons for the refusal of a request.

[10–685N] 27B Checklist for employers to preventing illegal working — guidance notes[1]

[10–685O] (*name*) Ltd — retirement policy

CHECKLIST (ILLEGAL WORKING) FOR INTERVIEWER OF PROSPECTIVE EMPLOYEES AND FOR RE-INTERVIEW OF EMPLOYEES WHERE REQUIRED

1 This procedure applies to all prospective employees[2].

It must be repeated in a re-interview before the end of each twelve month period for all employees who have produced a document or documents under List B.

2 Production of documents

Before the start of employment[3], require the prospective employee to produce any document or combination of documents (they must be originals, not copies) from

—   either List A[4] below,

—   or List B[5].

Employees who have produced a document or documents under List B must on re-interview be required to produce any document or combination of documents (they must be originals, not copies) from List B.

3 Examination of documents[6]

(a)   You must take all reasonable steps to check the validity of the documents and that they have not been tampered with.

(b) You must be satisfied that the any photographs is consistent with the appearance of the interviewee.

(c) You must be satisfied the dates of birth in any document are consistent across documents and correspond with the appearance employee.

(d) You must take reasonable steps to check that the interviewee is the rightful owner of the document. If, for instance, the interviewee gives you two documents which have different names, you must ask for a further document to explain this, eg a marriage certificate, a divorce decree, a deed poll or statutory declaration.

(e) You must check that any expiry dates have not been passed.

(f) You must check information showing the interviewee's entitlement to enter or remain in the UK and undertake the work in question. NB Nationals of the EEA (see below) are not restricted in their work but recent accession countries may be subject to registration and authorisations: see below

4 Copying and recording documents[7]

Documents produced must be copied in a format that cannot be altered and a record must be kept of them. The copies must be retained securely for a period of not less than two years after the employment has come to an end.

Documents should be copied in full, but if the document is a passport or other travel document, the following pages of that document are what needs to be copied.

(i) the front cover;

(ii) any page containing the holder's personal details including nationality;

(iii) any page containing the holder's photograph;

(iv) any page containing the holder's signature;

(v) any page containing the date of expiry; and

(vi) any page containing information indicating the holder has an entitlement to enter or remain in the UK and undertake the work in question.

You must also complete a record form for each interviewee.

EUROPEAN UNION AND EUROPEAN ECONOMIC AREA [10–685P]

Nationals of the following EEA countries can work in the UK without restriction, as also may nationals form Switzerland.

Austria, Belgium, Cyprus, Denmark, Finland, France, Germany, Greece, Iceland, Ireland, Italy, Liechtenstein, Luxembourg, Malta, Netherlands, Norway, Portugal, Spain. Sweden and the UK.

NEW EU COUNTRIES — ACCESSION STATES [10–685Q]

On 1 May 2004, ten new countries joined the European Union and became part of the EEA.

A Worker Registration Scheme monitors the participation of workers from eight of these countries in the UK labour market. Workers from these countries are entitled to work but should register with the Borders and Immigration Agency not later than one month after starting work. they will require evidence of the employment (contract of appointment letter) and the employer should take and retain a copy of the application form. These countries, the A8 Counties, are:

Czech Republic, Estonia, Hungary, Latvia, Lithuania, Poland, Slovakia and Slovenia.

For the other two, Bulgaria and Romania (the A2 Countries), there is requirement for authorisation to work and so workers from them must hold a valid accession worker authorisation document or evidence of exemption from authorisation, eg a registration certificate that they have unconditional access to the UK labour market.

[10–685R] LIST A

1   A passport showing that the holder, or a person named in the passport as the child of the holder, is a British citizen or a citizen of the United Kingdom and Colonies having the right of abode in the United Kingdom.

2   A passport or national identity card showing that the holder, or a person named in the passport as the child of the holder, is a national of the European Economic Area or Switzerland.

3   A residence permit, registration certificate or document certifying or indicating permanent residence issued by the Home Office or the Border and Immigration Agency to a national of a European Economic Area country or Switzerland.

4   A permanent residence card issued by the Home Office or the Border and Immigration Agency to the family member of a national of a European Economic Area country or Switzerland.

5   A Biometric Immigration Document issued by the Border and Immigration Agency to the holder which indicates that the person named in it is allowed to stay indefinitely in the United Kingdom, or has no time limit on their stay in the United Kingdom.

6   A passport or other travel document endorsed to show that the holder is exempt from immigration control, is allowed to stay indefinitely in the United Kingdom, has the right of abode in the United Kingdom, or has no time limit on their stay in the United Kingdom.

7   An Immigration Status Document issued by the Home Office or the Border and Immigration Agency to the holder with an endorsement indicating that the person named in it is allowed to stay indefinitely in the United Kingdom or has no time limit on their stay in the United Kingdom, when produced in combination with an official document giving the person's permanent National Insurance Number and their name issued by a Government agency or a previous employer.

8   A full birth certificate issued in the United Kingdom which includes the name(s) of at least one of the holder's parents, when produced in combination with an official document giving the person's permanent National Insurance Number and their name issued by a Government agency or a previous employer.

9   A full adoption certificate issued in the United Kingdom which includes the name(s) of at least one of the holder's adoptive parents when produced in combination with an official document giving the person's permanent National Insurance Number and their name issued by a Government agency or a previous employer.

10   A birth certificate issued in the Channel Islands, the Isle of Man or Ireland, when produced in combination with an official document giving the person's permanent National Insurance Number and their name issued by a Government agency or a previous employer.

11   An adoption certificate issued in the Channel Islands, the Isle of Man or Ireland, when produced in combination with an official document giving the person's permanent National Insurance Number and their name issued by a Government agency or a previous employer.

12   A certificate of registration or naturalisation as a British citizen, when produced in combination with an official document giving the person's permanent National Insurance Number and their name issued by a Government agency or a previous employer.

13   A letter issued by the Home Office or the Border and Immigration Agency to the holder which indicates that the person named in it is allowed to stay indefinitely in the United Kingdom when produced in combination with an official document giving the person's permanent National Insurance Number and their name issued by a Government agency or a previous employer.

LIST B   [10–685S]

1   A passport or travel document endorsed to show that the holder is allowed to stay in the United Kingdom and is allowed to do the type of work in question, provided that it does not require the issue of a work permit.

2   A Biometric Immigration Document issued by the Border and Immigration Agency to the holder which indicates that the person named in it can stay in the United Kingdom and is allowed to do the work in question.

3   A work permit or other approval to take employment issued by the Home Office or the Border and Immigration Agency when produced in combination with either a passport or another travel document endorsed to show the holder is allowed to stay in the United Kingdom and is allowed to do the work in question, or a letter issued by the Home Office or the Border and Immigration Agency to the holder or the employer or prospective employer confirming the same.

4   A certificate of application issued by the Home Office or the Border and Immigration Agency to or for a family member of a national of a European Economic Area country or Switzerland stating that the holder is permitted to take employment which is less than 6 months old when produced in combination with evidence of verification by the Border and Immigration Agency Employer Checking Service.

5   A residence card or document issued by the Home Office or the Border and Immigration Agency to a family member of a national of a European Economic Area country or Switzerland.

6 An Application Registration Card issued by the Home Office or the Border and Immigration Agency stating that the holder is permitted to take employment, when produced in combination with evidence of verification by the Border and Immigration Agency Employer Checking Service.

7 An Immigration Status Document issued by the Home Office or the Border and Immigration Agency to the holder with an endorsement indicating that the person named in it can stay in the United Kingdom, and is allowed to do the type of work in question, when produced in combination with an official document giving the person's permanent National Insurance Number and their name issued by a Government agency or a previous employer.

8 A letter issued by the Home Office or the Border and Immigration Agency to the holder or the employer or prospective employer, which indicates that the person named in it can stay in the United Kingdom and is allowed to do the work in question when produced in combination with an official document giving the person's permanent National Insurance Number and their name issued by a Government agency or a previous employer.

[10–685T] 1 On 29 February 2008 ss 15–25 of the Immigration, Asylum and Nationality Act 2006 came into force, replacing the Asylum and Immigration Act 1996, s 8. Employers of illegal migrants who started work before 29 February 2008 remain liable for prosecution under the Asylum and Immigration Act 1996, but any statutory defence established under s 8 of that Act will remain as long as the person's employment continues.

By s 15(1) of the Immigration, Asylum and Nationality Act 2006 'it is contrary to this section to employ an adult subject to immigration control if he has not been granted leave to enter or remain in the United Kingdom, or his leave to enter or remain in the United Kingdom is invalid, has ceased to have effect (whether by reason of curtailment, revocation, cancellation, passage of time or otherwise), or is subject to a condition preventing him from accepting the employment'. An employer who acts contrary to this section may be made liable to a penalty not exceeding the prescribed maximum (£10,000, SI 2008/132, reg 2), but may be excused if he shows that he complied with any prescribed requirements in relation to the employment. The Immigration (Restrictions on Employment) Order 2007, SI 2007/3290, which came into force on 29 February 2008, reg 3 prescribes that an employer is excused from paying a penalty (1) if the employee produces any of the documents in list A in the schedule to the regulations and the employer complies with reg 6 of them. By reg 4 the employer may be excised for twelve months if the employee produces any of the documents in list B and the employer complies with reg 6. There is no statutory obligation for the employer to make any checks, but he will not have an excuse if he does not establish it before the start of the employment. The checks are no excuse from prosecution if the employer knows that the employee is not permitted to do the job and may be prosecuted under s 21.

For further guidance see http://www.ukba.homeoffice.gov.uk/employers (accessed 04/10/09).

2 An employer who applies these checks selectively may be guilty of racial discrimination: Race Relations Act 1976, s 4(1)(a). It is safer to apply it to all applicants.

3 Where employees transfer under TUPE, the document check must be made by the new employer within the 28 days following the transfer.

4 This list applies to persons who are not subject to immigration control of have no restriction on their stay in the UK. An excuse established on the basis of List A lasts for the whole of the person's employment.

5 This list applies to person whose stay in the UK is time limited. The check must be repeated at least once in every year in order for the excuse to be retained.

6 The requirements under this and the 'copying' heading are based on the requirements listed in SI 2007/3290, reg 6 and guidance issued by the Home Office (UK Border Agency) at www.ukba.homeoffice.gov.uk/sitecontent/documents/employersandsponsors/preventingillegalworking/.

7 See note 6 above.

[10–685U]

27C   Record form of interview to avoid illegal working[1]

(*name*) Ltd

Record of interview and documents produced and copied pursuant to the Immigration, Asylum and Nationality Act 2006

1	date of interview	
2	place of interview	
3	name of interviewer	
4	name of interviewee	
5	address of interviewee	
6	title of job offered	
7	if interviewee is for new employment, intended start date	
8	if interviewee is an existing employee a) start date of employment b) date of previous interview	
9	nationality of interviewee	
10	documents produced by interviewee NB these must be one or more documents from either List A or List B. See lists in guidance notes. Ring the number of each of the documents produced.	List A 1, 2, 3, 4, 5, 6, 7, 8, 9, 10, 11, 12, 13 List B 1, 2, 3, 4, 5, 6, 7, 8
11	Details of any other documents produced by the interviewee.	
12	Write 'Yes' in the right column to indicate that the documents produced were originals.	
13	Write 'Yes' in the right column to indicate that the documents produced appear to be valid and not been tampered with. Otherwise write details in that column	
14	Write 'Yes' in the right column to indicate that you have confirmed with the interviewee that the documents are his or hers and a note of anything said in support.	

15	Write 'Yes' in the right column to indicate that any photographs in the documents are consistent with the appearance of the interviewee. If not consistent, not the fact in that column.	
16	Write 'Yes' in the right column to indicate that any dates of birth in the documents are across documents and with the appearance of the interviewee. If not consistent, not the fact in that column.	
17	Write 'Yes' in the right column to indicate that any expiry dates in the documents produced have not passed. Otherwise write details in that column	
18	Write 'Yes' in the right column to indicate that you have checked in the documents produced the interviewee's entitlement to enter or remain in the UK and undertake the work in question. Otherwise write details in that column	
19	If you have any grounds for doubting the interviewee's entitlement entitlement to enter or remain in the UK and undertake the work in question, write details in the right column.	
20	signature of interviewer	

[10–685V] [1] See precedent [10–685N] above and the notes to it. Although this has been prepared as a stand-alone form it may be incorporated in the employers other interview forms.

[10–686] PART V: WORKING TIME DOCUMENTS

[10–687] ## 28 Agreement to disapply the 48-hour maximum working week[1]

[10–688] [1] This agreement is made under regs 4(1) and 5 between the employer and the individual worker. There is no need for a relevant agreement, or a collective or workplace agreement, but nothing prevents this disapplication from being dealt with by one of these agreements. NB: There is no provision to contract out cf reg 5A (inserted by SI 2002/3128) under which a young person's working time shall not exceed eight hours a day or 40 hours a week. The

Working Time (Amendment) Regulations 2009, SI 2009/1567, amends reg 25A of the 1998 Regulations (as inserted by SI 2003/1684) by increasing the maximum working week for trainee doctors employed in the bodies listed in the new Sch 2A from 48 to 52 to hours with effect from 1 August 2009 to 31 July 2011.

2 'Employee' is the expression more usually used in employment documents and will usually be appropriate, but the regulations use 'worker'.

29 Workforce agreement

[10–689]

SCHEDULE [11] – ANNUAL LEAVE[9]

[regs 13, 14 and 15] [NB this may be in any other relevant agreement]

[10–701]

The start date for the holiday year shall be (date).

The amount of holiday pay in lieu of holidays at end of employment shall be calculated as follows.

(a)   If, when the worker's employment is terminated, the number of days of main holidays which he or she has taken in the relevant year differs from his or her entitlement (calculated at [1 $\frac{1}{4}$ (*or*) 1 2/3^{rds} (*or*) 2 (*or*) 2 1/3rd] days for each complete month of employment in the holiday year), then, a payment for the number of days' difference will be either paid to him or her or refunded by him or her, depending whether the amount actually taken is less or greater than his or her entitlement. The amount paid or refunded will be the number of days difference multiplied by the daily equivalent of the worker's annual basic salary (on the basis of [240 (*or*) 365] days a year).

(b)   The worker will not be entitled to a payment under sub-paragraph (a) if the Company is entitled to and does terminate his or her employment summarily or if he or she refuses to take any holiday entitlement during his or her notice period.

(*or*)

The amount of holiday pay in lieu of holidays at end of employment shall be calculated in accordance with each worker's contract.

1   Workforce agreements, when first introduced, were a means of disapplying some of the provisions of the Working Time Regulations 1998, SI 1998/1833, reg 23, but their application has been extended to the following:

[10–702]

— Merchant Shipping and Fishing Vessels (Health and Safety at Work) (Employment of Young Persons) Regulations 1998, SI 1998/2411 (permitting young person to work in rest periods);

— Maternity and Parental Leave etc Regulations 1999, SI 1999/3312 (alternative provisions for parental leave);

— Fixed-term Employees (Prevention of Less Favourable Treatment) Regulations 2002, SI 2002/2034 (modify the effect of successive fixed term contracts);

— Merchant Shipping (Hours of Work) Regulations 2002, SI 2002/2125 (exceptions to minimum hours of rest);

— Merchant Shipping (Working Time: Inland Waterways) Regulations 2003, SI 2003/3049 (definition of night worker and agreeing a reference period other than 17 weeks);

— Civil Aviation (Working Time) Regulations 2004, SI 2004/756 (definition of working time);

— Fishing Vessels (Working Time: Sea-fishermen) Regulations 2004 SI 2004/1713 (definition of night worker); and

— Road Transport (Working Time) Regulations 2005 SI 2005/639 (to agree a reference period other than 17 days, extend a reference period or extend a period of night work beyond ten hours).

The conditions for a workforce agreement are contained in Sch 1 to the Working Time Regulations, which are repeated the other regulations. Each of the working time matters capable of being dealt with by a workforce agreement are dealt with in a separate schedule in this precedent. All these matters may also be dealt with by a collective agreement. A workforce agreement maybe made only for workers, whose terms and conditions are not provided for, wholly or in part, by a collective agreement. In addition certain matters may also be dealt by a relevant agreement, as indicated where applicable in the schedules to this precedent. A relevant agreement is defined in reg 2 as a workforce agreement, a collective agreement 'or any other agreement in writing which is legally enforceable as between the worker and his employer'. The matters, which are not so indicated can be dealt with only by a workforce or collective agreement.

2   The default night time is from 11 pm to 6 am: reg 2(1).
3   The default reference periods for the calculation of average weekly hours and night workers' average normal hours are any periods of 17 weeks: regs 4(3)(b) and 5(3)(b).
4   The default night hours are eight in each 24 hours averaged over the reference period (normally 17 weeks): reg 6(1).
5   The default night hours in these circumstances are eight in each 24 hours and averaging is not allowed.
6   The default daily rest period for adults is eleven consecutive hours in every 24 hours: reg 10(1).
7   The default weekly rest periods are an uninterrupted 24 hours in each seven-day period or two 24-hour periods or one 48-hour period in each 14-day period: reg 11(1), (2).
8   The default rest breaks for adult workers are 20 minutes uninterrupted and if possible away form the workstation if the daily working time is over six hours.
9   The minimum of four weeks (increased for any holiday year beginning after 23 November 1999 from three weeks) is the only right under the regulations which cannot be disapplied. The election promise by Tony Blair in March 2005 (to ensure workers get bank holidays on top of paid leave if Labour won the next general election) was not wholly implemented. The Working Time (Amendment) Regulations 2007, SI 2007/2079, made pursuant to the Work and Families Act 2006, s 13, inserts a new reg 13A into the Working Time Regulations 1998, which increases a worker's annual leave entitlement from four to 5.6 weeks, an increase of eight days for a full time worker. This is introduced in two stages: the first 0.8 weeks applied from 1 October 2007, and the second will apply from 1 April 2009. A new reg 26A is added to the existing regulations to provide that reg 13A does not apply to a worker whose employer already provides an entitlement to additional annual leave of 1.6 weeks or 8 days (whichever is the lesser), as at 1 October 2007, by virtue of a relevant agreement. Only (broadly speaking) the holiday year, the timing of holiday and the calculation of pay in lieu of holiday on the termination of employment can be disapplied. The default holiday year is each year starting on 1 October 1998 or, if later, the date on which the worker starts employment: reg 13(3)(b). The default formula for pay in lieu of holiday is a time apportionment according to the formula in reg 14(3). In default of agreement on the times when holidays are taken, the notice procedure in precedent [10–703] will apply. The [1 ¼ (*or*) 1 2/3rds (*or*) 2 1/3rd] days in sub-paragraph relate to statutory annual leave of 3, 4, 4.8 and 5.6 weeks respectively at five days per week. Employees on long-term sick leave, who were not in receipt of any pay, were entitled to present claims to an employment tribunal for unlawful deduction of pay, when their employer dismissed them without a payment in lieu of annual holidays not taken: *Revenue and Customs v Stringer (sub nom Ainsworth v IRC)* [2009] UKHL 31, [2009] ICR 985.

12 Partnership

PRELIMINARY NOTES

AGE DISCRIMINATION

Retirement from partnership is dealt with in two specimen clauses, clause 24 [12-039] in precedent 2 (Partnership deed between persons setting up in business as a new partnership) [12-006] and clause 25 [12-082] in precedent 4 (Limited liability partnership agreement) [12-064]. The latter is linked to the following footnote:

12 The Employment Equality (Age) Regulations 2006, SI 2006/1031 (Age Regulations), as amended by SI 2006/2408, came into force for all purposes except pensions on 1 October 2006 and, by reg 17, apply to partnership as well as employment. While 65 (or over) may be a compulsory retirement age for employees, subject to their right to ask to work beyond that age, there is no corresponding provision for partnership. It is probably safer to omit this clause.

[12-000]

A little guidance on the application of these regulations to partnerships was given in the employment tribunal decision in *PJ Bloxham v Freshfields Bruckhaus Deringer* LTL 22/10/2007. The tribunal found that the reorganisation of the respondent's pension scheme for partners, to establish a more sustainable balance between active and retired partners, was a legitimate aim and that the 20% reduction suffered by the complainant by retirement at age 54 compared with a partner retiring at age 55 was not disproportionate. By reg 3 of SI 2006/1031, a person discriminates against another if, amongst other matters, he treats he treats that person less favourably than others on the grounds of his age and he 'cannot show the treatment or ... to be a proportionate means of achieving a legitimate aim'.

PRECEDENTS

PART I: ORDINARY PARTNERSHIPS

1   A partnership contract, in common with most other types of contract, may be formed in writing, orally or by conduct. In the absence of agreement on some other terms, partnerships are governed by the Partnership Act 1890, but their terms may be varied by the consent of all the partners (as any other contract may be varied): see Partnership Act 1890, s 19 which provides: 'The mutual rights and duties of partners, whether ascertained by agreement or defined by this Act, may be varied by the consent of all the partners, and such consent may be either express or inferred from a course of dealing.' In *Rajendra Chhotabhai Patel v (1) Euro Investments (UK) Ltd* [2005] EWHC 1075 (Ch), [2005] All ER (D) 438 (May), the claimant, who relied on oral evidence, failed to establish the existence of a partnership of any other interest in a disputed property. However, in *Rees v Dartnall* [2009] All ER (D) 244 (Feb) the fact that the two parties were joint signatories on business accounts and shared profits equally was sufficient to establish that they had been partners in a building merchant business. Proof of the existence of the partnership is the fact that the parties carry on a business in common, not the agreement to set up a business: *Khan v Miah* (1997) Times, 31 December, CA. This is the shortest practicable form of agreement and is intended for use where the Partnership is

[12-004]

governed principally by the Partnership Act 1890, but a 'bit of paper' is required to evidence its existence and, possibly, the shares of the parties, which, unless otherwise agreed, are equal.

PART II: LIMITED PARTNERSHIPS

[12-063A] **Note** References in the LLP precedents and the notes to them to the Companies Act 1985 remain unchanged for the time being. See Companies Act 2006 (Commencement No 3, Consequential Amendments, Transitional Provisions and Savings) Order 2007, SI 2007/2194, reg 12 (general savings) of which (2) reads 'Nothing in this Order affects any provision of the 1985 Act or the 1986 Order as applied by the Limited Liability Partnerships Regulations 2001 or the Limited Liability Partnerships Regulations (Northern Ireland) 2004 to limited liability partnerships'. There is a similar provision in reg 12 of the No 5 commencement order, SI 2007/3495.

[12-095]   1   The Limited Liability Partnerships Act 2000 created a new form of legal entity know as a limited liability partnership, which is a body corporate separate from its members and has unlimited capacity: LLPA 2000, s 1. The law relating to partnership does not apply to a limited liability partnership: LLPA 2000, s 1(5). The LPA 2000 and the Limited Liability Partnerships Regulations 2001, SI 2001/1090 envisage that the members will enter into a limited liability partnership agreement, but it is not obligatory to do so. The regulations have their main effect by amendments which they make, in relation to LLPs, of the applicable provisions of the Companies Act 1985. In default of agreement, the mutual rights and duties of the members and of the partnership and its members are governed by regs 8 and 9 of SI 2001/1090: LLPA 2000, s 5.

Two or more persons associated for carrying on a lawful business with a view to profit may form an LLP by subscribing their names to an 'incorporation document' (form IN01) and registering it with the Registrar of Companies. The LLP is incorporated by registration by the Registrar and the issue of a certificate of incorporation: guidance notes are published under the heading 'Guidance Booklets and FAQs' at www.companies-house.gov.uk.

In *Kovats v TFO Management LLP* [2009] ICR 1140, [2009] All ER (D) 116 (May), in which the claimant, who had entered into a deed of accession to join a limited liability partnership and had been removed from the partnership, claimed to have been unfairly dismissed, the EAT upheld the employment tribunal's decision that he was a partner in the partnership and, having considered the common law test, he was not an employee. See also the Limited Liability Partnerships Act 2000, s 4(4).

[12-124]   1   See notes at [12-055].

The Partnership must be registered with the Registrar of Companies, Companies House, Crown Way, Maindy, Cardiff. Registration is effected by filing application (Form No LP5), and in the event of a change in any of the details a further statement (Form No LP6) must be filed; Limited Partnership Rules 1907, SR&O 1907/1020 amended by Limited Partnerships (Amendment) Rules 1974, SI 1974 No 560. The Legislative Reform (Limited Partnerships) Order 2009, SI 2009/1940, aims to clarify the process by the insertion into the Limited Partnership Act 1907 of new sections 8, 8A, 8B and 8C and the amendment of s 5, with effect from 1 October 2009 for limited partnerships for which registration applications are received on or after that day.

[12-184]   # Prescribed forms[1]

Note The prescribed forms, which are to be used for filing from 1 October 2009, may be accessed on the forms pages of the Companies House website at www.companieshouse.gov.uk (accessed 30 September 2009).

LIMITED PARTNERSHIPS

Form	Name of form	Previous form
LP5	Application for Registration of a Limited Partnership	—
LP6	Limited Partnership Statement	—

LIMITED LIABILITY PARTNERSHIPS

Form	Name of form	Previous form
LL IN01	Application for the incorporation of a Limited Liability Partnership (LLP)	LLP2
LL AP01	Appointment of member of a Limited Liability Partnership (LLP)	LLP2288a
LL AP02	Appointment of corporate member of a Limited Liability Partnership (LLP)	LLP288a
LL AP02	Appointment of judicial factor (Scotland) to a Limited Liability Partnership (LLP)	—
LL CH01	Change of details of a member of a Limited Liability Partnership (LLP)	LLP288c
LL CH02	Change of details of a corporate member of a Limited Liability Partnership (LLP)	LLP288c
LL CH03	Change of service address for a judicial factor (Scotland) of a Limited Liability Partnership (LLP)	—
LL TM01	Termination of appointment of member of a Limited Liability Partnership (LLP)	LLP288c
LL TM02	Termination of appointment of a judicial factor (Scotland) of a Limited Liability Partnership (LLP)	—
LL AA0I	Change of accounting reference date of a Limited Liability Partnership (LLP)	LLP225
LL AA02	Notice of removal of auditor from a Limited Liability Partnership (LLP)	LLP391
LL AD01	Change of Registered Office Address of Limited Liability Partnership (LLP)	LLP2287
LL AD02	Notification of the single alternative inspection location (SAIL) of a Limited Liability Partnership (LLP)	—
LL AD03	Change of location of the records to the single alternative inspection location (SAIL) of a Limited Liability Partnership (LLP)	—

LL AD04	Change of location of the records to the registered office of a Limited Liability Partnership (LLP)	—
LL AD05	Notice to change the situation of an England and Wales Limited Liability Partnership or a Welsh Limited Liability Partnership (LLP)	LLP287a
LL AR01	Annual Return of a Limited Liability Partnership (LLP)	LLP363
LL DE01	Notice of change of status of a Limited Liability Partnership (LLP)	LLP8
LL NM01	Notice of change of name of a Limited Liability Partnership (LLP)	LLP3
LL DS01	Striking off of application by a Limited Liability Partnership (LLP)	LLP652a
LL DS02	Withdrawal of striking off application by a Limited Liability Partnership (LLP)	LLP652c
LL LQ01	Notice of appointment of an administrative receiver, receiver or manager by a Limited Liability Partnership (LLP)	LLP405(1)
LL LQ02	Notice of ceasing to act as an administrative receiver, receiver or manager by a Limited Liability' Partnership (LLP)	LLP405(2)
LL RP01	Replacement of document not meeting requirements for proper delivery for a Limited Liability Partnership (LLP)	—
LLP RP02A	Application for rectification by the registrar of Companies for a Limited Liability Partnership (LLP)	—
LL RP02B	Application for rectification of a registered office address by the Registrar of Companies for a Limited Liability Partnership (LLP)	—
LL RP03	Notice of an objection to a request for the Registrar of Companies to rectify the Resister for a Limited Liability Partnership (LLP)	—
LL VT01	Certified voluntary translation of an original document that is or has been delivered to the Registrar of Companies or a Limited Liability Partnership (LLP)	—
LL RT01	Application for administrative restoration of a Limited Liability Partnership (LLP) to the Register	—
LL MG01	Particulars of a mortgage or Charge created by a Limited Liability Partnership (LLP)	LLP395
LL MG02	Statement of satisfaction in full or part of mortgage or charge by a Limited liability Partnership (LLP)	LLP403a

LL MG04	Application for registration of .a memorandum of satisfaction that part (or the whole) of the property charged (a) has been released from the charge: (b) no longer forms part of the Limited Liability Partnership's (LLP's) property	LLP403b
LL MG06	Particulars of charge subject to which property has been acquired by a limited Liability Partnership (LLP)	LL MG06
LL MG07	Particulars for the registration of a charge to secure a series of debentures by a Limited Liability Partnership (LLP)	LLP397
LL MG08	Particulars of an issue of secured debentures in a series by a Limited Liability Partnership (LLP)	LLP397a
LL MG09	Certificate of registration of a charge comprising property Situated in another UK jurisdiction by a Limited Liability Partnership (LLP)	LLP398
LLP446	Particulars of an instrument of alteration to a floating charge created by a Limited Liability Partnership registered in Scotland	LLP466
LL MG01s	Particulars of a charge created by a Limited Liability Partnership (LLP) registered in Scotland	LLP410
LL MG02s	Statement of satisfaction in full or part of a fixed charge by a Limited Liability Partnership (LLP) registered in Scotland	LLP419a
LL MG03s	Statement of satisfaction in full or part of a floating charge by a Limited Liability Partnership (LLP) registered in Scotland	LLP419b
LL MG04s	Application for registration of a memorandum of satisfaction that part (or the whole) of the property charged (a) has been released from the fixed charge: (b) no longer forms part of the Limited Liability Partnership's (LLP's) property by an LLP registered in Scotland	LLP419b
LL MG05s	Application for registration of a memorandum of satisfaction that part (or the whole) of the property charged (a) has been released from the floating charge: (b) no longer forms part of the Limited Liability Partnership's (LLP's) property by an LLP registered in Scotland	LLP419b
LL MG06s	Particulars of a charge subject to which property has been acquired by a Limited Liability Partnership (LLP) registered in Scotland	LLP416

LL MG07s	Particulars for the registration of a charge to secure a series of debentures by a Limited Liability Partnership (LLP) registered in Scotland	LLP413
LL MG08s	Particulars of an issue of secured debentures in a series by a Limited Liability Partnership (LLP) registered in Scotland	LLP413a

PART V: 24-HOUR RETIREMENT AND RETURN TO WORK — MEDICAL OR DENTAL PRACTICE

[12–195A] **Note** The principle of the 24-hour retirement rule is that a member of the NHS Pension Scheme to whom the policy applies may receive retirement benefits from the scheme (pension and tax free lump sum) and return to work if these two conditions are satisfied:

1   retirement from NHS work for not less than 24-hours; and
2   that the retired member does not work for more than 16 hours per week in the first month after the pension becomes payable.

The second condition is in reg S1(1) in National Health Service Pension Scheme Regulations 1995, SI 1995/300, as amended, which are the rules which govern the scheme. The first condition appears to have no statutory authority but to be an administrative rule adopted by the NHS Pensions Agency to determine whether or not a member has resigned. Although in the private sector an occupational pension scheme may permit a member to start to take pension benefits without retiring from his or her employment, it cannot be said with any degree of certainly that a member of the NHS Pension Scheme may be treated as retired is he or she has made arrangements in advance to return to work, despite what appear to be practices to the contrary by some Primary Care Trusts. For a more detailed discussion, see 24-Hour Retirement by the general editor in the New Law Journal of 17 October 2008.

It is suggested therefore that medical and dental practices, which wish to permit or encourage flexible retirement by the use of the 24-hour retirement rule, do no more that agree a policy (precedent 1 below) and that only if it has been agreed with the relevant PCT and the NHS Pensions Agency ought 24-hour retirement to be incorporated in enforceable provisions of the Partnership agreement (precedent 2 below).

[12–195B] ## 16   Policy statement for 24-hour retirement[1]

(*name*), (*name*) and Partners

[12–195C] ### 24-HOUR RETIREMENT

This is a policy statement by the Partners. It is not a term of the Partnership agreement and does not give or impose any rights or óbligations on the Partners or any of them.

1So far as is consistent with their obligations to their patients, the Partners support the principle of flexible retirement, under which Partners may:
(a)   retire when they wish;

(b)   work full of part time hours as an alternative to wholly retiring from the Partnership; and

(c)   (to the extent permitted by the NHS Pension Scheme) receive payments of and tax free lump sums from the Pension Scheme even if after retirement they return to full or part time work.

2The Partners recognise that the ability to return to work after starting to receive pension benefits under para 1(c) above depends on complying with the Scheme's 24-hour retirement rule. The principle of the 24-hour retirement rule is that a member of the NHS Pension Scheme to whom the policy applies may receive retirement benefits from the scheme (pension and tax free lump sum) and return to work if these two conditions are satisfied:

(a)   retirement from NHS work for not less than 24-hours; and

(b)   that the retired Partner does not work for more than 16 hours per week in the first month after the pension becomes payable ('the Pension Date').

3A Partner ('the Retiring Partner') who wishes to retire under the 24-hour rule and return to work after his or her pension becomes payable may state so in his or her notice of retirement with his proposals for:

(a)   the date of his or her return to work;

(b)   if that return is in less than one month after the Pension Date, the hours that he or she is to work during that month or the remainder of it;

(c)   the hours that he or she is to work after the end that month;

(d)   the his or her status and terms on return to work (for instance Partner on the same terms as before his retirement, Partner on different terms, employee, freelance);and

(e)   any other terms which he or she wishes to agree.

4The Partners and the Retiring Partner will negotiate with each other in good faith about the proposed retirement and return to work, including but not limited to the proposals in para 3 above with a view to reaching agreement about these matters.

5No decision is to be taken on any matter without undertaking any necessary consultation with and obtaining any necessary agreement with the PCT and the NHS.

6Unless the PCT and the NHS agree the Partners and the Retiring Partner will not before the Retirement Date seek or make any agreement about the Retiring Partner's return to work.

7The Retiring Partner may at any time withdraw his or her proposals fro return to work and exercise his or her rights to retire.

[1]   Even though in practice 24-hour retirement may be operated with the agreement of the NHS Pensions Agency and PCTs, when there has been prior agreement with the retiring partners for his or her return to work or arrangement with the PCT (eg for cover during the 24-hour retirement and the four part time weeks), it cannot be said with certainty that the retirement is effective. It is therefore prudent to avoid any agreement or arrangement for return to work before the retirement and to have no more than a non-binding statement of policy.   **[12–195D]**

17 Resolution adopting policy statement for 24-hour retirement[1]   **[12–195E]**

The partners resolved [unanimously (*or*) by (*number*) for and (*number*) against) to adopt the policy statement for 24-hour retirement produced [to the meeting (*or*) with this written resolution.]

[1] The policy may be adopted by the partners either outside the partnership agreement, as in this form, or incorporated in the agreement as in the following form.

[12-195G] ## 18   Clause in partnership agreement adopting policy statement for 24-hour retirement

x Schedule (*number*) to this agreement contains a statement of the Partners' policy for 24-hour retirement.

[12-195H] ## 19   Clause in partnership for 24-hour retirement[1]

[12-195I] **x.1** In this clause 'the Policy' means the policy statement for 24-hour retirement [adopted by the Partners on (*date*) (*or*) contained in schedule (*number*) to this agreement] and expressions defined in it have the same meaning in this clause.

[12-195J] **x.2** If a Retiring Partner wishes to start his pension from the NHS Pension Scheme and as a result of consultation under the Policy reach an agreement with the other Partners for his retirement and return to work and record it in a memorandum of agreement[2], they shall take all steps as are necessary to ensure that the Retiring Partner:
— retires from the Partnership at midnight at the end of the day agreed;
— returns to work on the day agreed, which must be not less than 24-hours after his retirement;
— notifies the partners of his or her Retirement Date;
— does not work in the Partnership more than 16 hours in each of the four weeks immediately following the Retirement Date;
— takes leave of absence on such terms as is agreed instead of working all or any of those weeks;
— works after the end of those weeks as agreed; and
— is remunerated for his work as agreed.

[12-195K] [1] Note the warning in the note in [12–224] against using this or any contract for 24-hour retirement. It would be prudent to seek the agreement of the NHS Pensions Agency and relevant PCT before agreeing terms such as this.
[2] Although this clause reads superficially like an agreement to agree, it is not. If a memorandum is agreed the parties will then by contractually bound by it. There are so many permutations of the basis of work, remuneration and work status, that it would be excessively complicated, if possible at all for them to be provided for in the agreement.

[12-195L] ## 20   Specimen memorandum of agreement for 24-hour retirement[1]

[12-195M] **Memorandum of agreement**

(*name*), (*name*) and Partners ('the Partnership') and (*name*) ('the Retiring Partner')

Date of retirement	(*insert date*)
Date of return to work	(*insert date*)

In respect of the first four weeks (numbered 1 to 4) after the Pension Date[2]

— the number of each the week in which the will work	(*eg*) [weeks 1, 2, 3 and 4 (*or*) weeks 3 and 4]
— the number of hours to be worked by the Retiring Partner in each week	(*eg*) [week 1 to week 4 sixteen hours (*or*) week 3 eight hours and week 4 sixteen hours]
— remuneration in each week	(*eg*) [normal partnership share in each week (*or*) one third of normal partnership share in each week (*or*) salary at the annual rate of £ (*amount*) in each week (*or*) nil in weeks 1 and 2 and normal partnership share in each of weeks 3 and 4]
— status of Retiring Partner	(*eg*) [partner (*or*) employee (*or*) independent contractor]
In respect of the period after the first four weeks after the Pension Date	
— the number of hours to be worked by the Retiring Partner in each week	(*eg*) [full time (*or*) sixteen hours (*or*) such hours [being not less than 16] as the Partners reasonably request]
— remuneration	(*eg*) [normal partnership share (*or*) one third of normal partnership share (*or*) salary at the annual rate of £(*amount*) in each week (*or*) £(*amount*) for each hour]
— status of Retiring Partner	(*eg*) [partner (*or*) employee (*or*) independent contractor]
Other terms	[*as appropriate*]
Standard terms[3]	This memorandum incorporates the provisions of the agreement dated (*date*) by which the Partnership is governed (*or*) the terms of employment of which a specimen is attached (*or*) (as appropriates)] as modified by this memorandum.

Dated (*date*)

(*signed by the partners or authorised signatory and the retiring partner*)

---

[1] This is the memorandum to be made under the provisions in a partnership agreement for retune to work (see [12-230] preamble) but it could also be adapted as a free-standing agreement to be made only after the retirement. **[12–195N]**

[2] Note that as this agreement is intended to be made before retirement, the retirement date will not be known. Hence the obligation in [12-230] on the retiring partner to notify the other partners of the date.

[3] The memorandum in not inclusive of all relevant terms and it may be useful to annex to it a specimen of the standard terms which will be applicable.

13 Sale of shares and businesses

PRELIMINARY NOTE

Companies Act

References in this chapter to the Companies Act 1985 or provisions in it should be read as references to the 2006 Act and its corresponding provisions.

PRECEDENTS

PART I: SALES OF BUSINESSES

[13–001] **1 Business Sale Agreement — short form (eg) between connected companies: no warranties[1]**

Employees[11]

[13–023] **15.1** The (*Party-A*) and the (*Party-B*) acknowledge and agree that the sale pursuant to this agreement will constitute a relevant transfer for the purposes of the Transfer Regulations and, accordingly, the contracts of employment of, and collective agreements relating to the Employees will be transferred to the (*Party-B*) pursuant to the Transfer Regulations with effect from the Completion Date.

[13–024] **15.2** Each of the (*Party-A*) and the (*Party-B*) undertakes to the other that it has complied with all of its obligations under regulations 11 and 13 of the Transfer Regulations and to compensate the other for all losses, claims, costs, charges and demands, proceedings or judgements (including legal costs) arising out of any failure by it to comply with its obligations pursuant to regulations 11 and 13 of the Transfer Regulations.

15.3 The (*Party-B*) agrees it shall be responsible for and indemnify the (*Party-A*) against all costs, expenses, liabilities, claims, rights of action, compensation, awards, damages, fines, penalties and interest arising from or in connection with the employment of the Employees, whether arising before or after the Completion Date.

VAT

[13–029] **19.1** The purchase price for the transfer of the Sale Assets is exclusive of value added tax but the parties shall use their best endeavours to obtain the relief available under article 5 of the Value Added Tax (Special Provisions) Order 1995, SI 1995/1268, as amended.

[13–030] **19.2** If the relief is not available then the (*Party-B*) shall pay to the (*Party-A*) a sum equal to the value added tax at the appropriate rate in respect of such of the Sale Assets as are chargeable to value added tax immediately on receipt by

(*Party-B*) of a relevant tax invoice and a copy of confirmation from HM Revenue and Customs that VAT is payable.

Schedule [1], [2], [3] etc

(*plant and machinery*)   [13–036]

(*stock and materials*)

(*debts due to the Seller*)

(*sale contracts, orders, etc*)

(*purchase, hire-purchase, maintenance contracts, etc*)

(*patents, trade marks, etc*)

(*insurance policies*)

(*debts due by the Seller*)

(*employees*)

(*pensions*)

Adapt the pensions schedule in [13-302] *and* (*because of the risks arising from Beckmann v Dynamco Whicheloe Macfarlane Ltd C-164/00, [2002] ECR I-4893 and Martin v South Bank University C-4/01, [2003] ECR I-12859*) *add the following, the first as an additional warranty and the second as an indemnity:*

2.x The (*Party-A*)'s [Pension] Scheme[s] provides no benefits and none of the Employees has in respect of any other occupational pension scheme the right to any benefits (in both cases) other than for old age, invalidity and survivors benefits within the meaning of regulation 10 of the [Transfer Regulations];

2.y The (*Party-A*) shall compensate the (*Party-B*) in full on demand for all claims made against the (*Party-B*) in respect of any liabilities incurred by it in respect of any rights of any [Employee] in respect of the (*Party-A*)'s [Pension] Scheme[s] or any other occupational pension scheme which are transferred under the [Transfer Regulations].

12 See [13-302] and the notes to it. If the transferor company is a participating employer in a   [13–038]
    multi-employer occupational pension scheme, which provides salary related benefits, and as a
    result of the transfer, the transferor ceases to employ anyone in active membership of the
    scheme, the transferor may become liable to a pay its proportion of the scheme's deficit
    calculated on a wind-up basis: Pensions Act 1995, s 75 (as amended by the Pensions Act 2004,
    ss 271(6), 320, Sch 13, Pt 1); Occupational Pension Schemes (Employer Debt) Regula-
    tions 2005, SI 2005/678 (as amended by SI 2008/731). See also [13–306], note 5 and
    www.law-office.co.uk pension law article 25 (accessed 30 September 2009).

PART II: SALES OF SHARES   [13–039]

4 Agreement for purchase of whole of share capital of   [13–078]
company — basic form — fixed price

Definitions

1 In this agreement the following terms shall have the following meanings.   [13–080]

'Companies Act'   means the Companies Act 2006.

Completion agenda

[13–086] **7.0** On completion:

7.1 the (*Party-A*) shall deliver to the (*Party-B*):
— the certificates for the Sale Shares and signed transfers of them in favour of the (*Party-B*) or its nominees;
— a waiver in the agreed terms by all the members of the (*Party-C*) of any pre-emption or other rights which they have in respect of shares in the (*Party-C*);
— the written resignation in the agreed terms of (*specify names*) as directors and the secretary of the (*Party-C*);
— compromise agreements in the agreed terms for the purposes of the Employment Rights Act 1996 confirming the termination of the employments of (*names*[4]) without claim against the (*Party-C*);
— the written resignation in the agreed terms of (*name*) as auditors of the (*Party-C*) in accordance with sections 516 to 522 of the Companies Act 2006; and
— the certificate[s] of incorporation [and on change of name], seal and statutory registers of the (*Party-C*).[5]

[13–116]   [3] Stamp duty will be payable on the share transfer forms at the rate of 0.5% of the purchase price payable rounded up to the nearest £5. Provisions in the Finance Act 2008 exempt from stamp duty transfers of shares which attract a fixed duty of £5 or ad valorem duty of £5; these are where the consideration is £1,000 or less. These changes apply to instruments executed on or after 13 March 2008 and not stamped before 19 March 2008.

[10] This version of the clause is required only if the minimalist warranties in [13-205] are used, and may not be necessary even then if the buyer will be able to procure the target to exercise its power to remove the existing trustees (other that the member nominated trustees) and appoint new ones. Where a separate pensions schedule is used, only the first version of this clause will be necessary.

[13–117]   ## 5   Agreement for purchase by working directors of shares owned by controlling directors who retire[1]

[13–133]   [2] This note, attached to clause 4 (repayment of loan) was about financial assistance under s 151 of the 1985 Act which had been repealed. As there is no prohibition of financial assistance in respect of private companies, the note has been deleted.

[13–134]   ## 6   Option for purchases of shares

[13–147]   [1] This note, attached to clause 3 (grant of option – conditional on repayment of loan) was about financial assistance under s 151 of the 1985 Act which had been repealed. As there is no prohibition of financial assistance in respect of private companies, the note has been deleted.

PART III: ANCILLARY DOCUMENTS

[13–148]   ## 7   Specimen warranties by sellers of shares [or assets]

Returns

[13–158]   **10** The (*Party-C*) has made all proper returns and has supplied all relevant information to the HM Revenue and Customs authorities and to the appropriate authorities under the National Insurance Acts and there is no dispute or contemplated dispute at the date of this agreement with any such authorities.

Reconstructions and amalgamations

23 The (*Party-C*) has not obtained relief from stamp duty under the Finance   [13–171]
Act 1986, sections 75 or 76 (acquisitions: relief).

Returns

36 *Deleted*   [13–184]

PART 3: COMPANIES ACTS

37 All documents required by the Companies Acts to be filed with the   [13–185]
Registrar of Companies have been duly filed and that the Acts have been duly
complied with by the (*Party-C*).

38 The copy of the memorandum and articles of association of the (*Party-C*)   [13–186]
which are annexed to the Disclosure Letter are accurate and complete in all
respects and has embodied in it or annexed to it a copy of all resolutions and
agreements referred to in section 36(1) of the Companies Act 2006.

40 The (*Party-C*) has not received any notice of any application or intended   [13–188]
application under the provisions of the Companies Acts for the rectification
of its register of members.

46 The only directors of the (*Party-C*) (including persons deemed by sec-   [13–194]
tions 250 and 251 of the Companies Act 2006 to be a director) are the persons
whose name and address and other directorships are listed in schedule
(*number*) to this agreement.

104 No part of the Properties has been damaged as a result of mining   [13–252]
subsidence or is within the influencing distance of any past present or
proposed mineral workings.

105 The use of the Properties is in compliance with all requirements of the   [13–253]
planning legislation, the Factories Acts, the Health and Safety etc at Work
Act 1974, the Control of Asbestos Regulations 2006, SI 2006/2739 and the
Construction (Design and Management) Regulations 2007, SI 2007/320 (as
amended).

³   Section 108 of the Companies Act 1989 substituted new sections 35, 35A and 35B of the   [13–292]
Companies Act 1985 and substantially amended the doctrine of ultra vires. The commencement order has an explicit transitional and saving provision which preserves the status quo in
respect of any act by a company before 4 February 1991, consequently the doctrine of ultra
vires may not be relevant. Sections 35, 35A and 35B of the Companies Act 1985 were replaced
by sections 39 and 40 of the Companies Act 2006 with effect from 1 October 2009.

8   Schedule to agreement for sale of company: [13–293]
tax covenants¹

Definitions

Covenants by covenantors   [13–294]

3.3 In respect of payments made pursuant to the covenants contained within   [13–296]
paragraph 3 of this schedule:
(a)   all sums payable by the (*Party-A*) to the (*Party-B*) shall be paid free

and clear of all deductions, withholdings, set-offs or counterclaims whatsoever save only as may be required by law;

(b)   if any deductions or withholdings are required by any Taxation Authority law to be made from any sums, the (*Party-A*) shall be obliged to pay the (*Party-B*) such further amount as will, after the deduction or withholding has been made, leave the (*Party-B*) with the same amount as it would have been entitled to receive in the absence of such requirement to make a deduction or withholding; and

(c)   if any sum payable by the (*Party-A*) to the (*Party-B*) under paragraph 3 (including paragraph 3.2 and this paragraph 3.3) shall be subject by a Taxation Authority to taxation liability in the hands of the (*Party-B*), the (*Party-A*) shall pay to the (*Party-B*) such further sum equal to such taxation liability.

Financial time and other limitations

[13–299]   **6** The liability of the (*Party-A*) under paragraph 3 of this schedule shall be further limited or excluded in accordance with clause [14] (limitation of seller liability) of the agreement.

[13–302]   **9   Schedule to agreement for sale of company: pension and associated life assurance schemes or arrangements when members are to remain in seller's scheme for participation period[1]**

[13–306]   1   This schedule assumes that the target company and other subsidiaries of the seller participate in the seller's occupational pension schemes: the personal pension schemes, although expressed here to the seller's, are likely to 'belong' to the company. Where the employees in the target company are only part of the pension scheme membership and it is intended that they will remain in that scheme's membership for a limited period, it is usually convenient to include warranties and other necessary clauses in a separate pensions schedule. See [13-024]. As an alternative, when for instance only warranties are required, they could instead be included in the main warranties instead of a separate schedule: see [13-205] to [13-207]. Although there is a practice, particularly where the numbers involved are small or the scheme is not well funded, to provide expressly that the employees will cease to be members of the seller's scheme for the current service on completion, the buyer must beware of the risk that this, whether on completion or at an agreed later date, can trigger a debt on the employer: see [13–038] note 12 and note 3 below. This schedule may be adapted for use (a) where the target company is the principal employer (as in [13–205] to [13–207]) and (b) on the sale of assets. Express provisions for the calculation of transfer values are, in the present virtual absence of pension scheme surpluses, rare and usually unnecessary.

2   Any comforting but mistaken thought that occupational pension scheme were wholly exempt from transfer under TUPE were laid to rest by *Beckmann v Dynamco Whicheloe Macfarlane Ltd* [2002] ECR I-4893, [2002] All ER (EC) 865, followed by the similar case of *Martin and others v South Bank University* (Case C-4/01) [2003] ECR I-12859. In *Beckmann* the scheme provided a pension for members aged 50 and over with at least five years' service who were dismissed on certain grounds including redundancy. This was not a pension on age, invalidity or death, and so the obligation to provide this benefit passed under TUPE, even though no corresponding assets passed from the transferor's pension scheme. The *South Bank* case has been seen by some commentators to raise the spectre that ordinary early retirements might transfer under TUPE, but as these are ECJ decisions no one really know how they work in practice. See the editor's pension article 6 about them at www.law-office.co.uk.

3   Under the Occupational Pension Schemes (Employer Debt) Regulations 2005, SI 2005/678 an outgoing employer can be made liable for a share of the scheme's defect (see note 5). Former employers of a scheme in which there are no remaining members in active service are free from liability if the conditions in reg 9 are met.

4   For a note about the 'moral hazard' provisions of the Pensions Act 2004 see www.law-office.co.uk (pension article 28).

5   An employer leaving a pension scheme (ie ceasing to employ persons of the description of employment to which the scheme relates) becomes liable to a debt on the employer under section 75 of the Pensions Act 2004 unless steps are taken to employ a person who is in active service in the scheme (not likely to be practical in these circumstances), or one of several possible arrangements are made to deal with the debt: see pensions article 25 on www.law-office.co.uk (accessed 23 October 2009).

14 Assents

PRELIMINARY NOTES

FINANCIAL LIMITS ON INTESTACY

[14–000]   The former amounts of the surviving spouse's statutory legacy of £125,000 or, if there is no issue, £200,000 have been increased to £250,000 and £450,000 respectively in respect of deaths on and after 1 February 2009. The notes in [14–076] and paragraphs 1 and 2 in the notice in [14–117] are to be read and applied accordingly.

STAMP DUTY LAND TAX

Form SDLT 60 no longer exists and the references to it in [14–004] note 2 are to be ignored.

The note in [14–008] is replaced by the following.

[14–008]   There will be no stamp duty land tax on assents by deed as a result of the provisions of the Finance Act 2003, Sch 3, as amended. Where an SDLT is required, the form SDLT 1 must be completed by the person acquiring the interest certifying why no SDLT is payable. Stamp duty land tax came into force on 1 December 2003. As from 12 March 2008, an SDLT form is no longer required if the consideration for the transaction is under £40,000 (Finance Act 2003, s 77A(1), inserted by the Finance Act 2008, s 94(1), (2)). This should apply to most assents unless the beneficiary is paying a consideration. In that case it might be more appropriate to use a TR1.

16 Family

LASTING POWERS OF ATTORNEY

14 Each party shall execute an instrument in the form required by the Mental Capacity Act 2005 appointing the other party to be his or her attorney pursuant to that Act.[13]

[16–044]

[16–062]

1 Although this precedent is drafted to reflect the situation of cohabiting heterosexual couples there is no reason why it should not be adapted to suit the needs of gay or lesbian couples or any other family relationship, for example, a mother and son or two or more siblings.

2 This list can be amended indefinitely and could include holidays, joint recreation etc. Consider defining living expenses narrowly. Be wary of including variable items such as food, decorating etc which have no obvious reasonable limit.

3 To ensure a cohabitation agreement is enforceable basic contract law must be observed. The agreement needs to demonstrate an intention to create legal relations (hopefully implicit in the fact that the agreement is drawn up); show *consideration* (not necessary if drawn as a deed as anticipated here); be *certain* (clauses must be carefully drafted to avoid ambiguity of intention); include a severance clause to ensure if one clause fails for uncertainty the whole agreement is not rendered invalid; avoid duress/coercion (important to demonstrate on face of the agreement independent legal advice, arm's length negotiations and full and frank disclosure). The jurisdiction of the court cannot be ousted – any clause purporting to do so will fail.

4 For a specimen declaration of trust setting out beneficial interests see Trusts [19–233] or [19–252].

5 See the Law Reform (Miscellaneous Provisions) Act 1970, s 3 for the position in relation to gifts between engaged couples. If an engagement ring is a family heirloom it is an implied condition that it is not an absolute gift but conditional upon the marriage taking place. However, see *Cox v Jones* [2004] EWHC 1486 (Ch), [2004] 2 FLR 1010 where the judge rejected Mr J's argument that the engagement ring should be returned when the engagement was broken off.

6 The fact that a savings account is in the name of one cohabitant alone does not necessarily mean that the other has no claim to the funds or a share of the funds. In *Paul v Constance* [1977] 1 All ER 195, [1977] 1 WLR 527, CA, the words used by the account holder (that the money was as much his cohabitant's as his) were sufficient in the context of their relationship to constitute a declaration of trust.

7 Where contributions are unequal, in the absence of an express trust it may be possible to rebut the presumption of equal shares with evidence showing contrary intention. This clause therefore provides for any joint bank account to be expressly held by the parties as joint tenants. The rights of survivorship will therefore apply on death.

8 No attempt to regulate their own affairs can affect the liability of the parties either solely, or jointly and severally, as against the third party finance provider, hence the importance of obtaining an indemnity

9 See *Re Bishop, National Provincial Bank v Bishop Ltd* [1965] Ch 450, [1965] 1 All ER 249. It may be that if there is a joint mortgage, the building society or bank will require that repayments are made from a joint account.

10 See note 9 above.

11 But see the Life Assurance Act 1774, s 1 which requires the person for whose benefit a life assurance policy is made to have an insurable interest in the life assured; that is to say a financial interest. Married and engaged couples are seen to have an insurable interest but other relationships require an interest capable of valuation in financial terms and founded on a legally recognised obligation. This may be difficult to establish in a cohabiting relationship, although it is submitted that the duty to support is indirectly recognised by the upholding of trusts granting a share in property to a cohabitant who has contributed to its acquisition.

Cohabitants are establishing joint financial arrangements by virtue of the creation of an agreement between them. The mischief for which the 1774 legislation was intended was to prevent gambling on the death of another where there was no other interest. It is submitted that policies taken out by cohabitants are outside this and thus valid and legal. The difficulty if a policy is held to be void and illegal is that the policy holder may not be able to recover the premiums.

12 Benefits under personal pension schemes/retirement annuity contracts that arise in the event of the death of the policyholder prior to him/her drawing upon the fund can be written in trust. Some personal pension policies have a trust written into the scheme. In some cases the

scheme member would have already written death benefits under his or her personal pension policy/retirement annuity contract into a discretionary trust in which case the second option should be used.

13 If either party becomes seriously ill, the grant of a lasting power of attorney will enable the other to act on behalf of that party in relation to, for example, withdrawal of funds from a sole bank account or paying bills. The power may be revoked on the breakdown of the relationship. Note the obligation to register a lasting power of attorney if the party has become or is becoming mentally incapacitated. In contrast to enduring powers of attorney which lasting powers of attorney replace, these can now be registered immediately in the absence of incapacity. See Mental Capacity Act 2005.

14 This clause is included largely as an aide-memoire for advisers. Where there are children of the relationship, or a previous relationship, cohabitants may be advised as to the doctrine of mutual wills: see Trusts [19–278] for an agreement to make mutual wills and Wills [20–106] for a specimen mutual will; see also *Re Goodchild (decd), Goodchild v Goodchild* [1996] 1 All ER 670, [1996] 1 WLR 694. See also [16–099], note 4.

15 Note that since 1 January 1996 cohabitants of two years or more can now make a claim under the Inheritance (Provision for Family and Dependants) Act 1975, as well as in the capacity of dependant. Beware of the risk to the deceased cohabitant's estate resulting from a claim under the 1975 Act if inadequate provision is made for the surviving cohabitant. For courts' treatment of cohabitant claims under the Inheritance (Provision for Family and Dependants) Act 1975 post 1 January 1996 see *Re Watson (Deceased)* [1999] 1FLR 878 and *Gully v Dix* [2004] EWCA Civ 139, [2004] 1 FLR 918.

16 If the provisions of the deed were to continue on the marriage/civil partnership of the parties a pre-marital/pre-CIP agreement or contract would be created. Whilst presently such agreements are not binding see *K v K (Ancillary Relief): Pre nuptial Agreement* [2003] 1 FLR 120 and *Crossley v Crossley* [2008] 1 FLR 1467 for judicial moves towards greater respect for the terms of properly negotiated and drawn agreements. It is submitted that by analogy the same approach will be adopted to pre-CIPs on dissolution of civil partnerships.

17 The most important transitional provision on termination will be that governing rights of pre-emption or sale of jointly owned real property. For a declaration of trust between co-owners of property see Trusts [19–233] or [19–252].

18 The card owner will be the issuer of the card; e g the bank, building society or credit company.

19 Consider setting out the disclosure in summary form in an annexed schedule.

20 Historically cohabitation agreements would have been considered invalid on the grounds of immorality being against public policy, undermining marriage. Now it is unlikely enforcement by way of contract law would fail but see *Sutton v Mishcon de Reya* [2003] EWHC 3166 (Ch), [2004] 1 FLR 837 for enforceability of cohabitation agreements. Avoid making provision of sexual services or cohabitation itself the consideration for the agreement.

17 Gifts

PRELIMINARY NOTE

SETTLEMENTS

Under the new rules introduced in the Finance Act 2006 as from 22 March 2006 IHT may be payable: [17-007]

1   on the making of the settlement;[1]
2   for pre-22 March 2006 settlements on the death of a person beneficially entitled to an interest in possession;[2]
3   for pre-22 March 2006 settlements on the ending of the interest of such a person in his lifetime other than when he becomes absolutely entitled;
4   for post-21 March 2006 settlements on the making of a capital payment to a beneficiary under a discretionary or life interest settlement;[3]
5   on every tenth anniversary of the settlement of the property (excluding charitable, approved pension, trusts for bereaved minors and disabled persons trusts) at 30% of the rate which would be chargeable if the whole property had been distributed at that time ('the effective rate'). There is a reduction in the effective rate where the property within the trust has not been held within the trust for the whole of the ten year period; and
6   on the vesting of interests in pre-22 March 2006 accumulation and maintenance settlements from 6 April 2008 unless such trusts are brought to an end before 6 April 2008 or changed before that date so that they qualify for the new favoured tax treatment.

[1] From 22 March 2006 this would also include a lifetime life interest settlement for the benefit [17-008] of a spouse or civil partner. With effect from that date a person beneficially entitled to a life interest in a post-21 March 2006 settlement will not have that interest aggregated with his estate for IHT purposes unless the interest is:
(a) an immediate post death interest; or
(b) a disabled person's interest; or
(c) a transitional serial interest.
Instead the settlement will be taxed as though it were a discretionary trust.

[2] The pre-22 March 2006 rules continue to apply to life interests which were in existence at the time and will also apply to a life interest arising after 22 March 2007 but before 6 October 2008. This second life interest is known as the 'Second Serial Interest'.
[3] The exception to this are the trusts for bereaved minors or for a disabled person as defined in Sch 20 to the Finance Act 2006.

EXEMPTIONS, RELIEFS ETC

The following is a summary of the main current exemptions and reliefs: [17-009]

1   the band to which the nil rate of tax applies (from 6 April 2008 £312,000 and from 6 April 2009 £325,000);;
2   outright transfers between spouses (limited where the recipient spouse is non-UK domiciled) (IHTA 1984, s 18);
3   lifetime gifts to an individual (outright only), or to a disabled trust where the donor survives seven years (PETs);

199

4   transfers by any individual up to a total of £3,000 in any year with a carry forward of any unused balance for one year only (IHTA 1984, s 19);

5   regular gifts out of income which form part of the donor's normal expenditure (IHTA 1984, s 21) (see precedent [17–093]);

6   absolute lifetime gifts up to £250 to any individual (IHTA 1984 s 20);

7   gifts in consideration of marriage up to £5,000 by any parent of the parties, up to £2,500 by any party to the marriage or any remote lineal ancestor, and up to £1,000 in other cases (see precedent [17–016]) (IHTA 1984, s 22);

8   gifts in favour of the donor's children up to the age of 18 or undergoing full-time education for their maintenance, education or training (IHTA 1984, s 11);

9   gifts in favour of former spouses of the donor for their maintenance (IHTA 1984, s 11);

10   reasonable provision for a dependent relative (IHTA 1984, s 11);

11   100% or 50% reduction in value of qualifying business property or agricultural property as outlined above (the provisions relating to business property are contained within IHTA 1984, ss 103–114 and agricultural relief within ss 115–124);

12   woodlands under certain conditions (IHTA 1984, s 125);

13   national heritage, works of art etc (IHTA 1984, s 25);

14   charities (IHTA 1984, s 23);

15   limited relief for qualifying accumulation and maintenance settlements (IHTA 1984, s 71) following changes in Finance Act 2006. Settlements in existence before 22 March 2006 benefit from the old rules only until 5 April 2008. To continue to qualify for continued favourable status these settlements must be modified before 6 April 2008;

16   a deed of family arrangement or similar instrument made not more than two years after a death, which will result in IHT being payable as though the provisions of the deed were contained in the will, intestacy or otherwise. The parties must confirm in the variation that they wish the previous of these sections to apply (IHTA 1984, s 142); similarly for disclaimers made within two years of death (Disclaimers [20–164] and [20–166]);

17   property given to a legatee under a will subject to a wish that it be passed on to the others, if so passed on within two years of the death is treated as a gift by the testator and not two separate gifts (IHTA 1984, s 143);

18   transfer or failure of reversionary interests under settlements (see precedents [17–059] and [17–066]) (IHTA 1984, s 48);

19   protective trusts (IHTA 1984, s 88) if created before 22 March 2006;

20   trusts for disabled persons (see precedent [20–091]) (IHTA 1984, s 89, as amended by Sch 20 to the Finance Act 2006);

21   waiver of remuneration or dividend (IHTA 1984, ss 14 and 15); and

22   gifts to qualifying political parties (IHTA 1984, s 24).

CAPITAL GAINS TAX

[17–013]   [1]   The provisions of TCGA 1992, s 168 (Emigration of donee) should be noted. If the donee might emigrate within the time specified then a hold over election should not be considered unless adequate security for the donor can be given. In general hold over relief will not be available if the transfer is into a settlor interested trust. Taper relief applies to transaction up to 5 April 2008 to reduce the percentage of the chargeable gain subject to tax. From 6 April 2008 taper relief is no longer available.

STAMP DUTY AND STAMP DUTY LAND TAX

Most gifts will qualify for a complete exemption from stamp duty under the Stamp Duty (Exempt Instruments) Regulations 1987, SI 1987/516, provided a suitable certificate is included in the deed. The most frequently used category for the precedents in this section will be category L. If the gift is one of land, a stamp duty land tax form SDLT 1 must be completed to self certify that no stamp duty land tax is payable. If the land transaction is a gift the transaction will be exempt from stamp duty land tax under Sch 3, para 1 to the Finance Act 2003. As from 12 March 2008, an SDLT form is no longer required if the consideration for the transaction is under £40,000 (Finance Act 2003, s 77A(1), as amended by the Finance Act 2008, s 94). This should apply to gifts where there is valuable consideration for the gift. **[17–014]**

The change of form SDLT 60 to SDLT 1 applies also to [17–024] note 2, where it will be required if the consideration is over £40,000.

PRECEDENTS

2 Gift of land in consideration of marriage — registered title — modifications to HMLR form TR1[1] **[17–025]**

Note Because of a change in form TR1 references to Panels 9 and 12 are to Panels 8 and 11 in this precedent.[17–059]. **[17–025a]**

9 Gift by residuary beneficiaries (eg testator's children) of whole reversionary interest under wills to life tenant (eg surviving parent)[1] **[17–059]**

Note Because of a change in form TR1 references to Panels 9 and 12 are to Panels 8 and 11 in this precedent. **[17–059a]**

[1] The gifts of the reversionary interests are not chargeable transfers for IHT purposes since reversionary interests are generally exempt as 'excluded property' (IHTA 1984, s 48) and also no charge arises where the life tenant acquires such interests (IHTA 1984, s 53 subject to conditions introduced by the Finance Act 2006, Sch 20, Pt 3, para 14). Thus for post-22 March 2006 settlements there may be a charge to IHT where the life tenant acquires an interest under a settlement if the interest is not excluded property. If within two years of the death and the parties so elect an instrument varying the dispositions under a will may, for IHT purposes, be treated as contained in the will with IHT charged accordingly (IHTA 1984, s 142) but care must be taken to ensure the provisions of s 142 are met. **[17–065]**

Whilst interests under a trust or settlement are not chargeable assets for capital gains tax purposes there is a capital gains tax charge on all trust assets on an occasion when a person becomes absolutely entitled to such assets as against the trustee (TCGA 1992, s 71).

For a form where such a gift is made on intestacy and the assignment is made before the grant, see [17–085].

As equitable interests only are dealt with by this deed, it should be kept off the title. Notice of the assurance should be given to the personal representatives as soon as they have proved the will, or, if probate has been granted before the deed is executed, immediately after execution. The deed should be followed by a simple assent or transfer by the personal representatives, vesting the real estate in the donee (see Administration of Estates Act 1925, s 36). For an assent, see Assents [14–019]. If, however, the real estate has already been vested in the spouse as tenant for life pursuant to s 6(b) of the Settled Land Act 1925, a declaration of discharge by the trustees of the settlement will be required (see Settled Land Act 1925, s 17(1)).

2   The gift to the surviving spouse in the will is exempt from IHT provided it qualifies as an immediate post death interest (IPDI). Note the conditions that are quoted under the new s 49A of IHTA, 1984 introduced by the Finance Act 2006.

[17–085] ## 12   Assignment to the widow by other statutory beneficiaries under intestacy of all their shares and interests in the intestate's estate before grant of administration¹

[17–092] ¹   See [17-065], note 1 for IHT implications. With effect from 22 March 2006 the life interest trusts arising under an intestacy will qualify as an IPDI. The assignment here made is not new in form but it was the practice at one time to leave such assignments until after the grant had issued. Now in certain cases it is found more convenient to execute the assignment before the grant. The cases in question are those where the effect of the assignment is to merge the widow's life interest in the interests vested in her by the assignment so that she becomes absolutely entitled to the estate. Where this is so the grant can go to one administrator, who will in general be the widow and the administration of the estate is in consequence much simplified. The Probate Registry has by the issue of a direction removed all difficulty in the matter. The first difficulty was this: a subsequent purchaser finding a grant to one adminis-trator in respect of an estate valued at over £125,000 (this increased to £250,000 from 1 February 2009) where the intestate leaves issue or £200,000 (this increases to £450,000 from 1st February 2009) where there is no issue would probably raise objections on the ground that it was not clear that this was not a case in which the law required two administrators. It is probable that a purchaser is protected in such a case by the provisions of the Law of Property Act 1925, s 204(1), and see *Hewson v Shelley* [1914] 2 Ch 13, CA, and compare *Re Bridgett and Hayes' Contract* [1928] Ch 163, [1927] All ER Rep 191. But the precise effect of this section is not too clear on the authorities, see the decision in *Jones v Barnett* [1900] 1 Ch 370, CA. However, this matter has been avoided by a direction of the Registrar that the grant is to recite the assignment so that the reason for and the propriety of the grant to one administrator are apparent on the grant and on this point the purchaser will clearly have no ground for raising any requisition. It is understood also that where the widow is the sole statutory beneficiary this will be made clear on the grant and any difficulty (not, of course, connected with any assignment) so arising will be removed at the same time. For a form where such an assignment is made after the grant, see [17-059] and [17-066].

18 Powers of attorney

PRECEDENTS

14   Lasting power of attorney

[18–089]

Note: The Mental Capacity Act 2005 (MCA 2005) came into force for most purposes on 1 April 2007 and enacted, by s 66, that the Enduring Powers of Attorney Act 1985 ceases to have effect from 1 October 2007. No new enduring powers of attorney may be made from that date, although there are saving provisions for such powers created before it. In the place of the enduing power of attorney is the lasting power of attorney, which is defined in s 9 as:

'a power of attorney under which the donor ('P') confers on the donee (or donees) authority to make decisions about all or any of the following—

(a)   P's personal welfare or specified matters concerning P's personal welfare, and

(b)   P's property and affairs or specified matters concerning P's property and affairs,

and which includes authority to make such decisions in circumstances where P no longer has capacity.'

The main difference between an enduring and a lasting power of attorney is that the latter may include matters relating to the donor's personal welfare (eg medical treatment and accommodation) and not simply his or her property and affairs, and there are separate forms for these two purposes. It is not necessary for the same persons to be attorneys for both purposes. Only a natural person may be attorney under a welfare power, but the attorney under a property and affairs power may be either an individual or a trust corporation: MCA 2005, s 10(1).

A lasting power of attorney may have effect as a 'normal' power of attorney whilst the donor has full mental capacity or may be limited to have effect only when the donor no longer has capacity to make decisions. In both cases a power can be used only after being registered by the Office of the Public Guardian. The prescribed form includes prescribed information which must be read by or to the donor and an LPA certificate, in which a person, who has known the donor for at least two years immediately before the date of the certificate, certifies that, in his opinion, the donor understands the purpose and scope of the document he or she is signing: MCA 2005, Sch 1, para 2(1)(e).

That schedule states in para 1 that the power must be made in the prescribed form. The Lasting Powers of Attorney, Enduring Powers of Attorney and Public Guardian Regulations 2007, SI 2007/1253, reg 5 states:

'The forms set out in Parts 1 and 2 of Schedule 1 to these Regulations are the forms which, in the circumstances to which they apply, are to be used for instruments intended to create a lasting power of attorney.'

Subsequent schedules set out ancillary forms. Regulation 2 provides that 'any reference to a form in the case of a form set out in Schedules 2 to 7 to these Regulations, is to be regarded as also including a form to the same effect but which differs in an immaterial respect in form or mode of expression'. It must be taken that, as was the case with enduring powers, no deviation from the prescribed form will be permitted, so it is strongly recommended that only the printed forms are used.

Forms in the Lasting Powers of Attorney, Enduring Powers of Attorney and Public Guardian Regulations 2007, SI 2007/1253:

Ref	*Title*	*Source*
LPA-PA	Form for instrument intended to create a property and affairs Lasting Power of Attorney	Sch 2, reg 5
LPA-PW	Form for instrument intended to create a personal welfare Lasting Power of Attorney	Sch 2, reg 5
LPA 001	Notice of Intention to Apply for Registration of a Lasting Power of Attorney: limited power of attorney	Sch 2, reg 10
LPA 002	Application to Register a Lasting Power of Attorney	Sch 3, reg 11
LPA 003A	Notice to an attorney of receipt of an application to register a Lasting Power of Attorney	Sch 4, reg 13
LPA 003B	Notice to donor of receipt of an application to register a Lasting Power of Attorney	Sch 4, reg 13
LPA 004	Notice of registration of a Lasting Power of Attorney	Sch 5, reg 17
LPA 005	Disclaimer by proposed or acting attorney under a Lasting Power of Attorney	Sch 6, reg 20
EP1PG	Notice of intention to apply for registration of an Enduring Power of Attorney	Sch 7, reg 23
EP2PG	Application to Register an Enduring Power of Attorney	Sch 8, reg 24

[18–091A] **16 Power of attorney by a company for the execution of documents[1]**

[18–091B] THIS POWER OF ATTORNEY is made on (*date*) by (*name*) plc/Ltd a company registered in England and Wales with number (*number*) whose registered office is (*address*) ('Company').

1 The Company appoints (*name of attorney*) of (*address*) ('the Attorney') to be its attorney with authority to execute on its behalf any document [(except a cheque or other bill of exchange)] which is needed to further the Company's interests [and has been approved by a resolution of its directors] .

2 The Company intends that any deed executed on its behalf by the Attorney shall bind the Company and shall have the same effect as if it had been executed by the Company itself.

3 This power of attorney is governed by the laws of England and Wales.

[*executed as a deed*]

[1]   Although it cannot be doubted that a company has power to appoint agents as a means of carrying on its business, the Companies Act 2006, s 47, when it comes into force on 1 October 2009 will (regrettably) reinforce the drift of English towards the so-called continental principle (ie a broad understanding that person may not do anything unless expressly permitted by law, in contrast with the English notion that one may do anything not expressly forbidden), which will replace the Companies Act 1985, s 38 and extend it expressly to the giving of powers of attorney to execute documents in the UK.   [18–091C]

19 Trusts and trustees

PRELIMINARY NOTE

[19–001] See IHT note [17–007] at the start of the Private Client section. Converting existing accumulation and maintenance trusts into 18 trusts or 18–25 trusts could be achieved by the trustees' exercise of any overriding powers of appointment if there are such powers in the settlement. If there are no such powers then the trustees will have to rely of their powers of advancement under the Trustee Act 1925, s 32. In many settlements this power will be extended to cover all of the capital and not merely half.

[19–001A] The 2006 Budget contained some substantial changes to the taxation of certain types of trusts. Some of the changes contained in the Finance Act 2006 took effect from budget day, 22 March 2006. In view of these changes, there is no longer any tax advantages to limiting the age of vesting to 25. Discretionary trusts might also provide more flexibility and so may be preferable to non-discretionary trusts, but no longer for tax reasons. Capital gains hold-over relief will also be available for transfers into discretionary trusts unless the settlement is a settlor interested trust (TCGA 1992, s 169B–169G, as inserted by the Finance Act 2004, s 116, Sch 21, para 4 and amended). Any trust which includes as beneficiaries the infant unmarried children of the settlor would be a settlor interested trust. Income paid under a settlement to or for the benefit of the settlor's children who are unmarried and under the age of 18, will be treated as the income of the settlor under the Income Tax (Trading and other income) Act 2005, s 629 (as amended).

TRANSITIONAL RULES RELATING TO INTEREST IN POSSESSION TRUSTS IN EXISTENCE AT 22 MARCH 2006

[19–012] These can be summarised as follows:
1   Where the life tenant as at 21 March 2006 is alive and entitled to his or her interest then the old rules relating to life interest trusts of apply.
2   If that interest is terminated (whether during the lifetime or on death) prior to 6 October 2008 then a *transitional serial interest* (TSI) is created.
3   If the termination is during the lifetime of a life tenant then the creation of TSI is a PET by the life tenant.
4   If the termination is on death and the life tenant of the TSI is the surviving spouse or civil partner of the life tenant then the creation of that TSI has the benefit of the surviving spouse exemption (always assuming the other provisions of s 18 of IHTA 1984 apply). This applies whenever the termination or death occurs, even if it is after 5 October 2008.
5   The transfer terminating the life tenant's interest has to affect the whole of the life tenant interest. That interest could be transferred to more than one life tenant who would each have a TSI.

PRECEDENTS

1 Appointment of new trustees of will on the death of one trustee[1]

[1] Vesting of personal property subject to a trust in the trustees of a trust on the appointment of a new trustees will fall within category A of the Schedule to the Stamp Duty (Exempt Instruments) Regulations 1987. An appropriate certificate must be included within the deed. Where land is transferred the parties may need to complete an HMRC form SDLT 60 to self certify that SDLT is not payable. Unless the consideration exceeds £40,000 no SDLT 60 is now required.

As to appointment of new trustees, see the Trustee Act 1925, ss 36 and 37.

Under the Trustee Act 1925, s 40(1)(b), in any appointment made after 1925 a vesting declaration is implied extending to all estates, interests and rights with respect to which a declaration could be made, but excepting the cases mentioned in sub-s (4). An express declaration will therefore usually be omitted, but where included an additional clause will be added to the operative part of the deed, such as [19–599].

As regards leaseholds held under leases containing a provision against assignment without licence, the vesting declaration, express or implied, will not operate unless the requisite licence has been obtained or rendered unnecessary. Under the Landlord and Tenant Act 1927, s 19(1)(b), in the case of building or similar leases for terms of more than 40 years, with more than seven years unexpired, no licence need be obtained, even when there is express provision to this effect, if notice is given within six months after the assignment. It is difficult to say what is the effect of a vesting declaration in such a case, and it will be wise whenever possible to obtain a licence in the usual way. The section does not apply where the landlord is a government department, local or public authority, or statutory or public utility company.

29 Trust deed by registered holder of a share in a company where the company is the wholly owned subsidiary of another[1]

[2] The words in brackets are required only if the shares are numbered under s 543(1) of the Companies Act 2006 (formerly s 182(2) of the Companies Act 1985). If the shares had been converted into stock (Companies Act 1985, s 121(1)(c), repealed) the reference to the share should be to £1 [ordinary] stock ('Stock') in the capital of the Company' and the subsequent references to 'Share' changed to 'Stock'.

32 [Accumulation and maintenance] Settlement on discretionary trusts for settlor's existing and future children[1]

Beneficial interests

4 The (*Party-B*) shall hold the Trust Fund on trust:

—   to apply it under the power of discretionary appointment in this deed in such manner the (*Party-B*) in their absolute discretion at any time or times before the end of the Trust Period by any deed appoint; and

—   at the end of the Trust Period and in default of and subject to any such appointment for such of the Beneficiaries[5] as are then living [who attain the age of [twenty-five][6] years] and if more than one in equal shares per stirpes.

(*or, for an 18 trust*):

4 The Trustees shall hold the Trust Fund on trust:

4.1 to apply it under the power of discretionary appointment in this deed in such manner as the Trustees in their absolute discretion at any time or times before the end of the Trust Period by any deed appoint; and

4.2 if and to the extent that all or any part of the Trust Fund is not appointed
— for such of the Beneficiaries as reach 18 before the end of the Trust Period, and
— for such of the Beneficiaries under 18 as are living at the end of the Trust Period,
and if more than one in equal shares per stirpes.

[19–358]   1   See Preliminary Note at [19–001A]. This precedent may still be used as a discretionary trust. The whole of note 1, describing the tax advantages for which this precedent could formerly be used, is deleted.

[19–358A]   32A   Deed of appointment to convert an existing accumulation and maintenance settlement to an 18 trust or an 18–25 trust[1]

DATE AND PARTIES

[19–358B]   THIS DEED is made on (*date*) by (*name*) of (*address*), (*name*) of (*address*) and (*name*) of (*address*) ('the Trustees')

DEFINITIONS

[19–358C]   **1.1** In this deed the following terms shall have the following meanings.

'Children'   means the (Part-A's) children (*name*), (*name*) and (*name*) (and every other child of the Settlor born before the closing date but not including any child who is 18 on or before the date of this deed) and the word 'Child' shall be construed accordingly.

[NB Omit the above definition is this deed is to rely on the definition of, eg, Beneficiaries in the Settlement.]

'Closing Date'   means the earlier of
the date on which the first child reaches 18,
such date as the Trustees specify by deed, and
the date on which the Trust Period expires.

'Settlement'   means a settlement created by deed dated (*date*) and made between the Settlor and (*name*) and (*name*).

'Settlor'   means (*name*).

[19–358D]   **1.2** Words and expressions used in this deed have the same meaning as in the Settlement.

APPOINTMENT

[19–358E]   **2** The Trustees in exercise of their powers of appointment under clause [x][2] of the Settlement [ir]revocably appoint and declare that the [Trust Fund (*or*) such part of the Trust Fund as is specified in the schedule to this deed] are from the date of this deed held on the following trusts
2.1   for such of the [Children (*or*) Beneficiaries] as reach 18 before the end of the Trust Period, and

    2.2   for such of the [Children (*or*) Beneficiaries] under 18 as are living
           at the end of the Trust Period
and if more than one in equal shares [per stirpes].

THE SETTLEMENT

3 The Settlement shall remain effective in all respects except as expressly   [19–358F]
altered by this deed [and the schedule].

[*attestation as a deed*]

[THE SCHEDULE]

(*Description of the part of the Trust Fund to which this appointment applies.*) [19–358G]

¹ Accumulation and maintenance settlements existing before 22 March 2006 continue to enjoy [19–358H]
   the tax advantages of the pre-2006 regime: for a precedent see [19–341]. However, from 6 April
   2008 settlements which have not been converted into either 18 trusts or 18–25 trusts will be
   taxed under the relevant property regime and will be subject to the 10-yearly charge as well as
   exit charges. As the benefits of accumulation and maintenance trusts continue to apply until
   5 April 2008 practitioners might wish to convert as late as possible. However, once a
   beneficiary has obtained an interest in possession, conversion will not be possible so one
   might want to convert earlier if a beneficiary is nearing the age when he obtains an interest in
   possession.
² For a specimen power of appointment see the first part of [19–346] and [19–300].

34 Short form of settlement of money on child or children vesting at a specified age¹

[19–374]

¹ This precedent is drawn to provide the simplest practical form of trust instrument, for use in [19–386]
   cases where a small trust of unit trusts or stock exchange investments but not land or chattels
   is created for the settlor's children. Whilst tax planning is not primarily a consideration in this,
   the settlor should be advised that the income of his children under 18 will be treated as his
   income: Income Tax (Trading and other Income) Act 2005, s 629 (as amended by
   SI 2005/3229 and by the Finance Act 2006, s 89, Sch 13, para 34(1)), replacing Taxes
   Act 1988, s 660B as inserted.

34A Trustees' resolution¹

[19–386A]

the (*name*) Settlement   [19–386B]

minutes of a meeting of the trustees

date and time:

place:

present:

being [all (*or*) a sufficient majority to comply with the requirements of the
Settlement.]

in attendance:

[*Other business as necessary.*]   [19–386C]

The trustees resolved unanimously as follows.   [19–386D]

x Following the Finance Act 2006 the Trustees exercise their [power of [19–386E]
appointment under [clause x of the Settlement (*or*) the power to advance
capital under s 32 of the Trustee Act 1925 [as extended by clause x of the

209

Settlement]] so that the Settlement will from the date of this resolution qualify under the Finance Act 2006 as an [18 (*or*) 18–25] trust.

[19–386F] **x** In exercise of the power referred to above that the terms of the Settlement is amended so that
— each Beneficiary (as defined in the Settlement)[2] is absolutely entitled to his share of the Trust Fund on reaching [18 (*or*) 18–25], and
— each Beneficiary's share of income will be either paid to him or accumulated for his benefit[3].

[19–386G] **x** The Settlement shall remain effective in all respects except as expressly altered by this deed [and the schedule].

[19–386H] [1] It is not necessary to use a deed unless the original settlement provides that, for instance, the trustees exercise powers of appointment by deed.
[2] You may need to cut down or otherwise amend the class of beneficiaries depending on the terms of the trust you are amending.
[3] It was originally thought under the Finance Act 2006 provisions that each beneficiary's share (capital and income) had to be held or paid to him. It is now thought that whilst a beneficiary is under the age at which an interest in possession arises, income from his share could be applied for the benefit of other beneficiaries.

[19–402] ## 37   Deed of covenant short form: eg four-year covenant for payment of subscription to charity[1]

[19–404] [1] Covenants to charities were formerly income tax efficient. The period of four years was generally fixed for these covenants. The period had to be irrevocable within the three years: Income and Corporation Taxes Act 1988, s 347A (inserted by the Finance Act 1988, s 36 and amended). This favourable tax treatment was repealed by the Finance Act 2007 for payments made on or after 6 April 2007. These arrangements are no longer charges on income for income tax purposes. However the same benefit can be obtained using the gift aid system.

20 Wills

PRELIMINARY NOTE

[20–000]

TABLE OF NIL RATE TAX BANDS FOR INHERITANCE TAX[1]

Tax year	Nil rate bands
2009/10	£325,000
2008/9	£312,000
2007/8	£300,000
2006/7	£285,000
2005/6	£275,000
2004/5	£263,000
2003/4	£255,000
2002/3	£250,000

1   Amounts are cumulative over seven years and not yearly allowances.

[20–000a]

PRECEDENTS

2   Will of married person making various gifts and leaving residue to spouse absolutely with substitutional gift[1]

[20–007]

[20–019]

[11]   Despite the changes introduced by the Trustee Act 2000, Pt V (ss 28–33) which apply to deaths on or after 1 February 2001, it is recommended that a charging clause should be included. It should be noted that a sole trustee without a charging clause would not be able to charge unless all the beneficiaries agree or until he is able to appoint an additional trustee who will agree to his reasonable charges (see s 29(2) of the Trustee Act 2000). A solicitor, executor or trustee should obtain the testator's express instructions (in writing if possible) before inserting this clause (cf *Re Chalinder and Herington* [1907] 1 Ch 58). If a potential trustee is a witness to the will, he will no longer lose the benefit of the clause. As to beneficiaries contesting whether charges are reasonable, see *Re Wells, Wells v Wells* [1962] 2 All ER 826, [1962] 1 WLR 874, CA. The court has no jurisdiction to raise the general level of fees, unless they are derisory (as in *Re Codd* [1975] 2 All ER 1051n, [1975] 1 WLR 1139), but may authorise additional remuneration for work outside the scope of the duties originally expected to be undertaken: *Re Duke of Norfolk's Settlement Trusts, Earl of Perth v Fitzalan-Howard* [1979] Ch 37, [1978] 3 All ER 907; reversed by *Re Duke of Norfolk's Settlement Trusts* [1982] Ch 61, [1981] 3 All ER 220, CA. In the 1979 case, it was held the court's jurisdiction to authorise additional remuneration should be exercised sparingly and in exceptional circumstances. The Court of Appeal said in 1981 that the court had an inherent jurisdiction to increase or vary trustees' remuneration. The fees and commissions of a literary agent's company, when he was appointed as literary executor, may be charged under such a clause as this: *Re Orwell's Will Trusts, Dixon v Blair* [1982] 3 All ER 177, [1982] 1 WLR 1337.

[20–020]

3 Will of husband or wife: trusts for sale: payment of income to widow/er: remainder to children[1,2]

[20–021]

THIS IS THE WILL of me (*name*) of (*address*) [and formerly of (*address*)] [which I make on (*date*)].

REGULATION

[20–022]

1 I revoke all former wills and other testamentary dispositions made by me.

APPOINTMENT OF EXECUTOR

[20–023]

2 [*spouse and other*[*s*]*: see clause* [20–010]]

APPOINTMENT OF GUARDIANS

[20–024]

3 [*see clause* [20–011]]

FUNERAL DIRECTIONS

[20–025]

4 [*see clause* [20–012]]

PERSONAL CHATTELS[3]

[20–026]

5 I give to my [husband] (*name*[4]) of (*address*) free of the costs of transfer[5] all my personal chattels as defined by s 55 of the Administration of Estates Act 1925.

IMMEDIATE GIFTS TO SPOUSE

[20–027]

6 I give £(...) ((...) pounds) to my [husband] (*name*) [to be paid to [him] as soon as possible after my death in priority to all other gifts made by this will] and irrespective of the period for which [he] survives me.

SPECIFIC LEGACIES

[20–028]

7 [*specific legacies: clause* [20–013]]

RELEASE OF DEBT[6]

[20–029]

8 I release and forgive to (*name*) of (*address*) (*or*) if [he] predeceases me [his] personal representatives the debt of £(...) ((...) pounds) now owing by [him] to me or as much of it as at the time of my death remains owing and all interest on it and I direct that all securities for it be released and made over to [him] or [his] personal representatives and that all instruments necessary for this purpose be executed by my Trustees at the expense of my residuary estate.

REVERSIONARY INTEREST[7]

[20–030]

9 I give the [fifth] share [and all other shares (if any)] to which under the will dated (*date*) of (*name*) deceased I am at my death or afterwards entitled in reversion expectant on the death (*or*) remarriage of (*name*) in the residuary estate of (*name*) deceased to (*name*) of (*address*) and such of the issue of (*name*) as survive me and if more than one in equal shares per stirpes.

SPECIFIC GIFTS OF FREEHOLD AND LEASEHOLD[8]

10 I give my [share and interest in the] free (*or*) leasehold land and property known as (*address*) [and registered at HMLR with title number (*number*)][9] to [my [son]] (*name*) of (*address*) [free from all inheritance tax] [and in this clause exclude the operation of s 33 of the Wills Act 1837[10]].

[20–031]

CASH LEGACIES[11]

11.1 I give to be divided in equal shares per stirpes (*or*) capita amongst those of my children who survive me [and the issue of such children who predecease me[10]] an amount equal to the maximum[12] which can be given without incurring any liability for inheritance tax on my death [subject to a maximum of £(...) ((...) pounds) or if greater (*amount*)% of the value of my Residuary Estate after payment of funeral and testamentary expenses].

[20–032]

11.2 The amount given by this clause shall be reduced by the amount of any gifts made during my lifetime or any other gifts made by this will or any codicil to it which are liable to be taken into account on a calculation of inheritance tax payable on my death.

11.3 I declare that this clause shall only take effect if the gift to my spouse in clause [15] takes effect and qualifies for total exemption from inheritance tax under section 18 of the Inheritance Tax Act 1984.[11]

11.4 I declare that in calculating the amount in 11.1 the provisions of Inheritance Tax Act 1984, ss 8A–8C are [included/excluded].[12]

(*or*)

11.0-.5 [*see clause* [20–014]]

[20–033]

CHARITABLE LEGACIES

12.1/2 [*see clauses* [20–015] *and* [20–016]]

[20–034]

ANNUITIES[13]

13.1 I give to [my [brother]] (*name*) of (*address*) an annuity of £(...) ((...) pounds) [free of inheritance tax] payable by equal [monthly] payments on the [first] day of [each month] the first of such payments if necessary of an apportioned part of the said annuity to be made on the [first day of the month] next after my death.

[20–035]

13.2 My Trustees may if they think fit purchase in their names or in the name of [my [brother]] (*name*) from the government or some company of repute an annuity for the purpose of answering the annuity given to [my [brother]] (*name*) and any such annuity purchased in the names of my Trustees shall be paid to [him] in the same manner as the annuity answered by it.

[20–036]

TRUST FOR SALE OF RESIDUE[14]

14 I give the residue of my property to my Trustees on trust to sell it and after payment out of it of all legacies given by me and my debts and funeral and testamentary expenses[15] to hold it and the investments from time to time representing it [('my Residuary Estate')] on the trusts mentioned in the following clauses.

[20–037]

GIFTS OF RESIDUE[16]

[20-038] **15** My Trustees shall pay the income from my Residuary Estate to my [husband] during [his] life and on [his] death or if the gift to [him] lapses or fails for any reason[17] shall divide any Residuary Estate amongst all or any of my [legitimate[18]] children who are living at the date of my death (*or*[19]) the death of the survivor of my [husband] and me and attain the age of [18[20]] years and if more than one in equal shares.

TRUSTEES POWERS

The remainder of this precedent is a selection of commonly needed powers, which can be selected individually by each clause's own unique number or collectively as [20–300].

[20-039] **16** In addition to all powers given or implied by law my Trustees shall have the following powers.

(*set out*)

SURVIVORSHIP[21]

[20-040] **17** If any beneficiary under this will or any codicil does not survive me by [thirty days[22]] he or she shall be treated for the purposes of this will and any codicil to it as though he or she had died before me.

RESIDENTIAL PROPERTY[23]

[20-041] **18** My Trustees may [purchase and] permit [my [husband]] (*name*) (*or*) any person entitled to any interest in my Residuary Estate whether in possession or not and whether vested or contingent to reside in any house, flat or other dwelling [forming part of my Residuary Estate] for such period and on such conditions (if any) as to rent and other expenses and outgoings, insurance, maintenance, repairs, decoration and otherwise as my Trustees in their absolute discretion determine.

MAINTENANCE AND ADVANCEMENT

[20-042] **19.0** Section 31 of the Trustee Act 1925 in its application to this will shall be varied:

19.1 by the deletion of the proviso to subsection (1);

19.2 by the deletion in subsection (1) para (I) of the words 'as may, in all circumstances, be reasonable' and the insertion in their place of the words 'as my Trustees think fit'[; and]

[20-043] **19.3** All (*or*) all accumulations of income (and the property from time to time representing it) made pursuant to s 31(2) of the Trustee Act 1925 or otherwise shall be held on trust for [the beneficiary] absolutely.[24]

[20-043A] **19.4** During the accumulation period (which shall be the period of 21 years from the date of my death) as though references to the attainment of [21 or 25] years were substituted for references to the age of 18 years in that section (references to 'infancy' and 'minority' being construed accordingly.[24A]

ADVANCEMENT

20 My Trustees may at any time or times raise the whole or any part of the vested, contingent or presumptive share of any beneficiary under this will or any codicil to it and pay it to or use it for the advancement, maintenance, education or otherwise for the benefit of that beneficiary.

[20–044]

ACCOUNT OF LIFETIME GIFTS[25]

21 Every gift whether of money or property [of greater value at the date of the gift than £(...) ((...) pounds)] made by me after the date of this will to any child of mine and every sum of money or any property settled by me on any child of mine after the date of this will shall if my Trustees in their absolute discretion so decide be brought into account[25] by such child upon the division of my Residuary Estate at a value to be assessed either at the date of the gift or settlement or at the date of distribution of my Residuary Estate as my Trustees in their absolute discretion decide.

[20–045]

STATUTORY SUBSTITUTIONAL GIFT

22 Section 33 of the Wills Act 1837 shall not apply to any gift made by [clauses (*number*) and (*number*) of] this will [or any codicil to it].[26]

[20–046]

INHERITANCE TAX

23.1 If, after taking into consideration all relevant factors it appears to my Trustees to be advantageous so to do in respect of all or any of the [pecuniary] legacies given by [clause (*number*) of] this will, my Trustees may administer my estate on the basis that this will contains a direction that each or any legacy bears its own inheritance tax and the amount of each pecuniary legacy so treated shall be such sum as after deduction of tax amounts to the sum stated in my will or codicil.[27]

[20–047]

23.2 There shall be paid out of my Residuary Estate any additional inheritance tax payable on my death in respect of any gift or settlement made by me (*or*) the gift of (*amount*) made by me on (*date*) to (*name*) by reason of my death within seven years of the making of the gift [to the extent that provision for the payment of such additional tax has not been made by way of insurance effected for that purpose].[28]

[20–048]

23.3 I declare that if the share of any beneficiary in my Residuary Estate is not exempt from inheritance tax then the share of each beneficiary of my Residuary Estate [shall be of such amount that after the payment of inheritance tax on such share each share shall be the same amount] [shall bear its own inheritance tax so that each share shall be the same amount before the payment of inheritance tax].[29]

[20–049]

INVESTMENT CLAUSE[30]

24 My Trustees shall have the same unrestricted power of investing and changing investments (including investments not producing income) as they would have if they were beneficially entitled.

[20–050]

DELEGATION OF INVESTMENT POWERS[31]

25.0 My Trustees may:

[20–051]

25.1 delegate the operation of any bank or other account;

25.2 employ any investment advisor to advise on the investment of all or any part of my estate and the management of it; and

25.3 delegate to any investment adviser the management of all or any part of my estate at their discretion on such terms and subject to such conditions as my Trustees in their absolute discretion think fit without being liable for any loss arising as a result.

LAPSED SHARE[32]

26 If any gift made by this will lapses so that there could be an intestacy as to that gift it shall be primarily applied in or towards the payment of debts funeral and testamentary expenses[15] and pecuniary legacies given by this will, or any codicil to it before recourse is had to any other property given by this will or any codicil to it.

COMPANY RECONSTRUCTIONS[33]

27 Any testamentary gift made by me of any share or other security in any company shall be a gift of any share or other security owned by me at my death (in that or any company) resulting from any sale, amalgamation, reconstruction or issue or rearrangement of capital of the company or sale of its business.

TO CONTINUE BUSINESS[34]

28.1 My Trustees may carry on, discontinue and wind up any business in which I am engaged either alone or in partnership (*or*) my business of a (*description*) now carried on at (*address*) and for such purpose:
— employ in it any part of my capital or other property (whether already employed in it or not);
— employ any persons (including themselves) in or about the business at such remuneration as they think fit;
— and generally act in all respects in relation to the business or my interest in it as if they were its absolute owners;
— in ascertaining the profits of the business make all provisions for depreciation and reserves which they consider expedient; and
— (if any of my Trustees are employed in the business) to receive remuneration for employment in the business without being liable to account for it.

28.2 For the purposes of this clause carrying on business includes the exercise of any voting power in respect of any shares in any company owned by me and business includes any business conducted by any such company.

EXCLUSION OF TECHNICAL RULES OF ADMINISTRATION[35]

29 My Trustees may disregard the respective rules in *Howe v Earl of Dartmouth, Re Chesterfield's Trusts* and *Allhusen v Whittell* and the apportionment rules under the Apportionment Act 1870.

EXCLUSION OF TRUST OF LAND PROVISIONS

30 [*Exclusion Trusts* [19–371] *substituting* 'will' *for* 'settlement']

TO HAVE ACCOUNTS TAKEN[36]

31 My Trustees may exercise once in every year the statutory power to cause the trust accounts to be examined or audited by an independent accountant.

[20–058]

TO INSURE[37]

32 My Trustees may insure against loss or damage by fire and any other risk any property for the time being comprised in my estate or any trust fund created by this will or any codicil to it for any amount notwithstanding that any person is absolutely entitled to the property or any part of it and may pay the premiums for the insurance out of the income or capital of my Residuary Estate or out of the income or capital of that property or any trust fund comprising that property and any money received by my Trustees under any such policy shall be treated as though it were proceeds of sale of the property insured.

[20–059]

TO APPROPRIATE WITHOUT CONSENTS[38]

33 The power of appropriation conferred on personal representatives by section 41 of the Administration of Estates Act 1925 may be exercised by my Trustees in their capacity as trustees as well as personal representatives and in either case without the necessity of obtaining any of the consents required by that section [and for the purposes of this clause any property appropriated shall be valued as at the date of either my death or the appropriation as my Trustees in their discretion decide[39]].

[20–060]

EXERCISE OF DISCRETIONS BY TRUSTEES

34 Any of the powers, duties or discretions given by this will or any codicil to it or by operation of law imposed or conferred on my Trustees may be exercised by them although one or more of them is beneficially interested in the manner in which those powers duties or discretions are exercised.

[20–061]

TRUSTEES INCLUDE SUCCESSORS

35 The expression 'my Trustees' shall where the context so requires or permits include the executors named in this will and the survivor of them and any other executor or trustee for the time being of this will.

[20–062]

TO APPOINT TRUST CORPORATION[40]

36 If any trust corporation is at any time appointed as trustee (and whether as custodian or managing trustee) under this will it may act by its proper officers and may employ and pay solicitors, brokers and other agents to transact any business (including the receipt and payment of money) and may receive remuneration (free of inheritance or similar tax) in accordance with its scale of fees in force at my death.

[20–063]

POWER FOR TRUSTEE TO CHARGE

37 [*see clause* [20–018]]

[20–064]

POWER OF TRUSTEE TO PURCHASE TRUST PROPERTY

[20–065] **38** I authorise (*name*) notwithstanding that [he] is a trustee of this will at any time or times to purchase whether at any public auction or by private treaty all or any part of the property from time to time forming my Residuary Estate or property intended to fall into and form part of my Residuary Estate and I direct my Trustees subject to a proper price being obtained to agree to any such purchase.

PROTECTION OF TRUSTEES

[20–066] **39** Except as a result of his or her own fraud or dishonesty, no trustee shall be liable for any loss to my estate [and no Trustee shall be obliged to take any proceedings against another Trustee or former Trustee for any breach of trust by that Trustee or former Trustee.]

VARIATION

[20–067] **40** If my Trustees decide that it is necessary or desirable for the practical and economical administration of this will, they may at any time by deed alter or add to all or any of the administrative powers given by this will. This power does not permit them to make any alteration or addition, which would have any direct or indirect adverse effect on the amount, character or timing of any benefit payable to beneficiary under this will.[41]

41 I hereby exclude the provisions of the Trusts of Land and Appointment of Trustees Act 1996, s 11[12][19].[42]

[*Testimonium and attestation:* [20–340] *and* [20–346]]

[20–068]
1. This will may be used as a menu or master will. See the notes at [20–019].
2. Settled Land Act trustees should only be appointed where there is a settlement of freehold or leasehold property already in existence under the Settled Land Act 1925. Under any other trusts it will take effect as a trust of land (Trusts of Land and Appointment of Trustees Act 1996, ss 1, 2). In the case of any existing Settled Land Act settlement, if no appointment of Settled Land Act trustees is made, the personal representatives will be Settled Land Act trustees until others are appointed (SLA 1925, s 30(3)), so no great harm will be done if the appointment is omitted. Note that no new Settled Land can be created following the Trusts of Land and Appointment of Trustees Act 1996. Instead if Settled Land is purported to be created in a will it will take effect as a trust of land.
3. Clocks in an inherited collection are not articles of personal use in the definition of personal chattels by the Administration of Estates Act 1925, s 55 as amended: *Re Crispin's Will Trusts, Arkwright v Thurley* [1975] Ch 245, [1974] 3 All ER 772, CA. However, in *Re Collins' Will Trusts, Donne v Hewetson* [1971] 1 All ER 283, [1971] 1 WLR 37 a stamp collection, a coin collection and a motor car came within the expression 'personal effects'.
4. If the spouse has not been named before, insert the name in full. See [20–186], note 2.
5. Costs of packing and forwarding specific legacies are payable by the legatee (*Re Scott, Scott v Scott* [1915] 1 Ch 592, CA; *Re Fitzpatrick, Bennett v Bennett* [1952] Ch 86, [1951] 2 All ER 949). Where the estate is insufficient to pay the legacies in full these costs must in the absence of special provisions be borne by the legatees (*Re Sivewright, Law v Fenwick* (1922) 128 LT 416; *Re Leach, Milne v Daubeny* [1923] 1 Ch 161, [1922] All ER Rep 714).
6. A will should on no account contain a general forgiveness of debts, as it is impossible to foresee the effect, and the result may be to include sums due under debentures or mortgages held by the testator as investments. See *Re Neville, Neville v First Garden City Ltd* [1925] Ch 44, [1924] All ER Rep 377. A legacy expressed to be given to a creditor operates in satisfaction of the debt notwithstanding that the debt carries interest and the legacy does not (*Fitzgerald v National Bank Ltd* [1929] 1 KB 394, [1928] All ER Rep 596).
7. Where the reversionary interest may be affected by advances or the operation of accruer clauses, it is necessary in order to avoid disputes to include words in this clause which will make it certain that the beneficiary is to take the whole benefit of the reversionary interest subject to advances received by the present testator in his lifetime. This gift is confined to

reversionary interests and will not include vested interests under the will which have not been distributed at the time of the present testator's death, i e interests in the undistributed estate of the original testator which are vested but not distributed.

8   A gift of leasehold property will include the reversion, where the latter is acquired by the testator after the will was made: *Re Fleming's Will Trusts, Ennion v Hampstead Old People's Housing Trust Ltd* [1974] 3 All ER 323, [1974] 1 WLR 1552.

9   The testator must be advised of the risk of using these words instead of the general description in [20–242], [20–246] and [20–248]. A specific devise will fail by ademption if the testator disposes of the property in question before death. The will speaks from the testator's death, not the date of the will, as to the property comprised in it: Wills Act 1837, s 24. Where it is apparent that a residuary gift to charity is larger than was intended, the charity has power to give up part of the gift in favour of the beneficiaries, who were intended by the testator to have more than they were legally entitled to under the will: *Re Snowden, Shackleton v Eddy; Re Henderson, Henderson v A-G* [1970] Ch 700, [1969] 3 All ER 208.

10 The words in brackets will be omitted in most cases if the statutory substitutional gift applies. See [20–046] and note 26 below.

11 There is one scale of IHT (40%) payable on or within seven years of death, and the lifetime rates will be half the rates payable on death with tapering relief for gifts made more than three years before the death. From 6 April 2006 the upper limit for the nil tax band is £285,000. The nil rate band from 6 April 2009 is £325,000. The object of this clause is to enable a testator to leave his children the maximum possible sum on which no IHT is payable and the residue of his estate to his widow, which passes to her free of that tax provided s 18 of IHTA 1984 (as amended by SI 2005/3229) applies to it. Hence the restriction on the gift introduced by clause 11.3. Note that in certain circumstances (s 18(2) and (3)) the surviving spouse exemption will not apply to a gift, or all of a gift, to a spouse. Where the estate is large and the widow is adequately provided for, it may be advantageous to increase the children's legacy to an amount which, whilst becoming liable to tax, avoids needlessly increasing the widow's estate and effectively increasing the tax payable on her death.

12 One danger of this clause is that it could deplete the residuary beneficiary's share unexpectedly, because of changes in circumstances or tax rates or other factors, such as the exemption of significant assets from IHT. Where there is a risk of this occurring, a limitation should be included such as by the words in brackets. Care must be taken when using this clause to ensure the gift is not larger than intended by the Testator as a result of the introduction of the transferable nil rate band which applies to all deaths. For deaths on/after 9 October 2007, any deceased spouse's unused nil rate band (or proportion of it if part of the nil rate band has already been used by the first deceased spouse) can be claimed by the second deceased spouse. The first spouse's nil rate band is uplifted in value to the value at the time of the second death. Note that a claim must be made to HMRC by the personal representatives or any other person liable to the tax on the second death within two years of the end of the month in which the death occurred.

13 Having regard to the decision in *Re Pettit, Le Fevre v Pettit* [1922] 2 Ch 765, [1922] All ER Rep 163, that where a tax-free annuitant recovers relief by way of repayment of tax the testator's residuary estate is entitled to the repayment so far as it is referable to the annuity, it may be desirable in order to avoid practical difficulties where the annuitant's means are small to provide that the annuitant shall be entitled to any repayment of tax.

14 Any land will be held as a trust of land and subject to the provisions of the Trusts of Land and Appointment of Trustees Act 1996. The purpose of including a trust to sell is to incorporate a duty to sell under the implied power to postpone sale under s 3 of the Act. This duty overrides the power and provides a method of resolving disputes between trustees, i e they must sell if they cannot agree. Without this provision disputes can only by resolved by the court. However, if the intention is that the trustees should retain the property it may be better to leave out the trust to sell.

15 It appears for the reasons stated briefly below that it is unnecessary to include here the words '(including inheritance tax)'. The expression 'testamentary expenses' included, broadly, estate duty on personalty but not on realty, because formerly it was necessary to pay estate duty on only personal property in order to obtain probate, and therefore estate duty was to that extent a testamentary expense, as had formerly been the case with probate duty. Probate cannot be obtained until there is paid all tax which the personal representatives are liable to pay (Supreme Court Act 1981, s 109 as amended) except the instalments other than the first where election for payment by instalments has been made (IHTA 1984, ss 227 and 228 as amended). IHTA 1984, s 211 (re-enacting Finance (No 2) Act 1983, s 13, enacted following the Scottish case of *Re Dougal* [1981] STC 514) now provides that IHT, for which the personal representatives are liable so far as attributable to property in the UK which vests in them and

was not immediately before the death comprised in a settlement, shall be treated as part of the general testamentary and administrative expenses of the estate subject to any contrary intention shown by the deceased in his will.

Note that the Supreme Court Act 1981, s 109 (Refusal of grant where inheritance tax unpaid) is expected to be altered soon. (The Supreme Court Act 1981 was renamed the 'Senior Courts Act 1981' by the Constitutional Reform Act 2005, s 59(5), Sch 11, para 1.)

[16] If the life interest is to be in only part of the residuary estate or is to end or be reduced on remarriage, [20–076] and [20–077] should be used. This form assumes that the statutory substitutional gift to the testator's issue will apply: see [20–046] and the note to it. For a defeasible life interest as an alternative to terminating or reducing it on remarriage, see additional clause [20–290].

[17] See [20–079], note 3.

[18] See [20–303], note 1.

[19] See [20–079], note 5.

[20] See [20–079], note 6. If the age of 18 is chosen, the trust will be a bereaved minors trust. If an age greater than 18 is chosen, say 25, and the income interest does vest at 18 then if the testator and his spouse predecease the child, the trust would be an IPDI (immediate post-death interest) trust with no charge to IHT when the child reaches 25. However, there would be a charge to CGT, as hold over relief would not be available. If 9.4 is added then in the same circumstances the trust would not be an IPDI but the trust 18–25 rules would apply. CGT hold over relief would be available but there would be an IHT charge when the child reaches 25. The IHT exit charge is currently at a rate of 0.6% per annum for each year between the ages of 18 and 25. Thus is the child is entitled to capital at the age of 25 the charge at that time will be 4.2%. This is taxed on the excess over the nil rate band.

[21] This clause would include, for example, children, in the commorientes clause to provide for the death of most of the members of the family in, say, an air crash. This clause may be undesirable where there are, for example, grandchildren or other dependants of the testator's children, and the use of it is recommended only where the testator's family circumstances show a clear need for it.

[22] IHTA 1984, s 92 provides that, if the survivorship period is not more than six months the alternative disposition taking effect on the death of the primary donee within that period shall be treated as having effect on the death of the testator, avoiding double IHT. This applies if the alternative disposition is by operation of law and if there are separate dispositions of income. There may be circumstances in which it is preferable from the tax point of view, that there is no condition for survivorship, but it will be necessary to estimate the liability to tax in each case. See also [20–079], note 7.

[23] For specific gifts of a house to be occupied by a widow or widower, see [20–246] and [20–248].

[24] Under this clause the accumulated and capitalised income will belong indefeasibly to the child: *Re Delamere's Settlement Trusts, Kenny v Cunningham-Reid* [1984] 1 All ER 584, [1984] 1 WLR 813, CA. Whether the income is accumulated or paid to the child, it belongs to him and he is entitled to claim repayment of tax in respect of any otherwise unused personal reliefs, and there will be no additional tax on the trustees under ICTA 1988, s 686.

Note that ICTA 1988, s 686 is repealed by the Income Tax Act 2007, ss 1027, 1031, Sch 1, Pt 1, paras 1, 145, Sch 3, Pt 1 (with effect from 6 April 2007, for income tax purposes, for the tax year 2007–08 and subsequent tax years and, for corporation tax purposes, for accounting periods ending after 5 April 2007) subject to savings and transitional provisions in ITA 2007, s 1030(1), Sch.2.

On the child's death before the vesting of the capital the capital will pass according to the trusts of the testator's will, whilst the accumulated and capitalised income will pass as the child's estate under his intestacy or will. In order for a trust to qualify as an 18–25 trust it may be necessary to include a provision making clear that the income belongs to the particular beneficiary and no other person.

[24A] It would only be necessary to add this provision to the clause if the age of inheritance is greater than 18 and it is wished that the income interest would vest at age when the entitlement to capital arises.

[25] Although the Law Reform (Succession) Act 1995, s 1(2) abolished hotchpot in intestacy for deaths on or after 1 January 1996, there may still be circumstances in which a testator will wish to apply the principle of accounting for lifetime gifts on the distribution of the residue to ensure fairness when an advance has been made to one and not the others.

[26] By the Wills Act 1837, s 33 (substituted by the Administration of Justice Act 1982, s 19), gifts to a child of the testator or a class consisting of the children or remoter issue of the testator will take effect automatically as a gift in equal shares per stirpes to the issue living at the testator's death of that child or any child in the class, if the testator's child dies in his lifetime,

unless a contrary intention appears in the will. The contrary intention could be by an express exclusion as in this form or by a provision wholly or partially inconsistent with s 33.

27 Generally, this form is intended to be used in cases where the testator leaves it to the trustees of the will to decide in the circumstances then prevailing whether legacies should be treated as liable to bear their own tax. Unless the trustees do so act, the general rules will prevail, and the tax will ordinarily be payable out of residue. See also note 15 above.

28 Gifts within seven years prior to the death are liable to IHT at the full rate (40%), with tapering relief for gifts more than three years before the death, and other inter vivos gifts are taxed at half rate. The additional IHT could be reduced if the value of the gift falls between the time it was made and the death or its sale; IHTA 1984, s 131 as amended. By IHTA 1984, ss 199–204, the person liable to pay the tax is the donee, who should be advised to insure against the death of the donor within seven years. If the donee does not pay the Personal Representatives may be liable. However, the testator may direct that such additional tax is payable out of residue as in this form.

29 *Re Benham's Will Trusts* [1995] STC 210 confirmed that where shares of the residue of an estate are left to a mixture of exempt and non-exempt beneficiaries (e g charities and children or perhaps spouse and children) then, unless there is a provision to the contrary, the exempt beneficiaries will not bear any proportion of the IHT due on the estate. However, this will result in the grossing up of the non-exempt beneficiaries' shares so that after tax each beneficiary receives an equivalent proportion. If the will directs that the exempt beneficiaries are to bear a proportion of the tax, then there will be a smaller IHT bill overall and this may be closer to what the testator would have expected when giving his instructions. Thus always check this with the testator. This latter approach was the approach approved by the court in the later case of *Re Ratcliffe (deceased)* [1999] STC 262 which confirmed that the non-exempt beneficiaries should bear a proportion of the tax.

30 Following the Trustee Act 2000 which came into effect on 1 February 2001, Trustees (including Personal Representatives) are given a wide statutory power of investment under s 3. When investing, Trustees should have regard to the suitability of the investment to the trust and the need for diversification. These are the standard investment criteria referred to in s 4. Note the requirement for advice in s 5. The Trustee Act 2000 has substantially repealed the Trustee Investments Act 1961 as it applies to trusts whether created before or after the Act (Trustee Act 2000, s 7).

31 Part IV of the Trustee Act 2000 (ss 11–27) contain detailed provisions relating to the appointment of nominees, agents and the like and the extent to which Trustees' powers may be delegated. There are some restrictions on the functions that may be delegated (see ss 11(2) and (3)) and on the persons who may be appointed as agents (see s 12). However, where asset management functions are delegated there must be an agreement in writing with the agent under the terms of s 15. Note that a beneficiary cannot be appointed as an agent (s 12(3)). These provisions apply to trusts created before as well as after the Act.

32 There has been considerable discussion as to the effect of the Administration of Estates Act 1925, Sch 1, Pt II and this clause is intended to make the position clear.

33 A clause of this kind will not prevent the ademption of the bequest if the testator has before his death sold the substituted capital. It seems that bonus shares (and semble, shares acquired on a rights issue) do not pass with the gift, whether it is specific or general: *Re O'Brien, Little v O'Brien* (1946) 62 TLR 594.

34 A trustee with a controlling interest in a company must ensure that he receives adequate information to protect the interests of the beneficiaries and may be liable to compensate the beneficiaries for losses made as a result of hazardous investments by the company: *Bartlett v Barclays Bank Trust Co Ltd* [1980] Ch 515, [1980] 1 All ER 139. Where a trustee of shares in a private company appoints a manager, which in itself may be proper, he may be liable for breaches of trust arising out of the misconduct of the manager: *Re Lucking's Will Trusts, Renwick v Lucking* [1967] 3 All ER 726, [1968] 1 WLR 866. In the absence of express power the court may, in exceptional cases, allow a trustee to receive and retain remuneration, if it is in the interests that he be a director of the company and could not be expected to carry out those duties without additional remuneration: *Re Keeler Settlement Trusts, Keeler v Gladhill* [1981] Ch 156, [1981] 1 All ER 888. As to governors of a charity being unable to vote remuneration for themselves, see *Re French Protestant Hospital* [1951] Ch 567, [1951] 1 All ER 938.

35 For the individual rules and notes on them, see [20–328], [20–330] and [20–332].

36 See the Trustee Act 1925, s 22(4). The statutory power of audit may not be exercised more than once in every three years, unless the nature of the trust or special dealings with the property make a more frequent audit reasonable.

37 Section 34 of the Trustee Act 2000 inserts a new s 19 in the Trustee Act 1925 (a power to insure). This gives trustees power to insure that property and to pay the premiums out of

income or capital. It also applies to base trusts. The power applies to trusts created before as well as after the Act. It is subject to the trustees' statutory duty of care. In view of this new power to insure it may be appropriate in most cases to omit this provision altogether. In certain cases (where insurance cover might be difficult or expensive) consider a clause excluding the trustees from insuring.

[38] For capital gains tax purposes, the beneficiary who takes the asset in or towards satisfaction of a pecuniary legacy or a gift of residue, takes it as legatee and not as a disposal by the personal representatives, so that there is no charge to capital gains tax and the personal representatives' acquisition is treated as the legatee's acquisition: TCGA 1992, ss 62(4) and 64(3). Any other disposal by the personal representatives is charged in the ordinary way for capital gains.

[39] In the case of an appropriation towards the sum to which the widow was entitled under her husband's intestacy, the valuation was made as at the date of appropriation and not the death: *Robinson v Collins* [1975] 1 All ER 321, sub nom *Re Collins, Robinson v Collins* [1975] 1 WLR 309. The spouse of an intestate may, on agreeing to pay the excess, require the appropriation of the matrimonial home where its value exceeds the statutory legacy: *Re Phelps, Wells v Phelps* [1980] Ch 275, [1979] 3 All ER 373, CA.

[40] See [20–197], note 1. Where a bank was appointed managing trustee along with another and then separately appointed custodian trustee in order to secure remuneration, it is held that both appointments were bad: *Arning v James* [1936] Ch 158. As to the position where there are foreign assets, see *Re Sandys' Will Trust, Sandys v Kirton* [1947] 2 All ER 302, CA. Where under foreign law executors are entitled to 'agency commission', they may keep it for their own use and are not liable to account for it: *Re Northcote's Will Trusts, Northcote v Northcote* [1949] 1 All ER 442.

[41] See also Trusts [19–319] and the note to it.

[42] This clause excludes certain provisions of this Act. Section 11 is the obligation to consult beneficiaries, s 12 gives beneficiaries of land trusts a right to occupy the land and s 19 allows beneficiaries who between themselves are absolutely entitled to the trust property to appoint and remove trustees.

[20–068A]   **3A   Will of husband or wife: nil rate band trust legacy with residuary estate passing to surviving spouse absolutely or for life with remainder to children[1]**

[20–068B]   THIS IS THE WILL of me (*name*) of (*address*) [and formerly of (*address*)] [which I make on (*date*)].

REGULATION

[20–068C]   **1** I revoke all former wills and other testamentary dispositions made by me.

APPOINTMENT OF EXECUTOR

[20–068D]   **2** [*spouse and other*[*s*]*: see clause* [20–010]]

APPOINTMENT OF GUARDIANS

[20–068E]   **3** [*see clause* [20–011]]

FUNERAL DIRECTIONS

[20–068F]   **4** [*see clause* [20–012]]

PERSONAL CHATTELS[2]

[20–068G]   **5** I give to my [husband] (*name*[3]) of (*address*) free of the costs of transfer[4] all my personal chattels as defined by s 55 of the Administration of Estates Act 1925.

NIL RATE BAND GIFTS

6.1 In this clause the following meanings shall apply: [20–068H]
—   the Nil Rate Band Trustees shall mean the Trustees of the Nil Rate
     Band Trust
—   the Nil Rate Band Trust Fund shall mean
     the Nil Rate Band Legacy
     all property from time to time representing it
—   the Accumulation period means the period of 21 years from the date of
     my death
—   the Nil Rate Band Beneficiaries are:
     my spouse
     any civil partner of mine
     my children and remoter issue
     the spouses civil partners widows or widowers of my children and
     remoter issue
     any UK registered charity
     any person added to the class of Nil Rate Band Beneficiaries by my Nil
     Rate Band Trustees by deed. To exercise this power my Nil Rate Band
     Trustees must not be less than two in number).
—   the Nil Rate Band Legacy shall mean the maximum sum that I can give
     away under this provision without a charge to inheritance tax (or any
     other substituted tax) on my death[5]
—   the Trust Period shall mean:
     the period of 80 years from my death and it is the perpetuity period
     such earlier date as the Nil Rate Band Trustees shall by deed declare.

6.2 I give the Nil Rate Band Legacy to the Nil Rate Band Trustees to hold on [20–068I]
trust as to both capital and income for all or such one or more to the
exclusion of the other of the Nil Rate Band Beneficiaries in such shares and
generally in such manner as the Nil Rate Band Trustees shall in their absolute
and unfettered discretion think fit.[6]

6.3 Subject to the above at the end of the Trust Period the Nil Rate Band [20–068J]
Trustees shall hold the Nil Rate Band Trust Fund [upon the trusts of my
residuary estate] (or) [name absolutely]

6.4 This clause will only take effect if the gift to my spouse (or) civil partner in [20–068K]
clause [7] shall take effect and be exempt from inheritance tax under the
provisions of the Inheritance Tax Act 1984 or any statutory re-enactment or
modification of it.

6.5 In satisfying the Nil Rate Band Legacy the Nil Rate Band Trustees may: [20–068L]
—   leave the sum outstanding for as long as they think fit without any
     liability to the Nil Rate Band Beneficiaries for loss;
—   be required by my executors to accept a written undertaking or other
     promise to pay on demand from my spouse including such terms
     regarding interest index linking and security as my executors think fit;[7]
—   ignore the provisions of the Inheritance Tax Act, ss 8A–8C.

6.6 In satisfying the Nil Rate Band Legacy my executors may be required by [20–068M]
the Nil Rate Band Trustees to charge all or any part of my residuary estate
with the payment of all or any part of the Nil Rate Band Legacy including
such terms regarding index linking and security as the Nil Rate Band Trustees
think fit

[20–068N] **6.7** In satisfying the Nil Rate Band Legacy as above neither the executors nor the Nil Rate Bank Trustees shall be under any liability in relation to the payment or otherwise of the Nil Rate Band Legacy

[20–068O] **6.8** My executors may transfer any property so charged to my spouse who will not be liable personally for payment of the charged Nil Rate Band Legacy

[20–068P] **6.9** The Nil Rate Band Trustees must be at least two persons at all times and can be the same persons as my executors

[20–068Q] **6.10** The provisions of this clause are not exercisable by my spouse as a sole Nil Rate Band Trustee

[20–068R] **6.11** In administering the Nil Rate Band Trust the Nil Rate Band Trustees have the same powers are given to executors by the Will

IMMEDIATE GIFTS TO SPOUSE

[20–068S] **7** I give the remainder of my estate (my residuary estate) to my wife absolutely (*or*) during her life and on her death on shall divide my residuary estate amongst all or any of my [legitimate] children who are living at my death (*or*) on the death of the survivor of myself and my wife and attain the age of [18] years and if more than one in equal shares.

[20–068T] *[appropriate trustee powers eg [20–300]]*

[20–068U] 1   The aim of including a nil rate band legacy in a will is to make use of the nil rate band on the first death of a couple. By giving it to a class of beneficiaries including the testator's spouse or civil partner the survivor could have access to the trust funds (with the consent of the Nil Rate Band Trustees) if he or she requires additional assets The nil rate band trust only arises if there is a surviving spouse or civil partner. If the discretionary trust rules are followed, the assets in the trust should not be subject to IHT on the death of the surviving spouse. Consider the effect of the transferable nil rate band may have on this legacy, and if necessary specifically include or exclude the operation of these sections.

2   Assets held as collections may not necessarily be articles of personal use in the definition of personal chattels by s 55 of the Administration of Estates Act 1925: *Re Crispin's Will Trusts, Arkwright v Thurley* [1975] Ch 245, [1974] 3 All ER 772, CA. In *Re Collin's Will Trusts, Donne v Hewetson* [1971] 1 All ER 283, [1971] 1 WLR 37 a stamp collection, a coin collection and a motor car came within the expression 'personal effects'.

3   If the spouse has not been named before, insert the name in full. See [20–186], note 2.

4   Costs of packing and forwarding specific legacies are payable by the legatee (*Re Scott, Scott v Scott* [1915] 1 Ch 592, CA; *Re Fitzpatrick, Bennett v Bennett* [1952] Ch 86, [1951] 2 All ER 949). Where the estate is insufficient to pay the legacies in full these costs must in the absence of special provisions be borne by the legatees (*Re Sivewright, Law v Fenwick* (1922) 128 LT 416; *Re Leach, Milne v Daubeny* [1923] 1 Ch 161, [1922] All ER Rep 714).

5   The amount of the legacy would not be known until the testator's death as it depends on the inheritance tax rates and limits current at the date of death, the amount of any significant transfers made during the seven years prior to your death and the value of any other legacies made in your Will. The gift could be limited to a fixed sum instead of the full nil rate band. If an estate on death is valued at less than the nil rate band then the whole of the estate (after payment of any other legacies) will be held on discretionary trust. However, if an estate on death is valued at more than the nil rate band then only assets up to the value of the Nil be held on the trusts of residue.

6   The trustees would not be bound to share out the trust fund in any particular way but would have complete discretion as to who (among the class of beneficiaries) should benefit. Thus it is important to have a letter of wishes setting out how the testator wishes to benefit the beneficiaries.

7   The assets that can be placed in the trust include cash, investments, property, or a charge taken over a property for the value of the nil rate band legacy. The question of which assets to put into the nil rate band trust should be discussed with the surviving spouse and his/her co-executors after the first death and a decision is taken then as to the assets to put into the nil rate band trust. Where the family assets consist mainly of property it is possible to fund the nil

rate band trust by taking a charge (mortgage) over the property. There are various types of charge which could be taken over property, ie Fixed, Interest-Bearing or Indexed to the RPI.

7 Will providing for the maintenance of a spouse [who is a person suffering from mental disorder] with unlimited recourse to capital[1]

[20–091]

1   Where (i) a person is incapable of managing his affairs by reason of a mental disorder (Mental Health Act 1983, s 1 as amended by the Mental Health Act 2007, ss 1–3, 55, Sch 11, Pt 1); (ii) property is settled on trusts under which, during his life, no interest in possession subsists; and (iii) any of the settled property, which is applied during his life, is applied only or mainly for his benefit, then a distribution to that person is not a capital distribution and the periodic charge to tax shall be deferred until his death. Where the disabled person is the settlor, the making of the settlement and additions to it are not chargeable transfers: IHTA 1984, ss 74(1), (4), 89 as amended, inter alia, by the FA 2006 Sch 20 para 6(2). It does not appear to be necessary that the trusts are made for or even principally for the benefit of the disabled person, provided that any money which is applied is applied only or mainly for his benefit. Therefore it appears to be possible to use a discretionary settlement including, in the example of this precedent, the testator's children. The spouse may be in an institution so that all he will need will be extra comforts. He may, however, be discharged or for some time allowed out on licence. The form of will adopted gives the trustees power and opportunity to meet these varying circumstances if and when they happen. This will place some burden on the trustees but some relatives will usually be available and willing to undertake these duties. It is assumed that the estate is not a large one.

[20–098]

[1]   This precedent appears in the *Elderly Client Handbook, The Law Society's Guide to Acting for Older People*, by Gordon R Ashton (March 1994 edn) and contributed by Denzil Lush, solicitor. It is not a will and differs from wills in that it is intended to be used during the lifetime of the maker. It is also commonly called an advance directive or an advance decision to refuse treatment and its purpose is to give to others instructions about the sort of treatment that the maker would or would not want in the event of a serious illness or accident. The instructions in the will can take a number of general forms or may be a combination of the forms:

[20–175]

(a) a proxy directive — when the maker wishes others to make the decisions as to treatment for him. This is not yet enforceable in English law;

(b) a resist directive — where the maker expresses his wish as to the request he does not find acceptable; and

(c) an instruction directive — where the maker expresses his wish as to the treatment he does find acceptable.

So far as the latter two are concerned the directions must be clear, apply to the circumstances of the case, the maker must be of capacity when the directive was given and know the consequence of any refusal to be treated in a particular way, there must be no undue influence, the action required or not required must be unlawful, the directive must contemplate the circumstances that have arisen. It is difficult for any general directive to cover the above. In addition, if the directive is too specific it may not fully cover the circumstances. However, there is no doubt that such documents do give peace of mind to the maker and are invaluable in helping the next of kin who have very difficult choices to make when it comers to deciding the treatment of the gravely ill.

The Mental Capacity Act 2005 came into force in April 2007. Sections 24–26 deal with advance decisions to refuse medical treatment. Any person over 18 and with the necessary mental capacity can make an advance decision to refuse medical treatment. However, it will only be effective once the person loses his mental capacity. Health care directives can also now be given under a lasting power of attorney (replacing enduring powers of attorney) from 1 October 2007. Note that under the Act the advance decision will be revoked if the person making the advance decision gives health care decisions under a lasting power of attorney. Such an act may also revoke a living Will. See also the note on lasting powers of attorney at [18–089]. It must be in writing and signed and witnessed. It must also include a clause confirming that it applies even if life is at risk.

ADDITIONAL CLAUSES

Part 1: Introduction — name

Introduction to will — name and address of mentally disordered testator[1]

[20–179] THIS IS THE WILL of me (*name*) of (*address*) [and late of (*address*)] acting by (*name*) of (*address*) the person authorised in that behalf by an order of the Court of Protection dated (*date*) made under the Mental Capacity Act 2005.

[20–180] [1] A 'mentally disordered person' is now more properly referred to as a 'person lacking mental capacity': Mental Capacity Act 2005, s 2. See Mental Capacity Act 2005, ss 16, 18 and the testimonium and attestation clauses, [20–344] and [20–356], and the notes to them.

Use of any part of body for therapeutic purposes[1]

[20–224] **Note** This clause should be used with caution if at all pending expected changes in the law. The Human Tissues Act 1961 was repealed by the Human Tissue Act 2004 which is to be amended.

Use of (eg) eyes for therapeutic purposes

[20–226] **Note** This clause should be used with caution if at all pending expected changes in the law. The Human Tissues Act 1961 was repealed by the Human Tissues Act 2004 which is to be amended.

Use of any part of body for research, teaching or therapeutic purposes

[20–227] **Note** This clause should be used with caution if at all pending expected changes in the law. The Human Tissues Act 1961 was repealed by the Human Tissues Act 2004 which is to be amended.

Power to appoint foreign trustees[1]

[20–338] **x** My Trustees may appoint any person or corporation outside the jurisdiction of the courts of England and Wales to act as a trustee of this will in relation to any property situate outside England and Wales and may pay to that trustee or permit him to be paid out of the capital or income, of my Residuary Estate, or the property in respect of which he is appointed any fees or other remuneration which is customary in the country in which the foreign property is situate and make such arrangements generally with any such trustee as my Trustees deem expedient without being liable for any resulting directly or indirectly from the appointment.

Mentally disordered person[1]

[20–344] **In witness** of which this will is signed by me (*name*) acting by (*name*) pursuant to the above mentioned order on (*date*).

[20–345] [1] A 'mentally disordered person' is now more properly referred to as a 'person lacking mental capacity': Mental Capacity Act 2005, s 2. See Mental Capacity Act 2005, s 16, 18 and the beginning and attestation clauses, [20–179] and [20–356], and the notes to them.

Will of a mentally disordered person[1]

[20–356] **Signed** by (*name*) with the name of [name of testator] and with [his] own name pursuant to the said order in the presence of both of us and then by us in [his].

Sealed with the official seal of the Court of Protection on (*date*).

[1] This is an attestation clause of a will of a person lacking mental capacity. The powers of the   **[20–357]**
Court of Protection under the Mental Capacity Act 2005, s 16 include, under s 18(1)(i), the
execution of a will for a person lacking capacity. Sch 2, para 3 set out the requirements
relating to the execution of such a will, which must:
(a) state that it is signed by the patient acting by the authorised person;
(b) be signed by the authorised person with the name of the patient, and with his own name,
    in the presence of two or more witnesses present at the same time;
(c) be attested and subscribed by the witnesses in the presence of the authorised person; and
(d) be sealed with the official seal of the Court of Protection.

22 Easements and boundaries

PRECEDENTS

[22–016] 1 Stamp duty land tax return required where consideration is given for the grant and payment of duty where the consideration exceeds the threshold for duty to apply. An easement in fee simple or for a term of years absolute is a legal estate: Law of Property Act 1925, s 1(2)(a). The grant must in law be by deed: *Wood v Leadbitter* (1845) 13 M & W 838. By the Law of Property (Miscellaneous Provisions) Act 1989, s 2 there must be agreement in writing signed by or on behalf of the parties.

A legal easement cannot be registered as a separate title but only as appurtenant to a registered estate and the grant of an easement over registered land must be substantively registered as a disposition of the title of the servient tenement: Land Registration Act 2002, s 27(2)(d), Sch 2, para 7; Land Registration Rules 2003, SI 2003/1417, r 5(b)(ii), as substituted by SI 2008/1919, r 1(b).

If the grant for any reason takes effect as an equitable interest only (Law of Property Act 1925, s 1(3)), it is not registrable as a disposition nor is it an overriding interest under the Land Registration Act 2002, ss 11, 12, 29, Sch 1, Sch 3. An equitable easement that would be a land charge if the land affected were not registered therefore needs to be protected by entering a notice (Land Registration Act 2002, s 32) against the registered title of the servient property. In the case of unregistered land, an equitable easement should be registered as a Class D(iii) land charge (Land Charges Act 1972, s 2(1), (5)(iii)), and, if not registered, it is void against a purchaser for money or money's worth of a legal estate in the servient property (Land Charges Act 1972, s 4(6)). Once registered as a land charge, an equitable easement cannot be overreached (Law of Property Act 1925, s 2(3)). An easement may be validly reserved even though it does not expressly state the dominant tenement, if it is clear from the surrounding circumstances what the dominant tenement is: *Johnstone v Holdway* [1963] 1 QB 601, [1963] 1 All ER 432 and *St Edmundsbury and Ipswich Diocesan Board of Finance v Clark (No 2)* [1975] 1 All ER 772, [1975] 1 WLR 468, CA.

A grantor can by one deed convey land to one person, and subject it in his hands to a right of way (or other easement) in favour of another: Law of Property Act 1925, s 65.

As to a right of way of necessity where land is completely enclosed by grantor's land or nearly so: *Barry v Hasseldine* [1952] Ch 835, [1952] 2 All ER 317.

A land owner may build right up to the edge of a right of way: *Minor v Groves* (1997) 80 P&CR 136, CA.

The erection of a gate across a pedestrian rights of way (to secure small children from wandering onto a road) did not amount to a substantial obstruction to the easement, as the owners of the dominant tenements were supplied with keys: *Hall v Shepherd* (22 June 1993, unreported).

2 A right of way for all purposes is confined to the nature of the property at the time of the grant. Thus where the purpose at the time of grant was agricultural, an extension to purposes of a camping ground was an unjustifiable increase in the burden and not included in the grant: *RPC Holdings Ltd v Rogers* [1953] 1 All ER 1029; agriculture could include forestry but not storage of timber felled elsewhere: *Jobson v Record* (1997) 75 P & CR 375, CA. But a right of way is not lost where there was a mere increase in user and not user of a different kind or for a different purpose: *Woodhouse & Co Ltd v Kirkland (Derby) Ltd* [1970] 2 All ER 587, [1970] 1 WLR 1185; *Cargill v Gotts* [1980] 2 All ER 49, [1980] 1 WLR 521.

3 The benefit and burden of a repairing covenant intended to bind successors has been held to pass: *Halsall v Brizell* [1957] Ch 169, [1957] 1 All ER 371 — an obligation to pay costs of upkeep to enjoy a right of way. But consider other means to ensure payment, e g estate rentcharge.

4 The Law of Property Act 1925 provides that the rule against perpetuities does not apply to easements granted or reserved for certain purposes: LPA 1925, s 162(1)(d). However, the perpetuity rule is concerned with the vesting of the right, not with its exercise: in *Dunn v Blackdown Properties Ltd* [1961] Ch 433, [1961] 2 All ER 62, it was held that the grant of a right to use the sewers and drains 'now passing or hereafter to pass' was void for perpetuity since no drains or sewers were in existence at the date of the conveyance. Whilst the grant of a

future easement may be saved by the 'wait and see' rule of the Perpetuities and Accumulations Act 1964, s 3, this should not be relied upon and the grant of an easement to arise in the future should be framed so as to be exercisable only within the perpetuity period: eg a specified number of years (not exceeding 80) from the date of the deed: Perpetuities and Accumulations Act 1964, s 1(1).

5   To enable the easement to be substantively registered as a disposition of a registered title, application must be made for this in Land Registry Form AP1: Land Registration Rules 2003, SI 2003/1417, r 13, Sch 1, as substituted by SI 2008/1919.

1   An exchange is a land transaction and is therefore potentially subject to stamp duty land tax: **[22–078]**
Finance Act 2003, s 47. For this purpose the disposal of land on each side of the transaction is treated as if each is a distinct transaction separate from the other. A separate land transaction return is therefore required for each of the transactions comprising the exchange, where the value of the land on either side exceeds the threshold for duty to apply and an appropriate receipt for each of the returns issued by HMRC will need to be lodged at the Land Registry when application is made to register the land affected by the deed of exchange (the exchanges, being for value, will trigger the requirement for registration: Land Registration Act 2002, s 4(1)(a)(i)).

2   See [25–835], note 4, as to references to plans in conveyances. This is a case where the plans should be definitive and the 'more particularly delineated' is here correct. It may be necessary to have a survey and a new plan made.

23 Leases and tenancy agreements

PRECEDENTS

[23–098]

1   With effect from 28 February 1997 any new assured tenancy is automatically an assured shorthold tenancy (Housing Act 1988, s 19A, inserted by Housing Act 1996), except in the circumstances set out in Housing Act 1988, Sch 2A. There is no need for these new tenancies to have a minimum fixed term of six months or for there to be a prior landlord's notice. The court must make an order for possession on or after the tenancy comes to an end, if the landlord has given not less than two months' prior notice to the tenant stating that he requires possession. No reason need be stated. The notice may be given before or on the day on which the tenancy comes to an end: Housing Act 1988, s 21(2). If it is given to have effect when the tenancy has become periodic, it must end on the last day of a period of the tenancy: Housing Act 1988, s 21(4)(a).

Possession can be recovered during the tenancy but only on the grounds in Housing Act 1988, Sch 2, ie the grounds on which an assured tenancy can be terminated. This requires both express provision for termination (Housing Act 1988, s 7(6)(b), and see [23–810], [23–086], [23–087], [23–812]) and notice of intended application possession (form 3 in the Assured Tenancies and Agricultural Occupancies (Forms) Regulations 1997, SI 1997/194, as amended by the Assured Tenancies and Agricultural Occupancies (Forms) (Amendment) (England) Regulations 2003, SI 2003/260. For this reason assured shorthold tenancies are most advantageous for the landlord if made for an initial fixed term of six months, followed either by further fixed terms (which may be for less than six months) or a periodic weekly or monthly tenancy rather than for a longer term, which might require termination during the tenancy.

The Civil Procedure Rules, which came into force in October 2001, provide an accelerated possession procedure for certain assured shorthold tenancies only (Pt 55, Pt II). The conditions are set out in r 55.12, but for the court to make an order on the papers (ie without a hearing) the claim and defence forms must be prescribed forms and the Court must be satisfied that the landlord is entitled to an order for possession. In *Manel v Memon* (2000) 33 HLR 235, it was held that the tenant's allegation that a s 20 notice had not been served meant the accelerated procedure was not appropriate and the District Judge should not have made an immediate order for possession.

2   The tenancy many, but need not be for a fixed term. If on the coming to an end of an assured shorthold tenancy, a new tenancy comes into being between the same parties of the same or substantially the same premises and terms, it will be an assured shorthold tenancy, if and so long as it is an assured tenancy: Housing Act 1988, s 19A (or s 20(4) in respect of pre-Housing Act 1996 tenancies).

3   Generally tenants should not agree to preconditions to their rights to terminate a lease or tenancy other than, at most, payment of rent and other sums due and, if appropriate demanded, on the date of termination. Preconditions relating to performance or observance of covenants may be narrowly construed by a landlord, and could include once and for all breaches, which have been remedied. Note also the respective requirements that the landlord has given two month's notice to terminate (subject to the tenant's minimum six months' security of tenure) and that the tenant has served a notice to quit (see *Laine v Cadwallader* (2000) 33 HLR 397). This case established that as the Housing Act 1988 is silent on the point, the common law rule that a tenant can terminate a periodic tenancy only by giving a notice to quit equal to one period of the tenancy will apply (a statutory periodic tenancy arises at the end of the term of an assured shorthold – s 5(2)). This is subject to the four-week minimum period under s 5 of the Protection from Eviction Act 1977 although, in contrast to a notice served by a landlord on a tenant, there is no requirement that it contain prescribed information. However, the landlord may accept an offer to surrender, in which case the notice period will not apply, although any such acceptance by the landlord must be express.

4   The House of Lords dismissed actions in nuisance and for breach of the covenant for quiet enjoyment in *Southwark London Borough Council v Mills; Yvonne Elisabeth Baxter v Camden London Borough Council* [1999] 4 All ER 449, [1999] 3 WLR 939. It established that tenants cannot require landlords to install soundproofing to prevent ordinary everyday noises in

neighbouring premises being heard. The neighbours themselves were not creating a nuisance and so the Councils could not be liable for authorising them do to so. The covenant for quiet enjoyment does not imply a warranty that the premises are fit for any purpose. It is a prospective covenant so it applies to things done after the grant of a lease or tenancy, even though the consequences of pre-existing circumstances or conditions existing at the premises may continue to have an effect throughout the term of the lease. A lessor is not liable under the covenant for quiet enjoyment for the acts of strangers even though they purport to act under him unless the covenant is sufficiently widely worded to embrace them or it names particular individuals or identifies a person by reference to a particular interest in property: see *Queensway Marketing Ltd v Associated Restaurants Limited* [1988] 2 EGLR 49 in which earlier authorities are considered. It was held in *Matalan Discount Club (Cash and Carry) Ltd v Tokenspire* [2001] All ER (D) 260 (May) that a shopping centre landlord was not liable for a breach of the covenant for quiet enjoyment when repairs were carried out negligently by a roofing contractor, causing damage to tenants' goods.

5   Section 16 of the Housing Act 1988 implies into every assured tenancy an obligation on the tenant to allow the landlord access to the property and reasonable facilities for executing repairs.

6   The words 'without any deduction' were insufficient to exclude the tenant's equitable right of set off: *Connaught Restaurants Ltd v Indoor Leisure Ltd* [1994] 4 All ER 834, [1994] 1 WLR 501, CA. Also it was held in *Fuller v Happy Shopper Markets Ltd* [2001] 2 EGLR 32 that it is not possible to exclude any statutory rights to deduct amounts from rent and such provisions may contravene the Human Rights Act 1998.

See also note 23 below regarding the Office of Fair Trading Guidance on Unfair Terms in Tenancy Agreements.

7   Except in the case of a protected tenancy a deposit is not an illegal premium, but in order not to be a penalty it must be reasonable in relation to the potential liability for which it is paid. The Housing Act 2004, ss 212–214 came into force on 6 April 2007. Section 213 requires tenancy deposits to be held in accordance with a scheme authorised by the statute, and for certain prescribed information to be given to the tenant within fourteen days of the date on which the deposit is paid. See form [23–172A]. In relation to a shorthold tenancy, s 213(7) provides that no property other than money may be taken as a deposit.

8   The Landlord and Tenant Act 1985, s 11 implies certain conditions in the lettings for terms of less than seven years. The repairing provisions in ss 11 to 16 of the Landlord and Tenant Act 1985 may be left to take their course, and these clauses are for use only where the parties wish specifically to define their rights so far as the loose phrasing of the Act allows.

A lease is for less than seven years if it is determinable at the option of the landlord before the expiration of seven years from the commencement of the term. Except where the landlord has such an option, it is not for less than seven years if it confers on the tenant an option for a renewal for a term which with the original term amounts to seven years or more: Landlord and Tenant Act 1985, s 13(2). The period of the lease is to be calculated from the date of the lease and any part of the term before such date is to be left out of account (Landlord and Tenant Act 1985, s 13(2)), but the period may run from the date of the agreement for the lease: *Brikom Investments Ltd v Seaford* [1981] 2 All ER 783, [1981] 1 WLR 863, CA.

The obligations of the landlord are (a) to keep in repair the structure and exterior of the dwelling house (including drains, gutters and external pipes); and (b) to keep in repair and proper working order the installations (i) for the supply of water, gas and electricity, and for sanitation (including basins, sinks, baths and sanitary conveniences, but not other fixtures, fittings and appliances for making use of the supply of water, gas or electricity) and (ii) for space heating and heating water. These provisions must not be construed as requiring the landlord (a) to carry out any works or repairs for which the tenant is liable by virtue of his duty to use the premises in a tenant-like manner or would be so liable apart from any express covenant on his part; (b) to rebuild or reinstate the premises in the case of destruction or damage by fire, tempest, flood, or other inevitable accident; or (c) to keep in repair or maintain anything which the tenant is entitled to remove from the demised premises. As to making good inherent defects, see note 9 below.

The Landlord may not withhold his consent unreasonably to a request to carry out alterations to the Property: Landlord and Tenant Act 1927, s 19(2).

9   This clause is implied by the Landlord and Tenant Act 1985, s 11(6). If the term is less than seven years, the landlord of a dwelling house is responsible for the repairs stated in the Landlord and Tenant Act 1985, ss 11 to 16, as to which see note 7 above. The tenant's repairing obligations can extend to remedying inherent defects: *Ravenseft Properties Ltd v Davstone (Holdings) Ltd* [1978] QB 52, [1977] 1 All ER 47. However, the statutory duty of the landlord to repair under the Landlord and Tenant Act 1985 does not extend to improvements: *Quick v Taff Ely Borough Council* [1986] QB 809, [1985] 3 All ER 321. It has also been held

that it is not permissible to reinterpret the Landlord and Tenant Act 1985, s 11(1)(a) by virtue of the Human Rights Act 1998, s 3 in order to impose a general and unqualified obligation on local authorities in relation to their housing stock: *Ratcliffe v Sandwell Metropolitan Borough Council* [2002] EWCA Civ 06, [2002] 2 P&CR 322.

¹⁰ Insurance in respect of the risks of flooding and terrorism is currently of most concern in both commercial and residential lettings. Where the tenant is itself effecting or, by way of reimbursing the landlord, paying the premium, it may not wish to pay a significantly increased premium to include such risks. If either party covenants to insure in respect of risks specified in the lease, it should ensure that the obligation is limited to where such risks are insurable or insurable on reasonable terms in the marketplace, as some risks may become uninsurable at some point during the term. Alternatively, insured risks may be defined as those against which, more usually, the landlord has insured from time to time, with or without a list of possible or minimum risks, to give the landlord maximum flexibility. This is not satisfactory from the tenant's perspective, as it is uncertain, although this can be mitigated by the landlord agreeing to notify the tenant of any changes to the terms and risks insured under the policy. The parties should decide who is to bear the risk of there being a shortfall in the monies paid out by insurers and who is required to repair or reinstate if damage or destruction is caused by an uninsured or uninsurable risk. If necessary the tenant's repairing and service charge obligations should be qualified. A party may even consider back up insurance on their own (or a group) policy, where they agree to bear the risk of covenanting to reinstate the premises on the happening of certain events. For example, in commercial and industrial lettings it is possible to obtain cover for terrorism through the Pool Re scheme, which is backed by the government. Alternatively, either or both parties could have the ability to exercise a break option, if the premises are damaged or destroyed by an uninsured or uninsurable risk and/or not reinstated within an agreed period.

¹¹ Under Landlord and Tenant Act 1927, s 19, any provision against assigning, underletting, or parting with premises without consent is deemed to be subject to a proviso that such consent is not to be unreasonably withheld. The Landlord and Tenant (Covenants) Act 1995 introduced the ability of the parties to agree in advance and set out in the lease the circumstances in which the landlord could refuse consent to an assignment and any conditions to be satisfied (see clauses [23–831] to [23–845]). If it is desired fully to protect the landlord there must simply be a bare provision against assignment, underletting or parting with possession without any reference to consent by the landlord. The landlord may not refuse consent in order to achieve a collateral purpose unconnected with the terms of the tenancy (*Bromley Park Garden Estates Ltd v Moss* [1982] 2 All ER 890, [1982] 1 WLR 1019, CA). The landlord may be required to have regard to the consequences for the tenant of a withholding of consent: *International Drilling Fluids Ltd v Louisville Investments (Uxbridge) Ltd* [1986] Ch 513, [1986] 1 All ER 321. It was held in *Ashworth Frazer Ltd v Gloucester City Council* [2001] UKHL 59, [2002] 1 All ER 377 that whilst it is always a question of fact, a landlord may reasonably withhold consent to an assignment on the basis the proposed assignee intends to breach the user covenant.

The Housing Act 1988, s 15 implies into statutory and assured periodic tenancies a covenant not to assign, sub-let or part with possession of the whole or part of the property, if there is no express provision in the lease.

¹² In *Johnstone v Swan Estates Ltd* [1942] Ch 98, [1941] 3 All ER 446, it was held that the option to determine is independent of any obligation to repair so that the tenant may determine his lease although he has covenanted to repair and has not repaired. Where a lease contains terms that conditions, such as payment of rent or compliance with repairing covenants, must be complied with before a notice may be served, strict compliance is required.

¹³ See also notes 1 and 3 above regarding termination of the agreement by the parties.

¹⁴ The parties should be aware of the Property Litigation Association's 'Pre-action Protocol: Terminal Dilapidations Claims for Damages', which is an attempt to standardise or be a guide to best practice for terminal dilapidations claims. It provides a format for schedules of dilapidations, addresses the cap on damages arising from s 18 of the Landlord and Tenant Act 1927 and requires the tenant to provide valuation evidence. Due to the amount of detail required in the schedule which sets out the breaches of the tenant's repairing obligations, it is more likely to be used in higher value, consequently commercial lettings. The Protocol can be obtained online from the Property Litigation Association's website: www.pla.org.uk.

¹⁵ This sub-clause should be omitted in the case of long leases of residential property, which are likely to be used as security in a mortgage. The CML *Lender's Handbook for England & Wales*, introduced in 1999, contains comprehensive standard instructions to solicitors and licensed conveyancers. It was prepared by seven major lenders in consultation with the Law Society, and complies with r 6(3) of the Solicitors' Practice Rules 1990. It includes standard requirements relating to leasehold properties, for example, the minimum unexpired term and

that there must be no provision for forfeiture on the insolvency of the tenant or any superior landlord. A second edition of the handbook has been published and is to be used where instructions are received on or after 1 October 2002. The handbook can be obtained from the Council of Mortgage Lenders website: www.cml.org.uk.

16 This sub-clause should be included only where the tenancy is an assured tenancy. In an assured shorthold tenancy the reference to ground 2 (sale by mortgagee) should be omitted or qualified as in this form. Ground 2 is ambiguous, but it seems that it can be relied on only if notice is given under ground 1 (possession sought by owner occupier). There is therefore a risk that the prescribed form (see [23–810]) to be served before the start of the tenancy may not preclude the possibility that ground 2 (involving termination by the landlord) may be relied on in the first six months of the tenancy.

17 Both these dates must be within the preceding 12 months.

18 The tenancy must be for a term certain not exceeding eight months and the property must have been occupied under a right to occupy for a holiday within the period of 12 months ended on the relevant date. Where the tenancy is expressed to be for the purpose of a holiday the burden of proving that the tenancy is not for the purposes of a holiday rests on the tenant: *Buchmann v May* [1978] 2 All ER 993, CA.

19 The tenancy must be for a term certain not exceeding twelve months and the property must have been subject, at some time within the period of 12 months ended on the relevant date, to a tenancy granted to a student by a specified educational institute.

20 Any guarantors to the original lease should be party to any supplemental documents, as otherwise, any variations to it which are to the guarantor's detriment may release the guarantor.

21 Although likely to be more used in commercial lettings, there may be circumstances, such as where there is an impending disposal of the landlord's reversion, when a landlord may wish to obtain the tenant's qualified consent to release from the 'landlord covenants' in the lease or tenancy under ss 6–8 of the Landlord and Tenant (Covenants) Act 1995. This clause effectively does little more than draw to the tenant's attention its statutory obligations, but some may wish to include it nevertheless.

Under ss 6–8, a landlord may serve notice on a tenant requesting a release before or within four weeks of an assignment by it of the reversion. If the tenant does not object in writing within four weeks, the landlord is released to the extent mentioned in the notice. If the tenant does object, the landlord may apply to the court for a declaration that such a release is reasonable.

Under s 26(1)(a) nothing in the Act is to be read as preventing a party from releasing a person from a 'landlord covenant'. In *Avonridge Property Co Ltd v Mashru* [2005] UKHL 70, [2006] OEIG 100 the House of Lords considered the ability of the parties to agree to a provision in the lease limiting the lessor's liability upon assignment of the reversion. It was held that the 1995 Act was not intended to interfere with the parties' freedom of contract and that the provision didn't fall foul of the anti-avoidance provisions in s 25.

The case of *BHP Petroleum Great Britain Ltd v Chesterfield Properties Ltd* [2001] EWCA Civ 1797, [2002] Ch 194 addressed the distinction between 'landlord covenants' and personal covenants for the purposes of such a release. It was held that, despite the release from 'landlord covenants' under s 8, (defined in s 28(1) as covenants 'to be complied with by the landlord of premises demised by the tenancy'), personal covenants such as those relating to refurbishment works were not transmissible to the landlord from time to time entitled to the reversion.

Clearly landlords should consider obtaining a release from any personal covenants given in the agreement for lease, the lease itself or any other collateral agreements; as they fall outside the Act, they are not subject to the above restrictions.

22 Where the parties to an assured or assured shorthold agreement are involved in the provision of services as, respectively, a person carrying on business and a consumer and the terms of their agreements are not individually negotiated, they should be aware of the most recent Guidance On Unfair Terms In Tenancy Agreements. This was drawn up by the Office of Fair Trading and sets out standard clauses in assured and assured shorthold tenancy agreements, which, in its view, are potentially unfair under the Unfair Terms in Consumer Contracts Regulations 1999, SI 1999/2083. Although the courts would ultimately decide whether any term is unfair, the Guidance sets out the basis on which the OFT is likely to take enforcement action.

Examples of potentially unfair terms are those which: exclude or limit the landlord's liability in relation to the condition of the premises or appliances in them; transfer to the tenant liability which is the landlord's under statute; limit or exclude the tenant's right of set-off; enable the landlord to determine whether he is in breach of the agreement; give the landlord excessive rights of entry; provide the tenant should indemnify the landlord for legal costs, which should instead be costs reasonably incurred and also on the basis that the word 'indemnify' is legal jargon.

The Guidance can be found on the Office of Fair Trading website at www.oft.gov.uk.

[23–172A]   8A   Residential Tenancy Deposit: Notice of Prescribed Information[1]

DETAILS OF THE SCHEME ADMINISTRATOR OF THE AUTHORISED TENANCY DEPOSIT SCHEME THAT APPLIES TO THIS DEPOSIT

[23–172AA]   Name:

Address:

Telephone number:

E-mail address:

Fax number (if any):

INFORMATION CONTAINED IN A LEAFLET SUPPLIED BY THE SCHEME ADMINISTRATOR TO THE LANDLORD WHICH EXPLAINS THE OPERATION OF SECTIONS 212 TO 215 AND SCHEDULE 10

[23–172B]   The leaflet is attached. Paragraphs [ ] are especially relevant.

PROCEDURES THAT APPLY BY WHICH AN AMOUNT IN RESPECT OF A DEPOSIT MAY BE PAID OR REPAID TO THE TENANT AT THE END OF THE TENANCY

[23–172BA]   The leaflet is attached. Paragraphs [ ] are especially relevant.

PROCEDURES THAT APPLY WHERE EITHER THE LANDLORD OR THE TENANT IS NOT CONTACTABLE AT THE END OF THE TENANCY.

[23–172C]   The leaflet is attached. Paragraphs [ ] are especially relevant.

PROCEDURES THAT APPLY WHERE THE LANDLORD AND THE TENANT DISPUTE THE AMOUNT TO BE PAID OR REPAID TO THE TENANT

[23–172CA]   The leaflet is attached. Paragraphs [ ] are especially relevant.

FACILITIES AVAILABLE FOR ENABLING A DISPUTE RELATING TO THE DEPOSIT TO BE RESOLVED WITHOUT RECOURSE TO LITIGATION

[23–172D]   The leaflet is attached. Paragraphs [ ] are especially relevant.

INFORMATION ABOUT THE TENANCY IN RESPECT OF WHICH THE DEPOSIT HAS BEEN PAID

(i) Deposit [23–172DA]

amount of the deposit paid: [£] *paid on [insert date of payment]*[2]

(ii) The property to which the tenancy relates

Address:

(iii) The Landlord

Name:

(company/industrial & provident society number if applicable:)

Address:

Telephone number:

Any e-mail address:

Any fax number:

(iv) The Tenant

Details relevant now

Name:

Address:

Telephone number:

Any e-mail address:

Any fax number:

Details that should be used by the landlord or scheme administrator for the purpose of contacting the tenant at the end of the tenancy

Address:

Telephone number:

Any e-mail address:

Any fax number:

(v) Any person who paid the deposit on behalf of the tenant

Name:

Address:

Telephone number:

Any e-mail address:

Any fax number:

(vi) Circumstances when all or part of the deposit may be retained by the landlord

[Insert relevant excerpt of the terms of the tenancy, and refer to it by clause number]

(vii) Certificate by the landlord

The landlord certifies that

(aa) the information he provides in this notice is accurate to the best of his knowledge and belief; and

(bb) he has given the tenant the opportunity to sign this notice by way of confirmation that the information is accurate to the best of his knowledge and belief.

(*signed*)

Signed by the landlord

Date[3]

(*signed*)

Signed by the tenant

[23–172E] [1] Housing Act 2004, ss 212–214 came into force on 6 April 2007. Schedule 10 also applies. They require residential tenancy deposits to be held in accordance with a scheme authorised under the statute. Schemes may be custodial, where the deposit is held by the scheme administrator of the authorised scheme; or may be insurance schemes, where the landlord retains the deposit, but with insurance to cover the risk that the landlord will not comply with the directions of the scheme administrator. There are currently one custodian scheme and two insurance schemes that are authorised.

Section 213(5) requires prescribed information to be given to the tenant. The information has been prescribed by the Housing (Tenancy Deposits) (Prescribed Information) Order 2007, SI 2007/797. Section 213(6) requires the information to be given in prescribed form, but no form has been prescribed, and ministers do not intend to make an Order prescribing the form. It is not thought the inability to comply with s 213(6) will mean that deposits cannot be taken, so long as the prescribed information is given.

The sanctions for non-compliance in s 215 are serious. The landlord cannot serve a s 21 Notice (ie for recovery of possession on termination of shorthold tenancy under the Housing Act 1988, s 21) at a time when (a) the deposit is not being held in accordance with an authorised scheme, or (b) the initial requirements of such a scheme (see s 213(4)) have not been complied with in relation to the deposit. It might appear, therefore, that a landlord could remedy non-compliance by putting any such deposits into authorised schemes when he wanted to recover possession, and while this may be true, the sanction in s 214(4) means that in any proceedings where it is found that the deposit has not been held in accordance with an authorised scheme or where the prescribed information has not been given in the prescribed form or a form to the like effect (but NB, no form has been prescribed) then the court must also order the landlord to pay to the applicant a sum of money equal to three times the amount of the deposit within the period of 14 days beginning with the date of the making of the order.

These requirements apply to all landlords, public sector and registered social landlords as well as private sector landlords.

[2] This information is not required by the Housing (Tenancy Deposits) (Prescribed Information) Order 2007, SI 2007/797, but is essential to demonstrate that the notice of prescribed information has been given within the period of 14 days beginning with the date on which the deposit is received that is required by the Housing Act 2004, s 213(3).

[3] This must be within 14 days of the payment of the deposit.

[23–172EA] ## 8B   Clause for insertion in lease to give rights to a mortgagees in respect of forfeiture for want of repair[1]

[23–172F] **x.1** In this clause the following words and expressions have the meanings specified unless expressly stated to the contrary:

'Mortgagee'   the proprietor of any registered charge of the Property from time to time, or

— the owner of any legal mortgage of the property from time to time who has served written notice of the mortgage with an address for service on the (*Party-A*) [and

— the owner of any equitable mortgage of the property who has several written notice of the mortgage with an address for service on the (*Party-A*)].

x.2 It is a condition precedent to forfeiture or re-entry of the Property that the (*Party-A*) has served on the Mortgagee a copy of any notice served under section 146 of the Law of Property Act 1925 on the (*Party-B*).

x.3 The (*Party-A*) agrees that the Mortgagee will be entitled to remedy any breach specified in the notice mentioned in this clause that is capable of remedy.

x.4 The (*Party-A*) agrees that the Mortgagee will be entitled to the benefit of the Leasehold Property (Repairs) Act 1938 and will not treat any notice purportedly served under that Act by the Mortgagee as invalid merely because it has been served by the Mortgagee.[2]

x.5 Notwithstanding anything else in this Lease this clause is intended to benefit and to be enforceable by any Mortgagee.[3]

---

[1] The Rules of Court (PD55) require notice to have been served on any person whom the applicant knows to be entitled to apply for relief against forfeiture, and so a clause to the effect of the first part is not necessary. Not all mortgagees' solicitors are happy with this, and such a clause may offer them comfort; it can readily be adapted for use in a rentcharge with a right of forfeiture or re-entry annexed. **[23–172FA]**

[2] This is not a standard requirement of CML members or of other mortgages, which must be presumed to have taken informed and commercial decisions not to have such a requirement. Solicitors are generally not under a duty to volunteer commercial advice, and so such a clause should be used only in specific circumstances where especially required, perhaps where repair is a condition of a freehold rentcharge.

[3] For a note about the Contracts (Rights of Third Parties) Act 1999, see [2–242].

8C   Rent deposit agreement — a deposit paid to the landlord as part payment and security for future performance by the tenant   [23–172G]

Suggested terms for parties: [23–172GA]

(*Party-A*)	'Landlord'
(*Party-B*)	'Tenant'
(*Party-C*)	'Deposit Holder'

Date and parties

THIS AGREEMENT is made on (*date*) between (*name*) of (*address*) ('(*Party-A*)'), (*name*) of (*address*) ('(*Party-B*)') and (*name*) of (*address*) ('(*Party-C*)').   [23–172H]

Definitions and interpretation

1.1 In this agreement the following terms shall have the following meanings except when expressly stated to the contrary: [23–172HA]

'Bank'	the (*Party-A*)'s bankers from time to time.

'Deposit Balance'	the amount of money from time to time which is equal to the Initial Deposit less any Drawings plus any Interest which has not been paid to the (*Party-B*).
'Drawings'	the amount from time to time which the (*Party-A*) has drawn against the Deposit Balance under clause 0 and which has not been paid to the (*Party-A*) by the (*Party-B*) under clause 0.
'Initial Deposit'	£[....] [excluding VAT (*or*) including VAT of £[....]].[1]
'Interest'	the amount of money from time to time which is equal to the amount which has been credited by the Bank as interest in respect of the Deposit Balance less any tax required by law to be deducted from that amount and which amount of money has not yet been paid to the (*Party-B*) under clause 0.
'Lease'	a lease dated (*date*) and made between the (*Party-A*) and the (*Party-B*) by which the Property was let to the (*Party-B*).
'Property'	means the property known as (*address*) described in [the schedule to] the Lease and where the context so permits or requires any part of it.
'Rent Deposit Period'	[the term granted by the Lease howsoever it ends (*or*) the period commencing on (*date*) ending on (*date*).
'Rent Increase'	the amount by which the [Basic Rent] payable under the Lease is increased on with effect from each [Review Date[2]]
'Top Up Money'	the amount of money from time to time which is equal to [any or all of:] the Drawings of which the (Party-A) has given written notice to the (Party-B) [specify other amounts if appropriate, for rent increases and VAT for example]
'VAT'	value added tax chargeable under the Value Added Tax Act 1994 or any similar replacement or additional tax

1.2 The definitions and provisions as to interpretation in the Lease apply in this Deed [except where the context requires otherwise].

1.3 Except where the context renders it absurd or impossible every reference to any party to this (document) shall include his or her successors in title and personal representatives, by and against whom this agreement shall be enforceable as if they had been originally named as parties.

Background

[23–172I] **2.1** This rent deposit deed is supplemental to the Lease by which premises known as (*address*) described in [the schedule to] the Lease were let to the (*Party-B*).

2.2 The term granted by the Lease [is now (*or*) remains] vested in the (*Party-B*).

2.3 The reversion to the Lease [is now/remains] vested in the (*Party-A*).

Payment of initial deposit

3.1 The (*Party-B*) will pay the Initial Deposit to the (*Party-A*) on the date of [23–172IA] this Deed without any deduction or set off.

3.2 The (*Party-A*) is entitled to receive at the expense of the (*Party-B*) such evidence as the (*Party-A*) or the Bank requires regarding the source of the Initial Deposit with a view to avoiding any breach of the Terrorism Act 2000 the Financial Services and Markets Act 2000 or the Proceeds of Crime Act 2002 and the (*Party-B*) covenants to produce it within seven days of request.

The bank account

4 Following receipt both of the Initial Deposit and the information referred to [23–172J] in clause 3.2 the (*Party-A*) will place the Initial Deposit and any Top Up Money in an interest bearing account in its own name at the Bank.

Interest

5 The (*Party-A*) will pay Interest to the (*Party-B*) [annually or six monthly (*or*) [23–172JA] at the end of the Rent Deposit Period (*or*) within twenty eight days of having been notified of the crediting of interest by the Bank].

Drawings

6.1 The (*Party-A*) will not draw against the Deposit Balance other than to: [23–172K]
— remedy any breach by the (*Party-B*) of any covenant or condition in the Lease (including without limitation any non-payment of rent or other money due under the Lease); and
— make good on a full indemnity basis all costs and expenses (including legal and other professional fees) incurred or damages suffered by the (*Party-A*) because of or incidental to any of the events specified in clause 6.2.

6.2 The events for the purposes of clause 6.1 are:
— any breach by the (*Party-B*) of any covenant or condition in the Lease;
— any contemplated or actual forfeiture of the term granted by the Lease even if any right of re-entry or forfeiture has been waived by the (*Party-A*) or if the (*Party-B*) has been granted relief or if forfeiture is avoided otherwise than by relief granted by the Court;
— any contemplated or actual letting of the whole or any part of the premises demised by the Lease within [six months] of any forfeiture or disclaimer of the Lease;
— any contemplated or actual grant of any overriding lease pursuant to section 19 Landlord and Tenant (Covenants) Act 1995; or
— the implementation of arrangements under this deed including without limitation the service of notices and the calculation of Interest [but not the payment of any awards or costs ordered to be paid by the (*Party-A*) by an arbitrator under clause 12 or ordered by a Court or other tribunal of competent jurisdiction].

Top up money

7 The (*Party-B*) will pay Top Up Money to the (*Party-A*) without any [23–172KA] deduction or set off whatsoever within seven days of service by the (*Party-A*) on the (*Party-B*) of written notice of [*any or all of*] Drawings, a Rent Increase or VAT being payable on the supplies made by the (*Party-A*) under the Lease.

Assignment of the reversion

[23–172L] **8.1** If the (*Party-A*) assigns the reversion to the Lease during the Rent Deposit Period it is irrevocably authorised by the (*Party-B*) to pay the Deposit Balance standing at that time to its assignee (so long as the remaining provisions of this clause 8 are complied with).

8.2 The assignee of the reversion to the Lease [and the (*Party-B*)] must have entered into and delivered a Deed of Covenant under which the assignee of the reversion to the Lease covenants with the (*Party-B*) to observe and perform the obligations of the (*Party-A*) in this Deed.

8.3 If the (*Party-A*) assigns the reversion to the Lease and the provisions of clauses 8.1 and 8.2 have been complied with the (*Party-A*) will have no further obligation to the (*Party-B*) under this Deed.

8.4 If the (*Party-A*) assigns the reversion to the Lease during the Rent Deposit Period without procuring the deed referred to in clause 8.2 the (*Party-A*) will pay the Deposit Balance then standing at the time of the assignment to the (*Party-B*) and on doing so the (*Party-A*) will have no further obligation to the (*Party-B*) under this Deed.

Assignment of the lease

[23–172LA] **9** If the term granted by the Lease is lawfully assigned during the Rent Deposit Period then the obligations of the (*Party-A*) under this Deed will be owed to the assignee and the assignor (*Party-B*) will have no further claim against the (*Party-A*) under this Deed.

Payment to the (*Party-B*)

[23–172M] **10** The (*Party-A*) will pay the Deposit Balance to the (*Party-B*) within three months after the end of the Rent Deposit Period if the (*Party-A*) has no actual knowledge of any claim against the (*Party-B*) for any breach of any of the terms of the Lease.

No charge

[23–172MA] **11.1** The (*Party-B*) acknowledges that the Deposit Balance will be the property of the (*Party-A*) and that no trust or charge is created by this Deed.

11.2 The (*Party-B*) agrees and declares that the Initial Deposit is free from all security interests in favour of third parties [and will supply within seven days of demand and at its own expense such evidence as the (*Party-A*) requires in respect of it.]

Forfeiture right applies

[23–172N] **12** The (*Party-B*) acknowledges that the provisions of the Lease as to forfeiture of the Lease apply to any breach of this deed as well as to any breach of the terms of the Lease.

Notices³

13.1 Any notice given under this deed shall be in writing and may be served: **[23–192NA]**
—   personally;
—   by registered or recorded delivery mail;
—   [by email or [telex or] facsimile transmission (the latter confirmed by telex or post¹)]; or
—   by any other means which any party specifies by notice to the others.

13.2 Each party's address for the service of notice shall be [his] above mentioned address or such other address as [he] specifies by notice to the others [and until otherwise specified by notice those email addresses for the service of notices are as follows:
—   [(*Party-A*)] [*email address*] etc].

13.3 A notice shall be deemed to have been served:
—   if it was served in person, at the time of service;
—   if it was served by post, 48 hours after it was posted[; and
—   if it was served by email or [telex or] facsimile transmission, at [09.00 on the first working day after] the time of transmission].

13.4 [No notices may be served by email, [telex or] facsimile transmission.]

Disputes

14 All disputes, differences and questions which at any time arise between the   **[23–172O]**
parties touching or arising out of or in connection with this (document) or its subject matter shall be referred to a single arbitrator in accordance with the Arbitration Act 1996.

Contracts (*Rights of Third Parties*) *Act 1999*

15 Pursuant to s 1(2)(a) of the Contracts (Rights of Third Parties) Act 1999   **[23–172OA]**
the parties intend that no term of this agreement may be enforced by a third party within the meaning of that Act.

[*attestation clauses*]

¹   State the actual amount. Avoid formulae such as '£x plus a amount equal to the annual rent   **[23–172P]**
   plus VAT payable on it'. You know the amount upfront.
²   Use the defined terms used in the Lease.
³   See the note at [2–283].

8D   Agreement for rent deposit to be held on trust   **[23–172PA]**

Suggested terms for parties: **[23–172Q]**

(*Party-A*)	'Landlord'
(*Party-B*)	'Tenant'
(*Party-C*)	'Deposit Holder'

Date and parties

THIS AGREEMENT is made on (*date*) between (*name*) of (*address*) ('(*Party*-   **[23–172QA]**
A)'), (*name*) of (*address*) ('(*Party-B*)') and (*name*) of (*address*) ('(*Party-C*)').

Definitions

[23–172R] **1.1** In this agreement the following terms shall have the following meanings except when expressly stated to the contrary:

'Account'	[a separate, designated interest bearing deposit account at (*name*) Bank plc [at its branch at (*address*)] in the name of the Landlord [*or insert details*].
'Default'	any failure on the part of the (*Party-B*) to perform or observe any provision of the Lease which he is required to perform or observe
'Deposit Balance'	the Initial Deposit and any other amounts from time to time standing to the credit of the Account.
'Initial Deposit'	£[....] [excluding VAT (*or*) including VAT of £[....]].
'Lease'	a lease dated (*date*) and made between the (*Party-A*) and the (*Party-B*) by which the Property was let to the (*Party-B*).
'Property'	means the property known as (*address*) described in [the schedule to] the Lease.
'Working Day'	any day from Monday to Friday inclusive except Good Friday and Christmas Day and a bank holiday within the meaning of the Banking and Financial Dealings Act 1971.

Payment of Initial Deposit

[23–172RA] **2.1** The (*Party-C*) acknowledges receipt of the Initial Deposit from the (*Party-B*).

2.2 The (*Party-C*) will place the Initial Deposit in the Account as soon as reasonably possible, but in any event within two Working Days after the date of this Deed.

Creation of trust

[23–172S] **3** The (*Party-C*) holds the Deposit Balance on trust for the (*Party-A*) in accordance with, and subject to, the terms of this deed.

Minimum amount maintained

[23–172SA] **4** At all times the (*Party-B*) will:
— maintain the Deposit Balance at a amount not less than the Minimum Amount; and
— promptly pay to the (*Party-A*) amounts necessary to achieve this if the amount in the Account is less than the Minimum Amount (which amounts will become subject to the terms of this deed).

(Party-C)'s powers and duties

[23–172T] **5.1** The (*Party-C*) is not obliged to secure any particular rate of Interest.

5.2 The duties of the (*Party-C*) as to investment and safeguarding the Deposit and all duties imposed by law legislation or equity on trustees will be deemed to have been fully discharged by the (*Party-C*)'s compliance with this deed.

5.3 The (*Party-C*) as trustee will not be liable to the (*Party-B*) for any loss to the Deposit Balance or any loss of Interest arising from any act or default made in good faith unless such loss arises from the wilful default or negligence of the (*Party-C*).

Interest and charges

6.1 The interest accruing on the Deposit Balance is to be left in the Deposit   [23–172TA]
Account and is to form part of the Deposit Account.

6.2 After reasonable intervals of not less than [six] months following the date of this deed or any payment made to the (*Party-B*) under this clause the (*Party-B*) may by notice require the (*Party-C*) to withdraw from the Deposit Account and pay to him within [21 days] an amount (less any tax required to be deducted) equal to the interest that has accrued on the Deposit Balance as at the date of the (*Party-B*)'s notice sent to the (*Party-C*).

No payment following Default

7 The (*Party-C*) will not have to pay out any interest under this clause if: [23–172U]
—   there is any Default at the date payment would otherwise be due; or
—   to the extent that doing so would cause the Deposit Balance to be less than the Minimum Balance.

Responsibility for tax

8.1 The (*Party-B*) is responsible for and will pay all tax on interest that accrues   [23–172UA]
to the Deposit Balance except to the extent that any tax has already have been deducted by the (*Party-C*).

8.2 The (*Party-B*) acknowledges that the (*Party-C*) may (but is not obliged) to withhold amounts that represent any tax that may be due lawfully on the Deposit Balance and to pay those amounts to the appropriate tax authority.

Indemnity for tax[1]

9 If the (*Party-C*) does not elect to withhold any amounts under clause 07.2   [23–172V]
the (*Party-B*) will indemnify the (*Party-C*) on demand against all tax payable in respect of any Interest accruing on the Deposit Balance.

Withdrawals

10.1 The (*Party-B*) irrevocably authorises the (*Party-C*) to withdraw amounts   [23–172VA]
at any time from the Deposit Account in accordance with this clause.

10.2 Before any withdrawal can be made by the (*Party-C*) there must have been a Default and the (*Party-C*) must have given the (*Party-B*) at least [14] days' notice of that default and his intention to make a withdrawal from the Deposit Account and the amount of the proposed withdrawal.

10.3 If the (*Party-B*) remedies the Default before the expiry of the period stated in clause 9.2 the (*Party-C*) may not make the withdrawal for the default complained of in the notice.

Top-up of the Deposit[2]

[23–172W] **11.1** Without prejudice, and in addition, to the (*Party-B*)'s other obligations in this deed, the (*Party-B*) will pay to the (*Party-C*) such amount as is necessary to ensure that the Deposit Balance is not less than the Minimum Amount within ten Working Days after each of the following:

— the date of every occasion upon which the (*Party-C*) serves notice in writing on the (*Party-B*) that the (*Party-C*) has made a withdrawal from the Account;

— the date upon which each and every review of the Principal Rent is settled in accordance with the terms of the Lease.

11.2 Where the (*Party-A*) serves notice in writing on the (*Party-B*) that the (*Party-A*) has made an election under Schedule 10 to the Value Added Tax Act 1994 for the Property, then the (*Party-B*) will pay to the (*Party-C*) such amount as is necessary to ensure that the Deposit Balance is not less than the Minimum Amount plus VAT.

11.3 The (*Party-C*) undertakes to pay any monies paid to it under to this clause 10 into the Account as soon as reasonably possible, but in any event within [two] Working Days following receipt.

Repayment of the Deposit[3]

[23–172WA] **12.1** Subject to the rights of the (*Party-A*) under this Deed, the (*Party-C*) will pay the Deposit to the (*Party-B*) within the earlier of:

— two months after the date of the expiry or sooner determination of the Term; and

— five Working Days after the date of a lawful assignment of the Lease by the (*Party-B*).

12.2 The (*Party-C*) is entitled to retain from the Deposit Balance repaid to the (*Party-B*) under this clause such proportion of it as is reasonably necessary to make good any outstanding Default.

The right of re-entry in the Lease

[23–172X] **13** The right of re-entry in the Lease will be exercisable if any covenant or condition contained in this deed falling to be complied with by the (*Party-B*) is breached, as well as if any of the events stated in the provision for re-entry in the Lease occur.

[attestation clauses]

[23–172Y] [1] The parties should take detailed tax advice at the time about the current tax implications of using a trust structure. Interest on the account will be income for the tenant and as such will attract corporation tax or income tax (depending on whether the tenant is a company or an individual). The landlord should not have to bear the tax and should have an absolute right to deduct any tax that is due. It is probably going to be liable to account to HM Revenue & Customs for it. The trust route is probably not appropriate for pension funds. The tax position there will be more complicated.

[2] Maintaining the deposit topped up to the right level is critical for the landlord. After a rent review resulting in an increase in the rent, the value of the rent deposit will be serious eroded unless the tenant is required to top up the deposit. Similarly, if the landlord has to make a withdrawal, the tenant should top up the deposit. The idea is that it is a continuing security for the landlord maintained at its original value relative to the tenant's obligations under the lease. Beware of the effect of VAT. If, when the lease is granted, there has been no VAT

election, it does not mean that rent will always be payable without VAT because it may become appropriate for the landlord to elect in the future. Clause 11 is therefore of crucial importance.

There is, however, a health warning to be given to the landlord. The tenant gets no benefit for these payments. They are therefore likely to be transactions at an undervalue and open to challenge on the tenant's insolvency. The landlord will end up spending money dealing with such challenge and may have to pay back any top-up made if the tenant then becomes insolvent. The payments might also be treated as a preference on tenant insolvency—with similar effect for the landlord.

3   This precedent does not provide for an automatic release when the tenant proves itself to be a responsible tenant (ie, there has been no default for a given period) or if a financial test has been met, such as the tenant showing in audited accounts pre tax profits for three consecutive years of more than three times the passing rent.

Energy performance certificates — clause for insertion in leases[1]   [23–847A]

Definitions

'EPC'   means an Energy Performance Certificate as defined by
                       Regulation 1 of the EPC Regulations

'EPC   means the Energy Performance of Buildings
Regulations'   (Certificates and Inspections) (England And Wales)
                       Regulations 2007, SI 2007/991.

Energy performance certificates   [23–847B]

1.1 When required (whether because of any works to the Property, because of any underletting of the whole or any part of the Property, or because of any other reason) by the EPC Regulations the (*Party B*) must obtain a valid EPC.

1.2 The (*Party B*) must deliver a clearly legible copy of any EPC obtained to the (*Party A*) (including without limitation clearly legible details of the reference number of the EPC) within [5/7] Working Days of the obtaining of the EPC.

1.3 If anything done by the (*Party B*) makes any EPC for the Property [or the Building] (or any part of it) held by the (*Party A*) [of which the Tenant has prior written notice] invalid or adversely affects the asset rating in any EPC then the Tenant must (at the option of the (*Party A*)):

   1.3.1   Obtain a valid EPC for the Property [or the Building] (or any part of it), or

   1.3.2   Indemnify the (*Party A*) against the [reasonable] expenses properly incurred in obtaining a new and valid EPC for the Property [or the Building] (or any part of it).

1.4 Without prejudice to anything else in the Lease the (*Party A*) and the (*Party B*) will

   1.4.1   allow access and to the parts of the Building that they respectively control for the purposes of this clause, and

   1.4.2   co-operate as far as reasonably necessary to enable compliance with this clause and with the EPC Regulations.

1   The Energy Performance Certificates of Buildings (Certificates and Inspections) (England   [23–847C]
and Wales) Regulations 2007, SI 2007/991 (as amended) are now in force. They may have a
continuing impact as between landlords and tenants during the term of a lease because of the
need to renew them periodically and a desire to allocate responsibility and cost as between
landlord and tenant, perhaps especially when the lease is of part of a building.

Reg 50 applies where the Regulations impose a duty on a person to make available, give or display an energy performance certificate or a display energy certificate in relation to a building, or to ensure that an air-conditioning system is inspected. It imposes a duty on every person with an interest in, or in occupation of, the building to allow access and to co-operate as far as reasonably necessary to enable compliance. It may be thought that in many cases this will suffice, especially if the lease contains a covenant to comply with legislation that is in force from time to time during the term. Some draftsmen may prefer express provision, such as the above clauses.

25 Sale of Land

PRELIMINARY NOTES

LAND REGISTRATION ACT 2002

This edition has been updated to take into account the impact of the Land [25–001] Registration Act 2002 and the Land Registration Rules 2003, SI 2003/1417. New forms were prescribed by the Land Registration Rules 2003. The prescribed forms are listed in table at the end of this note. Most of the precedents in this chapter are based on form TR1, which is the prescribed form of transfer of the whole of freehold or leasehold land and is reproduced in full with notes (as appears in the *Encyclopaedia of Forms and Precedents*) in precedent [25–118]. This form may also be used for transfers of the whole of unregistered land contained in one or more deeds. Application for first registration of title must be made on Land Registry form FR1 and must be lodged at the Land Registry together with all the documents evidencing the unregistered title under cover of Land Registry form DL.

TABLE OF FORMS [25–002]

Form	Description	Old form equiva-lent
313*	Who owns that property	313
ACD*	Application for approval of a standard form of charge deed and allocation of official Land Registry reference	114
AC1	Application for registration in farmer's name	None
AC2	Application for registration in name of an agricultural society	None
AC3	Application for cancellation of an entry in the register on proof of discharge	None
AC4	Application for a certificate that a registration has been cancelled	None
AC5	Application for a certified copy of the memorandum filed in the Register of Agricultural Charges under the Act	None
AC6	Application for an official search	None
AC7	Application for the rectification of an entry in the register	None
ADV1	Application for registration of a person in adverse possession under Schedule 6 LRA 2002	None

Form	Description	Old form equiva-lent
ADV2	Application to be registered as a person to be notified of an application for adverse possession	None
AN1	Application to enter an agreed notice	None
AP1	Application to change the register	AP1
AS1	Assent of whole of registered title(s)	AS1
AS2	Assent of charge	AS2
AS3	Assent of part of registered title(s) by personal representative	AS3
CC	Entry note of consolidation of charges	None
CCD	Application to cancel a caution against dealings	None
CCT	Application to cancel a caution against first registration	None
CH1	Legal charge of registered estate [use of this form is not mandatory]	None
CH2	Application to enter an obligation to make further advances	113
CH3	Application to note agreed maximum amount of security	None
CIT	Application in connection with court proceedings, insolvency and tax liability	112A, 112B and 112C
CN1	Application to cancel a notice (other than a unilateral notice)	CN1
CM1	Application to register a freehold estate in commonhold land	None
CM2	Application for the freehold estate to cease to be registered as a freehold estate in commonhold land during the transitional period	None
CM3	Application for the registration of an amended commonhold community statement and/or altered memorandum and articles of association	None
CM4	Application to add land to a commonhold registration	None
CM5	Application for the termination of a commonhold registration	None
CM6	Application for the registration of a successor commonhold association	None
CS	Continuation sheet for use with application and disposition forms	CS
CT1	Caution against first registration	CT1

Form	Description	Old form equivalent
DB	Application to determine the exact line of a boundary	None
DI	Disclosable overriding interests	None
DJP*	Application to remove from the register the name of a deceased joint proprietor	83
DL	List of documents	DL
DS1	Cancellation of entries relating to a registered charge	DS1
DS2	Application to cancel entries relating to a registered charge	DS2
DS2E*	Application to cancel entries relating to a registered charge	DS2E
DS3	Release of part of the land from a registered charge	DS3
EX1	Application for the registrar to designate a document as an exempt information document	None
EX1A	Reasons for exemption in support of an application to designate a document as an exempt information document	None
EX2	Application for an official copy of an exempt information document	None
EX3	Application to remove the designation of a document as an exempt information document	None
FR1	First registration application	FR1
HC1	Application for copies of historical edition(s) of the register/title held in electronic form	None
HR1	Application for registration of a notice of home rights	MH1
HR2	Application for renewal of registration in respect of home rights	MH2
HR3	Application by mortgagee for official search in respect of home rights	MH3
HR4*	Cancellation of a home rights notice	MH4
ID1*	Evidence of identity for a private individual	ID1
ID2*	Evidence of identity for a corporate body	ID2
ID3*	Evidence of identity [to be completed by an applicant attending a Land Registry office in person]	ID3
NAP	Notice to the registrar in respect of an adverse possession application	None

Form	Description	Old form equivalent
OC1	Application for official copies of register/plan or certificate in form CI [form CI is the replacement for old form 102]	109
OC2	Application for official copies of documents only	110
OS1	Application by purchaser for official search with priority of the whole of the land in a registered title or a pending first registration application	94A
OS2	Application by purchaser for official search with priority of part of the land in a registered title or a pending first registration application	94B
OS3	Application for official search without priority of the land in a registered title	94C
PIC	Application for a personal inspection under s.66 LRA 2002	111
PN1	Application for a search in the Index of Proprietors' Names	104
PRD1	Request for the production of documents	None
RD1	Request for the return of original document(s)	None
RX1	Application to enter a restriction	75/76
RX2	Application for an order that a restriction be disapplied or modified	None
RX3	Application to cancel a restriction	None
RX4	Application to withdraw a restriction	77
SC	Application for noting the overriding priority of a statutory charge	None
SIF	Application for an official search of the index of relating franchises and manors	None
SIM	Application for an official search of the index map	96
TP1	Transfer of part of registered title(s)	TP1
TP2	Transfer of part of registered title(s) under power of sale	TP2
TP3	Transfer of portfolio of titles [use TR5 if the portfolio contains *only* whole registered titles]	TP3
TR1	Transfer of whole of registered title(s)	TR1
TR2	Transfer of whole of registered title(s) under power of sale	TR2
TR3	Transfer of charge	TR3
TR4	Transfer of portfolio of charges	TR4

Form	Description	Old form equiva-lent
TR5	Transfer of portfolio of whole titles [use TP3 if the portfolio includes titles other than whole registered titles]	TR5
UN1	Application to enter a unilateral notice	None
UN2	Application to remove a unilateral notice	None
UN3	Application to be registered as a beneficiary of an existing unilateral notice	None
UN4	Application for the cancellation of a unilateral notice	None
UT1	Application for upgrading of title	6
WCT	Application to withdraw a caution	WCT

PRECEDENTS

PART I: CONTRACTS FOR SALE OF LAND[1]

1 Contract for sale of registered or unregistered freeholds incorporating the Standard Conditions of Sale 4th Edition[2]

[25–003]

[1] A contract for the sale or other disposition of land must be in writing, incorporating all the expressly agreed terms and signed by or on behalf of each party to the contract (in one or more parts): Law of Property (Miscellaneous Provisions) Act 1989, s 2, superseding LPA 1925, s 40. Section 2 (as amended) does not apply to leases for less than three years.

[25–033]

In *Record v Bell* [1991] 4 All ER 471, [1991] 1 WLR 853, the seller of land sought specific performance of a contract, whose parts were exchanged on the basis of last-minute letters between the parties' solicitors about the state of the title. The letters were not in identical form or referred to in the contract and so did not comply with s 2, but they were held to be a collateral warranty as to title, independent of the land contract and outside s 2; and judgment was given for the seller. Exchange is effected when each part of the contract duly signed is in the actual or constructive possession of the other party or his solicitor (telephone exchange): *Domb v Isoz* [1980] Ch 548, [1980] 1 All ER 942, CA. Any variation to a contract governed by s 2 of the Law of Property (Miscellaneous Provisions) Act 1989 must satisfy the same conditions as the contract: it must be in writing, must be signed by (or on behalf of) all the parties to the contract (or when exchanged each part must be signed by the other parties), and must contain all the terms, by reference or expressly.

At present, land contracts cannot be made electronically. However, the Land Registry consultation paper, *E-Conveyancing Secondary Legislation* (*Part 1*) contains proposals to insert a new section 2A into the Law of Property (Miscellaneous Provisions) Act 1989, to allow electronic sale contracts to be used in e-conveyancing.

In *First Post Homes Ltd v Johnson* [1996] EG 125, CA, the Court of Appeal held that a letter and a plan were two separate documents. The letter contained the sale terms, but only the plan had been signed. As a result, there was not a valid contract because s 2 of the 1989 Act had not been complied with.

In *McLaughlin v Duffill* [2009] EWCA Civ 1627, [2009] 34 EG 80, the Court of Appeal confirmed that s 2 does not require that an authority to sign a contract on behalf of a contracting party must be given in writing, but good practice dictates (and for evidential purposes it is obviously essential) that any such authority is confirmed in writing.

PART V: TRANSFERS OF FREEHOLDS – GENERAL PRECEDENTS

Form TR1

[25–118]

14 Specimen transfer (on Form TR1) of the whole of a registered or unregistered freehold title[1]

[25–141]   [1]   This form contains various clauses showing where they should be inserted in Land Registry form TR1. Some but not all of the clauses may be appropriate to any particular transaction: the clauses inserted in this form, when considered collectively, are not drafted to suit a particular transaction and each clause should be considered separately.

As to stamp duty land tax (SDLT) see the note on stamp duty in the preliminary pages. Payment of SDLT should be arranged prior to lodging the application for registration or first registration.

Form SDLT 60 (stamp duty land tax self-certificate) is no longer required for land transactions with an effective date on or after 12 March 2008: FA 2003 Pt 4 as amended by FA 2008.

PART XII: FREEHOLDS — RENTCHARGES

The paragraph about distress in the note [25–515] is rewritten as below in view of the prospective abolition of this remedy.

NOTE

[25–515] The remedy of distress for non-payment seems to be an essential incident of a rentcharge—without a right to distrain the payment would not be rent. The common law remedy of distress has been prospectively abolished by the Tribunals, Courts and Enforcement Act 2007 as from a date to be appointed by Order. It will be replaced in relation to commercial property with a process known as commercial rent arrears recovery (CRAR), the procedure for which is in Sch 12 to the 2007 Act, and will be registered by court rules. CRAR will require notice to be served on the defaulting tenant, and so may prove to be of limited liability, especially in relation to tenancies. Remedies implied into rentcharges by s 121 of the Law of Property Act 1925 are: distress; entry into possession; and demise to a trustee who can create a term to be mortgaged or sold. The rule against perpetuities does not apply to them. A right of re-entry or forfeiture may also be annexed to a rentcharge, and if annexed to a legal rentcharge may itself be a legal estate. It seems that the rule against perpetuities does not apply to it. These remedies may be made exercisable on condition broken.

PART XIII: TRANSFERS OF THE WHOLE OF REGISTERED OR UNREGISTERED FREEHOLD LAND TO A COMPANY OR CORPORATION

81 Deed of covenant between adjoining land owners[1]

[25–571]   [1]This heading should only be used where the deed relates to registered land.

[25–572] ## 82 HM Land Registry: Standard restrictions

Form S (Disposition by proprietor of charge—certificate of compliance required)

No [disposition *or specify type of disposition*] by the proprietor of the registered charge dated [*date*] referred to above is to be registered without a certificate signed by

[*choose one of the bulleted clauses*]

- a conveyancer

- the applicant for registration [or their conveyancer]

- [*name*] of [*address*] [or their personal representatives] [or [their conveyancer *or specify appropriate details*]]

- [*name*] of [*address*] [or their personal representatives] and [*name*] of [*address*] [or their personal representatives] [or [their conveyancer *or specify appropriate details*]]

- [*name*] of [*address*] and [*name*] of [*address*] or the survivor of them [or by the personal representatives of the survivor] [or [their conveyancer *or specify appropriate details*]]

- [*name*] of [*address*] or [after that person's death] by [*name*] of [*address*] [or [their conveyancer *or specify appropriate details*]]

- the proprietor for the time being of the sub-charge dated [*date*] in favour of [sub-chargee] [or [their conveyancer *or specify appropriate details*]]

that the provisions of [*specify clause, paragraph or other particulars*] of [*specify details*] have been complied with [or that they do not apply to the disposition].

102   Notice by one joint tenant to another severing the joint tenancy[1]

[25–663]

[1]   This notice is given under the Law of Property Act 1925, s 36(2), under which notice by one joint tenant to the other is sufficiently served to effect a severance of the equitable interest when it is sent to the premises by recorded delivery post but is received by the person on whose behalf it is served: *Re 88 Berkeley Road, London, NW9, Rickwood v Turnseck* [1971] Ch 648, [1971] 1 All ER 254. See also generally as to service of notices [2–284], note 1. A husband and wife being beneficial joint tenants of the matrimonial home, which W left, and W having signed a memorandum that H could sell the house and use the proceeds to provide a home for himself, it was held that the joint tenancy had not been severed: *Nielson-James v Fedden* [1975] Ch 222, [1974] 3 All ER 38. However, an oral agreement for one joint tenant to purchase the share of the other, albeit unenforceable, may be evidence that the parties no longer intend to be bound by the joint tenancy, which is automatically severed: *Burgess v Rawnsley* [1975] Ch 429, [1975] 3 All ER 142, CA. The division of a house into maisonettes occupied by the beneficial joint tenants separately does not sever the joint tenancy: *Greenfield v Greenfield* (1979) 38 P & CR 570.

[25–664]

In the case of registered land, application must be made to enter a restriction on the register pursuant to the Land Registration Rules 2003, SI 2003/1417, r 91(1), Sch 4, Form A, as substituted by SI 2008/1919 (the trustee proprietor restriction). Application should be made on Land Registry Form RX1.

PART XVI: ADDITIONAL CLAUSES

Vacant possession

Additional clause to contract for sale for the occupiers to join in the sale contract and covenant to enable the seller to give vacant possession[1]

Parties:

[25–735A]

(Add ('Occupant[s]' as a party)

The Occupant[s]

x.1 [Each of] the Occupant[s severally] confirm[s] to the Buyer that:

x.1.1   he will join with the Seller in giving the Buyer vacant possession in the Property on the Completion Date by moving out of the Property and removing his possessions from it by the Completion Date;

x.1.2   he has no interest in any part of the Property that will affect or bind the Buyer at or after actual completion;

x.1.3   there are no persons aged 17 or older other than the Occupant[s] in actual occupation of any part of the Property at the date of this agreement; and

x.1.4   he will immediately notify the Buyer's solicitors in writing if he becomes aware of there being any persons aged 17 or older other than the Occupant[s] in actual occupation of any part of the Property before actual completion.

x.2 The Seller acknowledges that [none of] the Occupant[s] will have any liability to the Buyer under this Agreement except for his own statements, acts, or defaults and in particular will have no liability for the statements, acts, or defaults of the Seller or any other person who is an Occupant.

[1]   Clients and solicitors must use their judgement when there are persons other than the seller in occupation of the property. Some buyers (but not many) may be happy to buy even if there is a person in occupation of the property so long as he will not have any overriding interests, and to carry on any litigation necessary to get vacant possession. Some buyers (but not many) may be happy to postpone completion until the seller is able to get and give vacant possession of the property, relying on the usual remedies for breach of contract: an order for specific performance, which will not be granted if the occupier has a right to be there that will not be overreached on the sale, compensation under the contract, and damages. Many buyers will want to ensure that persons (other than members of the seller's immediate family) who are in occupation of the property at least have an obligation to the buyer to have moved out, and that is most conveniently done by getting them to join in the contract and promising that they will move out. It does not guarantee that they will keep the promise, but does mean that there will be an obligation that can be enforced.

26 Associations

PRECEDENTS

3 Constitution of a proprietor's club (not in relation to licensed premises)

RULES OF THE [AB] CLUB

NAME

1 The name of the club is [The AB Club] ('the Club'). [26–084A]

PROPRIETOR

2 The Club is a proprietary club, owned by [(*name*) of (*address*) (*or*) [26–085]
(*name*) plc/Ltd a company registered in England and Wales with number
(*number*[1]) whose registered office is (*address*) ('the Proprietor').

OBJECTS

3 The objects of the Club are to encourage [*describe activity*, e g participation [26–086]
in the sport of CD (*or*) encourage the restoration, preservation and use of the
EF motor cars (*or*) the propagation, growing and care of GH] (the Activity"),
to support the Proprietor in the provision of goods and services necessary for
the Activity and enable Members to have access to those goods and services in
priority to and, when the proprietor thinks fit, on more favourable terms than
are offered to the public at large.

MEMBERS

3.1 Any person who supports the aims of the Club may apply for membership [26–087]
by giving or sending to the Proprietor a written application signed by him or
her accompanied by payment of the subscription specified on the application
form and becomes a member when, as the Proprietor may at [his (*or*) its]
discretion decline to do, the Proprietor accepts the application and notifies the
applicant that he or she is a member. The Proprietor may at [his (*or*) its]
discretion admit persons to membership on other terms.

3.2 The Proprietor may establish different classes of membership, determine [26–088]
their respective privileges and duties and set the amounts of their subscriptions.

3.3 The Proprietor shall keep a register of Members. [26–089]

3.4 A Member shall cease to be a Member: [26–090]
(a) if he or she gives to the Proprietor written notice of resignation of his
or her membership;

(b)   if he or she fails to pay any subscription within one month after the due date of payment; or

(c)   if the Proprietor at [his (*or*) its] removes him or her from membership, in which case the Proprietor shall refund to the Member the amount of the subscription (if any) paid him divided by 12 and multiplied by the number of months (including the month of removal) unexpired of the year for which the subscription was paid.

[26–091]   **3.5** Membership is not transferable.

SUBSCRIPTIONS

[26–092]   **4.1** The Club's membership year is from [1 January to 31 December].

[26–093]   **4.2** The annual subscription of the Club is such amount as the Proprietor from time to time determines and notifies to the members. The proprietor may fix a reduced subscription for a member who joins the Club during a membership year.

[26–094]   **4.3** A Member who gives notice of resignation under rule 3.4(a) or ceases to be a Member under rule 3.4(b) remains liable to pay his or her subscription for the whole of the membership year in which his or her cessation of membership takes effect.

[26–095]   **4.4** If the Proprietor increases the subscription by more than [10]% of the rate in the current membership year, a Member may decline to pay it. The membership of a Member who gives written notice to the proprietor declining to pay such an increase ceases on the service of that notice. A Member whose membership ceases under this rule does not become liable to any subscription not paid at that date or payable under rule 4.3.

BENEFITS OF MEMBERSHIP

[26–096]   **5** The benefits of membership, which the Proprietor makes available and can at any time vary by written notice to the Members are:

(a)   the increased likelihood that, as a result of the existence and support of its members, the Proprietor will remain in business and able to supply goods and service needed for the Activity;

(b)   the opportunity for Member, who wish to do so, to assist in the support of the Activity to help the Proprietor in the conduct of [his (*or*) its business on a voluntary or any other basis agreed with the Proprietor;

(c)   participation for Members who so wish in the Social Committee and activities arranged by it or the Proprietor;

(d)   the receipt of a magazine about the Activity produced by the Proprietor or the Social Committee or jointly by them; and

(e)   (so far as it is commercially viable, as to which the Proprietor is the sole judge) priority over other members of the public and preferential terms of business for the supply of goods and services by the Proprietor.

SOCIAL COMMITTEE

[26–097]   **6** The Proprietor encourages the formation of a Social Committee of the Members in accordance with the by-law attached to these rules

ASSETS AND LIABILITIES

7 The Members have no interest of any kind in any of the assets of the Club or the Proprietor's business, which are the property of the Proprietor, and have no liability for any of the liabilities of the Club or the Proprietor's business, for which the Proprietor is solely liable. The Proprietor is not an agent for any purpose of the Members or any of them and the none of the Members is an agent for the Proprietor for any purpose. No member is entitled to any accounts or other information about the Proprietor's business except any which [he (*or*) it] decides to disclose.

[26–098]

INFORMATION ABOUT MEMBERS

8.1 It is a condition of membership of the Club that each Member and applicants for Membership provide to the Proprietor all information which [he (*or*) it] at any time or from time to time reasonably requires in connection with his or her involvements with the Activity. The Proprietor shall not, except as required by law or agreed in writing by the Member, disclose to any person any information supplied by the member to [him (*or*) it] in connection with the Club or [his (*or*) its] business.

[26–099]

8.2 For the purposes of the Data Protection Act 1998 each Member consent to the Proprietor holding and processing personal data about his or her.

[26–100]

RULE CHANGES

8 The Proprietor may at any and from time to time revoke, vary, add to or alter the rules and by-laws of the Club and is the sole authority for interpreting them and for settling all disputes relating to the affairs of the Club and the conduct of the Members.

[26–101]

TERMINATION OF CLUB

9 The Proprietor may at any time by written notice to the Members terminate the Club and, if [he (*or*) it] does so with effect at any time before the end of a membership year, [he (*or*) it] shall refund to each Member the amount of the subscription (if any) paid him divided by 12 and multiplied by the number of months (including the month of termination) unexpired of the year for which the subscription was paid

[26–102]

NOTICES

10.1 Notices under these rules and by-laws may be sent by hand, by post or, where a Member has agreed in writing, by email or (where applicable to Members generally) may be published in any magazine distributed by the Club.

[26–103]

10.2 The address at which a Member is entitled to receive notices is the address noted in the register of members (or, if none, the last known address).

[26–104]

10.3 Any notice given in accordance with these rules is to be treated for all purposes as having been received:
(1)   24 hours after being sent by email or delivered by hand to the relevant address;

[26–105]

(2)   two clear days (excluding Sundays and public holidays on which no post is delivered) after being sent by first class post to the relevant address;

(3)   one after being sent by overseas post to the relevant address;

(4)   on the date of publication of the magazine containing the notice; or

(5)   on being handed to the Member personally

BY-LAWS OF THE SOCIAL COMMITTEE OF THE [AB] CLUB

OFFICERS

[26–106]   **1.1** The honorary officers of the Social Committee are a President, a Chairman, a Treasurer and a Secretary. All the officers (except the President) must be Members of the Club.

[26–107]   **1.2** Any officer may retire by giving one week's prior notice to the Proprietor, and all shall retire at the end of each annual general meeting, but shall be eligible for re-election at that meeting.

THE COMMITTEE

[26–108]   **2.1** The Committee consists of the Proprietor, the honorary officers (except the President) and not fewer than four and not more than eight other Members.

[26–109]   **2.2** Any casual vacancy on the Committee or of any office arising between annual general meetings may be filled by the Proprietor.

[26–110]   **2.3** Any member of the Committee may retire by giving 30 days' prior notice to the Proprietor, and all shall retire at the end of each annual general meeting, but shall be eligible for re-election at that meeting.

[26–111]   **2.4** Any person who fails to attend [three] consecutive meetings of the Committee without giving a reason acceptable to it shall cease automatically to be a member of the Proprietor.

[26–112]   **2.5** The Committee may with the agreement of the Proprietor arrange such events and do such things in connection with the Activities and they think fit, but shall not shall directly or indirectly cause the proprietor to insure any financial or other liability except to the extent (if at all) expressly authorised by him in writing.

[26–113]   **2.6** The Committee may make such arrangements as it with the agreement of the Proprietor thinks fit for its meetings and the conduct of its work and keep in its minutes a record of any such arrangements.

ANNUAL GENERAL MEETING

[26–114]   **3.1** The Committee may convene an annual general meeting to be held in every year and not more than 18 months after the previous annual general meeting. If the Committee does not convene an annual general meeting the Proprietor may do so. The Committee has no power to convene an annual general meeting for the year in question at any time after the Proprietor has issued notices to Members for that purpose.

[26–115]   **3.2** The business of the annual general meeting shall be:

— to receive the Proprietor's and Chairman's report of the activities of the Club during the preceding year;
— to elect officers and other members of the Committee; and
— to discuss any other business put before it.

3.3 Not less than twenty-one days' prior notice in writing of an annual general meeting shall be sent to every Member at his or her last known address. Members are entitled to attend annual general meetings of the Club in person but have no right to appoint a proxy of agent to attend on his or her behalf unless the Proprietor agrees otherwise in writing. [26–116]

3.4 Resolutions at annual general meetings shall be passed by a simple majority of the votes cast by the Members present at the meeting. [26–117]

3.5 In the event of equality in voting the Chairman (or acting chairman at that meeting) shall have a second or casting vote. [26–118]

[1] Strictly speaking, this is not or is unlikely to be a not for profit organisation, but is likely to be ancillary to a person's business, where that business caters for a particular interest group with a common interest to support the business. For example the participants of specialised sport or the owners of classic cars or other groups, whose demand for goods and services is insufficient to support a wholly commercial supplier, are often willing to support a specialist supplier by subscription or voluntary work either solely to ensure that supplies are available at all or to have access to them on more favourable terms than are available to the public at large. Clubs such as this may also operate a social Proprietor to promote the activities of their group. [26–119]

4 Application form to join proprietor's club[1] [26–120]

APPLICATION TO JOIN THE [AB] CLUB

to

(*name*)

(*address*)

as the proprietor of the [AB] Club ('the Club').

I the person named below:

1 apply to be a member of the Club;

2 enclose my subscriptions of £[....];

3 acknowledge that I have received a copy of the rules and by-laws of the Club and agree to abide by them; and

4 agree that this application is an offer to you and that on your acceptance of it, it and the rules and by-laws of the Club will be a contract between us.

signature of applicant   _____

name   _____

address   _____

    _____

    _____

date of application

[26–121]   1   See precedent 3 and the note to it. The proprietor may require further information from the applicant, which can be required by letter or an addition to this form. See rule 8.1 [26–099] in the previous precedent.

GENERAL TERMS AND CONDITIONS
FOR USE OF THE COMPACT DISC GOODS
AND MATERIALS CONTAINED THEREIN

This Licence Agreement is between Reed Elsevier (UK) Limited trading as LexisNexis ("**we or us**") and the individual or company ("**you**") to whom LexisNexis has agreed to supply the Compact Disc Goods ("the **Goods**") and the Materials and content contained therein ("the **Materials**"). The following terms and conditions govern your use of the Goods supplied by LexisNexis and the Materials available therein:

1.   LICENCE; RESTRICTIONS ON USE
1.1   You are granted a non-exclusive, non-transferable, limited licence to access and use the Goods and the Materials from time to time made available to you for the purposes only of (i) research or study, (ii) providing professional services to your clients, and (iii) providing academic services to students. This licence is subject to the following limitations:

(a)   The right to electronically display the Materials retrieved from the Goods is limited to the display of such the Materials primarily to one person at a time;

(b)   The right to obtain a printout of the Materials is limited to single printout of the Materials downloaded (collectively, "**Authorised Printouts**"). You are not permitted to sell these Authorised Printouts; and

(c)   The right to retrieve and store machine-readable copies of the Materials is limited to the retrieval of a single copy of the Materials included in the Goods and storage of that copy in machine readable form primarily for one person's exclusive use. You are not permitted to transfer the Goods or the Materials electronically or via any other medium for commercial profit or for resale.

1.2   To the extent expressly permitted by applicable copyright law, you may make copies of Authorised Printouts and distribute Authorised Printouts and copies.

1.3   Except as specifically provided in Sections 1.1 and 1.2, you are otherwise prohibited from downloading, storing, reproducing, transmitting, displaying, printing, copying, distributing, or using the Materials retrieved from the Goods.

1.4   All right, title, and interest (including all copyrights and other intellectual property rights) in the Goods and the Materials (in both print and machine-readable forms) belong to us or our third party suppliers. You acquire no ownership of copyright or other intellectual property rights or proprietary interest in the Goods, the Materials, or copies thereof.

1.5   Except as specifically provided herein, you may not use the Goods or the Materials retrieved from the Goods in any fashion that infringes the copyright or proprietary interests therein.

1.6   You may not remove or obscure the copyright notice or other notices contained in the Materials retrieved from the Goods.

2.   ACCESS TO SERVICES
2.1   Only you shall be entitled to access and use the Goods and the Materials ("**Authorised Users**").

2.2   Except for use incidental to occasional, short-term travel, you may not access the Goods and the Materials from outside the country for which it was issued.

2.3   Materials and features may be added to or withdrawn from the Goods and the Goods otherwise changed without notice.

2.4   You must ensure that each person having access to the Goods and the Materials:

(a)   is an Authorised User; and

(b)   is using those Goods and the Materials only in accordance with these General Terms and Conditions.

3.   LIMITED WARRANTY
3.1   We represent and warrant that we have the right and authority to make the Goods and the Materials available pursuant to these General Terms and Conditions.

3.2   EXCEPT AS OTHERWISE PROVIDED IN SECTION 3.1, THE GOODS AND THE MATERIALS ARE PROVIDED ON AN "AS IS", "AS AVAILABLE" BASIS AND WE MAKE NO EXPRESS WARRANTIES UNDER THIS AGREEMENT, INCLUDING WITHOUT LIMITATION THAT THE GOODS AND THE MATERIALS ARE OR WILL BE COMPLETE OR FREE FROM ERRORS OR THAT INFORMATION WILL CONTINUE TO BE AVAILABLE TO US TO ENABLE US TO KEEP THE GOODS AND THE MATERIALS UP-TO-DATE.

4.   LIMITATION OF LIABILITY
4.1   To the maximum extent permitted by law, a Covered Party (as defined below) shall not be liable for any loss, injury, claim, liability, or damage of any kind resulting in any way from (a) any errors in or omissions from the Goods or any Materials available or not included therein, (b) the unavailability or interruption to the supply of the Goods or any

features thereof or any Materials, (c) Any Authorised Users use or misuse of the Goods or Materials (regardless of whether you received any assistance from a Covered Party in using or misusing the Goods), (d) your use of any equipment in connection with the Goods, (e) the content of Materials, (f) any delay or failure in performance of the Goods, or (g) any negligence of a Covered Party or its employees, contractors or agents in connection with the performance of our obligations under this agreement.

4.2 "Covered Party" means (a) us, our affiliates, and any officer, director, employee, subcontractor, agent, successor, or assign of us or our affiliates; and (b) each third party supplier of the Materials, their affiliates, and any officer, director, employee, subcontractor, agent, successor, or assign of any third party supplier of the Materials or any of their affiliates.

4.3 Our liability to you for breach of any condition or warranty implied under any law which cannot be lawfully modified or excluded by this agreement shall, to the extent permitted by law, be limited at our option to supplying the Goods or the Materials again or paying for their re-supply. Nothing in this Agreement is intended to exclude liability for death or personal injury resulting from any negligence by us.

4.4 Our liability to you for loss or damage of any kind (including loss or damage caused by negligence) is reduced to the extent that you caused or contributed to that loss or damage.

4.5 SUBJECT TO CLAUSE 4.3, THE AGGREGATE LIABILITY OF THE COVERED PARTIES IN CONNECTION WITH ANY OTHER CLAIM ARISING OUT OF OR RELATING TO THE GOODS OR THE MATERIALS SHALL NOT EXCEED THE AMOUNT OF YOUR ACTUAL DIRECT DAMAGES. YOUR RIGHT TO MONETARY DAMAGES IN THAT AMOUNT SHALL BE IN LIEU OF ALL OTHER REMEDIES WHICH YOU MAY HAVE AGAINST ANY COVERED PARTY.

4.6 SUBJECT TO CLAUSE 4.3, THE COVERED PARTIES SHALL NOT BE LIABLE FOR ANY SPECIAL, INDIRECT, INCIDENTAL, OR CONSEQUENTIAL DAMAGES OF ANY KIND WHATSOEVER (INCLUDING, WITHOUT LIMITATION, LEGAL FEES) IN ANY WAY DUE TO, RESULTING FROM, OR ARISING IN CONNECTION WITH THE GOODS, THE MATERIALS, OR THE FAILURE OF ANY COVERED PARTY TO PERFORM ITS OBLIGATIONS, REGARDLESS OF ANY NEGLIGENCE OF ANY COVERED PARTY.

4.7 The Materials are provided for reference purposes only and are not intended, nor should they be used, as a substitute for professional advice or judgement or to provide legal advice with respect to particular circumstances.

4.8 Whilst reasonable efforts are made to make sure the Materials are up to date, you should obtain independent verification or advice before relying upon any piece of information in circumstances where loss or damage may result.

5. MISCELLANEOUS

5.1 These General Terms and Conditions may be changed from time to time as described below or by written agreement.

5.2 The failure of us or any third party supplier of the Materials to enforce any provision hereof shall not constitute or be construed as a waiver of such provision or of the right to enforce it at a later time.

5.3 You may not assign your rights or delegate your duties under these General Terms and Conditions without our prior written consent.

5.4 These General Terms and Conditions shall be governed by and construed in accordance with the laws of England.

5.5 Each third party supplier of the Materials has the right to assert and enforce these provisions directly on its own behalf as a third party beneficiary.

5.6 We will use personal information collected about Authorised Users for the purposes of (a) providing access to and use of the Goods to Authorised Users, (b) providing customer support, billing and other similar activities related to the Goods, and (c) keeping Authorised Users informed about products, services, offers and upcoming events and to improve our services. We may also provide personal information about Authorised Users to third parties for the purpose of providing Authorised Users with direct marketing offers which we think may be of interest. If you do not wish to receive information about other products, services, offers and events, notify us in writing.

5.7 In accordance with the Data Protection Act 1998 we will provide and export personal information about Authorised Users to other members of our company group, including Reed Elsevier Inc. in the United States, for the purposes of (a) providing access to and use of the Goods to Authorised Users, and (b) providing customer support, billing and other similar activities related to the Goods.

5.8 Save for the owners of any intellectual property supplied by us, no third parties shall acquire any rights under this Agreement and the provisions of the Contracts (Rights of Third Parties) Act 1999 are excluded.

5.9 All Rights Reserved © Reed Elsevier.